INTERMEDIATE ✔ KU-285-845

ANTI-CALVINISTS

The Rise of English Arminianism
*c.*1590–1640

NICHOLAS TYACKE

CLARENDON PRESS · OXFORD

Oxford University Press, Walton Street, Oxford OX2 6DP

Oxford New York Toronto
Delhi Bombay Calcutta Madras Karachi
Petaling Jaya Singapore Hong Kong Tokyo
Nairobi Dar es Salaam Cape Town
Melbourne Auckland

and associated companies in
Berlin Ibadan

Oxford is a trade mark of Oxford University Press

Published in the United States
by Oxford University Press, New York

British Library Cataloguing in Publication Data
Tyacke, Nicholas
Anti-Calvinists: the rise of English Arminianism c. 1590–1640.
1. England. Arminianism, history
I. Title   230'.49
ISBN 0-19-820184-2

Library of Congress Cataloging in Publication Data
Tyacke, Nicholas.
Anti-Calvinists: the rise of English Arminianism. ca. 1590–1640 /
Nicholas Tyacke.
p.   cm.
Bibliography: p.   Includes index.
1. Church of England—History—16th century.   2. Church of
England—History—17th century.   3. Arminianism—England—
—History—16th century.   4. Arminianism—England—History—17th
century.   5. Calvinism—England—History—16th century.
6. Calvinism—England—History—17th century.   7. Anglican
Communion—England—History—16th century.   8. Anglican Communion—
—England—History—17th century.   9. England—Church history—16th
century.   10. England—Church history—17th century.   I. Title.
BX5073.T93   1989
283'.42'09031—dc20   89-35135 CIP
ISBN 0-19-820184-2

Printed in Great Britain
at the Alden Press, Oxford

FOR MY FAMILY

'Arminianism [is] an error that maketh the grace of God lackey it after the will of man, that maketh the sheep to keep the shepherd, that maketh mortal seed of an immortal God.' Francis Rous, 26 January, 1629.

> (*Commons Debates for 1629*, ed. W. Notestein and F. H. Relf (Minneapolis, 1921), pp. 12–13)

'They delight, it seemeth, to bee called after men's names, for anon they sticke not to call themselves Calvinists . . ., [whereas] I am not nor would be accounted willingly Arminian, Calvinist, or Lutheran, names of division, but a Christian.'

> (Richard Montagu, *Appello Caesarem* (1625), p. 10)

'We are all so much Arminians now that it requires a great imaginative effort to think oneself back into the pre-revolutionary society which Calvinism dominated.'

> (C. Hill, *The World Turned Upside Down* (1972), p. 276)

Foreword to the Paperback Edition*

ARMINIANISM turns out to be almost as controversial a topic today as it was in the early seventeenth century. Even before *Anti-Calvinists* appeared in print its main arguments had become the subject of a vigorous debate, which still continues, in the journal *Past and Present*.[1] After publication the review in *The Times Literary Supplement* was followed by five consecutive weeks of correspondence.[2] Meanwhile assessments elsewhere have been similarly mixed, at one extreme finding hardly a good word to say and at the other concluding that 'here we have the heart of the matter'.[3] What then is the disagreement all about? Clearly more is involved than the perennial itch of historians to contradict. Nor is it, on the whole, a dispute conducted at the level of scholarship as opposed to interpretation. The issues in reality run deeper, not least because the book challenges a powerful, albeit late, foundation myth.

Readers of *Anti-Calvinists* will notice that the word 'Anglican' appears solely in the preface, and with the remark that it has been consciously avoided thereafter (p. xviii). My objection based on the fact that the term 'Anglicanism' was only coined some 150 years ago, by High-Churchmen, as part of a campaign to remodel the English Church. In the words of the future Cardinal Newman, 'it still remains to be tried whether what is called Anglicanism, the religion of Andrews, Laud, Hammond . . . , is capable of being professed, acted on and

---

* I am most grateful to my London University colleagues Dr Peter Lake and Professor the Earl Russell for their comments on draft versions of this Foreword.

[1] P. White, 'The Rise of Arminianism Reconsidered', *Past and Present*, 101 (1983), 34–54; W. Lamont, 'Comment: The Rise of Arminianism Reconsidered', *Past and Present*, 107 (1985), 227–31; P. G. Lake, 'Calvinism and the English Church 1570–1635', *Past and Present*, 114 (1987), 32–76; N. Tyacke and P. White, 'Debate: The Rise of Arminianism Reconsidered', *Past and Present*, 115 (1987), 201–29; S. Lambert, 'Richard Montagu, Arminianism and Censorship', *Past and Present*, 124 (1989), 36–68.

[2] K. Sharpe, 'How Far did the Reformation Go?', *Times Literary Supplement*, 14 Aug. 1987; C. Russell, K. Sharpe, I. Green, N. Tyacke, T. Cogswell, and C. Russell, Letters, ibid., 21 Aug.–18 Sept. 1987.

[3] C. Haigh, *EHR*, 103 (1988), 425–7; P. Collinson, *Proceedings of the Huguenot Society*, 25 (1987), 454–5.

maintained.'[4] The historiographical consequences of this
endeavour can be seen at their starkest in a volume compiled
and edited during the 1930s, by P. E. More and F. L. Cross,
under the title *Anglicanism*. It consists of an extremely selective
body of seventeenth-century writings, designed to illustrate
the 'thought and practice' of the English Church; Calvinists
are chiefly remarkable for their absence. Although there is a
section on predestination, the lone pre-Civil War writer quoted
is the Arminian Richard Montagu.[5]

Not, of course, that most of my critics are themselves pro-
tagonists in an ecclesiastical cause. Rather they are the secular
inheritors of an essentially partisan religious construct. A
further complicating factor is the modern school of historical
'revisionism'. Many would regard my work as belonging in
this camp, yet certain revisionists have turned out to be its
fiercest critics. One is led to conclude that from their point of
view the author of *Anti-Calvinists* counts as a closet Whig.[6]
(The response by opponents of revisionism has also been somewhat confused.)[7] Three points are worth making briefly in this
connection. Firstly, there is no necessary incompatibility
between emphasizing the importance of both Arminianism *and*
Puritanism, as readers of Macaulay may recall.[8] Secondly,
Anti-Calvinists covers at least fifty years (1590–1640). Thirdly,
the book is quite explicitly predicated on a conflict model,
with ideas given great prominence. These last two features
especially are not normally thought of as characteristic of
revisionism.

Anti-Calvinists has been read as an attempt to abolish
Puritanism. This, however, is a misreading.[9] Moreover,
Puritanism does have a continuous history from the

[4] O. Chadwick, *The Victorian Church* (1966–70), I. 171; J. H. Newman, *Lectures on
the Prophetical Office of the Church, viewed relatively to Romanism and Popular Protestantism*
(1837), pp. 20–31. In the 2nd edn., of 1838, Newman substituted 'Anglo-Catholicism'
for 'Anglicanism'.

[5] P. E. More and F. L. Cross (eds.), *Anglicanism* (1935), pp. xix, xxx, 307–16.

[6] This point is made quite explicitly by Professor J. P. Kenyon when, intending
the reverse of flattery, he brackets my views with those of S. R. Gardiner (J. P.
Kenyon (ed.), *The Stuart Constitution* (2nd edn., Cambridge, 1986), p. 134).

[7] R. Cust and A. Hughes (eds.), *Conflict in Early Stuart England* (1989), pp. 6–8,
23–6, 193–223. Andrew Foster correctly locates my work historiographically.

[8] T. B. Macaulay, *The History of England from the Accession of James II* (1849–61), I.
75–89.

[9] N. Tyacke, Letters, *Times Literary Supplement*, 11 Sept. 1987.

Elizabethan period. Thus a parliamentary campaign for further reformation, especially as regards modifying clerical subscription, is traceable from the 1570s to the 1620s. In so far as a change of gear occurred it was from presbyterianism to congregationalism.[10] Yet the attempt to suppress Calvinism, during the 1620s and 1630s, proved particularly serious for more moderate Puritans—leading them ultimately to reject episcopacy. But were Puritans ever Calvinists in the same doctrinal sense as leaders of the established Church? This central affirmation of *Anti-Calvinists* has been challenged on the basis of a distinction between so-called 'credal' and 'experimental' predestinarian theology. The assumption is that Puritans were experimentalists, holding that the elect could and should seek personal assurance of salvation, and in consequence clearly differentiated from members of the episcopal hierarchy.[11] Alas for this counter-argument it can be shown that two of King James's three appointees to the archbishoprics of Canterbury and York, between them spanning the years 1606 to 1633, were experimentalists. While the views of Archbishop Toby Matthew of York are quoted below (pp. 18–19), those of Archbishop George Abbot of Canterbury deserve fuller citation. 'Either youth or age, life or death, in him that is elected', so Abbot taught, 'shall apprehend the promises. Be it the ninth houre, or the eleventh houre, yet there shal be a time.' This 'it is which bringeth comfort unto the wounded soule and affliced conscience—not that Christ is a saviour, for what am I the better for that, but a saviour unto me' and 'mine inheritance [is] with the saints'.[12] Such teaching represents one variety of Calvinism.

None the less a number of reviewers have complained of what they see as a too crude 'polarity' between Calvinism and Arminianism. They prefer to think in terms of a 'spectrum' of views.[13] The obvious response is that for certain purposes we need to distinguish between colours; the difference between red and green, for example, can sometimes matter greatly. All discourse of an analytical kind involves both distinctions and

[10] This will be the subject of my 1990 Friends of Dr Williams's Library Lecture.
[11] R. T. Kendall, *Calvin and English Calvinism to 1649* (Oxford, 1979), pp. 79–80 and *passim*.
[12] George Abbot, *An Exposition upon the Prophet Jonah* (1600), pp. 231, 267.
[13] e.g. A. Milton, *JEH*, 39 (1988), 614.

generalizations. Doctrinal distinctions abound throughout the pages of *Anti-Calvinists*—supralapsarians, sublapsarians, hypothetical universalists, and the like—but so do attempts at generalization on the basis of what is perforce usually imperfect evidence. A good illustration of the problems involved is my much contested identification of Archbishop Laud as an 'Arminian', which he himself denied. (It is incidentally worth remarking that in the calmer waters of the late seventeenth century this description would not have seemed nearly so pejorative; even Archbishops of Canterbury can then be found agreeing.)[14]

My appendix on Laud's Arminianism prints three especially relevant documentary excerpts (pp. 266–70). Two others now need adding. The first comes from a court sermon by Laud, of March 1622, and raises the possibility that even the elect can fall finally from grace. As such it strikes at the heart of absolute predestination. God's promise that David 'shall not miscarry' (Psalm 21: 7) is doubly *conditional*, both on the 'religious heart' of David and on divine 'mercy'. The 'providence' of God 'knows not how to forsake till it be forsaken', yet mercy 'will not profit any man that doth not believe and trust in it'. Particularly striking is that Laud here cites the *Collationes* of John Cassian, a fifth-century Church father, on the changeableness of the human will. For Cassian was generally regarded in the early seventeenth century as the founder of 'Semi-Pelagianism', a movement born in reaction to the teaching of St Augustine on the unconditional nature of predestination and which contemporaries justifiably assimilated to modern Arminianism.[15]

The second additional excerpt is Laud's answer to the resolution against Arminianism by the House of Commons, in January 1629, which 'avowed for truth the sense' of the Thirty-nine Articles according to 'the general and current exposition of the writers of our Church' Laud replied that 'the current

[14] Gilbert Burnet, *An Exposition of the Thirty-nine Articles* (1699), pp. i–ii, 152. The Archbishops in question were John Tillotson and Thomas Tenison. A few years later, in 1718, Archbishop William Wake also described Laud as an 'Arminian' (N. Sykes, *William Wake: Archbishop of Canterbury, 1657–1737* (Cambridge, 1957), II. 33).

[15] Willliam Laud, *Works*, ed. W. Scott and J. Bliss (Oxford, 1847–60), I. 55–7; O. Chadwick, *John Cassian* (2nd edn., Cambridge, 1968), p. 127 and ch. 4 *passim*. For the year 1622 as a Jacobean turning-point, see below, pp. 46, 102–3.

exposition of the Fathers themselves hath sometimes missed
"the sense of the Church"'. He added that 'consent of writers
. . . may and perhaps do go against the literal sense'.[16] Clearly
his aim was to circumvent the previously dominant Calvinists.
It is also highly significant that in mid-1622 Hugo Grotius, a
leading advocate of the Dutch Arminian cause, presented Laud
with a copy of his *Disquisitio* on Pelagianism. This treatise is
in reality a criticism of St Augustine and his Calvinist
expositors on the subject of predestination. The other reci-
pients were Lancelot Andrewes and Samuel Harsnett—
English anti-Calvinists of the previous generation.[17] So the
dossier builds up.

Evidence exists, however, that the views of Laud, like those
of his patron Bishop Neile, had changed. Indeed during the
first decade of the seventeenth century Laud appears to have
been a Calvinist, defending the view of John Calvin that the
'regenerate' cannot fall into final impenitency.[18] At the same
time, his mature (Arminian) views on predestination are only
one facet of a complex body of thought; in some ways more
novel were Laud's attitudes to the sacraments.[19] Should we
therefore prefer the term 'Laudian' to 'Arminian'? There are
a number of reasons why not. For a start 'Laudian' is not at
all easy either to define or to apply. Moreover, there are those
who deny that Laud was a Laudian.[20] But the great advantage
of 'Arminian' as a descriptive label is that it alerts us to the
theological dimension.

Yet it is precisely the connection between predestinarian
theology and the sacraments that some reviewers have questioned.[21] *Anti-Calvinists*, however, rehearses numerous cases,
like that of Robert Shelford (pp. 53–5), where this link was

[16] Laud, *Works*, VI. 11–12.
[17] Hugo Grotius, *Disquisitio an Pelagiana sint ea Dogmata quae sub eo Nomine traducuntur* (Paris, 1622), and *Briefwisseling*, ed. P. C. Molhuysen and B. L. Meulenbroek (The Hague, 1928–81), II. 241.
[18] Laud, *Works*, VI. 704. By 1615 Laud was known as an anti-Calvinist, which helps date his comments on this 1596 volume of Bellarmine's *Disputationes*. See below, p. 70.
[19] For a discussion of this and other aspects of Laud's thought see my essay in K. C. Fincham (ed.), *The Early Stuart Church*, Problems in Focus forthcoming.
[20] This, as I understand it, is one of the themes of a forthcoming book by Dr Julian Davies.
[21] e.g. J. P. Sommerville, 'Actions Speaking Louder than Words?', *History Today*, 37 (Sept. 1987), 58.

made explicitly by contemporaries. It is also those on the
Arminian side of the predestinarian debate who were in the
forefront of the ceremonial changes connected with the conversion of communion tables into altars. Some possible exceptions
to this generalization are discussed (pp. 210–13), although
genuine 'Calvinist ceremonialists' seem very rare birds.[22]
Attitudes to ceremonies more generally are beside the point.
Equally irrelevant are the examples of the Dutch Arminians
and the General Baptists, where no such sacramental connection occurs. For the peculiar circumstances of the English
Church, notably the existence of the Prayer Book, provide the
crucial variable. But even this does not mean that anti-
Calvinism in England *had* to take a sacramental form. What
we can say is that in the early seventeenth century it often
did. On such a basis the formal propagation of Arminian
doctrine was unnecessary, given the universal availability of
saving grace in the sacraments. The official ban by Charles I
on all predestinarian teaching was not, however, the innocent
action which my critics suggest. Here an analogy may help.
Were a modern government to forbid all discussion of Marx-
ism, on the grounds that dialectical materialism was likely to
give people the wrong ideas, it would not generally be regarded
as behaving impartially. Silence can be a very effective weapon.

   At this point I am obliged to deal in more detail with one
particular critic—Christopher Haigh, writing in the *English
Historical Review*.[23] Dr Haigh comments that my general thesis,
as originally propounded, 'won acceptance primarily because
historiographically it was a convenient one'. Revisionists
allegedly needed 'the rise of Arminianism' in order to explain
the English Civil War, whereas now 'it begins to look like a
necessary fiction'. Yet changing interpretations of the Civil
War do not affect the reality of the religious developments
described in *Anti-Calvinists*. Dr Haigh goes on to dismiss the

---

[22] Since my critics fail actually to name anyone in this category it is difficult to
respond directly. At the same time it is important to note that all bishops, during
the 1630s, were under pressure to endorse the new ceremonies.

[23] C. Haigh, *EHR*, 103 (1988), 425–7. A puzzling feature of this review is that Dr
Haigh is on recent public record as maintaining (1) that 'insistence' on 'predestination'
was a hallmark of Elizabethan Protestantism and (2) that the successors of those
who rejected such teaching provided grass-roots support for the 'Arminian doctrine'
of the 'Laudian Church' (C. Haigh (ed.), *The Reign of Elizabeth I* (1984), p. 219; C.
Haigh (ed.), *The English Reformation Revised* (Cambridge, 1987), pp. 6, 74).

silencing of Richard Montagu's Calvinist critics in 1626 as a 'petty piece of censorship', while failing to point out that Calvinist teaching at Cambridge University had already been suppressed on the basis of the same royal proclamation (pp. 48–9). Furthermore, *Anti-Calvinists* documents in detail the consequences of the new policy for teaching, preaching, and publishing. The 1626 proclamation and even more the 1628 declaration were not the ineffective orders that Dr Haigh implies. By the beginning of the 1630s university theological teaching had been transformed, along with the preaching at Paul's Cross. Press censorship too was biting increasingly hard. Loopholes of course remained, especially the freedom until 1637 to republish previously licensed works. The chaplains of Archbishop Abbot, who lived on until August 1633, also conducted a rearguard action as licensers for the press.[24] Yet the attitude of officialdom had undoubtedly altered. Thus Daniel Featley, himself a former licenser and chaplain to Abbot, suffered the indignity in 1636 of having his own collected sermons blue-pencilled as regards 'those things which were against Papists and Arminians'.[25]

Just how far the pendulum had swung can be illustrated by the publishing history of the works of Thomas Jackson—the premier English Arminian theologian of the 1630s. Only from the late 1620s onwards did Jackson feel able to express his true views in print. Even so a certain reluctance remained which was not finally overcome until 1638, when two sermons of his about predestination were published on the initiative of William Milbourne. The latter was curate to John Cosin and the work was licensed by a chaplain of Bishop Juxon. In these sermons Jackson refuted Calvinist teaching on both election and reprobation.[26] By May 1640 he had completed a more elaborate statement of his views, incorporating verbatim one of the aforementioned sermons, and presented it for licensing by the Vice-Chancellor of Oxford University. But political

---

[24] *A Transcript of the Registers of the Company of Stationers of London, 1554–1640*, ed. E. Arber (1875–94), IV. 533. The licensing role of Abbot's chaplains Robert Austin and Thomas Buckner looks to have been important here.

[25] HMC House of Lords, NS II. 433–4.

[26] William Milbourne (ed.), *Sapientia Clamitans* (1638), pp. 1–250; John Cosin, *Correspondence*, ed. G. Ornsby (Surtees Soc., 52, 55, 1868–72), I. 222–3; Arber, IV. 375. Milbourne had discussed the publication of these sermons with Cosin.

circumstances had now changed dramatically and the Vice-Chancellor, Accepted Frewen, turned to Archbishop Laud for guidance. Laud replied, on 22 May, in the following remarkable terms:

> You must contrive the handsomest way you can for some *delay*, for certainly this is no time to publish any thing that may give offence, as that will certainly do if it be so expressly against His Majesty's declaration [of 1628] as you write.[27]

The implication is that in more normal times there was little objection to publishing such an Arminian work.[28]

My account of English Arminianism up to 1640 traces a particular thread running through the often labyrinthine religious history of the period. Naturally other approaches are possible, for example from the standpoint of ecclesiology.[29] Nevertheless, the interpretative framework of *Anti-Calvinists* is not the arbitrary invention of the author. Instead it represents an interplay between the surviving evidence and various seventeenth-century attempts, from most points of the religious compass, to chronical the doctrinal evolution of the English Church. A particularly interesting example of this latter genre is Bishop Gilbert Burnet's *Exposition of the Thirty-nine Articles*, first published in 1699 and regularly reprinted well into the nineteenth century. (The work was unknown to me at the time of writing *Anti-Calvinists*.) Burnet was himself an Arminian or, as he chose to put it, a follower of 'the doctrine of the Greek Church from which St Austin departed'. He categorizes the 'first reformers' of the English Church as 'generally' sublapsarian 'Calvinists' and 'in the main points' indistinguishable from St Augustine. Partly under the influence of Dutch events, however, English opinion subsequently grew divided.

---

[27] Thomas Jackson, *Works* (Oxford, 1844), IX. The sermon is on pp. 448–504; Laud, *Works*, V. 268 (my italics). Cautious as always, Laud went on to say that Frewen should, if necessary, invoke the strict letter of the 1628 declaration.

[28] For the very different treatment meted out to Calvinist doctrine, see particularly the case of Richard Clerke in 1636 (HMC House of Lords, NS II. 434–5). Cf. S. Lambert, 'Richard Montagu, Arminianism and Censorship', *Past and Present*, 124 (1989), 64–8. The argument of Miss Lambert, concerning religious censorship, is vitiated by the fact that she fails to analyse the content of the published works which she instances. Censorship was *not* by author, but of views expressed.

[29] Dr Anthony Milton is currently completing such a study.

The Abbots [George and Robert] adhered to St Austin's doctrine; while Bishop Overal, but chiefly Archbishop Laud, espoused the Arminian tenets. All divines were by proclamation required not to preach upon those heads. But those that favoured the new opinions were encouraged, and the others were depressed.[30]

Thereby hangs the tale of the following book.

University College, London   N.T.

May 1990

---

[30] Burnet, *An Exposition of the Thirty-nine Articles*, pp. vi, 149, 151–2. Burnet also integrates the teachings of John Cassian into his account. Ibid., pp. 148–9.

Preface

DEBTS crowd in on the author of a first book. My dedication seeks to acknowledge a primary and continuing obligation. But here pride of place must go to Anne Whiteman, who first taught me the discipline of historical research. A kindly critic for even longer has been Christopher Hill. Many fellow scholars over the years have given me references, and I trust that all their names are duly acknowledged in the footnotes. They, and others who have from time to time discussed aspects of the work with me, include Simon Adams, Michael Archer, Peter Clark, Patrick Collinson, Claire Cross, Richard Cust, Lord Dacre, Alan Davidson, Julian Davies, John Fielding, Kenneth Fincham, Anthony Fletcher, Andrew Foster, Caroline Hibbard, the late Joel Hurstfield, Peter Lake, William Lamont, John Macauley, John Morrill, Harry Porter, Wilfrid Prest, Conrad Russell, Paul Seaver, Bill Sheils, Frederick Shriver, Koenraad Swart, Lady de Villiers, and R. B. Wernham. Particularly to be thanked are Patrick Collinson, Kenneth Fincham, Andrew Foster, Peter Lake, Conrad Russell, and Koenraad Swart, all of whom have read and commented on parts of the book in draft. Keith Thomas, acting in an editorial capacity, has also provided welcome help and encouragement. Of the numerous librarians and archivists who have patiently answered my queries and made their books and manuscripts available to me, it is invidious to name names. Nevertheless, I would be churlish not to mention my neighbours the staff of the Dr Williams's Library. A number of secretaries have wrestled with my successive revisions, notably Nazneen Razwi. Among much kindness and hospitality encountered on the way, a weekend spent with the Dyott family at Freeford stands out.

The present book had its distant beginnings in a doctoral thesis. While the original framework—a mixture of the episodic and the thematic—has been largely retained, a great deal of the evidence now provided is new. This is especially true of the last chapter and the two appendices. Some of the interpretations offered are similarly novel. Many individuals also feature either for the first time or much more prominently than before; one facet of this is the fuller treatment of lay religious attitudes. The argument remains that the rise of English Arminianism, and the consequent outlawing of Calvinism during the 1620s, both destabilized the religious status quo and provided a cutting edge to the increasingly acrimonious politics of Charles I's reign. Puritans, who had been at least partially reconciled to the established church, were as a result driven into renewed opposition. It follows that the Scottish rebellion impinged on an already volatile situation. The categories Arminian, Calvinist and Puritan all have contemporary warrant. 'Anglican', by contrast, is anachronistic to the point of being positively misleading and I have, therefore, avoided using the term.

N.T.

University College, London
February 1986

ADDENDUM

On page 71, below, I offer an explanation as to how the 'Good Shepherd' chalice got to St. John's College, Oxford. It now seems to me much more likely that this was the chalice bequeathed to the college, in 1631, by Bishop John Buckeridge (PRO, PROB. 11/160, fo. 17). Nevertheless, the chalice still stands as evidence of the eucharistic thinking of William Laud's immediate circle.

September 1986

Contents

List of Plates and Map

Abbreviations and Symbols

Arber   *A Transcript of the Registers of the Company of
                         Stationers of London, 1554–1640*, ed. E. Arber
                         (5 volumes, 1875–94)
BIHR   *Bulletin of the Institute of Historical Research*
BL   British Library
CU Arch.   Cambridge University Archives
CUL   Cambridge University Library
Cal. SP Venetian   *Calendar of State Papers Venetian*
Clark, *Register*   *The Register of the University of Oxford*, ed.
                         A. Clark (Oxford Hist. Soc., 10, 1887–9), I
Commons Debates, 1625 *Debates in the House of Commons in 1625*, ed.
                         S. R. Gardiner (Camden Soc., NS 6, 1873)
DNB   *Dictionary of National Biography*
EHR   *English Historical Review*
HMC   Historical Manuscripts Commission
JBS   *Journal of British Studies*
JEH   *Journal of Ecclesiastical History*
OU Arch.   Oxford University Archives
PRO   Public Record Office
Staffs. RO   Staffordshire Record Office
TRHS   *Transactions of the Royal Historical Society*
VCH   *Victoria County History*

*   Denotes my translation from Latin
†   Denotes my translation from French
‡   Denotes my translation from Greek

Introduction

THE ideas of a past society challenge our understanding, because they are often alien to more modern ways of thought. This is especially the case as regards that area of human experience which we call religious. In Elizabethan and early Stuart England religion bulked large. The Protestant saints, God's storm-troopers, were bent on conquering the devil, the flesh, and the world. Divinely elected before birth, they set their eyes on a heavenly kingdom but conceived it as their earthly duty to vindicate God's choice. England was for them a new Israel, her preachers akin to the prophets of the Old Testament, and events were in the hands of God who would not fail his chosen followers at the last. Sin and temptation, however, were everywhere and the saints needed to be on permanent alert, for God was a jealous and a punitive creator. This vision of reality was fed by a literal interpretation of the Bible yet clearly also had contemporary roots, the Spaniards being seen as legionaries of the papal Antichrist, and dearth, trade depression, and plague interpreted as divine judgements on a sinful people. Fear of failure and defeat, measured by terrestrial standards, was countered by the claim to eternal victory for the saints who lived in the world although they were not of it.[1]

The characteristic theology of English Protestant sainthood was Calvinism, centring on a belief in divine predestination, both double and absolute, whereby man's destiny, either election to Heaven or reprobation to Hell, is not conditioned by faith but depends instead on the will of God. Calvinism, so defined, was no mere speculation of the study; according to

---

[1] An example of this way of thinking is *A Necessarie and Godly Prayer appoynted by the Right Reverend Father in God John [Aylmer], Bishop of London, . . . for the Turning Away of God's Wrath* (1585). I discuss below the kindred views of Francis Rous, a layman, pp. 138–9. Much related material is also contained in K. Thomas, *Religion and the Decline of Magic* (1971). For some of the economic realities see B. E. Supple, *Commercial Crisis and Change in England, 1600–1642* (Cambridge, 1964).

Izaak Walton, 'the very women and shopkeepers were able to
judge of predestination'.[2] Particularly important here was the
Genevan Bible, first published in 1560, the marginal notes of
which contained Calvinist comments on the relevant scriptural passages. Similar Calvinist marginalia occur in the
Bishops' Bible of 1568, the officially authorized English version. Thus the Genevan Bible comments on Romans 9 that 'as
the only will and purpose of God is the chief cause of election
and reprobation, so his free mercy in Christ is an inferior
cause of salvation and the hardening of the heart an inferior
cause of damnation'. Glossing this same chapter, the Bishops'
Bible says that 'the will and purpose of God is the cause of . . .
election and reprobation. For his mercy and calling through
Christ are the means of salvation and the withdrawing of his
mercy is the cause of damnation.'

Between 1579 and 1615 at least thirty-nine quarto editions
of the Genevan Bible, *all* printed in England, had a predestinarian catechism bound with them. This catechism runs in
part as follows.

Question: Are not all ordained unto eternal life?
Answer: Some are vessels of wrath ordained unto destruction, as
    others are vessels of mercy prepared to glory.
Question: How standeth it with God's justice that some are appointed
    unto damnation?
Answer: Very well because all men have in themselves sin which
    deserveth no less, and therefore the mercy of God is wonderful in
    that he vouchsafeth to save some of that sinful race and to bring
    them to the knowledge of the truth.
Question: If God's ordinance and determination must of necessity
    take effect, then what need any man to care; for . . . he that liveth
    ill must needs be saved if he be thereunto appointed?
Answer: Not so, for it is not possible that either the elect should
    always be without care to do well or that the reprobate should
    have any will thereunto. For to have either good will or good work
    is a testimony of the spirit of God, which is given to the elect
    only . . .
Question: Cannot such perish as at some time or other feel these
    motions within themselves ['of spiritual life, which belongeth only
    to the children of God']?

---

[2] Izaak Walton, *The Life of Mr Richard Hooker* (1665), p. 59. Walton purports to be
quoting the comments of an Italian visitor to England in the 1580s.

Answer: It is not possible that they should, for as God's purpose is not changeable so he repenteth not the gifts and graces of his adoption. Neither doth he cast off those whom he hath once received.[3]

Most of these Genevan Bibles were printed by the royal printers Christopher and Robert Barker, or their deputies.

Evidence of the successful propagation of Calvinism among the laity is furnished by numerous wills in which the testator claims to be an elect saint.[4] As far as the clergy were concerned, Calvinist teachings became a major item of university diet and also found favour with leaders of the established church. During the 1590s absolute predestination was endorsed by the archbishops of Canterbury and York, John Whitgift and Matthew Hutton, as well as by successive bishops of London: John Aylmer, Richard Fletcher, and Richard Bancroft.[5] Indeed, it is not an exaggeration to say that by the end of the sixteenth century the Church of England was largely Calvinist in doctrine—something which is abundantly illustrated by the publications of the printing press. Part of this printed evidence, which includes information on university teaching, was assembled by William Prynne in his book *Anti-Arminianisme.*[6] My own investigation of the Paul's Cross sermons fully bears Prynne out.[7] Yet this situation had come about through default of any alternative interpretation of the Elizabethan religious settlement, and its confessional basis remained insecure. Granted that the Thirty-nine Articles, the English confession of faith, favoured the Calvinists, none the less the Elizabethan Prayer Book needed careful exposition in order not to contradict predestinarian theology; Prayer Book descriptions of the baptized Christian as 'a member of Christ, the child of God, and an inheritor of the Kingdom of Heaven', and of penitent communicants as 'very members incorporate' in 'the blessed

[3] C. Eason, *The Genevan Bible* (Dublin, 1937), pp. 8–9, 22–3.
[4] It has been calculated that between 1571 and 1650 some 20 per cent of surviving Manchester wills were of this type. R. C. Richardson, 'Puritanism in the Diocese of Chester to 1642', Manchester Ph.D. thesis, 1968, pp. 283–300.
[5] J. Strype, *The Life and Acts of John Whitgift* (Oxford, 1822), II. 280–1; E. Arber, *A Transcript of the Registers of the Company of Stationers of London, 1554–1640* (1875–94), II. 264, III. 43ᵛ.
[6] William Prynne, *Anti-Arminianisme* (1630), pp. 77–213, 240–62.
[7] See Appendix I.

company of all faithful people', might seem to run counter to the assertion of the Articles that 'predestination to life is the ever-lasting purpose of God, whereby (before the foundations of the world were laid) he hath constantly decreed by his counsel, secret to us, to deliver from curse and damnation those whom he hath chosen in Christ out of mankind . . .'

In the early and middle years of Elizabeth's reign Calvinism keyed in fairly convincingly with political reality. To begin with, the existence of a large body of English Catholics lent credence to the identification of Protestants with the elect.[8] Later, as relations with Spain deteriorated, Calvinism was transferable to the international plane, and Englishmen were now portrayed as chosen by God to do battle for the true religion.[9] But as political circumstances eased, so the way was opened for undermining Calvinism from within. In the course of the 1590s the external threat from Spain appeared to diminish and the prospect of an internal revolt by English Catholics seemed increasingly remote. A united Protestant front was, therefore, less essential. At the same time English Calvinist teaching was itself becoming more extreme, in line with continental religious developments.[10] Reaction came from those who have been called Arminians *avant la lettre*,[11] because not until the early seventeenth century were the major works of the Dutch theologian Jacobus Arminius published. So systematic, however, was his refutation of Calvinism that he gave his name to the anti-Calvinist movement generally.[12] Flash point occurred at Cambridge University in 1595, when William Barrett, a college chaplain, publicly challenged the Calvinist predestinarian schema. Archbishop

[8] Even towards the end of Elizabeth's reign there was a tendency to equate Catholics with reprobates. *The Recantation of Thomas Clarke* (1594), sigs. A4ᵛ–A6, B2–B4, D5ʳ⁻ᵛ.
[9] *A Forme of Prayer thought fitte to be dayly used in the English Armie in France* (1589), sigs. B1ᵛ–B3.
[10] B. Hall, 'Calvin against the Calvinists', *Proc. Huguenot Soc.* 20 (1962), 284–301 and R. T. Kendall, *Calvin and English Calvinism to 1649* (Oxford, 1979), pp. 13–76.
[11] H. C. Porter, *Reformation and Reaction in Tudor Cambridge* (Cambridge, 1958), p. 281.
[12] Jacobus Arminius, *Writings*, tr. J. Nichols and W. R. Bagnall (Grand Rapids, 1956), i. p. iii. What finally determined that the name of Arminius, rather than that of any other theologian, became synonymous with anti-Calvinism was the Synod of Dort. This international Calvinist gathering condemned the doctrines of Arminius and his disciples in 1619.

Whitgift was forced to intervene and, after consulting with his fellow primate, Archbishop Hutton of York, he approved a set of doctrinal rulings which came to be known as the Lambeth Articles. These are unequivocally Calvinist and provide an accurate index of received Church of England teaching, although they incurred the displeasure of Queen Elizabeth.[13] The upshot was that Arminianism before Arminius was for the time being suppressed, and Calvinism remained dominant in England throughout the first two decades of the seventeenth century.

An insight into the early Jacobean religious situation comes from a remarkable pamphlet written in 1613, by a Catholic convert called Benjamin Carier. He addressed his remarks to King James in the form of an open letter, and claimed that the Calvinism of the English Church had driven him into the arms of Rome. Carier's intellectual odyssey was probably similar to that of many English Arminians, most of whom, however, stopped short of conversion to Catholicism. By his own account born the son of a Protestant 'preacher' in 1566, Carier was resident in Cambridge for some twenty years (1582–1602), first as a student then as a fellow of Corpus Christi College. Thereafter he became a chaplain to both Archbishop Whitgift and King James, and a canon of Canterbury. In his apologia, he recalls that from about 1590 he concentrated exclusively on the study of 'church historie, and of the ancient fathers'. As a result he found 'the current opinions of our great preachers to be every where confuted', and on examining the matter further he concluded that they also 'wrong[ed] the Church of England . . ., for [in] the doctrine of predestination, sacraments, grace, freewill, synne, etc. the new catechismes and sermons of those preachers did run wholy against the Common Prayer Booke'. Carier had hoped 'to prove that the religion established by law in England was the same, at the least in part, which now was and ever had bin held in the Catholicke Church . . ., as an introduction unto farther peace and unitie with the Church of Rome'. But his

---

[13] Porter, *Reformation and Reaction*, pp. 344–90. The most recent and convincing treatment of Cambridge developments is by Dr P. Lake, in his *Moderate Puritans and the Elizabethan Church* (Cambridge, 1982), pp. 201–42. For my own discussion see below, pp. 29–33.

hopes were dashed by events during the early years of King
James's reign; instead of reconciliation, Gunpowder Plot had
rekindled the fires of Protestant extremism. In consequence
John Calvin's *Institution* is still 'the only current divinitie in
court and countrie'. Yet Calvinist teaching on predestination,
says Carier, makes both priest and sacraments redundant and
Calvinist bishops, those who 'goe in rochets', are traitors to
the clerical estate. The English monarchy, moreover, is in
danger of being turned into a 'Helvetian or Belgian popular-
ity', because 'if they ['the Calvinists'] can make their bourgers
princes and turne old kingdomes into new states it is lyke
ynough they will do it'. 'I beseech Your Majestie lett not Calvin's "church of the predestined"* deceave you.' 'Calvinisme'
is unfit 'to keepe subjects in obedience to their soveraigns', for
soon 'they will openly maintayne that God hath as well predestinated men to be trayters as to be kinges'.[14]

   The official reply to Carier, written by George Hakewill,
acknowledged the so-called 'Calvinisme' of the English
Church. At the same time Hakewill pointed out that this
teaching, 'rightly understood', was that of St Augustine. Faith
and works are not 'causes' but 'markes and effects infallible of
our predestination'. Hakewill went on to quote St Augustine
against 'their vaine manner of reasoning who defend the
foresight of God against the grace of God, affirming that wee
were therefore chosen before the foundation of the world
because God foresaw wee would be good [and] not that himselfe would make us good'. Reprobation is to be distinguished
'into a negative and positive act; the negative is God's will of
not saving men, the positive his will of damning men'. Faith is
'an assured perswaision' that 'wee are predestinate'. Such are
'the opinions of the Church of England (which you call Calvinisme) maintained as well by the pens as the tongues of
those church-men who sit at the sterne and in the most emi-
nent places of the Church'.[15]

   Nevertheless much of what Carier had to say was only an
extreme version of thoughts already forming in the mind of

   [14] Benjamin Carier, *A Treatise written by Mr. Doctour Carier* (Liège, 1614), pp. 10–14,
26–7, 37, 49–52. I have followed contemporary usage in referring to the English translation of Calvin's famous work as *Institution* rather than *Institutes*.
   [15] George Hakewill, *An Answere to a Treatise written by Dr. Carier* (1616), pp. 285–91.

William Laud. For it was in 1615 that Laud first came out against Calvinism,[16] and the publication of Carier's pamphlet may even have hastened that decision. Certainly in 1615 an Oxford colleague of Laud, John Howson, was referring sympathetically to the Carier case: 'hee would have beene a Protestant yett, if hee had not beene ill used.'[17] Laud, like Carier, so elevated the role of sacraments, and the grace which they conferred, as effectively to supplant the grace of predestination. Similarly he deplored the political consequences of predestinarian teaching.[18] These same years, however, also saw the development of a more philosophical critique of Calvinism. Here, too, clerics were prominent, although the lay appeal was potentially greater. An important early figure was the Oxonian Thomas Jackson, who in 1613 can be found writing that 'much would it avail to be resolved whether all things fall out by fatal necessity, or some contingently; how fate and contingency (if compatible each with other) stand mutually affected, how both subordinate to the absolute immutability of that one everlasting decree'. Originally intended to be a Newcastle merchant and subsequently the' university protégé of Lord Eure, Jackson was to have a direct religious influence on members of the parliamentary gentry.[19] Moreover, a notable feature of Jackson's arguments against unconditional predestination was his use of mathematical imagery.[20] But during the second decade of the seventeenth century English Arminians were still unable to publish their views in print, and Calvinists continued to control the English Church.

That Calvinism was the *de facto* religion of the Church of England under Queen Elizabeth and King James may surprise those brought up to regard Calvinists and Puritans as one and the same. Such an identification, however, witnesses to the posthumous success of the Arminians in blackening the reputation of their Calvinist opponents; until the 1620s Puritan, as a technical term, was usually employed to describe

---

[16] Peter Heylyn, *Cyprianus Anglicus* (1671), p. 62.

[17] PRO, SP 14/80, fo. 177ᵛ.

[18] William Laud, *Works*, ed. W. Scott and J. Bliss (Oxford, 1847–60), vi. 57, 245–6.

[19] Thomas Jackson, *Works* (Oxford, 1844), i. pp. xxxix–xl, lv–lvi, lxiii and see below, pp. 141–4. Eure may have introduced Jackson to Lord Spencer, whose sons Richard and Edward became his pupils at Corpus Christi College, Oxford.

[20] Jackson, *Works*, v. 203–9.

those members of the English Church who wanted further
Protestant reforms in liturgy and organization.[21] Only there-
after was the definition of Puritanism publicly extended so as
to include Calvinist doctrine.[22] Thus in 1626 the Calvinist
Bishop Carleton could write, in reply to the Arminian Richard
Montagu: 'this is the first time that ever I heard of a Puritane
doctrine in points dogmaticall, and I have lived longer in the
Church than he [Montagu] hath done.'[23] Yet much more was
involved than a redefining of terms, for the accession of
Charles I in 1625 meant the overthrow of Calvinism. This
Arminian revolution, its genesis and working out, is the sub-
ject of the present book.[24]

---

[21] The term Puritan is so used throughout this book. It was also, of course,
employed as an abusive epithet to cover any and every aspect of Protestant religiosity.

[22] One of the begetters of the new definition was Bishop Overall, who during the
second decade of the seventeenth century can be found describing the Dutch opponents of Arminianism as Puritans. Porter, *Reformation and Reaction*, p. 410.

[23] George Carleton, *An Examination of those Things wherein the Author of the late Appeale
[Richard Montagu] holdeth the Doctrines of the Pelagians and Arminians to be the Doctrines of the
Church of England* (1626), p. 78. The first historian of Arminianism, Peter Heylyn, was
clear that Calvinists and Puritans were not one and the same. *Cyprianus Anglicus*,
p. 119.

[24] I have not attempted to discuss the emergence of Arminian or 'General' Baptists. For their limited activities prior to 1640 see C. Burrage, *The Early English Dissenters in the Light of Recent Research* (Cambridge, 1912), I. 251–80.

I

The Hampton Court Conference and Arminianism *avant la lettre*

I

WHY begin a study of English Arminianism with the Hampton Court Conference of 1604? Traditionally the conference is associated with an attempt by the Puritans to modify the rites and discipline of the established church. But the doctrine of predestination was also discussed there and I have chosen this starting-point, in preference to the predestinarian disputes at Cambridge University during the 1590s, because before 1604 the challenge to Calvinism never fully escaped from the university confines. At Hampton Court anti-Calvinism received, for the first time, an airing at national level. Therefore, the conference provides a better standard of comparison than do the Cambridge disputes by which to judge subsequent religious developments within the English Church. Even more important, the Hampton Court Conference was the last time when the predestinarian question was handled, by English religious leaders, in an atmosphere largely free from continental Arminian influences.

The conference, which met in January 1604, had resulted from a burst of Puritan activity at the accession of James I. Puritan clergy and gentry entertained high hopes of the new King, and sent an emissary to him while still in Scotland.[1] Some initiative also came from the Scottish Church, especially in the person of Patrick Galloway, former Moderator of the General Assembly, who travelled south with James.[2] *En route* to London, in April 1603, the Puritans presented the King with what is known as the Millenary Petition.[3] One of several similar approaches, this petition was perhaps the most

[1] HMC Salisbury, xvii. 620–1.
[2] David Calderwood, *The History of the Kirk in Scotland*, ed. T. Thomson (Edinburgh, 1842–9), vi. 222, 241–7.
[3] For this dating see *The Answere of the . . . Universitie of Oxford* (Oxford, 1603), sigs. ¶3. ¶4ᵛ.

influential in bringing about the Hampton Court meeting
between representatives of the English hierarchy and the Puritans. The two parties were authorized to discuss the general
state of the English Church, at a conference to be presided
over by the King. In the event, the Puritan reformers failed to
obtain from James a new religious settlement significantly
more to their liking.[4]

While much of the debate at Hampton Court turned on
matters at issue for most of Elizabeth's reign, it also saw the
introduction of a new doctrinal element. This took the form of
a Puritan request that the Lambeth Articles of 1595 be given
confessional status. These Calvinist rulings had resulted
from Archbishop Whitgift's arbitration of the Cambridge
predestinarian disputes during the mid-1590s and they were
originally conceived as a local solution. At Hampton Court,
however, the Puritan John Reynolds asked that the Lambeth
Articles be added to the existing English confession of faith—
the Thirty-nine Articles. Unfortunately for the historian, this
request came during a session at which comparatively few
representatives of the ecclesiastical hierarchy were present to
register a response. Nevertheless, when taken in conjunction
with views expressed on the related topic of baptism, at a
more fully attended previous session, the ensuing discussion
about predestination provides the best single guide to contemporary Church of England teaching. For at this period the
degree of emphasis placed by an English theologian on predestination was usually in inverse proportion to that which he
put on baptism, thus bearing out Max Weber's dictum that
'every consistent doctrine of predestined grace inevitably
implied a radical and ultimate devaluation of all magical, sacramental and institutional distributions of grace, in view of
God's sovereign will'.[5] Indeed the grace of predestination and
the grace of the sacraments were to become rivals for the
religious allegiance of English men and women during the
early seventeenth century.

The standpoint of many participants at Hampton Court

[4] M. H. Curtis, 'The Hampton Court Conference and its Aftermath', *History*, 46
(1961), 1–16; F. Shriver, 'Hampton Court Revisited: James I and the Puritans', *JEH*,
33 (1982), 48–71; P. Collinson, 'The Jacobean Religious Settlement: the Hampton
Court Conference', in *Before the Civil War*, ed. H. Tomlinson (1983), pp. 27–51.

[5] M. Weber, *The Sociology of Religion*, tr. E. Fischoff (1966), p. 203.

can also be established independently of accounts of the conference. But if the views of those attending are to be treated as
representative of opinon at that time, it is worth asking on
what grounds they were chosen to take part. Most had probably received a letter of summons from the Privy Council, the
only surviving example apparently being one transcribed in
the *Life* of Richard Field by his son Nathaniel. This letter is
dated 27 August 1603 from Basing, and it is signed by privy
councillors Robert Cecil, Devonshire, Henry Howard, Mar,
and Northumberland.[6] These five seem to have been the inner
ring of the Privy Council at this date, and between them they
also represent the two factions which were to characterize
James's government for most of his reign.[7] Since the bishops
were summoned as a party to the intended debate, it is not
unreasonable to assume that James turned for advice to his
courtiers about the selection of representatives. My suggestion, then, is that many of the clergy at Hampton Court can
appropriately be regarded as the nominees of aristocratic
patrons, especially of leading privy councillors.[8]

Lord Henry Howard, later Earl of Northampton, was a
Catholic and the Earl of Northumberland was sympathetic to
Catholic recusants.[9] Both are known to have been hostile to
Puritanism. At the conference Howard drew the King's attention to nonconformist practices in Emmanuel College
chapel,[10] and subsequently Northumberland condemned Puritan petitioning as tantamount to rebellion.[11] On the other
hand, the Earl of Devonshire, formerly Lord Mountjoy, was
regarded as a potential supporter of the Puritans in the 1604
parliament.[12] That same year a sabbatarian tract was dedicated to him by George Widley, who was soon afterwards

[6] Nathaniel Field, *Some Short Memorials concerning the Life of . . . R. Field*, ed. J. Le
Neve (1717), p. 9.

[7] D. H. Willson, *The Privy Councillors in the House of Commons, 1604–1629* (Minneapolis, 1940), pp. 17–18, 22.

[8] This does not rule out the influence of Archbishop Whitgift, who was also a privy
councillor, nor does it assume that the five signatories of the letter to Field were all
equally interested in the matter.

[9] *Correspondence of King James VI of Scotland with Sir Robert Cecil and Others in England*,
ed. J. Bruce (Camden Soc., 1st ser. 78, 1861), pp. 36, 47, 56.

[10] R. G. Usher, *The Reconstruction of the English Church* (1910), II. 338.

[11] *Les Reportes del Cases in Camera Stellata 1593 to 1609*, ed. W. P. Baildon (1894),
p. 190.

[12] Bodleian, Tanner MS 75, fo. 109.

suspended for nonconformity.[13] In addition Devonshire describes himself in his will of 1606 as 'assuredly considering' that he is one of the 'elect'.[14] Of not dissimilar outlook to Devonshire was the Earl of Mar. In Scotland he had been one of the leading presbyterian lords. He was exiled during 1584–5, for political activities, and his residence in England coincided with that of Patrick Galloway, the later Scottish presbyterian agent.[15] Both had made contact with the English Puritans during this period and, with the accession of James, Mar was considered by some as likely to favour further reforms in the English Church.[16] In a category on his own was Robert Cecil, at this date Baron of Essendon. Recently he had given a measure of protection to individual Puritans, for example shielding Stephen Egerton, the lecturer at Black-friars, from prosecution by the ecclesiastical authorities,[17] and in 1605 Andrew Willet, in a book dedication to Cecil, considered it worth recommending to him a policy of 'brotherly connivence' towards Puritan nonconformists.[18] Yet Cecil in his will, made in 1612, went out of his way to emphasize the importance of sacraments, writing of the eucharist as a source of 'speciall nourishment and lief and graces whatsoever' to a penitent receiver.[19] Moreover, his chaplain Richard Neile was, after Cecil's death, to become the organizing genius of early English Arminianism.[20]

On the assumption that these five privy councillors had some say in the selection of conference members, those chosen might be expected to vary considerably in their religious attitudes. An analysis of those attending the conference in fact reveals a divergence of views among the representatives both of the hierarchy and the Puritans. There is, however, still some doubt as to whom precisely the Puritan contingent

[13] George Widley, *The Doctrine of the Sabbath* (1604), sigs. A2–A4; W. H. Mildon, 'Puritanism in Hampshire and the Isle of Wight from the Reign of Elizabeth to the Restoration', London Ph.D. thesis, 1934, p. 45.

[14] PRO, PROB. 11/108, fo. 1.

[15] G. Donaldson, 'Scottish Presbyterian Exiles in England, 1584–8', *Recds Scottish Church Hist. Soc.*, 14 (1960), 67–80.

[16] Miles Mosse, *Scotland's Welcome* (1603), sig. A3ʳ⁻ᵛ and pp. 60–6.

[17] HMC Salisbury, XVII. 38.

[18] Andrew Willet, *Hexapla in Genesin* (Cambridge, 1605), ii, sig. Kk1ᵛ.

[19] PRO, PROB. 11/119, fo. 389ᵛ.

[20] See below, Chapter 5.

included. William Barlow in his official account, written originally at Whitgift's request, lists four. These are Laurence
Chaderton, John Knewstubb, John Reynolds, and Thomas
Sparke. Other contemporary sources indicate that the number
should be raised to five by the addition of Richard Field. It is
clear that he attended the conference but the difficulty is to
establish in what capacity. On a list of proposed representatives compiled in late 1603, Field is named as an alternative to
Arthur Hildersham, a notorious nonconformist. Furthermore,
an anonymous but contemporary account of the subsequent
conference considers Field's silence in the Puritan cause
worthy of remark, and Galloway writes of *five* 'bretheren' representing the Puritans at Hampton Court.[21] If Field previously
was a Puritan, perhaps by the time of the conference he had
changed his mind.[22] There is also the anomalous case of John
Gordon, made Dean of Salisbury in 1603. He was a Scot, with
Huguenot connections, whom Barlow lists as a supporter of
the established church. Nevertheless, one of Gordon's
recorded interventions at Hampton Court was to question the
antiquity of signing with the cross in baptism and to judge by
a comment some months afterwards, from John Chamberlain,
he would in January 1604 have ranked as of nonconformist
tendency.[23]

Chaderton, Knewstubb, and Reynolds had all been participants in the classical movement of the 1580s.[24] Yet, unlike
Chaderton, Reynolds endorsed a form of episcopacy. So did
Sparke, who had been Archdeacon of Stow and claimed to
have conformed even before the conference.[25] Knewstubb's
position was probably similar to that of Chaderton. The signs
are that these four clergy were all Calvinists.[26] But more

[21] E. Cardwell, *A History of Conferences . . . connected with the Revision of the Book of Common Prayer* (Oxford, 1840), pp. 170, 213; PRO, SP 14/6, fo. 44; *DNB* s.n. Hildersham,
Arthur; Usher, *Reconstruction*, II. 338.
[22] It is possible that Field was summoned simply as an expert witness, although his
book *Of the Church* had not yet appeared.
[23] *DNB* s.n. Gordon, John (1544–1619); Cardwell, *Conferences*, pp. 170, 197; John
Chamberlain, *Letters*, ed. N. E. McClure (Philadelphia, 1939), I. 206.
[24] BL Harleian MS 6849, fo. 231ʳ⁻ᵛ; P. Collinson, *The Elizabethan Puritan Movement*
(1967), p. 320.
[25] John Reynolds, *The Summe of the Conference betwene John Rainoldes and John Hart*
(1584), p. 535; Laurence Chaderton, *A Fruitfull Sermon* (1584), pp. 41–2; Thomas
Sparke, *A Brotherly Perswasion* (1607), sigs. B3–B4.
[26] Laurence Chaderton, *An Excellent and Godly Sermon* (1580), sig. E1; John

problematic is the case of Richard Field. Shortly after the
Hampton Court meeting he clarified his position in a sermon.
Religious disputes, he said, fell into three categories—'things
indifferent', 'things mistaken' and 'matters of fayth'; only the
last was a legitimate source of conflict. As examples of the first
two categories, he instanced 'the contentions of some in our
church, about round and square, white and black, sitting,
standing and kneeling', and the differences between Lutherans and Calvinists 'touching the losing or not losing of grace
once had, and touching predestination'. Field's apparent
moderation with regard to the predestinarian question is especially striking. Yet he cannot on the doctrinal evidence of his
other published writings, which appeared between 1606 and
1610, be styled an anti-Calvinist.[27]

By mid-1603 the most likely court patron of Puritans was
Devonshire, upon whom the mantle of the Earl of Essex had
descended. During the last years before his rebellion Essex
increasingly associated with Puritan clergy, and it is suggestive that a former secretary of Essex, William Temple, can be
found writing to Devonshire in May 1604 that 'the worthiest
preachers in this land . . . expect at your Lordship's hands an
endeavour to relieve them' from 'unjustifiable conformity'.[28]
In support of Essex's scheme for expediting the accession of
King James, Devonshire had planned to bring over troops
from Ireland, and Mar, whose Puritan connections we have
already remarked, was involved as a diplomatic intermediary.[29] Of the Puritan representatives at the Hampton
Court Conference their 'foreman' Reynolds had been maintained by Essex in a special university lectureship at Oxford,
and while under house arrest in April 1600 Essex twice
requested permission to confer with him.[30] Back in the 1580s
Knewstubb was patronized by Ambrose Dudley, Earl of War-

Knewstubb, *A Sermon preached at Paules Cross* (1579), sigs. Q2, S2. This sermon is
appended to *A Confutation of Monstrous and Horrible Heresies* (1579); Cardwell, *Conferences*, p. 178; Sparke, *A Brotherly Perswasion*, p. 3.

[27] Richard Field, *A Learned Sermon preached before the King at Whitehall* (1604), sigs.
B5–B7 and *Of the Church* (Cambridge, 1847–52), IV. 429–32.

[28] Bodleian, Tanner MS 75, fo. 109.

[29] *Correspondence of King James VI of Scotland*, ed. Bruce, pp. xxi–xxix.

[30] John Reynolds, *De Romanae Ecclesiae Idolatria* (Oxford, 1596), sig. ¶3ʳ⁻ᵛ; *HMC
Salisbury*, x. 124, 127.

wick, and Sparke by Lord Arthur Grey of Wilton.[31] Similarly
in 1584 Chaderton had been chosen by Sir Walter Mildmay to
be first Master of Emmanuel College, Cambridge. Given that
the Puritan aristocracy 'chose both their wives and their
friends from within the clan',[32] these Puritan clergy are likely
to have been moving within the same patronage circles at the
start of the new reign.

II

Of the representatives of the hierarchy at the Hampton Court
Conference, Barlow lists seventeen bishops and deans (including Gordon) as attending. But it is necessary to add George
Abbot, Dean of Winchester, since his name appears in three
other contemporary accounts.[33] The nine bishops due to
attend had been selected by late August 1603. The list of
deans, however, remained incomplete until the eve of the
meeting.[34] There was also one archdeacon—John King of Nottingham. Among the bishops, Richard Bancroft of London
revealed himself at Hampton Court as thoroughly hostile to
the Puritan requests, at times disagreeing with his own metropolitan, Archbishop Whitgift, and with the King. Bancroft
and Thomas Bilson of Winchester had probably resisted the
idea of any such meeting from the start. Certainly to the
organizers of the Puritan agitation Bishop Bilson seemed
among their most formidable enemies prior to the conference
and they wrote, for instance, of his attempts to discredit Galloway with the King.[35] At Hampton Court both these bishops
defended the administration of baptism by lay persons 'in case
of necessity'. Bancroft put the case

that the state of the infant dying unbaptized being uncertain, and to
God only known, but if it die baptized there is an evident assurance
that it is saved, who is he, that having any religion in him, would not
speedily by any means procure his child to be baptized, and rather

[31] Knewstubb, *A Confutation*, sig. *2; Thomas Sparke, *A Sermon preached at Cheanies* (1585), sig. Aii.
[32] L. Stone, *The Crisis of the Aristocracy, 1558–1641* (Oxford, 1965), p. 742.
[33] Cardwell, *Conferences*, pp. 169–70; Usher, *Reconstruction*, II. 337, 341; HMC Beaulieu, p. 33.
[34] PRO, SP 14/3, fo. 87.
[35] BL, Sloane MS 271, fo. 23.

ground his action upon Christ's promise than his omission thereof upon God's secret judgement.

In support of Bancroft, Bilson affirmed 'that the denying of private persons in cases of necessity to baptize were to cross all antiquity'.[36] Bishops Thomas Dove of Peterborough and Anthony Watson of Chichester also appeared actively hostile to the Puritans and their requests. Watson had taken a prominent part in arresting some Puritan petitioners in late 1603,[37] while at the conference Dove 'alledged out of the ecclesiastical writers that an ancient father in case of necessity baptised with sand instead of water'.[38] A few months earlier Dove's commissary, Richard Butler, had caused a furore by maintaining that infants dying unbaptized were damned.[39]

But of the bishops at Hampton Court Bancroft was unique in his direct criticism of predestinarian views. Replying to the Puritan request that official teaching about the perseverance or continuance in faith of the saints be strengthened, he 'took occasion to signifie to His Majesty how very many in these daies, neglecting holinesse of life, presumed too much of persisting of grace, laying all their religion upon predestination— "if I shall be saved, I shall be saved", which he termed a desperate doctrine'.[40] This kind of criticism, which stressed the antinomian perversion of Calvinism, was to become a familiar Arminian argument in later years, and one reason for Bancroft taking such a line at the conference may have been his fear of predestination as a political ethic. Thus he had earlier pointed out that the English millenarians who in 1591 proclaimed the return of Christ, and attempted to seize power for the saints, defended their action on grounds 'of predestination, as though (by the abuse of that doctrine) they meant to have had the blame of all the wicked and intended mischiefes, both of themselves and of their partakers, removed from themselves, and layde uppon the Lorde's shoulders—as though he should have moved them to such lewd attemptes'.[41] Neverthe-

---

[36] Cardwell, *Conferences*, pp. 175–6, 180.
[37] HMC Salisbury, xv. 262–3.
[38] Usher, *Reconstruction*, II. 342.
[39] BL Add. MS 8978, p. 94.
[40] Cardwell, *Conferences*, p. 180.
[41] Richard Bancroft, *Dangerous Positions* (1593), p. 162. The fullest account of the Hacket conspiracy is by R. Bauckham, *Tudor Apocalypse* (Abingdon, 1978), pp. 191–204.

less, even in Bancroft's case it would be a mistake to assimilate his position to that of Arminianism. For at Hampton Court he also spoke of the 'true doctrine of predestination, wherein we should reason . . . thus: "I live in obedience to God, in love with my neighbour, I follow my vocation, etc., therfore I trust that God hath elected me and predestinated me to salvation"'.[42] Moreover, as Bishop of London Bancroft had in 1598 personally licensed an English translation of a Calvinist treatise entirely devoted to the predestinarian controversy. Written by Jacobus Kimedoncius of Heidelberg, this work denied that Christ had died for all mankind and asserted the doctrine of unconditional predestination.[43]

Significantly different, however, were the collective attitudes of Bishops Babington of Worcester, Robinson of Carlisle, Rudd of St David's, and Matthew of Durham—all of whom attended the Hampton Court Conference. On 30 November 1603 Stephen Egerton wrote from London that the first three 'are turned Puritans, to whom I doubt not but Durham will joyne'.[44] This is a statement to which little attention has been paid, in spite of the fact that it came from a well-informed source. For Egerton was one of those who had presented the Millenary Petition to the King, and during May 1604 he was to petition convocation in similar terms.[45] His characterization of these bishops therefore merits serious consideration. Information about Gervase Babington's disposition towards Puritanism is lacking, but Henry Robinson, as Provost of Queen's College, Oxford, had in the 1580s held religious views probably identical with those of the Puritan Reynolds.[46] Anthony Rudd, during the 1604 convocation, was to advise against the enforcement of ceremonies such as signing with the cross in baptism, since both the Puritans and their opponents agreed 'in substance of religion'.[47] Earlier Toby Matthew, about whom Egerton had reservations, can be

[42] Cardwell, *Conferences*, pp. 180–1.

[43] Jacobus Kimedoncius, *Of the Redemption of Mankind . . . wherein the Controversie of the Universalitie of Redemption and Grace by Christ, and of his Death for All Men, is largely handled. Hereunto is annexed a Treatise of God's Predestination* (1598); Arber, III. 43ᵛ.

[44] BL Sloane MS 271, fos. 23ᵛ–4.

[45] Thomas Fuller, *The Church History of Britain*, ed. J. S. Brewer (Oxford, 1845), v. 265; D. Wilkins, *Concilia* (1737), IV. 379.

[46] Collinson, *Elizabethan Puritan Movement*, pp. 459, 504.

[47] BL Harleian MS 7049, fos. 284–5ᵛ.

found writing to Robert Cecil regarding 'the scandalous circumstances of the execution of the nowe Church's discipline'.[48] As Archbishop of York, from 1606, Matthew was to protect individual Puritan ministers.[49] Yet to dub such bishops Puritans was to confuse tolerance with agreement, although in the light of later usage it is interesting that they also tended to be strong Calvinists.[50]

Bishop Babington, for example, held views more unyielding than those embodied in the Lambeth Articles, as can be seen from a Paul's Cross sermon of 1590 where he stated that 'salvation or damnation' are according to the 'good pleasure' of God. 'Esau and Jacob, Peter and Judas with the two theves at the death of Christ, and many mo[re], declare thus much in example to us. God hath loved and God hath hated, God hath elected and God hath rejected, God hath saved and God hath cast away for ever.' At Hampton Court, in opposition to Bancroft and Bilson, Babington denied the legality of lay baptism with its implication of utmost urgency. His view, rehearsed earlier in print, succinctly illustrates the connection between baptism and predestination: 'no elect can be damned, wee knowe it a principle whatsoever foolish men do prattle, but some unbaptized are elect (a thing that no man will deny) therefore some unbaptized cannot be damned.'[51] Similarly Matthew's Calvinist theology emerges clearly from a sermon preached in 1592 before the Earl of Huntingdon, where he rebuts the charge that

we so preach the doctrine of God's eternal predestination that we make thereof a mere stoical and fatal necessity, and teach the people that if they be predestinate they shall be saved do what they list, [while] if they be not predestinate they may not be saved do what they can. Whereas our doctrine is this: that whether a man be predestinate or no, yet he should live so much as may be in a holy obedience. Because if he be predestinate he must make his election sure by well doing, working out his salvation in fear and trembling;

[48] PRO, SP 14/4, fo. 205.
[49] R. A. Marchant, *The Puritans and the Church Courts in the Diocese of York, 1560–1642* (1960), pp. 29–51.
[50] Cf. P. Lake, 'Matthew Hutton—A Puritan Bishop?', *History*, 64 (1979), 182–204.
[51] Gervase Babington, *A Sermon preached at Paules Crosse* (1591), p. 8 and *Certaine Plaine, Briefe, and Comfortable Notes upon Everie Chapter of Genesis* (1592), fo. 62ᵛ; Cardwell, *Conferences*, pp. 174–5.

for he that hath that hope that he is one of God's sons doth purify himself, and being a vessel of honor must keep himself fair and clean for the use of his Master, being sanctified and prepared unto every good work. But if he find not himself to be predestinate yet may he not loose the reins to the lusts of concupiscence, as do the Gentiles which know not God, but rather bridle and restrain both his actions and passions, yea his very affections and perturbations that he receive not . . . deeper damnation, . . . [and] that it may be easier for him in the day of judgment, being ascertained that in the world to come there are degrees as well of torment as reward.

Speaking of Catholic baptism, in this same sermon, he asks 'have they not admitted and allowed women, that weak vessel, to be lawful administers thereof—an ancient heresy?' That Matthew was well aware of the inverse relationship between the grace of predestination and that of the sacraments emerges from a form of recantation sanctioned by him in 1613 for a renegade Catholic priest. Among the errors abjured on this occasion was the 'efficacie of sacramentes to the overthrowing of the misterie of God's election'.[52]

Lastly there is the case of Archbishop Whitgift. He had been responsible for the final form of the Lambeth Articles and at the Hampton Court Conference he stated that 'the administration of baptism by women and lay persons was not allowed in the practice of the [English] Church, but enquired of by bishops in their visitation and censured.'[53] Under Elizabeth John Whitgift had initially supported the noncon- formists and in 1574 he could still write of religious cere- monies that 'we (but only for obedience sake) do not much esteeme of them'.[54] His subsequent severity, however, towards Puritans, as archbishop, made it unlikely that he would sup- port any call for their toleration in the new reign, and this events bore out. Thus the bishops at Hampton Court fall into two groups, with the more committed Calvinists among them apparently milder in their attitudes to Puritan nonconformity.

---

[52] 'Two Sermons, hitherto unpublished, of Dr Tobie Matthew . . .', *Christian Observer*, 47 (1847), 728, 777–8; Borthwick Institute, York Chancery Act Book 1613–18, fo. 41ᵛ. I owe this last reference to Dr P. Tyler. Matthew's notion of 'degrees' of torment was the same as that of William Perkins, *Workes* (1612–13), I. 358.

[53] Cardwell, *Conferences*, p. 174.

[54] P. Collinson, 'The "nott conformytye" of the young John Whitgift', *JEH* 15 (1964), 192–200; John Whitgift, *Works*, ed. J. Ayre (Cambridge, 1851–3), II. 6.

The eight deans (excluding Gordon) and the solitary
archdeacon at the conference were on average ten years
younger than the bishops,[55] and it is among them rather than
their seniors that we might expect any new intellectual ten-
dencies to show up. Three of these eight deans, Lancelot
Andrewes of Westminster, William Barlow of Chester and
John Overall of St Paul's, had during the 1590s adopted doctrinal positions more moderate than the Lambeth Articles.
Andrewes, in his extant comments on these articles, was not
prepared, he said, to condemn the view that election was 'according to faith foreseen' and he also denied that reprobation
was 'absolute'".[56] In February 1599 Barlow, who also composed the official account of the Hampton Court Conference,
wrote privately to Overall criticizing his teaching that in the
case of the elect grace works 'infallibly, . . . whereby mee
thinkes you inforce that the elect cannot incline much lesse fall
into capitall sinnes, or such as they call "the ruin of conscience"''.[57] Yet at the same time Overall himself was under
attack from Calvinists at Cambridge for his interpretation of
the doctrine of perseverance which, as has been said, introduced an element 'of freedom of choice'.[58] The views of these
three, however, remained unpublished, and in so far as they
had a common continental inspiration it was the Danish
Lutheran Niels Hemmingsen or Hemmingius. Barlow, for
example, in his letter to Overall of 1599, quoted Hemmingsen
on the subject of free will. Only gradually did they make contact with Dutch Arminianism; and Andrewes alone survived
to see English Calvinism defeated during the 1620s. Nevertheless, by 1612 the Dutch Arminian Petrus Bertius can be found
soliciting the religious support of Barlow and the following
year Hugo Grotius visited Andrewes and Overall on behalf of
the same anti-Calvinist cause.[59]

[55] This 'average' represents the difference between the median age of the bishops
and their junior colleagues.

[56] Lancelot Andrewes, *Works*, ed. J. P. Wilson and J. Bliss (Oxford, 1841–54), VI.
295–6, 298. Confusion has been caused here by Professor New who cites the second of
the Lambeth Articles as if it were Andrewes's own comment. J. F. H. New, *Anglican
and Puritan* (1964), p. 12 and Andrewes, *Works*, VI. 290.

[57] CUL MS Gg/1/29, fo. 42 (from back).

[58] Porter, *Reformation and Reaction*, pp. 402–3.

[59] Trinity College Dublin MS 143, fos. 1–26ᵛ; Hugo Grotius, *Briefwisseling*, ed. P. C.
Molhuysen and B. L. Meulenbroek (The Hague, 1928–81), I. 230–6.

Of the five remaining deans, James Montagu, of the Chapel Royal, had sided with the Cambridge Calvinists in 1596 and he was to maintain this doctrinal stand until his death in 1618.[60] As Master of Sidney Sussex College he did not enforce conformity until after the conference and still expressed the wish that 'the sign of the cross were left out in the liturgy'.[61] His brother, Sir Edward Montagu, was to intervene on behalf of Northamptonshire Puritans at the start of the 1604 parliamentary session.[62] George Abbot, Dean of Winchester, was another staunch Calvinist. Preaching at Oxford University during the mid-1590s he offered the same cold comfort to reprobates as had Bishop Matthew. 'But suppose that thou belong not to him [God] . . . yet flie from sinne and do morall vertues, and that at least shall ease some part of the extremity of those torments which thou shalt have in Hell fire.' He had also opposed the practice of lay baptism.[63] In 1601 Abbot fell into temporary disgrace with Bishop Bancroft over the proposed renovation of Cheapside Cross; being asked for his opinion, as Vice-Chancellor of Oxford, Abbot had condemned the project as 'unlawfull in true divinity', and the five Oxford doctors concurring in this judgement included the Puritan leaders John Reynolds and Henry Airay.[64] Thomas Ravis, Dean of Christ Church, was a similarly committed Calvinist predestinarian. He speaks of himself in his will of 1609 as 'confidently beleeving' that he shall 'enjoy eternall lief among the sainctes and holy elect'.[65] The religious beliefs and attitudes however of Thomas Eedes, Dean of Worcester, and Giles Thompson, Dean of Windsor, remain obscure. This leaves Archdeacon John King, who had taught at York in 1594 that God 'having power over his clay may worke at his pleasure, either in judgement to make it a vessell of dishonour or of honour in mercy'.[66] As Bishop of London, in 1611, King

---

[60] Porter, *Reformation and Reaction*, p. 376 and see below, pp. 42–3.

[61] *Two Elizabethan Puritan Diaries*, ed. M. M. Knappen (Chicago, 1933), p. 130; HMC Salisbury, XVII. 29.

[62] HMC Buccleuch, III. 80–1.

[63] George Abbot, *An Exposition upon the Prophet Jonah* (1600), pp. 532–3 and *Quaestiones Sex* (Oxford, 1598), pp. 68–98.

[64] *Cheap-Side Crosse Censured and Condemned by a Letter* (1641), pp. 2, 12.

[65] PRO, PROB. 11/115, fo. 60ᵛ. Ravis, as Bishop of London, nevertheless took a very firm line with Puritan nonconformists. *Two Puritan Diaries*, ed. Knappen, p. 31.

[66] John King, *Lectures upon Jonas* (Oxford, 1597), p. 255.

was personally to license a Calvinist work on the permanency of justifying grace.[67]

Patronage evidence concerning these clergy, like that for their Puritan counterparts, is fragmentary. Robert Cecil was clearly a patron of Bishop Matthew[68] and latterly also of Bishop Bilson.[69] Bishop Watson was a protégé of the Catholic sympathizer, Lord Lumley[70] and Bishop Babington owed his original preferment to the second Earl of Pembroke.[71] Among the deans, Abbot[72] and Ravis[73] had Lord Treasurer Buckhurst for a patron while Sir Fulke Greville, the future Lord Brooke, had been instrumental in securing their posts for both Andrewes and Overall in 1601.[74] Archdeacon King was chaplain to Lord Chancellor Ellesmere.[75] Such links help to explain the presence of particular bishops and lesser church dignitaries at Hampton Court in January 1604.

III

The actual course of the conference, compared with the uncertainty which surrounds the selection of participants, is well charted. Some points nevertheless need stressing. At the conference Reynolds was the main spokesman for the Puritans. His manner of handling their case, however, departed widely from the original blueprint for discussion, as laid down in the Millenary Petition. Whereas doctrine occupied a minor position in the petition, two short sentences among a mass of other items mainly ceremonial,[76] at the conference it had pride of place, with Reynolds listing as his first request that 'the doctrine of the Church might be preserved in purity, accord-

[67] Charles Richardson, *The Repentance of Peter and Judas* (1612); Arber, III. 213ᵛ.

[68] A. G. R. Smith, *Servant of the Cecils: the Life of Sir Michael Hickes, 1543–1612* (1977), pp. 74–7.

[69] HMC Salisbury, XI. 386, XII. 527.

[70] R. B. Manning, *Religion and Society in Elizabethan Sussex* (Leciester, 1969), pp. 205–6.

[71] DNB s.n. Babington, Gervase.

[72] P. A. Welsby, *George Abbot* (1962), pp. 17–18.

[73] HMC Salisbury, VI. 195.

[74] R. A. Rebholz, *The Life of Fulke Greville, First Lord Brooke* (Oxford, 1971), pp. 142–3.

[75] King, *Lectures upon Jonas*, sigs. ˙3–˙6.

[76] 'That there may bee an uniformity of doctrine prescribed. No popish opinion to bee any more taught or defended.' *The Answere of the . . . Universitie of Oxford*, p. 3.

ing to God's word'. Elaborating on this, he suggested some clarification of the teaching of the Thirty-nine Articles and that the Lambeth Articles should be incorporated wholesale. Although Prayer Book reform remained on the agenda, a number of Millenary complaints, like bowing at the name of Jesus, were omitted and others, such as the ring in marriage and the clerical cap, were explicitly repudiated as grievances.[77]

This change in emphasis probably represents, among other things, a tactical decision on the part of Reynolds. To ask that the Lambeth Articles be given confessional status was not unrealistic given that both English primates had acknowledged their truth, and in 1615 the Irish Convocation was in fact to implement this request.[78] By obtaining majority support in the first instance, Reynolds may have hoped to smooth the way for his later and more radical proposals; it is noticeable that his last suggestion, for a modification of the episcopal system, was also his most far reaching.[79] At the same time there seems to have been a genuine anxiety for the future of English Calvinism. Here one continuing focus of concern was Richard Hooker's *Laws of Ecclesiastical Polity* (1594–7) which in 1599 had been criticized on doctrinal grounds, including predestination and the necessity of baptism.[80] The controversy was revived in two works, by Andrew Willet, published in the months between the Millenary Petition and the Hampton Court Conference.[81] Reynolds had been Hooker's Oxford tutor and is likely to have been particularly worried by the charges of heterodoxy involving his late pupil. More generally he was well aware of the recent Cambridge disputes about predestination. Reynolds thus began by handling the sixteenth of the Thirty-nine Articles, which concerned the doctrine of perseverance, and asked for it to be stated clearly that an individual once having attained to a state of grace could fall away 'neither totally nor finally'. We have already

---

[77] Cardwell, *Conferences*, pp. 178, 200–1.

[78] *Articles of Religion agreed upon . . . in the Convocation holden at Dublin* (Dublin, 1615).

[79] Cardwell, *Conferences*, pp. 201–2.

[80] *A Christian Letter of Certaine English Protestants* (n.p. 1599), pp. 7–8, 11–12, 15–17, 30–3.

[81] Andrew Willet, *An Antilogie or Counterplea* (1603), sigs. A3[r–v] and *Ecclesia Triumphans* (1603), pp. 90–2.

noticed the hostile response this elicited from Bancroft, but King James felt it necessary to qualify the Bishop's remarks, lest 'God's omnipotency might be called in question by impeaching the doctrine of his eternal predestination'. Moreover the King, as ultimate arbiter, 'left it to be considered whether anything were mete to be added, for the clearing of the doctor [Reynolds] his doubt' about this particular article.[82]

The proposal that the Lambeth rulings as a whole, 'the nine assertions orthodoxal', be officially adopted was at first ignored, to be again raised by Reynolds. This led to a discussion of their Cambridge University origins and in turn prompted Dean Overall, who was also the Cambridge Regius Professor of Divinity, to make a personal statement on the predestinarian question. He began by alluding to 'a controversie between him and some other in Cambridge, upon a proposition which he had delivered there', presumably referring to events in 1599. The disagreement had hinged on Overall's differentiation between justified believers and the elect; the former after receiving 'good affections and motions of grace' *may* through negligence 'fall away and end in the flesh', whereas the latter never become 'destitute of all the parts and seed' of grace and despite their sins repent of necessity and are saved. King James does not seem to have accepted this distinction, which implicitly denied reprobation to be the inevitable fate of all the non-elect, for in reply he 'entred into a longer speech of predestination and reprobation, than before, and of the necessary conjoyning repentance and holinesse of life with true faith, concluding that it was hypocrasie, and not true justifying faith, which was severed from them'.[83] There is no admission here that truly justifying as opposed to counterfeit faith could be the property of any except the elect, and as it stands this statement looks like orthodox Calvinist teaching.

Under the heading of doctrine Reynolds also included the question of baptism by lay persons, only to be told by King James that the matter was already in hand. Considerable time had been spent debating this point at an earlier session, from which the Puritans were excluded, and, while the bishops dis-

[82] Cardwell, *Conferences*, pp. 178, 181.
[83] Ibid., pp. 185–6; Porter, *Reformation and Reaction*, pp. 399–400, 402–3.

agreed among themselves as to the propriety of lay baptism, even in emergency, James was adamant that baptism 'was necessary to be had where it might be lawfully had, . . . ministered by lawful ministers' and by them 'alone'. According to him, bishops like Bancroft ascribed 'too much to baptism', and he had recommended that the Prayer Book rubric be altered so as clearly to exclude 'all laikes' from baptizing. This appears to underline the Calvinist orthodoxy of King James in the matter of predestination.[84]

The original list of changes agreed at Hampton Court includes the provision that the 'Articles of Religion . . . be explained and enlarged'.[85] Within three weeks of the end of the conference, however, this had been abandoned, as can be shown from a subsequent list emended by the King's 'own hand'.[86] The most likely influence at work here was that of Bancroft, yet the fact that the request was even entertained distinguished the new supreme governor of the church from the old. Similarly distinctive were the 1604 Prayer Book changes concerning the sacrament of baptism which, by limiting the administration to a clergyman whatever the circumstances, effectively detracted from its essential saving role, and the new prayer for the royal family, which invoked the doctrine of divine election.[87] Moreover the failure of Reynolds's bid in 1604 to have the Lambeth rulings grafted on to the Thirty-nine Articles has an epilogue, because four years later, in March 1608, his request was to some extent met by the publication of *The Faith, Doctrine and Religion, professed and protected in the Realme of England and Dominions of the Same*. This was a semi-official commentary on the Thirty-nine Articles from the pen of Thomas Rogers, who in his analysis not only explained but, under the guise of listing erroneous doctrines, enlarged on the articles in a Calvinist sense. The commentary was based on an earlier work by the same author, entitled *The English Creede* and published at London in two parts between 1585 and 1587. Some of the most interesting alterations in the 1608 version relate to the question of predestination. The

---

[84] Cardwell, *Conferences*, pp. 174–6, 179, 181.

[85] PRO, SP 14/6, fo. 45.

[86] Cardwell, *Conferences*, pp. 213–16.

[87] 'Almightie God which hast promised to be a Father of thine elect, and of their seede, we humbly beseech thee . . .'

error that 'the very elect may fal utterly from grace and be damned' was changed to read 'the very elect, *totally and finally*, may fall from grace and be damned'. Also, while both versions teach the doctrine of double and absolute predestination, Rogers added as an error in 1608 that 'no certaine companie be foredestined unto eternall condemnation'. Furthermore the statement 'Christ thus suffered' was altered to read 'Christ for his elect hath suffered', so restricting the atonement.[88]

This revised version of Rogers' commentary nevertheless raises certain problems. According to the title page, it was 'perused and by the lawfull authoritie of the Church of England allowed to be publique'. The book was also dedicated to Bancroft, now Archbishop, whose chaplain Rogers was.[89] Given the views expressed by Bancroft only four years before, this seems an odd situation. But a clue may be provided by the place of publication, which was Cambridge. In the circumstances the choice was an unusual one. For between 1590 and 1610 the Cambridge press published an annual average of eight books,[90] a tiny output compared with London and mostly the work of resident academics, whereas Rogers was an Oxford man none of whose other numerous works emanated from Cambridge. Precedent, however, existed for publishing at Cambridge an extreme Calvinist work which had been refused a London licence.[91] In 1608 the Cambridge licenser would be Robert Some, as Vice-Chancellor, who in the 1590s had been a leading defender of Calvinism in the university.[92] Yet the problem of the dedication to Bancroft remains, for it is

[88] Thomas Rogers, *The English Creede* (1585–7), I. 62, 64 and *The Faith, Doctrine and Religion, professed and protected in the Realme of England and Dominions of the Same* (Cambridge, 1607), pp. 74–5. The preface of the latter is dated 11 March 1607/8. My italics. For the text of the Lambeth Articles, see below, pp. 30–1.

[89] Writing in 1624, William Laud described the book as the judgement of a 'private man'. By contrast Cornelius Burges, five years later, claimed that it 'came abroad with injunction from the Archbishop that was [Bancroft] that there should be one of them bought for every parish in the province of Canterbury'. Laud, *Works*, II. 54; Cornelius Burges, *Baptismall Regeneration of Elect Infants* (Oxford, 1629), p. 68.

[90] This arithmetical mean is based on G. R. Barnes, *A List of Books Printed in Cambridge at the University Press: 1521–1800* (Cambridge, 1935).

[91] CUL MS Gg/1/29, fo. 104.

[92] J. Le Neve, *Fasti Ecclesiae Anglicanae* (Oxford, 1854), III. 605; Porter, *Reformation and Reaction*, pp. 317–19. For Rogers's stormy relations with Puritanism see P. Collinson, 'The Beginnings of English Sabbatarianism', *Studies in Church History*, ed. C. W. Dugmore and C. Duggan (1964), I. 219–21.

unlikely to have been entirely without permission. Perhaps Bancroft considered that permitting a dedication was a lesser evil than granting a licence to publish at London.[93]

Whatever the personal attitude of the Archbishop, it is probable that a further shift in royal policy lay behind the appearance of Rogers's commentary in 1608, which partly implemented an agreement abandoned in 1604. On that first occasion James was originally in favour of explaining and enlarging the Thirty-nine Articles, and Bancroft not. The project had been dropped and Bancroft became Archbishop. These two events were connected for, as the extent of Puritan organization, and the involvment of many leading gentry, became clear to the King in the course of 1604, so a policy of no concessions had emerged.[94] Bancroft's anti-Puritan reputation recommended him as director of the new strategy. Unlike modern biographers of Bancroft, however, his contemporaries did not consider him the obvious successor to Whitgift. The most hotly tipped candidate was Bishop Matthew.[95] But, after some months of wavering, fear of Puritanism as a political force seemingly induced the King to promote Bancroft to Canterbury in October 1604.[96] Since that time certain changes had occurred which might explain a more conciliatory royal attitude by 1608. There had been, for instance, an attempt by James to impose a new oath of allegiance on his Catholic subjects.[97] This tended to distract attention from the possible dangers of Puritanism. Arguably more important was the Midland Revolt in May 1607, the most serious agrarian disturbance of the reign. Located principally in Northamptonshire, the revolt had initially been blamed by some on the 'Puritane faction'. The denouement, however, had been its

[93] An alternative explanation is that Rogers presented the Archbishop with a *fait accompli*. This was what Bancroft said had happened over the dedication to him of Cowell's *Interpreter*, which was published at Cambridge in 1607. *Proceedings in Parliament, 1610*, ed. E. R. Foster (New Haven, 1966), I. 29, 188. For a general discussion of licensing, see W. W. Greg, *Some Aspects and Problems of London Publishing between 1550 and 1650* (Oxford, 1956), pp. 41–62.

[94] B. W. Quintrell, 'The Royal Hunt and the Puritans, 1604–1605', *JEH* 31 (1980), 41–58.

[95] Strype, *Whitgift*, III. 408–9; BL Lansdowne MS 89, fo. 19.

[96] John Harrington, *A Briefe View of the State of the Church of England* (1653), p. 11. Perhaps as a consolation prize, Matthew became Archbishop of York in 1606 where he remained until his death in 1628.

[97] P. Milward, *Religious Controversies of the Jacobean Age* (1978), pp. 89–94.

ruthless suppression at the hands of a local contingent under the command of Sir Edward Montagu and Sir Anthony Mildmay.[98] In so doing Montagu, a leading Puritan agitator in the parliament of 1604, and Mildmay, son of the founder of Puritan Emmanuel College, testified convincingly to the political loyalty of the Puritan gentry. The moment was certainly opportune for a renewed approach to the King on the subject of elaborating the Thirty-nine Articles.

For most of James's reign Calvinism was in fact to enjoy greater royal favour than it had under Elizabeth. On the other hand, among the younger participants at the Hampton Court Conference the makings of a future Arminian party are already discernible. Compared, however, with the Calvinists these Arminian precursors were much less assertive. They lacked both leadership and an explicit body of doctrine, tending to avoid rather than deny the more positive teaching of their opponents. Indeed one of them, William Barlow, seemingly felt it necessary publicly to affirm his essential Calvinist orthodoxy in the summer of 1599.[99] Moreover the sacramental counter-argument to determinism remained undeveloped, almost nobody claiming as yet that saving grace was universally bestowed in baptism and predestination therefore conditional upon faith.[100] In 1604 the initiative indubitably still lay with the Calvinists, and subsequent royal support was considerably to strengthen their position. But as a result the latent Arminian opposition was under increased pressure to define itself. English theology, never since the Reformation independent of continental developments, was in addition soon to receive the impress of Dutch religious disputes. By this process English Arminianism proper was to emerge. The new movement first appeared in the universities and to these the next two chapters are devoted.

[98] E. F. Gay, 'The Midland Revolt and the Inquisitions of Depopulation of 1607', *TRHS* 18 (1904), 215–16.

[99] See below, p. 37.

[100] W. Goode, *The Doctrine of the Church of England as to the Effects of Baptism in the Case of Infants* (1850), pp. 278–80, 322–5, 328, 335–7.

Cambridge University and Arminianism

I

DURING the early 1590s English Calvinism had been very much in the ascendant, and nowhere was that ascendancy more obvious than at Cambridge University. Symptomatic of the situation is the publication there in 1590 of William Perkins's *Armilla Aurea*, translated the following year as *A Golden Chain . . . containing the Order of the Causes of Salvation and Damnation*. The author, a fellow of Christ's College, soon became one of the most widely read English writers. His book, the English translation of which was personally licensed by Bishop Aylmer of London,[1] asserted the doctrine of absolute predestination against its critics. The 'cause of the execution of God's predestination is his mercy in Christ, in them which are saved, and in them which perish the fall and corruption of man: yet so as that the decree and eternal counsel of God concerning them both hath not any cause beside his will and pleasure'. It is clear from the diagram which accompanies *A Golden Chain* that Perkins was a supralapsarian, teaching that God had divided mankind unconditionally into elect and reprobate even before the fall of Adam. Perkins was here indebted to the second-generation exponents of Calvin, such as Theodore Beza.[2]

Paradoxically, however, the propagation of such views also helped fuel anti-Calvinist sentiment. At Cambridge direct confrontation came about due to a university sermon delivered on 29 April 1595, by William Barrett. For Barrett, a chaplain of Gonville and Caius College, used the occasion to criticize at length the deterministic teaching of the Cambridge Calvinists. In so doing he was probably influenced by the Lady Margaret Professor of Divinity and French Protestant

---

[1] Arber, II. 264.
[2] *The Work of William Perkins*, ed. I. Breward (Abingdon, 1970), pp. 82–3, 85, 168–9, 613–32.

exile, Peter Baro, who privately held that 'God has predestined such as he from all eternity foreknew would believe on Christ' and 'hath likewise from all eternity reprobated all rebels, and such as contumaciously continue in sin'.[3] According to Baro, therefore, election and reprobation are conditional. The decision of Barrett to reply to the Cambridge Calvinists at this time was most likely prompted by a development two months earlier, when on 27 February William Whitaker, Regius Professor of Divinity, delivered a public lecture 'against the advocates of universal grace'.[4] Whitaker's audience included three earls and five barons, as well as many gentry, and it has been plausibly argued that Barrett 'had little choice' but to protest. 'Heavily outnumbered in the upper echelons of the university as they were, the anti-Calvinists, had they allowed things to go much further, would have found themselves confronted by a *fait accompli*, their case defeated without a hearing.'[5]

Barrett, in consequence of his sermon, was called before the Cambridge Consistory Court and forced to recant. Yet the matter did not rest here, because Barrett then appealed to Archbishop Whitgift. In the ensuing discussions the Archbishop's initial sympathy for Barrett waned as the wider implications of his sermon became clear.[6] The case culminated in November 1595 with Whitgift agreeing to a set of Calvinist propositions—the Lambeth Articles, which he described as 'uniformly professed in this Church of England and agreeable to the Articles of Religion established by authority'. The Lambeth Articles, in translation, assert that

i God from eternity has predestined some men to life, and reprobated some to death.

ii The moving or efficient cause of predestination to life is not the foreseeing of faith, or of perseverance, or of good works, or of anything innate in the person of the predestined, but only the will of the good pleasure of God.

iii There is a determined and certain number of predestined, which cannot be increased or diminished.

iv Those not predestined to salvation are inevitably condemned on account of their sins.

[3] Porter, *Reformation and Reaction*, pp. 344, 388.
[4] Peter Baro, *Summa Trium de Praedestinatione Sententiarum* (Harderwijk, 1613), pp. 30–43.   [5] Lake, *Moderate Puritans*, pp. 202, 205.   [6] Ibid., pp. 205–18.

v A true, lively and justifying faith, and the sanctifying Spirit of God, is not lost nor does it pass away either totally or finally in the elect.

vi The truly faithful man—that is, one endowed with justifying faith—is sure by full assurance of faith ['plerophoria fidei'] of the remission of sins and his eternal salvation through Christ.

vii Saving grace is not granted, is not made common, is not ceded to all men, by which they might be saved, if they wish.

viii No one can come to Christ unless it be granted to him, and unless the Father draws him: and all men are not drawn by the Father to come to the Son.

ix It is not in the will or the power of each and every man to be saved.[7]

Some modern historians, however, have questioned the Calvinism of the Lambeth Articles.[8] On the other hand they were to prove anathema to English Arminians during the 1620s.[9] Moreover, the articles derived from a draft prepared by William Whitaker, himself a supralapsarian Calvinist.[10] In their final form they are quite clear that election—'predestination to life'—is unconditional. 'Justifying faith' cannot be lost and 'saving grace is not granted . . . to all men'. Alone of the Lambeth Articles, number iv might seem to open the door to an anti-Calvinist interpretation. But in reality it is the logical corollary of the other eight articles. Two categories of person, and no more, are envisaged, the saved and the damned. The cause of salvation is 'the will of the good pleasure of God', whereas those not predestined to life are 'inevitably condemned on account of their sins'. Yet even Perkins, as we have seen, granted that the reprobate perished because of 'the fall and corruption of man'. Condemnation is the *inevitable* fate of the non-elect. That is the important point. The ambiguity of article iv lies in the fact that it can be interpreted in both a supralapsarian and a sublapsarian Calvinist sense, reprobation dating from either before or after the fall of Adam.

That Whitgift should have sided with the Cambridge Calvinists in 1595 is hardly surprising in the light of his previous

---

[7] Porter, *Reformation and Reaction*, p. 371. I am grateful to Dr Porter for allowing me to reproduce his translation of the Lambeth Articles.

[8] Notably Porter, *Reformation and Reaction*, pp. 366–71.

[9] Laud, *Works*, VI. 245–6.

[10] Porter, *Reformation and Reaction*, pp. 364–6. Whitaker's supralapsarianism emerges clearly from his last sermon. *Cygnea Cantio* (Cambridge, 1599), pp. 6–17.

doctrinal record. During the early 1570s Whitgift had quoted, with approval, Beza's distinction between those 'whom we call by the word of God reprobate and the vessels of anger . . . appointed to destruction' and 'those which are chosen in Christ by eternal election'. As regards the latter, 'it is not possible that they should perish'.[11] In the mid-1580s he personally licensed a Calvinist commentary on the Thirty-nine Articles, by Thomas Rogers.[12] Similarly in 1591 Whitgift had affixed his imprimatur to a Paul's Cross sermon, by Gervase Babington, which was largely taken up with demonstrating the truth of predestination, both double and absolute.

All men [were] at the first before the Lord in his eternall counsell, to receive an end or use according to his will, to life or death, to honour or dishonour, to salvation or damnation, to heaven or hell. In which good pleasure of his . . . he hath disposed of some one way, of some another. It being his glory in his house also to have vessells of divers sortes and not all to one use.[13]

In reaching his conclusions on the Barrett affair Whitgift seems to have paid special attention to the comments of his fellow primate, Archbishop Matthew Hutton of York. On 19 August he had written to ask Hutton for his opinion about reprobation, certainty of salvation, and the perseverance of the elect, which were the three specific questions at issue.[14] Hutton, in his reply, the covering letter dated 1 October, argued that the decree of reprobation related to man in a state of original sin and he thus rejected the supralapsarian teaching of the Cambridge followers of Beza. His own position was that of a sublapsarian Calvinist. Going on to discuss the certainty of salvation, he rejected the concept of 'security', another extreme Calvinist view which, like supralapsarianism, had been maintained against Barrett, and in writing of 'plerophoriam spei', full assurance of hope, he anticipated the sixth Lambeth article. As regards the doctrine of perseverance Hutton maintained that although in the elect 'faith can be

[11] Whitgift, *Works*, III. 142–3. I owe this reference to Dr Lake.
[12] Arber, 11. 201ᵛ, 217 and see above, pp. 25–6.
[13] Babington, *A Sermon*, pp. 8–9; Arber, 11. 279. For an analysis of this sermon, see below, pp. 251–2.
[14] Matthew Hutton, *Correspondence*, ed. J. Raine (Surtees Soc., 17, 1843), pp. 104–5; Porter, *Reformation and Reaction*, pp. 351–4.

shaken, injured, strangled, and apparently dead and buried, it never fails totally, much less finally".[15] This last judgement may well have persuaded Whitgift as to the truth of the fifth Lambeth article, since in June 1595 he had still considered it 'disputable' whether or not the elect could lose faith totally.[16] By November he was prepared to agree that 'justifying faith . . . is not lost nor does it pass away either totally or finally in the elect'. Both archbishops emerged during these debates as Calvinists, albeit moderates.

At the Cambridge Commencement in July 1595 George Downham, a future bishop, had denied that grace was either universal or that it could be lost.[17] His choice of subject was clearly meant to be topical. Similarly, although Whitgift described the Lambeth Articles as 'private judgements' and 'not as laws or decrees',[18] many of the Calvinist points in dispute came to be affirmed at the Oxford University Acts of 1596 and 1597 and echo the Cambridge controversy.[19] The Commencement and the Act were the high points of the academic year, and the divinity theses maintained on these occasions represented the official voice of the university. Oxford also contributed to Calvinist agitation in London, for on 6 February 1597 John Dove, who had incepted doctor at Oxford the previous July, devoted a Paul's Cross sermon to the subject of predestination. While he made no mention of Cambridge, his reference to the 'Lutherans of our times' must have had the Barrett affair in mind. During the recent Act, he had listened to his fellow-inceptors maintain Calvinist positions on reprobation, certainty of salvation, and perseverance. Now in February, modelling his sermon on an academic disputation, he chose to discuss the three conclusions that, 'It is not the will of God that all men should be saved. The absolute

---

[15] Matthew Hutton, *Brevis et Dilucida Explicatio . . . de Electione, Praedestinatione ac Reprobatione* (Harderwijk, 1613), pp. 1–3, 16–19, 33–4, 42.

[16] Porter, *Reformation and Reaction*, p. 351.

[17] BL Harleian MS 7038, p. 80. This manuscript contains an almost complete list of Commencement theses from the 1590s to the 1650s. I owe my knowledge of it to Dr K. Fincham.

[18] Porter, *Reformation and Reaction*, p. 372.

[19] See below, pp. 60–1. The Cambridge predestinarian disputes also found a local echo in Lincolnshire with the case of William Williams, Rector of Asgarby. Williams held views similar to those of Barrett. H. Beddow, 'The Church in Lincolnshire, *c.*1595–*c.*1640', Cambridge Ph.D. thesis, 1980, pp. 225–43.

will of God, and his secret decree from all eternitie, is the cause why some are predestinated to salvation, others to destruction, and not any foresight of faith, or good workes in the one, or infidelitie, neglect, or contempt in the other', and lastly that 'Christ died not effectually for all'. On this last point, Dove quoted St Augustine's interpretation of biblical references to the salvation of 'all men' as meaning some 'of all sortes'.[20]

Dove's sermon was dedicated to Lord Keeper Egerton, the later Ellesmere and, since the bishopric of London was temporarily vacant, Archbishop Whitgift, or his deputy, should by rights have licensed its printing. Although there is no record of such authorization, the indications are that Dove was in favour with the Archbishop, who a bare three months before the Paul's Cross sermon had presented him to the rectory of St Mary Aldermary.[21] Dove, however, was the protégé of Egerton as well and this influential layman perhaps seemed an even more suitable recipient of his published labours.[22] The Cambridge disputes of the mid-1590s might, therefore, have been expected to produce a religious explosion on a national scale, involving as they had in the Calvinist cause both Archbishops, Oxford University, the Paul's Cross pulpit, and now a leading minister of state. That this did not happen was due to the relative powerlessness of the opposition. Initially indeed it had looked as if the anti-Calvinists were rallying significant support at court, led by Lord Treasurer Burghley who was also Chancellor of Cambridge University.[23] By October 1598, however, the translator of a further Calvinist treatise dedicated to Egerton could claim the doctrinal backing of 'the governours of our [English] Church'.[24]

At the same time productions by both university presses in the last decade of the sixteenth century remained consistently Calvinist. Particularly striking in this connection is that between 1587 and 1601 there were four Cambridge editions of

[20] John Dove, *A Sermon preached at Paules Crosse* (1597), sig. A and pp. 18, 31. For an analysis of this sermon, see below, pp. 252–3.
[21] R. Newcourt, *Repertorium Ecclesiasticum Parochiale Londinense* (1708–10), I. 435–6.
[22] Dove, *A Sermon*, sigs. A2–A3.   [23] Lake, *Moderate Puritans*, pp. 232–3.
[24] Jacobus Kimedoncius, *Of the Redemption of Mankind* (1598), sig. A2ᵛ. The translator was Hugh Ince, preacher at Greenstead, Essex, and his work was personally licensed by Bishops Bancroft of London and Vaughan of Chester. Arber, III. 43ᵛ.

Jeremias Bastingius' exposition of the Heidelberg Catechism and five Oxford editions of Zacharias Ursinus' lectures on the same subject. According to Bastingius, a Dutchman, 'Christ's death is in deede sufficient for all mankinde, but effectuall only for the elect . . . whome he regenerateth by his holy spirite, whome he preserveth and in the ende shall crowne with everlasting glorie'.[25] Likewise Ursinus, of Heidelberg, taught that 'Christ's ransome though sufficient for all yet [is] not applied to all' and 'justifieng faith', which 'cannot faile finallie', is 'given to the elect alone'.[26] More punitive sanctions were also employed, for both William Barrett and his mentor Peter Baro were effectively driven out of Cambridge, Baro in 1596 and Barrett in about 1597. The latter went abroad and became a Catholic.[27]

Just as Barrett had been provoked by Whitaker's attack on the advocates of universal grace, so Baro was goaded by the Lambeth Articles into a counter-attack. His chosen medium also was a sermon, preached on 12 January 1596. Baro directed the main thrust of his criticism against those articles which limited the benefit of Christ's death to the elect. Unlike Barrett he was not forced to recant, but he failed in 1596 to be re-elected as Lady Margaret Professor and retired to London.[28] His successor was Thomas Playfere, whose sermons indicate that he held a Calvinist position more advanced than that of the Lambeth Articles. In those rulings Whitgift had persuaded the Cambridge Calvinists to omit their teaching on spiritual security. Nevertheless, preaching before the university, in May 1605, Playfere descanted on 'the securitie and felicitie of the faithfull'. Referring to the late Regius Professor of Hebrew, Edward Lively, he said 'we see how safe and secure the faithfull man is in Christ. He is a house to which the floods may come neere to shake it, but never to throwe it downe. He is a ship which the waves may come neere to tosse it, but never to turn it over.'[29] The Calvinist monopoly, however, remained incomplete because in December 1595 John Overall had been appointed Regius Professor of Divinity. We

[25] Jeremias Bastingius, *An Exposition or Commentarie* (Cambridge, 1589), fo. 22.
[26] Zacharias Ursinus, *The Summe of Christian Religion* (Oxford, 1587), pp. 281, 283, 638.　　　　　　　　　　　　　　[27] Porter, *Reformation and Reaction*, p. 362.
[28] Ibid., pp. 380–90; Lake, *Moderate Puritans*, pp. 230–6.
[29] Thomas Playfere, *Nine Sermons* (Cambridge, 1612), pp. 207, 214, 224.

have already noticed Overall's idiosyncratic opinions, and he
tended like Baro before him to become the Cambridge champion of a more liberal theology of grace.

II

To the extent that Overall and those who thought like him
looked to the Continent for guidance, or at least confirmation
of their views, after the turn of the century it was to the United
Provinces that they increasingly turned. One of the earliest
Englishmen to make direct contact with Dutch Arminianism
had been Richard or 'Dutch' Thomson of Clare College, Cambridge. We know this from a letter written by Thomson in
1605, to Dominicus Baudius of Leiden University, where he
remarks on once having known Arminius very well and that
others at Cambridge are now becoming aware of his doctrines.
'As a consequence our teachers enquire earnestly concerning
Arminius, whenever any [Leiden] students arrive here.'[30]
Born in Holland but studying at Cambridge from 1583,
Thomson was back on the Continent during the 1590s. In
1594 he visited Leiden and his acquaintance with Arminius,
then at Amsterdam, probably dates from the same decade.[31]
Overall later arranged for the posthumous printing, at
Leiden, of Thomson's tract *De Amissione*.[32] This had been
refused an English licence for publication in the late 1590s[33]
and taught that even the elect could lose the grace of their justification. Thomson also reasoned, in what was to become a
characteristically English fashion, that the universal efficacy
of baptism invalidated the idea of an absolute predestinarian
decree.[34] His patrons included Lancelot Andrewes, as Bishop
of Ely, and at Clare College he overlapped with Augustine
Lindsell, subsequently to be described as sitting 'at the sterne
of Popish Arminianism in England'.[35]

[30] Dominicus Baudius, *Epistolarum Centuriae Tres* (Leiden, 1620), p. 731.
[31] Isaac Casaubon, *Epistolae* (Rotterdam, 1709), nos. 12–13.
[32] Grotius, *Briefwisseling*, I. 230–6, 244.
[33] Robert Abbot, *De Gratia et Perseverantia Sanctorum* (1618), sig. C4ᵛ.
[34] Richard Thomson, *Diatriba de Amissione et Intercisione Gratiae et Justificationis* (Leiden, 1616), pp. 31–40, 45–126.
[35] *DNB* s.n. Thomson, Richard (d. 1613); John Cosin, *Correspondence*, ed. G. Ornsby (Surtees Soc., 52, 55, 1868–72), I. 162.

Overall first seems to have clashed at the official level with Cambridge Calvinism in 1599, as a result of his assertion that the perseverance of a truly justified man was conditional upon repentance for sin.[36] At the same time he and his allies distinguished their position from the more radical theology of Peter Baro. Thus at the 1599 Commencement William Barlow, who earlier in the year had chided Overall for his view that grace worked 'infallibly' in the elect, maintained that 'vessels made for contumely cannot become vessels of salvation'*.[37] The campaign against Overall ran on into the summer of 1600 and ended somewhat inconclusively. Archbishop Abbot wrote, in retrospect, of Overall's tenure of the Regius chair that he 'did infect as many as he could till by sharp rebuke and reproofes he was beate from the publique avowing those fansies'.[38] The climacteric was perhaps reached in 1606. That year Robert Kercher, fellow of Trinity College, chose to defend as a Commencement thesis the proposition that 'The decree of election and reprobation depends on the mere will of God'*. Overall, when replying, claimed that, in addition to the will of God, reprobation stems from sin and that to maintain Kercher's position imposes a necessity of sinning on the reprobate. This, he said, is 'utterly nonsensical'*.[39] It was the teaching of Kercher, however, and not that of Overall which prevailed at this time. The following year Overall resigned as Regius Profesor of Divinity, although he remained at Cambridge as Master of St Catharine's College until 1614.

The continuing involvement meanwhile of the laity with these religious questions needs stressing. For example in 1599 Roger Gostwycke, fellow of King's College, dedicated his translation of Amandus Polanus' *De Aeterna Dei Praedestinatione* to Sir Edward Ratcliffe, an Elizabethan MP and future Earl of Sussex. 'I have done into English this treatise of another man's', he wrote, 'that you whome God hath advanced to great place in your countrey [Bedfordshire] may both have yourselfe what to hold and also countenance the orthodoxall judgements of the learned about you, as occasion may serve.'

---

[36] Porter, *Reformation and Reaction*, pp. 398–403.
[37] BL Harleian MS 7038, p. 82; CUL, Sel. 1.11.2.
[38] PRO, SP 105/95, fo. 9ᵛ. I owe my knowledge of this letter book to Dr R. Schreiber.
[39] CUL MS Gg/1/29, fo. 98ʳ⁻ᵛ.

According to Polanus, a professor at Basle, 'predestination is the foundation and principall part of the Gospel'; both election and reprobation are unconditional and, moreover, predate the fall of Adam.[40] Similarly the Oxonian Richard Crakanthorpe was to comment on 'that right and interest which your selfe and every one of God's children have in God's election', when dedicating a sermon on absolute predestination to Sir Edward Barrett in 1620. He also recalled 'divers conferences' concerning the subject held at Barrett's house.[41] While on the anti-Calvinist side, William Cecil, Lord Burghley, had stated in 1596 that he conceived Peter Baro to have been persecuted for 'holding the truth'[42] Probably also in the same camp was Sir Robert Killigrew, an intimate of 'Dutch' Thomson. In January 1611 Isaac Casaubon records a day spent in the country with Thomson and Killigrew, at the house of the latter. 'There I read the book lately published by Petrus Bertius—*De Apostasia Sanctorum*.'* The copy of this notorious Dutch Arminian work had been furnished by Thomson, who also showed Casaubon the manuscript of his *De Amissione* which maintained the same position as Bertius.[43] Killigrew and Barrett were jointly to represent the Cornish borough of Newport in the parliament of 1621, and Killigrew sat in the four succeeding parliaments where Arminianism came increasingly under attack.[44]

At Cambridge in 1607 Overall was succeeded as Regius Professor of Divinity by John Richardson, fellow of Emmanuel College, who back in 1589 can be found petitioning against the expulsion of a leading university Puritan, Francis Johnson.[45] Yet, contrary to what one might assume, Richardson was an anti-Calvinist. There survive, in manuscript, 'Lectiones D. D. Richardsoni de Praedestinatione' which probably date from before 1610, when the major works of Arminius first began to appear in print, because the most

[40] Amandus Polanus, *Concerning God's Eternall Predestination* (Cambridge, 1599), sig. A3ᵛ, p. 1 and *passim*.
[41] Richard Crakanthorpe, *A Sermon of Predestination* (1620), sig. A2ʳ⁻ᵛ.
[42] Porter, *Reformation and Reaction*, p. 386.
[43] Isaac Casaubon, *Ephemerides*, ed. J. Russell (Oxford, 1850), II. 811–12 and *Epistolae*, no. 743.
[44] *Return of Members of Parliament* (1878–91), I. 450, 457, 463, 468, 474.
[45] Porter, *Reformation and Reaction*, pp. 209–10.

recent author cited is the Lutheran Niels Hemmingsen.
According to Richardson, salvation is available 'to all men in
general'. He 'who restricts the grace of God to the elect
removes any way for sinners to repent'*, whereas in truth
grace is offered to others beside the elect and can be accepted
or rejected. Moreover, as part of his argument, Richardson
invokes the universal application of the 'seal of the sacrament'*.[46] The occasion of these lectures is not known, but he
seems to have steered clear of religious conflict as Regius Professor for some ten years. This despite the fact that the Lady
Margaret professorship continued to be held by Calvinists,
since in 1609 Playfere was followed by John Davenant whose
teaching can be deduced from his published *Determinationes*.
For example, Davenant there quotes with approval the opinion of Calvin that God chooses out of the corrupt mass of mankind certain 'vessels of honour'*—the elect—and leaves the
rest as ignominious reprobates. Davenant's declared opponents, however, are the 'Papists'*, and not apparently until
1618 did he dispute against Arminians as such.[47]

Calvinism in the meantime continued to be endorsed officially at the Cambridge Commencement. Thus in both 1608
and 1611 it was maintained that the grace of justification cannot be lost, by William Pemberton and Michael Bentley
respectively.[48] Nevertheless, from 1612 onwards there existed
a standing challenge in the form of Arminius' posthumously
published *Examen* of the teaching of William Perkins on predestination. The modern biographer of Arminius has
described this book as 'the basic document of Arminianism',[49]
in that his theology of grace there receives its most detailed
exposition. Against Perkins Arminius argues that 'God truly
wills the salvation of all men, on the condition that they
believe', for God does not forcibly convert men but rather
moves them 'by mild and sweet persuasion'*.[50] The challenge

---

[46] BL Harleian MS 750, fos. 106ᵛ–108. By 1609 Richardson regarded Robert Cecil,
now Earl of Salisbury, as his patron. *HMC Salisbury*, XXI. 13–14.

[47] John Davenant, *Determinationes Quaestionum Quarundam Theologicarum* (Cambridge,
1634), pp. 119–22; Simonds D'Ewes, *Autobiography and Correspondence*, ed. J. O. Hal-
liwell (1845), I. 120.

[48] BL Harleian MS 7038, pp. 87–8.

[49] C. Bangs, *Arminius: A Study in the Dutch Reformation* (Nashville, 1971), p. 209.

[50] Jacobus Arminius, *Examen Modestum* (Leiden, 1612), pp. 196, 220.

was taken up in 1615 by John Yates, fellow of Emmanuel College, 'drawn unto it by considering how many runne after Arminius'. His book, *God's Arraignement of Hypocrites*, was published at Cambridge and consists in part of a defence of Perkins. 'I professe', he writes, 'against all the crew of Arminius's defenders that they do greatly derogate from the majestie of God', whose 'mercy and justice [is] not "on account of faith foreseen" or "sin"'*, but from the promise which was his meere good will and pleasure.' Yates concludes his remarks with a paean of praise to God who 'hath lately raised up such worthie bishops, the true defenders of orthodoxall truth and resolute enemies to all that oppose it'[51]—presumably a reference to men like Archbishop Abbot.

A second edition of *God's Arraignement* came out in 1616, and was most probably in the mind of Samuel Brooke, Professor of Divinity at Gresham College, London, when at Cambridge that summer he chose publicly to defend 'Doctor Arminius'. Brooke had left Trinity College, Cambridge, four years previously and his visit in 1616 may well have been at the invitation of the Regius Professor of Divinity, John Richardson, who was now Master of Trinity. On 27 June Brooke discussed, 'publicly in the Cambridge Schools', the question 'Whether it can happen that of two people, each having the same measure of grace, one nevertheless is converted, and believes, the other not'*. His answer was in the affirmative, and he explicitly rejected the views of Calvin, Beza, and Perkins.[52] Two years later Brooke presented a manuscript copy of his argument to the third Earl of Pembroke, deploring that such religious questions had returned 'from the Netherlands'* to sow discord among English divines and at the court itself.[53]

III

In the United Provinces relations between Count Maurice of Nassau and Oldenbarnevelt, Advocate of Holland, had steadily deteriorated since the Twelve Years Truce of 1609. Each

---

[51] John Yates, *God's Arraignement of Hypocrites* (Cambridge, 1615), pp. 91, 114, 157–8.

[52] CUL MS FF/5/25, fos. 94–112. It should be emphasized that this was *not* a Commencement thesis.

[53] CUL Add. MS 44 (16), fos. 1–5.

became identified with rival Dutch Calvinist and Arminian groups, Maurice championing the former and Oldenbarnevelt the latter. King James, via his ambassador at The Hague, supported Maurice as being more pro-English than Olden-barnevelt.[54] The political stance of James was, moreover, re-inforced by his religious sympathies. Basically a Calvinist in doctrine for most of his life,[55] the King's views blew hot and cold depending on what theologian or group of theologians had greatest influence over him at any given time; since 1611 Archbishop Abbot and James Montagu, now a bishop, had tended to push him into a position of Calvinist intransigence.[56] The price of Maurice's alliance with the Dutch Calvinists was a national synod, and by March 1617 King James had definitely come out in favour of such a meeting.[57] It was con-vened at Dort the following year, with English delegates in attendance, and set about condemning Arminianism. Clearly the motives of the King were mixed. Nevertheless, while the issue of the political struggle in the United Provinces remained in doubt, English unanimity on doctrinal matters was at a premium, especially in pronouncements by the uni-versities. At Oxford Robert Abbot, the Regius Professor of Divinity and brother of the Archbishop, had lectured against Arminianism as early as 1613.[58] Cambridge's acquiescence in official policy was even more important, since the university was so close to the favourite royal residences of Royston and Newmarket. At Cambridge the Regius professor of Divinity, John Richardson, was, as we have seen, a potential Arminian supporter and there a conflict between private belief and pub-lic allegiance seems to have led to his resignation, dated 25 September 1617.[59]

The evidence for Richardson's behaviour at this time derives mainly from a letter written on 6 December 1617 to

---

[54] J. den Tex, *Oldenbarnevelt* (Cambridge, 1973), II. 452, 490, 541–2, 569–70, 581, 614, and see below, pp. 87–91.

[55] James I, *A Meditation upon the Lord's Prayer* (1619), pp. 41–2, 92–3, 116–19, 122, 143, and see above, pp. 24–5.

[56] Casaubon, *Epistolae*, no. 743; Peter Heylyn, *Historia Quinqu-Articularis* (1660), i. 71.

[57] Dudley Carleton, *Letters*, ed. P. Yorke (1775), p. 123.

[58] Robert Abbot, *De Gratia et Perseverantia Sanctorum*, pp. 1–14.

[59] CU Arch., Guard Book 39/2 (Regius Professor of Divinity), no. 2.

James Ussher, the future Archbishop of Armagh. The author, Sir Henry Bourchier, writes from London that

> about a fortnight since the heads and others of the University of Cambridge were summoned to appear before His Majesty at Newmarket, where, at their coming, they were required to deliver their opinions concerning Mounsieur Barneveldt's confession, lately sent over to the King. To which, as I am informed, many of them did subscribe and principally Dr. Richardson, the King's Professor, for which he either hath already or is in some danger of losing his place.[60]

There was such a meeting on 15 November,[61] but it had been called because of an Arminian sermon delivered in October in the presence of King James at Royston. The preacher was Edward Simpson, fellow of Trinity College. His chief offence was to have expounded Romans 7 in the same sense as Arminius,[62] thereby casting doubt on the perseverance of the saints. Calvinists interpreted the words of St Paul, 'I am carnal, sold under sin', as having reference to a regenerate man. Simpson, like Arminius before him, denied this. 'Some it seemes have beene of opinion that in those that are regenerate freedome from sinne and thraldome under sin may consist and concurre together in the same subject . . . thus they wold confound our spirituall man and the carnall man together, but how liberty can stand with any the least degree of bondage or captivity I cannot yet conceive.' The 'regenerate person', Simpson argued, 'doth for the most parte prevaile against his carnall lustes and get the victory in this combate between the flesh and the spirit', yet sometimes 'he castes away his weapons out of his handes, begining the fight in the spirit but ending in the flesh.'[63]

According to Simpson's own account, Bishop James Montagu, after hearing the sermon, wrote to the Vice-Chancellor, who happened to be Richardson, complaining that it contained Arminian tenets.[64] A copy was sent to the King, who

[60] James Ussher, *Works*, ed. C. R. Elrington (Dublin, 1847–64), xv. 130.
[61] CU Arch., U.Ac.1(3), fo. 1.
[62] Jacobus Arminius, *De Vero et Genuino Sensu Cap. VII Epistolae ad Romanos Dissertatio* (Leiden, 1612).
[63] BL Add. MS 5960, fos. 49ᵛ, 52ᵛ.
[64] *Praestantium ac Eruditorum Virorum Epistolae Ecclesiasticae et Theologicae*, ed. C. Hartsoeker and P. Limborch (Amsterdam, 1684), pp. 397–400. Simpson says that

referred it back to the Vice-Chancellor and Cambridge heads. Their initial censure was considered inadequate and the various parties were summoned to Newmarket, where a fuller judgement was hammered out; having first written that Romans 7 'may be understood "of a regenerate person", howsoever the preacher restrayned it "to someone unregenerate"*', they now stated 'we thinke that the Apostle did not intend to describe the person of a carnall or unregenerate man'. They also went on to assert that while 'godly men fall often . . . into sinnes' God none the less 'delivers them out'.[65] It was probably at this Newmarket meeting that 'Barneveldt's confession' was mentioned. The latter had recently been sent over to England, via the Dutch Ambassador, and consists of a rather non-committal statement by Oldenbarnevelt apropos the Dutch Arminian controversy—phrased 'in generall fashion', as Archbishop Abbot complained. Indicative of coincidence in time is that Abbot appended a copy of the confession to a letter, dated 12 December, which also mentioned Simpson's sermon.[66] Yet, as previously noted, Richardson had already resigned the Regius chair on 25 September. Therefore, unless his resignation is backdated, neither Oldenbarnevelt nor Simpson can have been the cause. Perhaps Richardson simply anticipated trouble and sought to avoid it.

What amounts to a refutation of Simpson was published at London in early 1618 with a dedication to Buckingham, the new royal favourite. The author, Anthony Cade, had taught Buckingham at Billesdon School in Leicestershire. His pamphlet, *St. Paul's Agony*, originated as a sermon preached at Leicester and his purpose in publishing was, he says, 'to oppose the spreading of those opinionate and fansifull younglings, who drawing bad juyce from Arminius . . . beginne to bud and blossome in our Academie'. (Cade had been at Cambridge in the 1580s.) As to Romans 7 he expounds St Paul as teaching that 'our corruptions though abated yet are not extinguished by regeneration, but our mind and will continue still partly flesh and partly spirite, that is partly grace and partly corruption; reformation begunne but not finished, like

---

previously he had taught the same doctrine in a university sermon without receiving any censure.

[65] BL Add. MS 5960, fos. 56ᵛ, 57ᵛ, 60ᵛ.　　　[66] PRO, SP 105/95, fos. 16–17.

the ayre in the dawning of the day, neyther wholy yet enlightned nor wholly remayning darke . . . ' The marginal note reads 'sanctification begun, not completed'*, for St Paul's experience is, according to Cade, that of all 'God's blessed children' on earth.[67]

Meanwhile, at Cambridge, Richardson was replaced as Regius Professor by Samuel Collins, the Provost of King's College. In his only published sermon, one of 1607, Collins underwrote the suppression of Puritanism by Archbishop Bancroft, whose chaplain he then was. But he also rebutted the 'dearling freewill' of the 'Pelagian', against whom he taught that 'it is God's finger alone that can import a consent, though we can imprint a conceit. He bowes the neck of the inner man, and puts our feet into wisdomes fetters, our handes into her links and chaines, mollifies and intenerates . . . the iron synew of our unbeliefe.' God, furthermore, 'which hath begunne the good work in you will fulfill it unto the end'.[68] Such views appear to have fitted Collins better than Richardson to cope with the outside pressures now being felt in the university, as plans took shape for a Calvinist gathering—the Synod of Dort—to settle the religious questions so much agitated in the United Provinces. The synod, which met in late 1618, brought direct Cambridge involvement because of the four English delegates initially sent two were resident academics. One was John Davenant, Lady Margaret Professor of Divinity and Master of Queens' College. The other was Samuel Ward, Master of Sidney Sussex College and soon to succeed Davenant in the Lady Margaret chair.[69] The single Scottish delegate was also a Cambridge resident—Walter Balcanqual, fellow of Pembroke College. Perhaps as a conscious prologue to the synod, it was maintained by Francis White at the Commencement in 1618 that 'Predestination to grace is not on account of works foreseen'*.[70]

---

[67] Anthony Cade, *St. Paul's Agony* (1618), sig. A3ᵛ, pp. 2, 16; G. Cuming, 'The Life and Works of Anthony Cade, B.D., Vicar of Billesdon, 1599–1639', *Leics. Archæological and Hist. Soc.*, 45 (1969–70), 39–56.

[68] Samuel Collins, *A Sermon preached at Paules Crosse* (1607), sig. A4, pp. 6–12, 58–62.

[69] Davenant and Ward both defended the *jure divino* theory of episcopacy at the Synod of Dort, although the latter had earlier inclined to nonconformity. Walter Balcanqual *et al.*, *A Joynt Attestation* (1626) and *Two Puritan Diaries*, ed. Knappen, pp. 39–44.   [70] BL Harleian MS 7038, p. 92.

Proceedings at Dort are discussed in a later chapter and here it suffices to say that, for Cambridge, participation in the synod by some of its leading theologians meant a sharper focusing of attention on the religious questions at issue. As a result, existing differences of opinion grew more bitter. A foretaste of conflicts to come was afforded by the contested election to the Pembroke College mastership in early 1619. Bishop Andrewes supported the candidature of Jerome Beale, a former fellow of Pembroke and prebendary of Ely. The opposition in the college, led by Ralph Brownrig, accused Beale of Arminianism. Counter-accusations of Puritanism seem to have been made, and this rival lobbying elicited a royal message that the fellows should not elect anyone suspected of either 'Arminianisme or Puritanisme'. By the late 1620s Beale was a declared Arminian, but now in 1619, on 21 February, he was elected Master. Ironically his supporters included Balcanqual, currently engaged in condemning Arminianism at Dort, and King James expressed satisfaction at the result.[71] In this instance the influence of Andrewes, successor-elect to the late Bishop James Montagu of Winchester, was probably crucial. Archbishop Abbot recalled in 1613 that Andrewes 'heretofore inclined' to the view that a man 'truly justifyed and sanctifyed may "fall from grace"' . . . but being told the King's judgment of it had made shew to desist from broaching any such thing'.[72] Nevertheless, while distancing himself from the Dutch Arminians, Andrewes retained his independence and in a court sermon of May 1619 dared to speak of those 'with their new perspective' who 'think they perceive all God's secret decrees, the number and order of them clearly, are indeed too bold and too busy with them'.[73] His allusion is almost certainly to the canons of the Synod of Dort.

IV

All Cambridge dissent from Calvinism appears temporarily to have been silenced by royal support for the Dort rulings. The

[71] BL Harleian MS 7034, pp. 158–76 and see below, p. 97.
[72] Ralph Winwood, *Memorials*, ed. E. Sawyer (1725), III. 459.
[73] Chamberlain, *Letters*, II. 111, 141; Andrewes, *Works*, III. 328.

calm was probably prolonged by the election of Ward as Vice-Chancellor in 1620 and at the 1621 Commencement, with Davenant presiding, Ralph Brownrig maintained the thesis that 'Help sufficient to salvation is not granted to all men'*.[74] But from this time onwards the maintenance of good Dutch Calvinist relations played an increasingly subsidiary role in English diplomacy. Fresh efforts were now made to bring to a head the long-discussed project of a Spanish marriage alliance, Cambridge officially entertaining the ambassadors in February 1623.[75] Criticized by many prominent Calvinists, including Archbishop Abbot,[76] the revival of this policy tended to qualify their recent triumph. Conversely the proposed Spanish marriage had the support of Buckingham; and it may be significant that a chaplain of his, William Lucy, was the first to attempt a reversal of the Cambridge situation brought about by Dort. Preaching before the university on Commencement Sunday 1622, his sermon, according to Joseph Mead, was 'totally for Arminianisme, wonderfully boldly and peremptorily, styling some passages of the contrary by the names of blasphemie etc.'. Representations were made to the Vice-Chancellor, Leonard Mawe, and there was an attempt to stop Lucy's grace for the degree of BD. Mawe, however, who next year was sent to join Prince Charles and Buckingham in Spain, seems to have prevented any formal censure.[77]

The reported extremism of Lucy's sermon was perhaps sparked by one of the Commencement theses maintained that year by John Garnons—'The grace of conversion determines the will'*.[78] In his official handling of this thesis, Ward, now Lady Margaret Professor, argued against Arminius and the 'Dutch Remonstrants',[79] who leave man's will in a state of equilibrium 'either to turn to God or not'; their opinion, he said, completely overthrows the 'foundation of divine predestination'*.[80] The thesis is recorded in the minutes of the

[74] Le Neve, *Fasti*, III. 606; BL Harleian MS 7038, p. 93; Davenant, *Determinationes*, pp. 234–9.
[75] C. H. Cooper, *Annals of Cambridge* (Cambridge, 1842–1908), III. 154–5.
[76] Welsby, *George Abbot*, pp. 107–10.
[77] BL Harleian MS 389, fo. 213; *DNB* s.n. Mawe, Leonard.
[78] BL Harleian MS 7038, p. 94.
[79] Remonstrant was a synonym for Arminian.
[80] Samuel Ward, *Opera Nonnulla* (1658), pp. 127–30.

Consistory Court,[81] an abnormal proceeding which probably indicates that it was queried by some of the college heads before being allowed for affirmation. Anti-Calvinism within the university went no further for the moment, but was soon to find a national champion in Richard Montagu, an ex-fellow of King's College and scholarly collaborator of 'Dutch' Thomson.[82] Montagu's book—*A New Gagg for an Old Goose*, published at London in 1624—denied the credal Calvinism of the English Church; absolute predestination and unconditional perseverance were but 'private opinions'. Subsequently defending himself against those who 'would make the world beleeve that "the Church of England is Calvinist"*', Montagu, in his *Appello Caesarem* of 1625, rejected the authority of the Synod of Dort and went on to suggest that the English participants had prejudiced episcopacy in favour of presbyterianism. He also dubbed Calvinists 'Puritans'.[83] Among those replying in print to Montagu was John Yates,[84] who ten years before had defended Perkins against Arminius. That Montagu managed to get his own books licensed for the press is evidence of a remarkable shift now taking place in the balance of religious power.

Ward took up the specific charge of presbyterianizing, at the Commencement in 1625, and was able to demonstrate that Montagu had misrepresented the facts.[85] As regards doctrine, towards the end of 1625 Ward was occupied with 'illustrating and confirming' the perseverance of the saints,[86] and in January 1626 he preached at St Mary's Church an extended attack on Arminianism. Under the title *Gratia Discriminans* this sermon was licensed for the London press on 12 June,[87] by Thomas Goad, chaplain to Archbishop Abbot and like Ward a former English delegate at Dort. In it Ward claims to be defending 'the cause of God'* against Arminius and his

---

[81] CU Arch., V.C.Ct. 1/48 (Acta Curiae, 1622–3), fo. 19.

[82] *Sancti Gregorii Nazianzeni in Julianum Invectivae Duae*, ed. Richard Montagu (Eton, 1610), sig. ¶ 4ᵛ.

[83] Richard Montagu, *A New Gagg for an Old Goose* (1624), pp. 157–83 and *Appello Caesarem* (1625), pp. 59–60, 108.

[84] John Yates, *Ibis ad Caesarem* (1626).

[85] Ward, *Opera Nonnulla*, p. 114.

[86] Bodleian, Tanner MS 72, fo. 55.

[87] Arber, IV. 122.

followers, whose doctrine subverts the gratuitous basis of predestination. On this question, he says, the English Church
and its teachers have always agreed with St Augustine.[88] His
sermon elicited at least one full-length reply, consisting of an
interleaved copy with extensive manuscript comments on
almost every page. This has been attributed to Matthew
Wren, a one-time pupil of Jerome Beale[89] at Pembroke College
and now Master of Peterhouse. Wren appears highly critical
of the imperial 'we'* used by Ward in his doctrinal exposition.
Instead he cites a non-Augustinian tradition which had its
origin in Christian antiquity and continued across the Reformation, finding recent exponents in Overall and Richardson.
Wren also writes that Ward distorts the views of Arminius 'of
pious memory'* and seems drunk with Augustinian wine. His
own commentary shows a wide acquaintance with Dutch
Arminian writings.[90]

It had been intended at the 1626 Commencement to maintain the thesis that 'No one disputes, save in error, against
absolute predestination'*. This, however, was prevented by
the direct intervention of Bishop Neile, acting on the instructions of King Charles.[91] Neile's letter was dated 16 June, and
enclosed a royal proclamation of two days earlier for 'the
establishing of the peace and quiet of the Church of England'.[92] While the proclamation as printed does not mention
Arminianism by name, its authors clearly had in mind the
publications of Montagu and his critics. The view taken of
recent religious history is that excessive zeal in opposing
Catholicism had caused strife within the English church, and
disputants in future are forbidden either 'by writing, preaching, printing, conferences or otherwise' to 'raise any doubts, or
publish or maintain any new inventions, or opinions, concerning religion than such as [are] clearly grounded and war-

[88] Samuel Ward, *Gratia Discriminans* (1626), pp. 49, 53–4.
[89] Christopher Wren, *Parentalia* (1750), p. 49.
[90] Bodleian, 4° Rawl. 150, pp. 9, 22, 49, 54. Thomas Baker, the antiquary, has written in the front of this volume that 'the marginal or interleaved notes are in Mathew
Wrenn's hand, sometime Bishop of Ely, as I believe anyone will allow that knows his
hand, which I have often seen and once compared with these notes. I presume they
were added about the same time the sermon was printed.'
[91] CU Arch., Lett. 12 (1625–44), no. 6.
[92] A. W. Pollard and G. W. Redgrave, *A Short Title Catalogue of Books printed in England . . . 1475–1640* (1926), no. 8824.

ranted by the doctrine and discipline of the Church of England, heretofore published and happily established by authority'.[93] As interpreted by Bishop Neile and the Durham House group,[94] who now numbered the most influential ecclesiastics in royal circles, the proclamation meant the abandonment of doctrine officially taught in the universities from the Elizabethan period onwards. Furthermore, it opened the way for the discreet propagation of Arminianism. Criticizing this policy, while preaching before the King on 25 June 1626, Archbishop Ussher said that it sacrificed an orthodox majority to an Arminian minority and that silence should only have been imposed on the latter. He also deplored the novel branding of Calvinists with the 'odious name' of Puritans, and went on to predict for England the political disaster which had barely been avoided in the United Provinces.[95]

This muzzling of Cambridge Calvinism took place within a fortnight of the election of Buckingham as Chancellor and the two events are closely connected. One of Buckingham's chief canvassers had been Bishop Neile, in a contest won by only four votes, while Jerome Beale and Matthew Wren had also campaigned prominently on his behalf.[96] Neile wrote that the event would 'in a sort purchase His Majestie himself our royall patron and Chancellor'. Two years later, in recommending a successor to the late Buckingham, King Charles added 'not that wee shal cease to bee your Chanceler in effect'.[97] Thus from June 1626 Cambridge University came more directly under royal control than probably at any time since the accession of Elizabeth and it is revealing of Charles's views that Calvinism suffered accordingly. At Oxford, by contrast, Calvinist positions continued to be maintained at the Divinity Act as late as 1631.[98]

Despite Calvinism being effectively banished from the Commencement, Ward carried on the dispute in his ordinary lectures, writing in May 1628 that he had 'read this year and a

[93] *The Stuart Constitution*, ed. J. P. Kenyon (Cambridge, 1966), pp. 154–5. The original draft of this proclamation exists in manuscript and differs markedly from the printed version, being explicitly aimed against 'Richard Mountague' and 'Arminianisme'. PRO, SP 16/29, fo. 155. I owe this reference to Dr J. Macauley.
[94] See below, Chapter 5.
[95] Ussher, *Works*, XIII. 348–51, XV. 347–8.
[96] Cooper, *Annals*, III. 185–9.
[97] CU Arch., Lett. 12 (1625–44), nos. 1 and 14.
[98] See below, pp. 76–81.

half, at least, upon that point which I chiefly insist on in my
sermon in Latin [*Gratia Discriminans*]', concerning the irre-
sistibility of God's grace. In this same letter he reports that
'as for our university, none do patronage these [Arminian]
points, either in schools or pulpit; though because preferments at court are conferred upon such as incline that way
[this] causeth some to look that way'.[99] Ward in fact was
not openly opposed until after the issue in late 1628 of
Charles's declaration, prefacing a reissue of the Thirty-nine
Articles. This, unlike the earlier proclamation, specifically
forbade members of the universities to handle 'those curious
points in which the present differences lie', offenders being
threatened with High Commission. Moreover, the declaration abandoned the neutrality of the proclamation, ordering
that 'these disputes [be] shut up in God's promises, as they
be *generally* set forth to us in the holy scriptures'.[100] Charles I
thus glossed the Thirty-nine Articles in favour of the Arminians and their doctrine of universal grace. It apparently
emboldened Jerome Beale to confront Ward in the Consistory
Court and so reverse the position of the 1590s, with a Calvinist
now in the dock. 'Our first difference, and chiefe', wrote
Ward, 'grew upon the sensing of the 17th. Article of our
Confession, which I affirmed was repugnant to the Arminians
predestination "from faith foreseen"* and you denyed.' Their
discussions ranged over the true meaning of the Dutch
Arminian authors Petrus Bertius and Joannes Arnoldus
Corvinus, and the correct interpretation of St Augustine.
Galled to be told he had misunderstood the last named, Ward
chose for his exit line at one such meeting: 'I durst wager I
could produce more places out of St Augustine to confirme
that the trewly faithful and regenerate doe never finally fall
away, then you should to confirme the contrary assertion.' He
remained, moreover, confident that his was the 'receyved
opinion of the best divines of the Reformed Church' and of the
'best approved doctors in our Church since the beginning

---

[99] Ussher, *Works*, xv. 404. Someone whom Ward may have had in mind here was
his colleague Samuel Collins, the Regius Professor of Divinity. That September Collins wrote to congratulate Richard Montagu on his promotion to the episcopate.
PRO, SP 16/117, fo. 13.

[100] *The Constitutional Documents of the Puritan Revolution, 1625–1660*, ed. S. R. Gardiner
(Oxford, 1962), pp. 75–6. My italics.

of the Reformation'.[101] Ward's only concession was, in his lectures, to omit 'naming the authors (Remonstrants) whom I impugn'.[102]

<h1 style="text-align:center">V</h1>

The position of Cambridge Calvinism was, however, further weakened by the March 1629 dissolution of parliament in a manner which augured its long intermission. For a majority of the House of Commons had declared firmly in favour of Calvinism and on 17 February 1629 the Speaker had written, about Arminianism, to the Vice-Chancellors of both Oxford and Cambridge.[103] The letter originated in a motion by Sir Benjamin Rudyard and asked for

the names of all such persons within your universitie . . . as since the thirteenth yeare of Queene Elizabeth have taught, written or published, any points of doctrine contrary to the Articles of Religion established in that yeare, or contrary to the true and generallie recived sence of those Articles, or the current doctrine of the Church of England, and withall to certifie what actes, determinacions, censures, recantacions, submissions or other proceedings have been thereupon had or made, together with true copies of the same.[104]

Somewhat ambiguous as to the scope of the returns expected, the request was interpreted by the Cambridge heads in a decidedly restricted sense. Their findings were completed too late to be presented to the Commons and would have given little satisfaction. Of the fourteen cases listed only two, those of Barrett and Baro, were relevant to the Arminian issue and that of Baro apparently was only included at the insistence of Ward. Wren, as Vice-Chancellor, cautioned the investigating committee not to infringe the royal declaration of 1628, and the inadequacy of the university records further contributed to ensure that the return did less than justice to Calvinist claims. Doubt was thus cast on the authenticity of Barrett's recantation, since no copy could be found entered into any register.

[101] Bodleian, Tanner MS 71, fos. 10–11, 15, Tanner MS 72, fo. 314 and Tanner MS 80, fo. 143ʳ⁻ᵛ.
[102] Ussher, *Works*, xv. 500.
[103] *Commons Debates for 1629*, ed. W. Notestein and F. H. Relf (Minneapolis, 1921), pp. 23, 57.
[104] CU Arch., Lett. 12 (1625–44), no. 15.

This perhaps also explains the total omission of the censure of Edward Simpson. Furthermore a rider was added to the Baro case that, since no conclusion had been reached, it could not stand as evidence. The only college head refusing to sign the report on 2 April was Ward, but even he signed eighteen days later with some slight qualifications.[105]

June 1629 saw the first attempt to use the Commencement disputations for Arminian propaganda. The answerer, Edward Quarles of Pembroke College, chose the thesis 'All baptised infants are undoubtedly justified'', and this was, according to Ward, 'with a purpose to impugn the doctrine of perseverance, as they conceived, by an undeniable argument'.[106] Ward's representations to Wren, still Vice-Chancellor, were unavailing. He was, therefore, compelled in his Commencement determination to distinguish between the grace of justification bestowed in the baptism of all infants and a superadded grace of election necessary for the perseverance of adults.[107] But the original thesis indicates the sacramental thrust of English Arminianism, which in turn informs the ceremonial changes so characteristic of the 1630s. This link between free will and the externals of devotion is illustrated by a notable sermon of 1632. It was preached on 6 May at St Mary's Church by Nathaniel Barnard, a visiting London lecturer, who condemned both what he termed a growing Pelagianism in doctrine and a Romish superstition in worship. He later claimed that at the 1631 Commencement the preacher had argued against the absolute decree of reprobation and, although his other charges were undocumented, he presumably also had in mind the much publicized alterations at Durham and Winchester cathedrals.[108] The teaching of the sermon was, in addition, something of a political milestone. Barnard had spoken of treason, distinguishing between that against the blood royal and that against the church and nation, 'which last is by soe much the worst of them two, by how much the end is better than the meanes and the whole of greater consequence than any one part alone'. In his conclusion he was understood to have advocated withstanding reli-

---

[105] CU Arch., Guard Book 6/1, nos. 38 and 39.
[106] Ussher, *Works*, xv. 504; BL Harleian MS 7038, p. 97.
[107] Ward, *Opera Nonnulla*, pp. 53–4.   [108] See below, pp. 116–18, 214–15.

gious innovation by force, thus applying the Calvinist doctrine of resistance.[109] After a number of interviews in the Consistory Court, Barnard was handed over to the High Commission and apparently died in prison.[110]

As well, however, as the ceremonial implications of English Arminianism, there were others of a more overtly doctrinal character; thus, for example, the performance of good works acquired much greater importance when salvation came to be considered conditional on behaviour throughout life. Likewise the questioning of the absolute decree resulted in a new assertion of the power of a regenerate man to avoid sin. This ramification of the Arminian controversy is illustrated by the printing in 1635, at Cambridge, of *Five Pious and Learned Discourses*. Written by Robert Shelford, a former member of Peterhouse and now Rector of Ringsfield, in Suffolk, the book was 'published at the very Commencement'.[111] Archbishop Ussher wrote of it later in the year as 'rotten stuff', which was being exploited in Ireland by the Jesuits.[112] The fourth discourse is about the 'Divine Attributes'. God, says Shelford, 'hath given to man free will, and to maintain this he hath ordained contingencie and added his grace' which 'is like to the vertuous magnet the most remarkable of all stones, the guide of the diall and the direction for sea travell. For as the pin and needle of the diall being toucht with it the needle will stand no way but north and south, so the heart of man being toucht with God's grace in his regeneration will stand no way but to Heavenward.' By God's grace 'man travelleth either to his home of happiness or his home of heavinesse', because shipwreck is always possible on 'the ocean of contingencie'. He concludes by proving 'contingencie to stand with the Holy Scripture, against the men which attribute all to fate and necessitie'.[113]

---

[109] CUL MS Mm/6/54, fos. 1–24ᵛ. For the wider significance of Barnard's notion of treason see M. Walzer, *Regicide and Revolution* (1974), pp. 42–5.

[110] Cooper, *Annals*, III. 252.

[111] Henry Burton, *For God and the King* (1636), p. 123. *Five Pious and Learned Discourses* was not a posthumous work, despite the attempt by J. and J. A. Venn to kill off Shelford in 1627. *Alumni Cantabrigienses . . . Pt.I* (Cambridge, 1922–7), IV. 57. Shelford's will is dated August 1638. PRO, PROB. 11/180, fo. 34ᵛ.

[112] Ussher, *Works*, XVI. 9.

[113] Robert Shelford, *Five Pious and Learned Discourses* (Cambridge, 1635), pp. 193–4, 203, 207.

The bulk of Shelford's book, however, concerns religious questions which only came to the fore during the 1630s. Thus his second discourse is entitled 'Preferring Holy Charitie before Faith, Hope and Knowledge', and he appends a Commencement determination of 1633: 'Good works are efficaciously necessary to salvation.'*[114] The latter was the work of Eleazer Duncon, a Pembroke graduate and one of Neile's chaplains.[115] In 1634 Ward had successfully counter-attacked, and prevented another Pembroke man from maintaining a similar thesis at the Commencement. Instead he procured a member of his own college, William Flathers, to uphold the doctrine of justification by faith alone.[116] Accordingly the appearance of Shelford's book in 1635 once more reversed official teaching in favour of that most strongly canvassed at Pembroke College, two members supplying dedicatory verses.[117] 'Charitie', says Shelford, 'is the substance of Christianitie;' 'it is the divine seed of a Christian, by which we are born of God and freed from mortall sinne.' Moreover 'charitie is alwayes working, because it is the heart's pulse to Godward', and 'the more good works a Christian doth in the kingdome of grace the greater shall be his crown in the kingdome of glorie'. On this question he takes direct issue with Calvin and Beza.[118] Shelford's third discourse, about the 'Law's Possibilitie', again covers ground disputed at the Commencement in 1633, and reasserts the position then determined that 'A regenerate man is able to fulfill the law'*.[119] For, he argues, 'were the law impossible to be kept then all the exhortations and threatnings in God's word should be idle, then all men's labours would wax lazie and then good life which is after the rule would be exiled, for that no man would strive against the stream'. He also indicates how this teaching conflicts with the Calvinist doctrine of perseverance, exhorting 'let every one, as soon as he is down, presently rise again'.[120]

---

[114] Ibid., p. 120; BL Harleian MS 7038, p. 99.
[115] *DNB* s.n. Duncon, Eleazer.
[116] Ussher, *Works*, xv. 579–80; BL Harleian MS 7038, p. 100.
[117] Shelford, *Five Discourses*, sig. Aᵛ, A2.   [118] Ibid., pp. 98, 100, 105, 108, 115.
[119] Bodleian, Tanner MS 71, fo. 164. In 1633 Duncon had also interpreted Romans 7 in the Arminian sense, as referring to an unregenerate man. PRO, SP 16/243, fo. 47.
[120] Shelford, *Five Discourses*, pp. 129, 150. At the Commencement in 1637, Richard

But while discourses two to four largely overlap with Dutch
Arminianism,[121] discourses one and five part company and
serve to demonstrate the difference between the Dutch and
English movements. Thus in 'God's House', the first discourse, Shelford describes the 'holy altar', placed 'at the east
end' of a church, as 'the Sonne of God's seat' and the 'holy
font, at the nether end', as 'where the Holy Ghost is alwaies
ready to receive all into his kingdome'. He regrets, however,
that 'the beauty of preaching (which is a beauty too) hath
preacht away the beauty of holinesse', and urges men to set
about refurbishing God's sanctuary. Reverence also is owed to
God by 'bowing the knee' towards the altar—'the speciall
place of his residence'.[122] The underlying theology here can be
found in Shelford's second discourse, where he exclaims 'oh
the lamentation of our times! Who shall make our people to
beleeve that Christ's sacraments bestow grace? They say they
signifie onely and that faith cometh by hearing onely. Yet,
when they have heard what they can and beleeve what they
will, they shall never be saved without the grace of the sacraments.'[123] Shelford in fact substitutes sacramental grace for the
grace of predestination, an English Arminian mode of argument deriving from the Prayer Book. Similarly English is the
fifth and final discourse 'Shewing the Antichrist not to be yet
come', in which Shelford rejects a voluminous Protestant literature proving the Pope to be Antichrist.[124] At the same time it
has been suggested that the ideas of absolute predestination
and Antichrist 'stood or fell together', the two realms of elect
and reprobate implying two rulers—Christ and his opposite.[125] The demise of the papal Antichrist, however, also
meant a softening of Protestant attitudes towards Catholics
and for Shelford, at least, opened up the prospect of their general toleration. 'Let Protestants love the Papists because they
have kept the holy oracles and sacred mysteries for them, and
let Papists love the Protestants because they are descended
from them, wear the badge of the covenant with them and by

Holdsworth maintained that 'The fulfillment of the law is impossible in this life'* BL
Harleian MS 7038, p. 101.

[121] Arminius, *Writings*, I. 369–71, II. 202–3 and see above, pp. 39–40.
[122] Shelford, *Five Discourses*, pp. 12–13, 15, 17–18.
[123] Ibid., p. 66. [124] Ibid., pp. 282–8.
[125] C. Hill, *Antichrist in Seventeenth Century England* (1971), pp. 168–9.

a light and oblique dissent provoke them to better life and more refined learning.'[126]

Shelford's own case history is particularly interesting. A septuagenarian, he had studied at Peterhouse, Cambridge, during the 1580s, describing himself in 1635 as 'formerly secretary to the famous Perne''.[127] This association with Andrew Perne, a man who had complied with all the religious changes from Henry VIII to Elizabeth, served doubly to damn Shelford in the eyes of Archbishop Ussher, who commented that 'in his *Five Discourses* . . . he hath so carried himself "that the hand of Perne is all too recognisable"*'.[128] But, whatever may be the truth about Perne, his one-time secretary Shelford was certainly no turncoat. As early as 1596 he had come under criticism for advocating 'good nourture', by way of education, as the cure of corrupt nature.[129] Only at the very end of his life, however, did he emerge from obscurity, his views celebrated by Richard Crashaw in verses which begin

Rise then, immortal maid! Religion rise![130]

At Cambridge the religious turning-point is marked by a letter from Ussher to Ward, dated 30 June 1626, in which he writes that 'it behoveth all you who are heads of colleges and "likeminded"✝ to stick close to one another and, quite obliterating all secret distastes or privy discontentments which possibly may fall betwixt yourselves, with joint consent . . . promote the cause of God'.[131] His phrase 'the cause of God' echoes the title of Thomas Bradwardine's famous fourteenth-century treatise *De Causa Dei contra Pelagium*. This had been printed for the first time in 1618, on the eve of the Synod of Dort. Published by order of Archbishop Abbot, and dedicated to King James,[132] the book was clearly intended as English Calvinist propaganda—Bradwardine's cause being that of the irresistible grace of God. From an Arminian point of view, however, Bradwardine was an 'enemy of God'*, as

---

[126] Shelford, *Five Discourses*, pp. 240–1.
[127] Ibid., sig. ¶2ᵛ.
[128] Ussher, *Works*, XVI. 9.
[129] Robert Shelford, *Lectures . . . concerning the Vertuous Education of Youth* (1606), sig. A2ʳ⁻ᵛ and pp. 124–5. The first edition of this book is dated 1596.
[130] Shelford, *Five Discourses*, sig. A.   [131] Ussher, *Works*, XV. 346.
[132] Thomas Bradwardine, *De Causa Dei contra Pelagium* (1618), sig. a and title-page.

Matthew Wren called him.[133] Moreover, Arminians became
increasingly uninhibited in describing Calvinists as Puritans.
'Praedestination is the roote of Puritanisme', wrote Samuel
Brooke, now Master of Trinity College, in 1630, and
'Puritanisme the roote of all rebellions and disobedient
intractableness in parliaments etc. and all schisme and sauci-
ness in the countrey, nay in the Church itself'.[134] But it was
more truly the case that the victory of Arminianism meant the
recrudescence of militant Puritanism.[135]

[133] Bodleian, 4° Rawl. 150, p. 37.
[134] PRO, SP 16/177, fo. 13.
[135] During the 1630s the preaching of Arminianism apparently went unchecked at
Cambridge University. Thus it was subsequently alleged that John Pullen and John
Willington had both maintained 'falling from grace', without receiving any censure.
Bishops in turn—those 'mitred and scarletted prelates'—were coming under renewed
attack by 1632. BL Harleian MS 7019, fos. 63, 89. I owe my knowledge of this manuscript to Dr Lake.

3

Oxford University and Arminianism

I

THE fortunes of Calvinism at the two English universities followed broadly similar paths, but during the 1590s there was no Oxford equivalent to the Cambridge clash between Calvinist orthodoxy and emergent Arminianism. This difference is partly explained by the fact that anti-Calvinism, in the person of Anthony Corro, had been checked at Oxford some ten years earlier. An ex-monk from San Isidro near Seville, Corro taught at Oxford from about 1579 to 1586. He had come to England in 1568, via France and the Netherlands, first preaching to a group of Spanish Protestants in London and then lecturing at the Temple Church.[1] Shortly after his arrival in England Corro got involved in religious controversy, the echoes of which followed him at least to the end of his Oxford days.

Particular exception was taken to a broadside by Corro published in 1569 at Norwich and entitled *Tableau de l'œuvre de Dieu*.[2] This led some of Corro's fellow-clergy to question the soundness of his views 'about three heads of our religion—namely predestination, free will and justification by faith alone'.[3] The gravamen of the complaint against him is perhaps best understood by comparing his *Tableau* with one by Beza, first published in 1555.[4] Beza's table begins with the double decree of predestination whereas Corro ends with this—faith or its lack preceding election and reprobation. Having migrated to the Temple Church, Corro was then accused by the Master, Richard Alvey, of 'affirming free will

---

[1] For Corro's early career I have relied on W. McFadden, 'The Life and Works of Antonio del Corro, 1527–1591', Queen's University Belfast, Ph.D. thesis, 1953.

[2] There is a copy in the Cambridge University Library.

[3] *Ecclesiae Londino—Batavae Archivum*, ed. J. H. Hessels (Cambridge, 1887–97), III. 131.

[4] Theodore Beza, *Tractationes Theologicae* (Geneva, 1570–6), I. 170; F. Gardy, *Bibliographie des œuvres théologiques . . . de Théodore de Bèze* (Geneva, 1960), p. 47.

and speaking not wisely of predestination'.[5] The previous year, 1574, had seen the publication of Corro's *Dialogus Theologicus*, where he says that he has been called a Pelagian for countering 'false security'" with exhortations to do good works.[6] Also revealing, however, is that, when answering his critics, he appealed to the writings of the Danish Lutheran Neils Hemmingsen,[7] who during the late sixteenth century became something of an international spokesman for all those opposed to Calvinism.

In April 1576 Corro applied for and was refused an Oxford doctorate of divinity, until he should purge himself from charges of heresy.[8] The matter came up again in Convocation during June, plus the suggestion that Corro be appointed to a lectureship. Among those objecting to both proposals was John Reynolds, future Puritan spokesman at the Hampton Court Conference and at this date fellow of Corpus Christi College. He now wrote to the Vice-Chancellor, Laurence Humphrey, singling out the *Tableau* for attack as containing erroneous teaching on 'predestination and justification by faith, two of the chiefest points of Christian religion'. Reynolds moreover expressed the fear that Corro had subscribed to the Thirty-nine Articles 'in such sort as St Austin writeth of Pelagius . . . "forced to damn for fear of being condemned"'.[9] Opposition of this kind apparently sufficed to prevent Corro from ever proceeding to a doctorate, but in 1579 he was appointed Censor Theologicus at Christ Church and the same year is listed as Catechist of Gloucester Hall, Hart Hall, and St Mary's Hall.[10]

The campaign against Corro none the less continued. By 1580 his name can be found linked with that of Peter Baro,[11] who was already coming under Calvinist criticism at Cambridge, and for the remainder of his time at Oxford Corro seems to have been a man on probation—especially in the

---

[5] Matthew Parker, *Correspondence*, ed. J. Bruce and T. T. Perowne (Parker Soc., Cambridge, 1853), p. 476.   [6] Anthony Corro, *Dialogus Theologicus* (1574), fo. 107ᵛ.

[7] *Ecclesiae Londino—Batavae Archivum*, ed. Hessels, III. 131.

[8] *The Register of the University of Oxford*, ed. A. Clark (Oxford Hist. Soc., 10, 1887–9), i. 153.

[9] Anthony Wood, *The History and Antiquities of the University of Oxford*, ed. J. Gutch (Oxford, 1792–6), II, pt. i. 180–2.

[10] Christ Church, Oxford, Disbursement Books; Clark, *Register*, p. 156.

[11] *Ecclesiae Londino—Batavae Archivum*, ed. Hessels, II. 670, 672.

eyes of the university Puritans. His name disappears from the Christ Church records after 1586 and he probably ceased to teach in the university from that date. The evidence for Corro having positively influenced religious developments at Oxford is slight. Christ Church produced a number of early Arminians but of these only John Howson was Corro's contemporary, and he would appear to have been a Calvinist as late as 1602.[12] Another contemporary was Richard Hooker of Corpus Christi College, whose teaching was described as 'not unlike' that of Corro.[13] In this case, however, the 'not unlike' needs stressing because Hooker never broke completely with Calvinism and his posthumously published writings were to be cited by Calvinists against the Arminians.[14]

Certainly the influence of Corro did not result in any demonstrable Oxford support for the doctrines of William Barrett and Peter Baro when they were opposed at Cambridge in the mid-1590s. Nevertheless, it was unlikely that the Cambridge dispute would have gone unremarked by Oxford theologians and in fact most of the main tenets of the Lambeth Articles came to be affirmed during the Oxford Acts of 1596 and 1597. While such questions had provided thesis subjects earlier,[15] the phraseology and the particular emphasis on predestination are new. In July 1596 the Calvinist assertion was undertaken by two of the incepting doctors of divinity, Roger Hacket and Henry Parry. The following year Robert Abbot and Richard Field entered the lists. Hacket dealt with the question of reprobation, arguing that 'God of his own volition will repudiate some people' and that 'The reprobate, being excluded from all hope of eternal salvation, necessarily perish".[16] His theses comprise a gloss on the fourth Lambeth article. Similarly the theses maintained by Parry in 1596 con-

---

[12] John Howson, *A Sermon . . . in Defence of the Festivities of the Church of England* (Oxford, 1602), sig. A3. Howson speaks of 'that general and admirable benefite of our redemption which was sufficient for the whole world, but efficient to al the elect of God'.   [13] Richard Hooker, *Works* (Oxford, 1850), II. 662.

[14] The ambiguities of Hooker's position are apparent from the uncompleted reply to his critics, which he left in manuscript. Richard Hooker, *Of the Laws of Ecclesiastical Polity* (Cambridge, Mass., 1977–82), IV. 123–67. For a Calvinist citation of Hooker, see Prynne, *Anti-Arminianisme*, pp. 88, 97, 203–4.

[15] For example, in 1582 William Souch had maintained that 'the election of the saints is gratuitous' and that 'no one who is elect can perish'*. Clarke, *Register*, p. 195.

[16] Ibid., p. 197. For the text of the Lambeth Articles, see above, pp. 30–1.

cerned the question of perseverance, so much agitated at Cambridge and dealt with in the fifth and sixth Lambeth articles. Parry, who was to be made a bishop in 1607, asserted that a justified man could not lose faith finally or for a time, and could be certain of his salvation in perpetuity.[17]

In 1597 Robert Abbot, later Regius Professor of Divinity and ultimately a bishop, maintained a version of the first Lambeth article: 'The eternal predestination of God comprises the election of some to life eternal and the reprobation of others to death.'[18] Linked with this was the defence of Calvin's own teaching by Field, who argued that 'The doctrine of predestination formerly delivered by Augustine, and in our times by Calvin, is the same, containing nothing contrary to Catholic truth or to the rule of faith'.[19] None of the incepting doctors handled the seventh and eighth Lambeth articles on the extent of man's redemption by Christ. But in December 1595 this had been discussed in a St Mary's sermon by Sebastian Benfield. Citing St Augustine, as well as William Perkins's *A Golden Chain*, he taught that salvation was restricted to 'the elect and chosen of God', and that Gospel promises to 'all men' must be understood as referring to 'all sorts of particulars, not each particular of all sorts'. He went on to assert that 'God's will and pleasure is the onely chiefe cause why hee electeth some and reproveth the rest'.[20] Benfield was to become Lady Margaret Professor of Divinity in 1613. More generally Henry Airay, preaching at about this time in Oxford, commented on the current predestinarian disputes

in our Church what cockatrice egges be now a hatching, what outworne errors of Pelagianisme be now a broaching? Libertie of will, universalitie of grace, salvation of all men, and other like damnable errours must now be set on foot againe, though the whole Church bee set on fire therewith . . . by contentious men, which cannot abide to agree with the Church in the received truth.[21]

---

[17] Clark, *Register*, p. 198.

[18] This is the version given by William Prynne, and differs slightly from that in the Congregation register. I have preferred the former, since Prynne was relying on the printed Act programmes which probably reflect more accurately the final version of the thesis as maintained. Prynne, *Anti-Arminianisme* (1630), p. 242; Clark, *Register*, p. 199.

[19] Ibid.   [20] Sebastian Benfield, *Eight Sermons* (Oxford, 1614), pp. 4, 7.

[21] Henry Airay, *Lectures upon the Whole Epistle of Saint Paul to the Philippians* (1618),

'Throughout the 1590s', it has been said, 'the Calvinist message rang loudly and clearly from the Oxford pulpits.'[22] The
sermons of Sebastian Benfield are a case in point, where he
reiterates that the offer of salvation is limited to 'the elect' and
adds that 'the saints of God . . . fal not finally in the end nor
utterly at any time'.[23] Meanwhile Zacharias Ursinus' lectures
on the Heidelberg Catechism remained 'a standard Oxford
textbook'.[24] They include a section on predestination, where
Ursinus states that neither 'anie good foreseene' nor 'sin' is
the 'efficient cause' of election and reprobation but 'the most
free good pleasure of God'.[25] A fifth edition of these lecturers
was printed at Oxford in 1601. Among English authors published by the Oxford press in the first years of the seventeenth
century was George Abbot, the future archbishop. Replying to
a Catholic adversary, Thomas Hill, Abbot took occasion to
point out that, when in the Bible it is said that God wishes the
salvation of all men, the word 'all intendeth many, or diverse
of diverse sorts, not universally every one'.[26] Likewise Calvinist theses featured regularly at the annual Oxford Act.
Thus in 1603 Cadwallader Owen maintained that the salvation of the elect is 'simply gratuitous'', and in 1605 John Har-
mar denied that someone truly justified could fall from grace.[27]

II

Outwardly Oxford University continued to present a uniform
Calvinist face until 1607. That year an anti-Calvinist pro-
tagonist first emerged in the person of Humphrey Leech, a
chaplain of Christ Church. He developed his views in a
number of sermons, culminating with one preached on 27
June 1608. The ostensible question at issue was his defence of
'evangelicall counsayles', or works of supererogation, such as
poverty and chastity. 'Precepts are of necessitie, counsailes

p. 302. These lectures were clearly an Elizabethan product because Airay refers
throughout to the monarch as a female.

[22] C. M. Dent, *Protestant Reformers in Elizabethan Oxford* (Oxford, 1983), p. 222.
[23] Benfield, *Eight Sermons*, pp. 19, 40, 148.
[24] Dent, *Protestant Reformers*, p. 186.
[25] Ursinus, *The Summe of Christian Religion*, pp. 642–3.
[26] George Abbot, *The Reasons which Doctour Hill hath brought* (Oxford, 1604), p. 19.
[27] Prynne, *Anti-Arminianisme*, p. 244; Clark, *Register*, p. 204.

arbitrarie [and] left to our free choice. Both ayme at the marke of Heaven, by shootinge at the butte of Christian perfection, but differ in the manner. Both levell at the meanes of salvation, that is perfection of charitie, yet counsailes after a more exquisite and excellinge perfection.'[28] Leech's premiss, however, is explicitly anti-Calvinist—men having it in their power to do both more and less than the minimum necessary for salvation.[29] He also warns against 'sinfull secure presumption of Heaven'[30] and his case in a number of ways recalls that of William Barrett at Cambridge. Therefore it is probably significant that at the ensuing Act, in July, three doctors of divinity[31] all affirmed the final perseverance of the saints, two linking this with the assertion that believers could be 'certain'* of their salvation.

Following his final sermon Leech was summoned before the Vice-Chancellor, John King, and he claimed retrospectively to have been the victim of a 'Calvinist'[32] faction whereas 'the best learned in Oxford concurred with me in this point'.[33] Silenced by the Vice-Chancellor, Leech then appealed to higher authority in the person of Archbishop Bancroft, 'in regard of his academicall soveraignty over me and them, being our honourable Chancellour, and much more in respect of his archiepiscopall dignity'.[34] Bancroft had been elected Chancellor of Oxford that April and Leech apparently expected a sympathetic hearing from him, as one 'averse from Calvinisme', although he was to be bitterly disappointed. Indeed he writes of Bancroft as 'falling into Calvin's false and absurd exposition' on the subject of evangelical counsels.[35] Shortly thereafter Leech fled abroad and turned Catholic. His case was referred to by Bancroft when writing to the university in January 1609. Alluding specifically to the Leech case, Bancroft warned Oxford men to be 'very wary and circumspect that they broach not or mainteyne not, out of singularitie or a spirit of contention, any opinions contrarie to the receaved doctrine of the Church of England coming verie

[28] Humphrey Leech, *A Triumph of Truth* (Douai, 1609), p. 39.
[29] Ibid., pp. 2–3, 31–5.
[30] Ibid., p. 34.
[31] Nicholas Simpson, Thomas Allen and John Lee. Clark, *Register*, pp. 205–6.
[32] Leech, *A Triumph of Truth*, p. 62.
[33] Ibid., pp. 59–60. [34] Ibid., p. 116.   [35] Ibid., pp. 80, 116.

neare unto Poperie, albeit a little they seeme to mince and
qualifie it'. For a likely consequence said Bancroft would be
'shipwracke of a good conscience' by desertion to 'the common enemy'.[36]

This letter seems to bear out the contention of Leech that he
had supporters in Oxford. They may have included John Williams, Lady Margaret Professor of Divinity until his death in
1612, who was said to have denied that the Pope was Antichrist[37]—a remarkably advanced position at the time. One of
the most likely candidates, however, is William Laud, who the
same year as Leech's sermon was addressed in print by Joseph
Hall under the guise of 'Mr W. L.'.

Today you are in the tents of the Romanists, tomorrow in our's, the
next day betweene both, against both. Our adversaries thinke you
our's, wee their's. Your conscience findes you with both, and
neither. I flatter you not. This of your's is the worst of all tempers.
Heat and cold have their uses. Lukewarmnesse is good for nothing
but to trouble the stomach.[38]

In this same collection of epistles Hall summed up the essence
of 'all Popery' as tending 'to make nature either vainly proud
or carelessly wanton'.[39] But once Leech had declared in favour
of Catholicism he became a source of embarrassment to his
former allies. Thus John Overall who was cited by Leech as
having been in basic agreement with him was quick to deny
any such thing.[40]

While the nexus of intellectual relationships surrounding
Leech at Christ Church is probably irrecoverable, it has
proved possible to trace the prehistory of Arminianism in
another Oxford college. At Corpus Christi College, in May
1607, the death of the President, John Reynolds, unleashed a
fierce faction fight among the fellows. The conflict within the
college, however, was not explicitly religious. Centre of the
storm was Daniel Featley, son of the late President's cook and
now a fellow of the college. In the opinion of his opponents,

---

[36] OU Arch., Reg. K. 22, fo. 31.

[37] PRO, SP 14/80, fo. 177ᵛ; Hill, *Antichrist in Seventeenth Century England*, pp. 31–40.

[38] Joseph Hall, *Epistles* (1608), ii. 55–6; Heylyn, *Cyprianus Anglicus*, p. 50.

[39] Hall, *Epistles*, ii. 33.

[40] Leech, *A Triumph of Truth*, pp. 77–9; Daniel Price, *The Defence of Truth* (Oxford, 1610), pp. 288–95. In replying to Leech's sermon of June 1608, Price counters that the truly righteous 'cannot fall finally and totally from God'. Ibid., p. 125.

Featley, under the patronage of Reynolds, had acquired a dis-
proportionate share of college emoluments. Social edge may
also have been given to the struggle in that the opposition was
directed by one of the few gentlemen among the fellows,
Walter Browne.[41] The dispute began over the assignment of
scholars to college tutors. Bryan Twyne attempted to wrest
Francis Allen from Featley and, being thwarted, urged that
the case be tried before the Visitor, Bishop Bilson of Winchester. According to Featley this was 'by the advise of Mr Browne
without whome he [Twyne] is thought to do nothing'. A similar move was made by Thomas Jackson over the tutoring of
another scholar—Matthew Colmore.[42] Relations then seem to
have deteriorated so badly that only the intervention of
Bishop Henry Parry, an alumnus of the college, saved Featley
from dismissal.[43] But what is of primary interest here is the
theological alignment of the two groups. Having become
chaplain to Archbishop Abbot in about 1615, Featley was to
write and campaign against Arminianism during the 1620s.[44]
His protector Bishop Parry, as we have noted, had in 1596
defended two of the central positions of the Lambeth Articles,
and Featley's circle of correspondents was almost exclusively
confined to committed Calvinists.[45]

By contrast the leader of the opposing faction at Corpus
Christi, Walter Browne, was among the earliest Oxford
theologians conversant with continental Arminian thought,
and probably belonged to that school himself. An inventory of
his library, drawn up in April 1613, includes five of Arminius'
writings. These comprise the *Disputationes*, the *Orationes*, the
Examen against the teaching of Perkins on predestination,
which also incorporates Arminius' exposition of Romans 9,

[41] Browne matriculated, in 1590, as of Surrey, gentleman. J. Foster, *Alumni Oxonienses, 1500–1714* (Oxford, 1892), I. 198. He was probably the grandson of Sir Matthew Browne of Bechworth Castle. J. P. Yeatman, *The Brownes of Bechworth Castle* (1903), p. 49.
[42] Bodleian, Rawlinson MS D.47, fos. 55ʳ⁻ᵛ. Featley writes of 'Mr Jackson'. As how-ever he also describes him as one of the 'fellowes', Thomas not Henry Jackson must be meant.
[43] Ibid., fos. 62–63ᵛ.
[44] Daniel Featley, *A Second Parallel . . . against the Appealer* (1626); William Loe, *A Sermon preached . . . at the Funerall of . . . Daniel Featley* (1645), p. 25.
[45] These correspondents included John Prideaux, John King, Robert Abbot, and Thomas Morton. Bodleian, Rawlinson MS D.47, fos. 16ʳ⁻ᵛ, 35, 39ᵛ–40, and 50ᵛ.

and the *Dissertatio* on Romans 7.[46] Both the *Examen* and the
Dissertatio were first printed at Leiden in 1612, and their rapid
appearance in England may have owed something to the fact
that Arminius was published by an English expatriate,
Thomas Basson, and his Dutch-born son Govert.[47] While it is
rash to deduce the views of a man from the contents of his
book-shelves, in this case other evidence suggests that Browne
was no enemy to Arminius. Most important he was labelled as
a suspected 'Papist' by Oxford Calvinists, and on his death
some of his papers were impounded by the Vice-Chancellor.[48]
Furthermore the balance of the library—over five hundred
books are listed—is tilted against the Calvinists. Calvin is only
represented by the *Institutio* and the works of William Perkins,
the leading English Calvinist writer, are completely unrepre-
sented. But Browne did possess the *Concordia* by Ludovicus
Molina and the *De Gratia* by Leonardus Lessius;[49] between
them these two Jesuit writers were the leading Catholic advocates of free will. Very different was an inventory taken two
months later of a library similar in size, belonging to John
English of St John's College.[50] This contained nine works by
Calvin as well as the complete works of Perkins. Arminius was
absent, as were Molina and Lessius. Apart from the strictly
theological emphases of these two libraries, both were strong
in the writings of classical antiquity. Browne, however, possessed much more in the way of vernacular literature, as well
as a number of recent scientific works.[51]

According to Thomas Jackson's subsequent recollections, it
was some two years before these stirs at Corpus Christi College that he became disenchanted with Calvinism. Interest-
ingly, however, Jackson hardly ever quotes Richard Hooker

---

[46] OU Arch., Hyp. B.20, fos. 18ʳ⁻ᵛ. This important inventory was overlooked by M.
H. Curtis, *Oxford and Cambridge in Transition, 1558–1642* (Oxford, 1959), p. 285.

[47] J. A. van Dorsten, *Thomas Basson, 1555–1613: English Printer at Leiden* (Leiden,
1961), pp. 52–4, 61, 95, 98–9. The *Examen* and the *Dissertatio* were the work of Govert
Basson, who continued publishing Arminius until 1629.

[48] PRO, SP 14/80, fo. 177ᵛ; OU Arch., Hyp. B.20, fo. 21; Laud, iv. 318.

[49] OU Arch., Hyp. B.20, fo. 15ʳ⁻ᵛ.

[50] W. C. Costin, 'The Inventory of John English, B.C.L., Fellow of St John's College', *Oxoniensia*, 11–12 (1946–7), pp. 102–31.

[51] These included the *Tractatus de Globis* by Robert Hues, *The Navigator's Supply*,
probably by William Barlow, *The Art of Navigation* and *The Art of Dialling*. Browne also
owned the *De Re Anatomica* by Realdo Colombo. OU Arch., Hyp. B.20, fos. 16ᵛ, 19ᵛ.

throughout his voluminous writings, and there is no suggestion that he regarded him as a theological ancestor. Defending
his own views, 'lately published' in 1628, he recalled that 'for
these three and twenty years' his patience had been tried by
preachers 'of absolute election or reprobation'.[52] In 1605 he
would have been a master of arts in his mid-twenties. By 1612
Jackson himself was preaching against Calvinist determinism,[53] although he did not air such views in print until the
mid-1620s and these early sermons were apparently confined
to the college chapel.[54] Jackson argued in terms of man's
mutability, and that the state of election or reprobation was
not a constant one.[55] Brian Twyne, on the other hand, was still
an orthodox Calvinist in 1610, from the evidence of his own
theological notebook,[56] and to what extent his views developed
thereafter is unclear. Apart from Jackson and possibly Twyne,
Browne's theological concerns may have been important for a
number of other members of the college. Henry Mason, a
chaplain of Corpus Christi from 1602 to 1611, was to be joint
author during the early 1630s of an Arminian work on universal grace,[57] and Gabriel Bridges, who graduated in 1611 and
became a fellow of the college, was to deny absolute predestination from the university pulpit in 1623.[58] Influences of this
kind also extended to lay members of the college, and produced the two most prominent parliamentary defenders of
Arminianism during the 1620s—Richard Dyott and Richard
Spencer.[59]

Names closely associated with Walter Browne by hostile
Oxford contemporaries are William Laud and John Howson.
Both admitted being acquainted with him.[60] Together with
John Buckeridge, Laud and Howson were in 1625 specifically
to oppose the Calvinist teaching contained in the Lambeth

For the wider context of Browne's interests see M. Feingold, *The Mathematicians'
Apprenticeship* (Cambridge, 1984).

[52] Jackson, *Works*, IX. 354, 377.
[53] Writing in 1638, Jackson says these sermons were delivered 'about twenty-six
years ago'. Jackson, *Works*, VIII. 256.
[54] Ibid., IX. 441 and see below, p. 121.   [55] Jackson, *Works*, IX. 495–9.
[56] Corpus Christi College, Oxford, MS E.259, fos. 60, 66–7, 80–2.
[57] *God's Love to Mankind* (1633). For Mason's part in writing this book, see William
Twisse, *The Riches of God's Love* (Oxford, 1653), ii. *passim*.
[58] OU Arch., Reg. N.23, fos. 157ᵛ–8.   [59] See below, pp. 140–5.
[60] Laud, *Works*, IV. 318; PRO, SP, 14/80, fo. 177ᵛ.

Articles.[61] Religious differences of this sort may, therefore, underlie Laud's contested election to the presidency of St John's College, Oxford, in 1611, as successor to Buckeridge, who had been elevated to the bishopric of Rochester. The names of those voting in the election and the way their votes were cast are known,[62] although very little information survives as to the views of the individual electors. John English, one of those voting against Laud, was probably a Calvinist, judging from the contents of his library to which reference has already been made. On the other side Christopher Wren, brother of Matthew and a correspondent of Hugo Grotius in the early 1620s,[63] was perhaps an Arminian in the making. Another supporter of Laud was William Juxon, who by 1627, as Vice-Chancellor, was turning a blind eye to Arminianism.[64] Such evidence permits no firm conclusions to be drawn. Yet the manner in which the contest was conducted does suggest a mobilization of Calvinist forces against Laud. The first opposition candidate, one of the senior fellows of St John's, had been dropped in favour of John Rawlinson, who was an ex-member of the college and a much superior choice. Rawlinson was already Principal of St Edmund Hall and chaplain to Ellesmere, who in turn was Chancellor of Oxford and a favourer of Calvinism.[65] The deputy Vice-Chancellor in 1611 was the Calvinist Sebastian Benfield, a protégé of Archbishop Abbot[66] and, it transpired, a supporter of Rawlinson. As a pre-election move he prevented four of the non-graduate fellows of St John's from proceeding BA, three having declared for Laud, and thus deprived them of the right to vote for a college president.[67] Despite these measures, however, the floating vote of one of the fellows, John Towse, secured the St John's election for Laud. Towse had at one stage favoured Rawlinson but, ultimately, under the influence of both Bishop Richard Neile and Laud, changed sides.[68] The defeated party then appealed

[61] Laud, *Works*, VI. 245–6.   [62] St John's College, Oxford, Register II, p. 486.
[63] Grotius, *Briefwisseling*, II. 246–7.
[64] Thomas Crosfield, *Diary*, ed. F. S. Boas (1935), p. 11.
[65] See above, p. 34.
[66] Sebastian Benfield, *Doctrinae Christianae Sex Capita* (Oxford, 1610), sigs. *2–*3ᵛ. This work includes Benfield's reply to Humphrey Leech.
[67] Bodleian, Tanner MS 338, fos. 330, 370. This manuscript contains a wealth of detail about the contest. Cf. H. R. Trevor-Roper, *Archbishop Laud, 1573–1645* (1965), pp. 42–3.   [68] Bodleian, Tanner MS 338, fo. 330ʳ⁻ᵛ.

to the Visitor of the college and matters eventually came to a royal hearing, when Neile probably played an important role in gaining confirmation of Laud's election.[69]

John Howson, a canon of Christ Church, was in trouble with Oxford Calvinists as early as 1612. About September of this year he chose to devote a university sermon to criticizing the marginal notes of the Genevan Bible. This latter had been, in the late sixteenth and early seventeenth centuries, the most potent single tool for disseminating Calvinism in England. Its marginalia, and the predestinarian catechism bound up with many editions, roundly asserted the doctrinal teachings of Calvin and his expositors, which the Dutch Arminians were by now remonstrating against. But Howson did not choose to protest on Arminian grounds. Instead he maintained that these same marginalia undermined the divinity of Christ and the doctrine of the Trinity, by glossing away Old Testament proofs of both.[70] Howson may have felt that he was effectively sealing the fate of the Genevan Bible, its survival already threatened by the King James's Bible of 1611. This particular sermon was apparently one of a series, two others being said by Howson to be 'in the custodye' of Bishop Neile.[71] Outraged Calvinist feelings on the subject were vented in a letter from Sir Thomas Bodley to Thomas James, keeper of the university library, dated 16 September.

I repute it a matter much importing the honour and credit of the university, and to say the very truth the whole church of this realm, that he [Howson] should be censured severely, and either made to recant his malicious taxations of those he termeth glossers or should not be suffered to dwell and hatch his new-fangleness in the university, nor injoy those livings that he possesseth in the state, as a person well affected to religion here authorized.[72]

Bodley was the son of one of those responsible for getting the Genevan Bible printed in England, which perhaps gave a special vehemence to his tone. Three years later, in an interview

---

[69] Ibid., fos. 346, 356–7; Heylyn, *Cyprianus Anglicus*, p. 56.
[70] Bodleian, Rawlinson MS D.320, fos. 47–63; Wood, *History*, p. 312.
[71] PRO, SP 14/80, fo. 175.
[72] Sir Thomas Bodley, *Reliquiae*, ed. T. Hearne (1703), p. 353.

with the King, Howson confirmed that at the time he was 'censured for sermons "less than orthodox"'[73] As with Laud, so in the case of Howson, support by Neile is likely to have been important. A Christ Church colleague of Howson was Richard Corbett, whose poem 'The Distracted Puritane' probably dates from the same decade and includes a derisory reference to the 'black lines of damnation' contained 'in Perkins's tables'. The allusion is to *A Golden Chain* by William Perkins, which incorporated a diagram or table of predestination.[74]

Seemingly, however, it was Laud who now took the anti-Calvinist initiative. In a sermon on Shrove Sunday 1615, at the university church of St Mary's, he is said, by Peter Heylyn, to have 'insisted on some points which might indifferently be imputed either to Popery or Arminianism as about that time they began to call it'. Robert Abbot replied in a sermon on Easter Sunday, charging that 'in the points of free will, justification, concupiscence being a sin after baptism, inherent righteousness, and certainty of salvation, the Papists beyond the seas can say they [Laud and his like] are wholly theirs'.[75] From the evidence of Laud's later writings it is clear that he believed in universal grace,[76] while rejecting Calvinist teaching on reprobation and perseverance.[77] Furthermore, in 1625 he signed a letter which referred to the 'fatal opinions' contained in the Lambeth Articles.[78] His mentors Buckeridge and Neile were in 1618 to be suggested by the Dutch Arminians as suitable English representatives at the Synod of Dort.[79] During the early 1620s he made theological contact with Hugo Grotius, via the Dutch Arminian exile Francis Junius the younger.[80] Laud also, in 1624, wrote a tract, no longer extant, with the suggestive title of 'Doctrinal Puritanism'.[81] In consequence there is good reason to believe

[73] PRO, SP 14/80, fo. 175.

[74] Richard Corbett, *Poems*, ed. J. A. W. Bennett and H. R. Trevor-Roper (Oxford, 1955), p. 58.

[75] Heylyn, *Cyprianus Anglicus*, pp. 61–2.

[76] Laud, *Works*, III. 304–5.　　　　　　　　　　　　　　　　[77] Ibid., VI. 132–3.

[78] Ibid., VI. 245–6. For a fuller discussion of Laud's Arminianism, see Appendix II.

[79] Johan von Oldenbarnevelt, *Bescheiden*, ed. S. P. Haak and A. J. Veenendaal (The Hague, 1934–67), III. 440.

[80] Grotius, *Briefwisseling*, II. 241.

[81] Laud, *Works*, III. 155–6. The very concept of 'Puritan', i.e. Calvinist, doctrine

that by 1615 he was in the vanguard of Oxford Arminianism. That Laud survived the wrath of the university Calvinists, however, owed much to Neile.[82]

Further light is possibly shed on Laud's religious views by a remarkable communion chalice now in the possession of St John's College, Oxford. This has been dated to 'about 1615', which suggests that it was acquired during the presidency of Laud.[83] Whereas the Elizabethan period had seen the systematic destruction of chalices and their replacement by communion cups, the St John's College chalice is the earliest known surviving example of a subsequent 'gothic revival' which was 'well established' by the 1630s. It is a particularly interesting piece in that the outside of the bowl of the chalice is engraved with a picture of Christ as the good shepherd and the cover, which also serves as a paten, depicts on its top the wise men's star (plate 1). The iconography is identical to that on a chalice listed as being in the chapel of Bishop Lancelot Andrewes. According to Andrewes, the 'lost sheep' on Christ's shoulders 'is the image of us all' and the star 'leads us thither to his body there'.[84] If Laud was the donor, or otherwise instrumental in acquiring the chalice, this would certainly help explain his very exalted view of the sacraments. Also relevant is that among the books given to the college by Laud, as President, was a copy of the Sarum Missal, a work which was later to provide one of the sources of Caroline liturgical experiment.[85]

was a neologism at this date, and is indicative of Laud's hostility. According to Heylyn, Laud's tract included a discussion, from an anti-Calvinist point of view, of 'the five points' concerning 'predestination and the concomitant thereof'. Heylyn, *Cyprianus Anglicus*, p. 119.

[82] Laud, *Works*, VII. 3–4; Heylyn, *Cyprianus Anglicus*, pp. 60, 63.

[83] C. Oman, *English Church Plate, 597–1830* (1957), p. 313 and plate 80. The 'good shepherd' chalice is not included in a list of St John's College plate dated 1618, whereas two other 'communion cups' are. St John's College, Oxford, Muniment XC.1., p. 88. For help in this matter I am indebted to Dr M. Mendelson and Dr M. Vale. An alternative explanation to that advanced above is that this chalice was among the 'chapel plate' bequeathed by Laud to St John's College. Laud, *Works*, IV. 442.

[84] Oman, *English Church Plate*, pp. 133–46, 205–6, 226–7; Andrewes, *Works*, I. 247, III. 89–90, XI. p. xcvii. Oddly, Oman failed to note the star engraved on the cover of the St John's College chalice.

[85] St John's College, Oxford, Benefactors' Book, col. xciv. This gift is dated 1620. See also below, p. 198.

III

By 1611 Thomas Holland, Regius Professor of Divinity, was guarding against any manifestation of 'Arminianism'* in the Oxford Divinity Schools.[86] His successor, Robert Abbot, lectured regularly against the Dutch Arminians from 1613 onwards. That year he rebutted, in the form of an Act lecture, the teaching of Arminius' leading Dutch disciple—Petrus Bertius, on the potential apostasy of the elect.[87] At the next Act, in 1614, he turned his attention to Arminius and the question of universal grace. Abbot denied that divine grace was 'promiscuously'* available to all.[88] He singled out for criticism four of Arminius' own works, including the famous *Declaratio* of his views, and also cited works by the Dutch Arminians Joannes Arnoldus Corvinus and Nikolaas Grevinchovius. In addition Abbot provided an English dimension to the controversy by quoting from Peter Baro's *Summa Trium de Praedestinatione Sententiarum*, first published in 1613.[89] He continued his anti-Arminian theme at the 1615 Act.[90] Made a bishop in October, he was succeeded as professor by John Prideaux, who kept up the Calvinist tradition. For his first Act lecture, in 1616, Prideaux asserted the absolute decree of reprobation.[91] It was in these years, too, that Sebastian Benfield, now Lady Margaret Professor of Divinity, devoted a course of lectures to defending the Calvinist doctrine of the perseverance of the saints. One of his particular concerns was to refute the claim by the Dutch Arminians that their teaching was in accord with the Thirty-nine Articles of the Church of England.[92]

A marked quickening of interest as regards these questions is evident from the Act theses defended at this time. In 1612 John Prideaux denied that 'grace sufficient for salvation'* was granted to all men. He also argued that 'the regenerate'* could never forfeit grace completely. On this same occasion William White affirmed that those 'justified by faith' could be 'certain

---

[86] BL Add MS 22, 962, fo. 226.
[87] Robert Abbot, *De Gratia et Perseverantia Sanctorum*, pp. 1–14.
[88] Ibid., p. 24.
[89] Ibid., pp. 15–16, 19, 21.
[90] Ibid., pp. 25–44.
[91] John Prideaux, *Lectiones Novem* (Oxford, 1625), pp. 1–22.
[92] Sebastian Benfield, *De Perseverantia Sanctorum* (Frankfurt, 1618), pp. 102–6.

of salvation"*.[93] In 1614 George Carleton, soon to be made a bishop, opposed the notion that grace was 'simply universal"*.[94] Another inceptor in divinity, John Charlett, denied that the regenerate could fall from grace, while affirming that 'predestination to life' was 'purely gratuitous' and that God had eternally reprobated some people 'only on account of his good pleasure"*. A third inceptor, Edward James, maintained the certainty of salvation and that 'faith once had cannot be lost"*.[95] The following year, 1615, Samuel Radcliffe defended the same Calvinist views as had Edward James.[96] In 1616 the certainty of salvation and perseverance were again affirmed, by John Hampden and John Flavell respectively.[97] During the 1617 Act three more inceptors maintained Calvinist positions. John Mosely affirmed the doctrine of perseverance. Richard Lloyd denied that election was 'due to foresight of works' and asserted that 'the decree of reprobation' was 'absolute"*. Finally Daniel Featley argued apropos the 'grace of regeneration' that neither was it offered 'to everyone' nor could it be 'resisted"*.[98] All told in this six-year period eleven Oxford doctors of divinity entered the lists in defence of Calvinism.

At Exeter College, where Prideaux was Rector, eighteen theses aimed against Arminianism were set for disputation in 1617. The first concerned the correct interpretation of Romans 7, and may link with the controversy on this topic at Cambridge in November. It was now determined, in opposition to Arminius, that St Paul 'spoke of himself as a regenerate person"*. Arminius' 'analysis' of Romans 9 also came under attack. Unconditional predestination, perseverance and the certainty of salvation were affirmed. The universality and resistibility of grace were denied, and Arminianism was said to be the same as 'Semi-Pelagianism"*.[99] During the Act of 1618 Prideaux lectured against universal grace and Richard Etkins denied final falling away from grace.[100] Moveover this

[93] Clark, *Register*, p. 209.
[94] Bodleian, Wood 276A, fo. 412.
[95] Clark, *Register*, p. 210.
[96] Ibid., p. 211.
[97] Ibid., p. 212.
[98] Prynne, *Anti-Arminianisme*, p. 246.
[99] William Prynne, *Canterburies Doome* (1646). p. 156.
[100] Prideaux, *Lectiones Novem*, pp. 49–68; Clark, *Register*, p. 214.

was the year of the Synod of Dort. King James, as we have seen, supported the Dutch Calvinists from a mixture of motives and agreed to the sending of English delegates to the proposed synod. In August 1618 Sir Henry Savile, Warden of Merton College, wrote to Sir Dudley Carleton, English Ambassador at the Hague, advising him to consult Prideaux on the finer points of the Arminian dispute.[101] Robert Abbot was now dead but his anti-Arminian lectures, together with his reply to the English Arminian Richard Thomson, came out in a memorial edition, dedicated to Prince Charles. An Oxford man, George Carleton—now Bishop of Llandaff, was chosen to head the delegation to Dort. Carleton had shown himself the most active of the bishops, apart from Robert Abbot, in refuting the Dutch Arminians.[102] While, on behalf of the Oxford Arminians, Richard Corbett versified privately in December 1618:

> Wee know allready how will stand the case
> With Barnavelt, and universall grace.[103]

IV

Between 1619 and 1622, Oxford theology continued to mirror English policy in the United Provinces. During these years Prideaux lectured on conversion, justification, perseverance, and the certainty of salvation, all in refutation of Arminianism.[104] At the Act in 1619, with the Synod of Dort fresh in their minds, two doctors of divinity affirmed Calvinist teachings. Roger Bates and Thomas Isles both denied that the faith of true believers could be lost, Isles adding that God's efficacious grace was irresistible.[105] The perseverance of the regenerate was again affirmed in 1621, by Robert Robotham.[106] Not until 1623 did there occur an Arminian reaction at Oxford when, on 19 January, Gabriel Bridges delivered a university sermon against absolute predestination—

[101] PRO, SP 14/98, fo. 117.
[102] PRO, SP 14/93, fo. 235ᵛ.
[103] Corbett, *Poems*, p. 63.
[104] Prideaux, *Lectiones Novem*, pp. 69–170.
[105] Clark, *Register*, p. 215; Prynne, *Anti-Arminianisme*, p. 248.
[106] Clark, *Register*, p. 216.

asserting instead universal grace and the co-operation of man's free will in conversion. As at Cambridge, where an equivalent Arminian sermon had been preached six months earlier, this development perhaps owed something to the changing international preoccupations of the government—specifically the desire for closer links with Spain, which Calvinists opposed. Bridges' temerity, however, resulted in his being summoned before the Vice-Chancellor, William Piers, and seven other doctors of divinity: Thomas Anyan, Samuel Fell, Thomas Isles, Richard Parker, Robert Pincke, John Prideaux, and John Rawlinson. Their number included the head of his own college, Anyan, and they proceeded to censure him 'with unanimous consent', charging him with 'false and offensive doctrine'. Bridges was ordered to maintain for his forthcoming BD theses that predestination was not conditional and that grace sufficient to salvation was not granted to all men. On 23 January he also read a public submission.[107] The same year the Calvinist articles of Dort, as confirmed by the 'Reformed Churches of France', were published at Oxford.[108]

In 1624, however, there appeared *A New Gagg for an Old Goose*, by Richard Montagu. Despite the slightly different language, the book seemed to defend the same Arminian propositions which the Oxford doctors had recently condemned.[109] As such it was a veritable bombshell. Understandably, academics like Prideaux supported complaints made to the House of Commons, and may even have instigated proceedings.[110] For there were many links between the Calvinist divines of the university and their lay counterparts in parliament. It was John Pym, an Oxford man, who that May introduced the petition against Montagu for debate in the Commons.[111] At about the same time, Bishop Carleton was writing to Archbishop Abbot complaining that, 'in diverse places the doctrin of generall grace is published with such confidence as if it were a doctrin of the Church of England', and

---

[107] OU Arch., Reg. N.23, fos. 157ᵛ–8.
[108] *Articles agreed on in the Nationall Synode of the Reformed Churches of France* (Oxford, 1623). This was reprinted in 1624.
[109] Montagu, *A New Gagg*, pp. 177–83.
[110] Cosin, *Correspondence*, I. 50.
[111] *Commons Journals*, I. 788.

asking that either the articles of Dort or the articles of Lambeth be approved by convocation.[112] Calvinist clergy and laity were clearly working in parallel and probably in conjunction. Despite their efforts Montagu issued a second book in justification of the first—*Appello Caesarem*. The publication of this Arminian defence, with what purported to be royal approval, was an even more serious challenge to the Calvinists.[113] It coincided with the printing at Oxford of Prideaux's own anti-Arminian Act lectures. There one participant in a BD disputation, in May 1625, went so far as to utilize some of the arguments from *Appello Caesarem* on the subject of falling from grace. This resulted in the Regius Professor admonishing all theology students present to be wary of such books,[114] and during the Act it was affirmed by Edward Meetkerk that predestination was not 'due to foresight of faith or works'.[115] That August parliament was adjourned to Oxford, because of the plague, and the Montagu case was taken up during the second day's proceedings in the Commons.[116]

Whereas at Cambridge June 1626 saw Calvinism henceforth outlawed from the Commencement, on the basis of royal proclamation, it survived at the Oxford Act for another six years. This was mainly thanks to the third Earl of Pembroke, Chancellor Oxford since 1616. On 6 July 1626 he wrote to the university, on the occasion of Prideaux's retirement as Vice-Chancellor. Pembroke particularly emphasized

those painfull endeavors wherewith hee [Prideaux] hath discharged the place of Regius Professor, to the great and generall satisfaction of all such as are well affected to the true religion, keeping by his sound doctrine the fountaine theare from the erronious tenets and opinions, which are apt to disturbe the peace and quiet both of the Church and Commonweale, wherein I cannot enoughe commend his care and integritie.

His reference to 'the peace and quiet' of the English Church

[112] PRO, SP 14/164, fo. 19ᵛ. Bishop Carleton added that 'in myn own diocess I shall take order with some of these humorests'.

[113] In dedicating his *Appello Caesarem* to Charles I, Richard Montagu claimed the approbation of James I. *Appello Caesarem*, sig. a3.

[114] Wood, *History*, pp. 354–5. A hostile report of Prideaux's conduct on this occasion was sent to Laud, now Bishop of St Davids, by Thomas Turner of St John's College. PRO, SP 16/27, fo. 68.

[115] OU Arch., Reg. O.14, fo. 241.   [116] *Commons Journals*, 1. 809–10.

echoes the title of Charles's recent proclamation on the Arminian question, while interpreting that pronouncement in favour of Prideaux and the Oxford Calvinists.[117] When Sebastian Benfield resigned as Lady Margaret Professor of Divinity in 1626, he was replaced by another Calvinist—Samuel Fell.

Prideaux's successor, as Vice-Chancellor, was William Juxon, President of St John's and a supporter of Laud from early days. In March 1627 he was called upon to deal with an Arminian sermon preached by Nicholas Brookes of Wadham. The latter seems to have received some form of censure, but Juxon managed to be 'out of towne'. His absence was, as a contemporary diarist commented, 'suspicious'.[118] On the other hand the Act in July saw a new burst of Calvinist activity, no doubt inspired by Prideaux. Cornelius Burges, a well-known London preacher and royal chaplain, came to take his doctorate and for his theses defended Calvinist positions on the certainty of salvation and perseverance.[119] Another Calvinist spokesman in 1627 was Accepted Frewen, son of a Puritan clergyman but a future archbishop of York. For his doctoral theses he maintained that predestination to salvation was not on account of faith foreseen and was moreover immutable, and that grace sufficient to salvation was not conceded unto all men.[120]

Juxon, as Vice-Chancellor, appears to have been powerless to alter the doctrinal complexion of the Act. At the end of his second term of office, in July 1628, Calvinism was again endorsed, Anthony Saunders maintaining absolute reprobation.[121] Only outside interference was capable of changing this situation. Hence the importance of the royal declaration in late 1628, which banned all university disputing on points at issue between Arminians and Calvinists.[122] This new ruling could not ultimately be evaded. There seems, moreover, to have been something of a concerted effort at this time to capture Oxford for the Arminians. Bishop Neile, for example, attempted to secure the presidency of Corpus Christi College

---

[117] OU Arch., Reg. N.23, fos. 226ᵛ–7; *Stuart Constitution*, ed. Kenyon, pp. 154–5.
[118] Crosfield, *Diary*, p. 11.
[119] OU Arch., Reg. O.14, fo. 242.
[120] Prynne, *Anti-Arminianisme*, p. 250.
[121] OU Arch., Reg. O.14, fo. 244.
[122] *Constitutional Documents*, ed. Gardiner, pp. 75–6.

for the Arminian, Thomas Jackson. According to Featley, the
intention was the Jackson should become Regius Professor of
Divinity. Replying to a letter from Prideaux, he commented
that the 'Jack (you write of) would faine have bene cast into
the troubled waters at CCC that, upon an inundation of prae-
ferment sweeping you away, he might more easily swimme to
your chaire there to spawne yong Arminians'.[123] It was probably in connection with these plans that in November 1627
Jackson dedicated an Arminian work to the Earl of Pembroke.[124]

V

During 1629 the Oxford Arminians went on to the offensive,
by raising the question of the confessional basis of English
Church teaching. Members of the House of Commons having
agitated unsuccessfully against Arminianism, even to the
extent of attempting to define orthodoxy, it was now argued at
the Act that the 'definition of controversies belongs to synods'*
in which the laity have no suffrage. The respondent was
Thomas Laurence—an Arminian.[125] Stormy scenes ensued,
with a notable outburst from Prideaux. 'You talk of synods!
Wee are concluded under an anathema to stand to the Synod
of Dort against the Arminians. Why doe not you and your fellowes stand to it?'[126] The answer was, of course, that the Dort
rulings had never been adopted in England. Therefore the
Thirty-nine Articles, passed by convocation in 1563, remained
the doctrinal standard of the English Church and as regards
Arminianism they were not clear-cut.

The dethronement of Oxford Calvinism was, however,
incomplete in 1629. The new Vice-Chancellor was Accepted
Frewen. That year he licensed a work by Cornelius Burges,
his fellow inceptor of 1627, entitled *Baptismall Regeneration of
Elect Infants, professed by the Church of England.* Dedicating the
book to the fourth Earl of Bedford, whose family had long

---

[123] Bodleian, Rawlinson MS D.47, fo. 16.
[124] Jackson, *Works*, v. 3–5.
[125] PRO, SP 16/146, fo. 95. For Laurence's Arminianism, see below, p. 83.
[126] Lambeth Palace Library, Lambeth MS 943, p. 134.

been his patrons, Burges in his concluding pages turned his attention to the Arminians, and their objections to the 'doctrine of God's absolute election' and the 'comfortable doctrine of finall perseverance'. He replied, and presumably Frewen as licenser agreed, that

> wee can tell them that they, who are elected to the end, are elected to the meanes, and to a conscionable use of the means wherby the end may be attained. So also the doctrine of perseverance teacheth that though perseverance be certaine yet it is also of the nature of that grace, in which men persevere, to make and keepe them diligent in the use of all good means, wherby they may, and do, persevere and worke out their salvation with feare and trembling.[127]

Moreover Pembroke was still Chancellor, whom Daniel Featley described as having prevented the 'pretious "deposit"' of saving truth' from being 'embased by any Semi-Pelagian alloy'.[128] Printed in 1630 these words provided an unwitting epitaph, for the Earl died that April. Yet in the scramble for a successor Frewen did not join with Prideaux and Bishop John Williams of Lincoln in an attempt to elect Pembroke's brother and heir, and supported instead the successful candidature of William Laud.[129] The reasons behind Frewen's action are unclear. Ambition certainly entered into it, two petitions for preferment being presented to the King on behalf of Frewen in October 1629. The intermediary was Endymion Porter, an influential courtier with close Arminian connections, and Frewen subsequently became Dean of Gloucester in 1631.[130]

Another defector from the Calvinist camp was Christopher Potter, Provost of Queen's College. In 1618 he had edited, with apparent enthusiasm, a volume of sermons by Henry Airay which took a firm Calvinist line. God, Airay taught, has 'chosen thee and refused him', has 'made thee a vessell of honour and him a vessell of dishonour', simply of 'his good pleasure'. For there is 'nothing in us to move' God.[131] Nevertheless, by March 1629 Potter was commending the

---

[127] Burges, *Baptismall Regeneration*, sigs. ¶2–¶4ᵛ, pp. 341–3.

[128] Daniel Featley, *The Grand Sacriledge of the Church of Rome* (1630), sig. A3ᵛ.

[129] Heylyn, *Cyprianus Anglicus*, p. 197.

[130] PRO, SP 16/150, fos. 73, 74. For Endymion Porter's links with Arminian clergy, see Cosin, *Correspondence*, i. 99, 106.

[131] Airay, *Lectures*, p. 418. This work is dedicated by Potter to Archbishop Abbot. Sigs. ¶2–Aᵛ.

'latitude' of the English Church concerning these questions.[132] Although not voting for Laud, Potter probably bears some responsibility for his election as Chancellor in 1630. Supporting neither Laud nor the fourth Earl of Pembroke, he campaigned instead on behalf of Lord Keeper Coventry, and may well have attracted votes that would otherwise have turned Laud's majority of nine into a defeat.[133] Some two months later, in June, he addressed the fellows of Queen's on the subject of the Arminian controversy. He criticized the failure of members of the college to bide by the royal declaration of 1628, describing the doctrines at issue 'as matter of opinion, not of faith, disputable problems, not necessary Catholike verities'. He instructed them 'not to be confident where they were ignorant, [and] to moderate the deepe censures of men in opinions which they did not yet fully understand'. For further enlightenment they should turn to Bible study and read the ancient authors, as well as 'the best writers of this age of all parties'. To this end Potter offered 'to furnish the library of the colledge (as other houses have done) with the best and choicest writers of both sides in these controversies'.[134]

As a consequence, rumour flew round the university that Potter had declared himself an Arminian. According to his own account fingers were pointed at him during the 1630 Divinity Act, and 'I now suffer in vulgar opinions as a temporiser, a timeserver, a courtier, an ambitious man, and I knowe not what'. Certainly his claim that not one in a hundred clergy, nor one in a thousand laymen, understood the Arminian controversy was not calculated to endear him to committed Calvinists. 'I find', he wrote, 'that Arminians have told us some faults that in my opinion deserve to be mended, and for my part I cannot see many arguments answered which they urge against some vulgar tenents.' Particularly offensive was the doctrine of absolute reprobation.[135] Potter seems genuinely to have changed his mind about Arminianism,

---

[132] Christopher Potter, *A Sermon preached at the Consecration of the Right Reverend Father in God Barnaby Potter* (1629), pp. 65–8.

[133] Crosfield, *Diary*, p. 42.

[134] Bodleian, Rawlinson MS A.419, fos. 37ᵛ–38. The libraries of both Balliol College and Queen's College acquired books relevant to the Arminian controversy at this time. Balliol College, Benefactors' Book, p. 26; Queen's College, MS Arch. E.23.

[135] Bodleian, Rawlinson MS A.419, fos. 38–39ᵛ.

independently of altered circumstances. Elsewhere he recalled that

for some yeares in my youth, when I was most ignorant, I was most confident. Before I knew the true state or any grounds of these questions, I could peremptorily resolve them all, and upon every occasion, in the very pulpit, I was girding and railing upon these new heretiques the Arminians . . . Yet all this while I tooke all this that I talkt upon trust, and knew not what they said or thought but by relation from others, and from their enemies.[136]

His own subsequent reading of Dutch Arminian writings 'convicted mee not so farre as absolutely to yeeld unto them, or take part with them in any faction, . . . but so farre as not rashly to censure, damne or anathematize them till I can see their pretensions voided'.[137] By 1629 Potter was a self-styled 'moderate'.[138]

An example of Arminian partisanship, of the kind which Potter wished to avoid, is afforded by a book published at Oxford in 1630. This was *The Schysmatical Puritan*, by Giles Widdowes. Dedicated to the Duchess of Buckingham, it listed among various Puritan types the 'presuming predestinatist', whose 'purenes is an inspired knowledge that hee shal be saved by God's absolute election. He is so sure of his salvation, as if he were now in Heaven [and] as if there were no life in him but God's essentiall glory.'[139] Such a caricature of the teaching of Burges, licensed the previous year, indicates the rapidity of change now overtaking Oxford theology under the chancellorship of William Laud. Moreover, almost overnight Calvinism had been rechristened Puritanism, and after 1631 Calvinist doctrine disappeared from the Oxford Act.[140] To be fair to Laud, however, he did require the Vice-Chancellor to judge 'impartially' as between Arminian and Calvinist offenders, against King Charles's moratorium on disputes

[136] Christopher Potter, *His own Vindication of Himselfe*, appended to John Plaifere, *Appello Evangelium* (1652), pp. 414–15.
[137] Ibid., p. 421.
[138] Ibid., p. 433.
[139] Giles Widdowes, *The Schysmatical Puritan* (Oxford, 1630), sigs. A2ʳ⁻ᵛ, C2ᵛ. A second edition was printed at Oxford in 1631.
[140] The Calvinist doctrine of final perseverance was maintained at the Acts of 1630 and 1631, by John Stubbinge and Thomas Mason. OU Arch., Reg. P.15, fos. 274, 275.

about predestination, 'that neither one nor the other may have cause to say that you favour a party'.[141] But the suppression of Calvinism meant inevitably a redressing of the balance in favour of Arminianism. This Prideaux and his supporters found hard to bear. Potter described them as having 'so farre engaged themselves, on the contrary part in the quarrell, that they are ashamed or can hardly with honesty retract'.[142] Matters came to a head in mid-1631 with a crop of Calvinist-inspired sermons castigating Arminianism in high places. The first, by Thomas Hill, was said to have disparaged 'the whole order of bishops . . . making them the favourers of unsound and erronious doctrine'. Hill was disciplined but similar sermons followed. The preachers refused to acknowledge the authority of the Vice-Chancellor, William Smith, and in so doing had the support of Prideaux. One of them, Thomas Ford, appealed to Congregation. His appeal was sustained, by a committee which included Prideaux, and Smith then petitioned the King. Predictably Charles found in favour of the Vice-Chancellor, during a hearing at Woodstock. A number of expulsions from the university followed, and Prideaux apparently only retained his professorial chair through the intervention of the fourth Earl of Pembroke.[143] It was probably on this same occasion that Charles recommended to the Oxford 'faculty of divinity' the subject of 'Jesus Christ and him crucified'.[144]

Meanwhile Potter wanted both Calvinist and Arminian parties to agree that their doctrinal differences were not fundamental. With this in view he arranged for the Oxford publication, in early 1631, of a work by the Italian irenicist Jacobus Acontius, entitled *Stratagematum Satanae*.[145] Arguing that doctrinal dissension was the work of the Devil, Acontius advocated the reduction of religious truths to a minimum and the mutual toleration of diversity of belief.[146] Originally published in 1565, Acontius' book had already been invoked on behalf of

---

[141] Laud, *Works*, v. 48. On the other hand, during the 1630s, Laud's chaplains can be found licensing Arminian sermons. See below, pp. 217, 265.
[142] Crosfield, *Diary*, p. 51.
[143] Wood, *History*, pp. 372–7, Laud, *Works*, v. 50–6; Crosfield, *Diary*, p. 56.
[144] Jackson, *Works*, vii. 3.   [145] Crosfield, *Diary*, p. 50.
[146] W. K. Jordan, *The Development of Religious Toleration in England* (1932–40), i. 318–23, 334–42.

the Dutch Arminians,[147] although its message continued to be unacceptable from the point of view of dogmatic Calvinists. Furthermore, the hotter sort of English Arminians were themselves unwilling to rest in silence. It is true that extreme statements of Arminianism still tended to land preachers in trouble.[148] Nevertheless, as early as Christmas Eve 1633 anti-Calvinist remarks were being made with impunity from the university pulpit of St Mary's Church. On this occasion Thomas Browne, student of Christ Church, spoke of a 'sort of heretiques in the primitive church' who were known as 'the "predestined"'. They taught that 'no sinne whatsoever could endanger the state of him that was justified and predestinated by God'. Browne concluded that 'so long as we are in this world, he that now standeth should feare least he fall. The mercies of God are not for lives. He does not entayle salvation upon his children . . . but that our prodigall presumption may cutt it off. If we would be secure of Heaven, let us take heed of security.'[149] This sermon was printed at Oxford in 1634. Preaching at the Act that same year Thomas Laurence echoed Browne's remarks about 'the "predestined"', who 'presumed upon a fatallity of their election and would needs have Heaven promised without the condition of workes'.[150] Laurence's sermon was printed at Oxford in 1635.

Arminian doctrine is also to be found in the works of Thomas Jackson, published at Oxford during the later 1630s. Jackson had returned to Oxford in 1631, as royal nominee to the presidency of Corpus Christi College.[151] 'Many in our days', says Jackson, and 'some of this Church of England have . . . taught that Christ died for none but the elect.' Others have distinguished between the 'sufficiency' and 'efficiency' of Christ's death, limiting its extent to 'some of all sorts of men'. But in reality, claims Jackson, Christ 'redeemed not only every one of us in particular, but all mankind'.[152] Elsewhere he argues that it can only occasion hatred of God to teach that

---

[147] Simon Episcopius, *Apologia* (n.p. 1629), fo. 11.

[148] Wood, *History*, pp. 370–1, 381–2, 385.

[149] Thomas Browne, *The Copie of the Sermon preached before the Universitie at St Maries in Oxford . . . the XXIV of December 1633* (Oxford, 1634), pp. 39, 51–2.

[150] Thomas Laurence, *Two Sermons* (Oxford, 1635), i. 10–11. For further anti-Calvinist comments by Laurence, see pp. 15 and 22 of this sermon.

[151] PRO, SP 16/182, fo. 64ʳ⁻ᵛ.   [152] Jackson, *Works*, VIII. 217–18.

'he hath reserved judgment without mercy to some men as they are men, or that he hath destinated them to inevitable destruction before he gave them life or preservation'.[153]

Other novel teachings came to the fore during these years. For example, in 1637 Adam Airay denied, as an Act thesis, that it was 'superstitious to worship God by bowing towards the altar'*.[154] The communion table in the university church had already been moved back, by Laud's order, to a permanent altarwise position in the chancel.[155] One of those objecting to the new ceremonial requirements was Edward Corbet, on the ground that 'he that does more than canon requires is as great a Puritan as he that does less'. Laud in turn contended that 'the Church of Christ had ever certain customs which prevailed in her practice, and had no canon for them; and if all such may be kicked out, you may bid farewell to all decency and order'.[156] Yet there was also a theological rationale at work here—eucharistic grace versus that of absolute predestination. As Thomas Laurence put it in 1634, 'where God is there is a propitiatory and an altar. Wee are therefore no more idolatrous by our prostration towards the table of the Lord then the Jewes were by their's towards the . . . mercy seate in the Temple.[157]

At the same time the cause of Arminian 'moderation' continued to be propagated at Oxford. Potter followed up the reprinting of Acontius by a work of his own—*Want of Charitie*. Published at Oxford in 1633 and primarily addressed to Roman Catholics, the book defined 'fundamental points of faith' in terms of the Apostles Creed and specifically excluded from this category 'Calvinist' views regarding predestination.[158] William Chillingworth expanded on the same theme in his *The Religion of Protestants*, published at Oxford in 1638. Writing of those who believed themselves 'predestinate', he said that 'we conceive a charitable judgement of our brethren and their errors, though untrue, much more pleasing to God than a true judgement, if it be uncharitable'. Rather than condemn their views, it was better 'to hope well of their hope',

[153] Ibid., vi. 108–9.
[154] OU Arch., Reg. Q.16, fo. 179.   [155] Laud, *Works*, v. 156.
[156] Ibid., v. 205–6.   [157] Laurence, *Two Sermons*, i. 37.
[158] Christopher Potter, *Want of Charitie* (Oxford, 1633), ii. 77–8, 116–17.

despite the fact that 'a great multitude of very potent arguments' had been marshalled against them.[159] Chillingworth's book had the general approval of Archbishop Laud, who arranged for Richard Baylie, in his capacity as Vice-Chancellor, and the two professors of divinity, Prideaux and Fell, each to affix his imprimatur.[160] (Later it was to be alleged that Prideaux's seal of approval was insincere.)[161] During 1638 Fell was succeeded as Lady Margaret Professor by the Arminian Thomas Laurence, who in a sermon of four years earlier had urged 'mistrust even [of] what thou knowest', concluding ''tis enough for thee to hold the foundation'.[162]

By the 1630s William Laud's own attitude to the predestinarian question was studiedly moderate. 'I have left no stone unturned in my efforts to prevent the public discussion of these intricate and thorny problems, lest, while pretending zeal for truth, we should offend against religion and charity. I have ever counselled moderation . . .'*[163] So Laud had written about the Arminian controversy in a private letter of July 1629. It may be that growing responsibility for ecclesiastical policy had cooled his earlier Arminian ardour. None the less there had always been a moderate wing to Arminianism, as can be illustrated by a passage from Grotius's elegy on Arminius.

> And whether that the truth ows much to thee,
> Or as by nature's lot man cannot see
> All things, in some part thou didst slip (judge they
> Who have that knowing pow'r, that holy key).

Having recorded this open verdict concerning the doctrines of Arminius, Grotius proceeded, in the same poem, to enrol him in the ranks of 'moderation' as one

> Who keeping modest limits now doth please
> To speak for truth, now holds his tongue for peace.[164]

The English translation of this elegy was itself probably an

[159] William Chillingworth, *The Religion of Protestants* (Oxford, 1638), pp. 406–7.
[160] Ibid., sig. S4ᵛ; Laud, *Works*, v. 165–6.
[161] Anthony Wood, *Athenae Oxonienses*, ed. P. Bliss (1813–20), III. 91.
[162] Laurence, *Two Sermons*, ii. 32.
[163] Trevor-Roper, *Archbishop Laud*, p. 94; Laud, *Works*, VI. 265.
[164] William Cartwright, *Plays and Poems*, ed. G. B. Evans (Madison, 1951), pp. 497–9.

Oxford product of the 1630s, but the moderate Arminian course which Laud sought to steer, in these years, remained full of hazard. Indeed, from a Calvinist point of view, the suppression of 'the truth of God' concerning predestination was to be compounded by the allied growth of 'superstitious ceremonies', and together might seem to discredit the very order of episcopacy.[165]

---

[165] *Constitutional Documents*, ed. Gardiner, pp. 138–9.

4

The British delegation to the Synod of Dort

I

THE presence of an official British delegation at the Synod of Dort was a crucial episode in the rise of English Arminianism. For this international Calvinist gathering, which condemned the doctrines of the Dutch Arminians in 1619, acted as a catalyst on the English religious thought of the early seventeenth century. Thomas Goodwin later recalled how 'the noise of the Arminian controversy in Holland, at the Synod of Dort, and the several opinions of that controversy, began to be every man's talk and enquiry'.[1] More generally, Peter Heylyn claimed that 'the predestinarian quarrels in the Belgick Churches' wakened Englishmen out of a 'dead sleep'.[2] One result was that differences among English theologians, hitherto often implicit, were brought out into the open. Similarly suspension of judgement on the nature of the relationship between grace and free will became harder, and doctor and student alike directed their studies especially to resolving this problem. Dissenters from Calvinism came increasingly to be identified as a group, and they in turn felt obliged to seek out allies in defence of a common cause. Indeed the Synod of Dort was, to an extent, responsible for the creation of an Arminian party in England.

The holding of this synod marked the culmination of a continuing English concern, from 1611 onwards, with religious disputes in the United Provinces. As the Dutch Church had become increasingly divided, partly as a result of the greater intellectual freedom allowed after the 1609 truce with Spain, so both Calvinists and Arminians began to seek for outside support. Because of the close Anglo-Dutch political ties which existed at the time, it was only natural that England should be one of the countries canvassed. England under Elizabeth had

---

[1] Porter, *Reformation and Reaction*, p. 409.   [2] Heylyn, *Cyprianus Anglicus*, p. 122.

played a central role in gaining independence from Spain for the seven northern provinces, and any threat to their continued survival as a nation remained the concern of English governments. To some observers the Dutch Arminian movement seemed to pose for the United Provinces a danger of internal dissolution. Thus the English Ambassador warned the States General in 1611 of 'the great danger now threatening the nation, if you allow the Arminian schismatics to continue in such favour with the chief towns of Holland'†.[3]

The nature of the English response to the Dutch religious crisis was, however, conditioned by a number of other factors besides politics. King James himself was possessed of a genuine interest in theology and his Archbishop of Canterbury was the Calvinist George Abbot. In 1611 the Dutch Arminian Petrus Bertius had made the mistake of appealing to Abbot only to be rebuffed.[4] Less straightforward by comparison was the attitude of the King. His personal views were more subject to *raison d'état* than those of his metropolitan, and, although at this date sympathetic to Calvinist doctrine, he was less inclined to be dogmatic. Moreover the early reactions of James to Dutch Arminianism were coloured by its association with the Vorstius affair. Conradus Vorstius, a German theologian, was the Arminian candidate for the Leiden professorship vacated by the death of Arminius in 1609. Those opposed to his appointment had charged him with heretical views concerning the Deity. As a result of reading the *Tractatus Theologicus de Deo*, by Vorstius, James claimed to have been enlisted in the campaign against him. Thus the support of Vorstius by the Dutch Arminians made them particularly unpopular with King James, and he described Arminius to the States General in 1611 as 'of little better stuff' than his would-be successor. Arminius himself was 'an enemie of God', and the 'first in our age that infected Leiden with heresie'.[5]

James was encouraged in these views by the English Ambassador at The Hague, Sir Ralph Winwood, who had his

[3] Winwood, *Memorials*, III. 305.
[4] Casaubon, *Epistolae*, no. 743.
[5] *His Majestie's Declaration . . . in the Cause of D. Conradus Vorstius* (1612), pp. 5, 15, 18. Cf. F. Shriver, 'Orthodoxy and Diplomacy: James I and the Vorstius Affair', *EHR* 85 (1970), 449–74.

own definite ideas about the Dutch religious controversy. In 1611 he reported to Salisbury that the

points in question are about predestination, universall grace, originall sinne, freewill, [and the] perseverance of the saintes. In all which Arminius, a Professor of Divinity in Leyden, lately deceased, who first did broach these doctrynes, clearly doth dissent from the Churches of England [and] Scotland, and the Reformed Churches in France and Germany.[6]

Winwood finally returned to England in 1614 and continued there to wield influence on behalf of the Dutch Calvinists. He was replaced by Sir Henry Wotton, sent as a special ambassador to try to resolve the Julich–Cleves succession dispute in which the Protestant candidate was backed by the United Provinces. Wotton was another Calvinist, who when he came to make his will in 1637 wrote of Christ's death as being 'sufficient satisfaction for the sins of the whole world and efficient for his elect, in the number of whom I am one by his mere grace and thereof most unremoveably assured'.[7] He went back to his earlier post at Venice in 1616, being succeeded by Sir Dudley Carleton who was cast in a similar religious mould. Carleton did not demur at his instructions to support the 'true professors' of religion—that is to say the Calvinists—against those holding 'erronious opinions', and subsequently he described the canons of Dort as being in defence of 'God's cause'.[8] Given these circumstances, it is perhaps surprising that the Dutch Arminians made any diplomatic headway at all in England. But, despite the setback of the Vorstius affair, they continued to work for English support. Their leaders did not despair of converting the King, and in 1613 his pronouncements seemed more favourable. They also began to try to build up an Arminian following among the English clergy, and the most active supporter to emerge was John Overall.[9] From 1616 the Dutch Arminians also had a friend in Sir Thomas Lake, one of the two secretaries of state.[10]

This is the English background against which international developments shortly preceding the Synod of Dort need to be

[6] PRO, SP 84/68, fo. 34[r].
[7] L. P. Smith, *Life and Letters of Sir Henry Wotton* (Oxford, 1907), i. 215.
[8] Carleton, *Letters*, p. 6; PRO, SP 84/89, fo. 208[v].
[9] Grotius, *Briefwisseling*, i. 234–6, 240–4.   [10] Carleton, *Letters*, pp. 37, 127, 197.

seen. So far as Dutch events were concerned, almost built into the 1609 truce with Spain had been the subsequent power struggle between Maurice and Oldenbarnevelt, the military and political leaders respectively of the republic. Each came to be identified with rival foreign policies. Oldenbarnevelt favoured a closer French alliance, and no trading concessions to the English. Maurice would have preferred a more aggressive policy towards Spain and the maintenance of existing ties with England, even at the expense of admitting an English presence in the East Indies. As early as February 1612, King James had confided to Winwood that he understood Oldenbarnevelt to be 'completely alienated', depending 'wholly'[†] on France, whereas Maurice was reportedly well affected to English interests.[11] The King followed this up by arranging for Maurice to be invested, in 1613, with the Order of the Garter.[12] In the event of any Dutch internal crisis, these known preferences were likely to influence English government attitudes.

Just such a crisis developed in 1617. The Habsburg threat, which had come into renewed prominence during the Julich–Cleves dispute, was once more in abeyance. Maurice now came out more openly in support of the increasingly militant Calvinists. In lieu of separate adjudication between the religious parties, by each provincial state, he favoured a national synod, under the patronage of the States General. Oldenbarnevelt was against this and events rapidly escalated into a direct political confrontation. During 1617 many Holland towns appointed their own militia or *waardgelders*. Originally intended to suppress local religious disturbances, these forces came to be perceived as a challenge to central authority. In July 1618 the States General ordered the disbandment of the *waardgelders*, threatening force if necessary. This was followed by the arrest of Oldenbarnevelt and a purge of Holland town councils, the latter by Maurice at the head of regular troops.[13]

With this turn of events, it was predictable that King James would support Maurice's action and his allied decision to hold

---

[11] Winwood, *Memorials*, III. 339. For some slightly later evidence of divergent Dutch attitudes towards trade see *Calendar of State Papers East Indies, 1617–21*, pp. 206, 211–12.

[12] Den Tex, *Oldenbarnevelt*, II. 490.

[13] Ibid., II. 554–645.

a national synod for settling the Dutch religious disputes. True to earlier form, the French interceded on Oldenbarnevelt's behalf and prevented Huguenot delegates from attending the synod.[14] In May 1618 Sir Thomas Lake had been disgraced, for reasons unconnected with the United Provinces. At various times in the recent past he had questioned the wisdom of supporting Maurice, and written of the proposed synod 'I wish it better than I fear'.[15] His political demise was, therefore, a considerable loss for the Dutch Arminians. Among the English bishops only Overall continued openly to defend the Dutch Arminians, arguing their near-agreement with the Church of England up to the eve of the synod.[16] Other potential supporters, like Lancelot Andrewes,[17] now tended to dissociate themselves from the increasingly unpopular cause. During December 1618 Archbishop Abbot wrote to Sir Dudley Carleton, summarizing what he claimed was both his own and the King's opinion of the Dutch Arminians.

They deny the true properties of God's election and the true manner of his grace, making that to be a cause of his forechoosing which is indeed a consequent, and placeing our perseverance not in God's hands but in our owne, and so adde unto it that a man who is truly faithfull, or regenerate and sanctified (for it cometh to the same head), may fall from grace both 'finally' and 'totally'. The King is marvelously inflamed against these graceless positions, and I acknowledge unto you that so am I.[18]

In August 1617 Maurice had suggested that English delegates be sent to the proposed national synod.[19] From then on, with plans being made for French, German, and Swiss delegations, this remained a serious proposition. During July 1618 the invitation was officially delivered. According to the Venetian Ambassador, Archbishop Abbot was given the task of selection.[20] Abbot, however, only claimed responsibility for one of the four initially sent. This was George Carleton,

[14] 'Autobiographie de Pierre du Moulin', *Bulletin de la Société de l'Histoire du Protestantisme Française*, 7 (1850), 470; PRO, SP 84/87, fo. 124[r-v].

[15] Carleton, *Letters*, p. 197.

[16] PRO, SP 14/99, fo. 160; Cosin, *Correspondence*, I. 5.

[17] Chamberlain, *Letters*, II. 111.

[18] PRO, SP 105/95, fo. 49.

[19] Carleton, *Letters*, p. 166.

[20] *Cal. SP Venetian, 1617–19*, p. 281.

Bishop of Llandaff.[21] Of the three other Englishmen, Joseph Hall, Dean of Worcester, had entered the court circle in 1607 as chaplain to Prince Henry, and in 1617 accompanied the King on his Scottish progress.[22] The remaining two, John Davenant, Master of Queens' College, Cambridge, and Samuel Ward, Master of Sidney Sussex College, were both royal chaplains by 1618.[23] How far the sending of these three to Dort was a matter of King James exercising his own preference is uncertain, the most likely instance of a personal appointment being that of Hall. Ward and Davenant would have tended to come in contact with the court on the frequent occasions when James stayed near Cambridge, at either Royston or Newmarket. As Calvinist theologians they may have first attracted James's attention in late 1617, during the investigation of the Cambridge Arminian Edward Simpson.[24] Given the major role played in those proceedings by Bishop James Montagu, there is the further possibility that Ward at least was his Dort nominee. For Montagu, who died in July 1618, was Ward's patron, appointing him his chaplain and to various posts in the diocese of Bath and Wells.[25] After the synod had begun, the Dutch invited James to send a Scottish delegate. His choice, perhaps a personal one, was Walter Balcanqual, a Scot resident in England, and thereafter it becomes proper to speak of a 'British' delegation. A final complication is that Joseph Hall fell ill during the synod and was replaced by Thomas Goad, chaplain to Archbishop Abbot and recommended by him.[26]

The supposition that Samuel Ward owed his presence at the Synod of Dort to Bishop James Montagu is strengthened by Ward's surviving correspondence over the Dort period. What emerges from these letters is the existence of an important clerical connection based on the bishopric of Bath and Wells, which Montagu had vacated in 1616. The group comprised Ward, in his capacity as Archdeacon of Taunton, Dean John Young of Winchester, who was also Chancellor of Wells, and

[21] PRO, SP 14/109, fo. 271.
[22] *DNB*, s.n. Hall, Joseph.
[23] PRO, SP 84/86, fo. 89ᵛ.
[24] See above, pp. 42–3.
[25] *Two Puritan Diaries*, ed. Knappen, pp. 41, 131.
[26] PRO, SP 14/109, fo. 271.

their diocesan Bishop Arthur Lake.[27] The views of this group were to have considerable influence on the doctrinal stand ultimately adopted by the British delegation at Dort, mainly due to the close relations existing at the time between the Scottish Dean Young and King James. Writing to Ward in January 1619 Young, while disclaiming actual rivalry with Archbishop Abbot, described himself as handling some of the King's correspondence about proceedings at Dort.

It is good reasone that things should first be imparted to my Lord Grace [Archbishop Abbot], and by him to his Majesty, but I have the relatione of these things as they passe still from his Majesty and the readinge of the letters as they come from the Embassadore their. For lightly his Majesty is pleased to putt them into my hand.[28]

When later a doctrinal disagreement arose among the British delegation, it was Young who successfully advocated to King James the cause of Ward, in spite of Archbishop Abbot.

II

On 24 September the original four English delegates to the Synod of Dort assembled at Hampton Court to receive their written instructions, having been briefed previously by Archbishop Abbot.[29] Two days later Ward wrote to Bishop Lake on the subject of the forthcoming synod. He expressed particular concern about difficulties likely to arise in connection with the Arminian doctrine of universal grace. The substance of his letter consisted of three queries about the relationship between man's redemption by Christ and absolute predestination.[30] Ward followed this up with a more explicit request to the bishop for advice.

I shal be very glad to have your Lordship's advise for the better carriage of business in this action, as alsoe your Lordship's resolution in some difficulties. I mentioned one or two in the last letter, as they came into my mynde. If your Lordship's leasure will permitt you to

---

[27] Bishop Lake was the brother of Sir Thomas Lake, the two men apparently holding opposed religious views.

[28] Bodleian, Tanner MS 74, fo. 180.

[29] Ibid., fos. 128, 132. These instructions are printed in Thomas Fuller, *The Church History of Britain*, ed. J. S. Brewer (Oxford, 1845), v. 462–3.

[30] Bodleian, Tanner MS 74, fo. 132.

sett down the 'steps of reasoning'* which are in the order of predestination, uppon the supposall of the fall, I should take it as a great
favour, desireing your Lordship's censure of the order inclosed in
this paper. There are sundry pointes, worthy the scanning, which in
probabilitie will come to be debated. But I cannot now enlarge as I
would .[31]

Attached was what Lake, in his reply of 12 October, described
as a 'concatenation of the branches of God's decree'.[32]

Lake's answer, sent to Dort, stressed that Ward must be
guided by the 'princelie instructions' of the King, but added
that the synod should try to avoid 'laime problemes, that mai
bee canvassed pro and con'. Turning to the theological questions involved, he wrote that

> the reconcilinge of God's justice and mercie, in dealing wih man-
> kinde, is the upshott of all this deliberation, and everie one studdies
> so to frame the decree as that the reconciliation of theise two maie
> bee the issue of his delineation, and what doth each except against
> the other but that he derogates either from the freedom of mercie or
> evennesse of justice.[33]

A comparison of the two letters indicates that Lake, as distinct
from Ward, was advocating what is known as a 'hypothetical
universalist' view of Christ's atonement. The concept of
hypothetical universalism was evolved by a number of Calvinist theologians, in an effort to counter the Arminian criticism that their teaching on predestination derogated from the
work of Christ's sacrifice through restricting it to the elect. To
avoid this difficulty they asserted that Christ had indeed died
on behalf of all mankind without exception. Hypothetical universalists, however, went on to distinguish between the original sin of Adam and the continuing depravity of his posterity.
Universal or 'common' grace only applied to the former, while
predestination still determined unconditionally who was to be
saved. Thus Lake wrote that the 'apostacy of man' had
rendered 'particular what began as universal'*.[34] The stricter
Calvinist view placed absolute election and reprobation prior
to God's providing fallen man with a means of redemption by
Christ, so limiting the atonement from the outset. In basing

[31] Ibid., fo. 132ᵛ.   [32] Ibid., fo. 134.
[33] Ibid., fo. 134ᵛ.   [34] Ibid., fo. 135ᵛ.

his 'concatenation' on this stricter scheme, Ward was probably adopting a debating position. For he was soon to demonstrate his agreement with Lake, and he had been discussing problems raised by Arminius regarding redemption since at least 1613.[35]

The surviving evidence for Ward's doctrinal position prior to Dort cannot be paralleled for any of the other British delegates. Their various theological standpoints only become apparent in the reports sent from Dort to Sir Dudley Carleton, first by his chaplain John Hales and latterly by Walter Balcanqual.[36] During the early sessions matters coming under discussion were not of a kind to cause dispute. The Dutch Arminians did not arrive at Dort until late November. The period of waiting was taken up with schemes for Bible translation and a standardized catechism, helped out with a series of sermons. One of the preachers was Joseph Hall, and in the course of his sermon he chose to cite a passage from King James's instructions that the Dutch Church should bide by its existing Calvinist confessions of faith. 'How fit it was', Hales wrote, 'to open so much of their commission, and thus to express themselves for a party against the Remonstrants your Honour [Sir Dudley Carleton] can best judge.'[37] This comment helps to confirm the Calvinist nature of James's intentions at this time, and indicates the chief criterion for selection as a delegate.

When the Arminians finally did appear at the synod their participation turned out to be a farce. Treated from the outset as the accused, under the leadership of Simon Episcopius they resorted to various procedural ploys. The intention seems to have been one of playing for time, presumably in the hope that the political situation would change in their favour. As it was, the Arminians effectively prevented any judgement at Dort until early January, when they were dismissed. The synod then proceeded to condemn them *in absentia*. Their doctrinal views were extracted from their published writings, and divided into the five main topics under which the Arminian controversy had already by tradition come to be handled. The

---

[35] Ibid., fo. 29ᵛ.
[36] John Hales, 'Letters from the Synod of Dort', in *Golden Remains* (1673).
[37] Ibid., p. 13.

first was predestination and this presented no major problems
to the delegates. Franciscus Gomarus, finding himself in a
minority, failed to press his supralapsarian views on the
synod. General agreement was reached on the unconditional
nature of the double decree, of election and reprobation, subsequent to the fall of Adam.[38] One of the Bremen delegates,
however, Matthias Martinius, chose to contest a subsidiary
thesis. He maintained, with the Arminians, that Christ was
both author and executioner of election, while rejecting the
Calvinist position that 'God first of all resolved upon the salvation of some singular persons and in the second place upon
Christ, as a mean to bring this decree to pass'. With this first
serious threat of a division of opinion among the delegates,
some of the foreign divines attempted to mediate and a meeting took place at Bishop Carleton's lodgings. Martinius was
there prevailed upon to keep his views to himself.[39] Nevertheless this potential disagreement seems to have laid the foundation of a future alliance between him and Ward.

The synod now moved on to the second general topic, that
dealing with man's redemption by Christ. Walter Balcanqual
was one of those chosen to open discussion, with the question
'Whether the death of Christ was intended indifferently for all,
or only for the elect'. The latter view was orthodox Calvinist
teaching, but Martinius of Bremen, in line with his earlier
stand, was again found in opposition. This, moreover, was the
subject on which Ward had sought advice from Bishop Lake
and he was soon reported as siding with Martinius.[40] The evidence points to Ward as being the prime mover on this issue
among the British delegates. According to Sir Dudley Carleton, 'it beganne with Dr Warde and he gained somewhat on
Dr Davenant'.[41] A succinct account of the subsequent division
of opinion is furnished by Balcanqual, who at the end of
January took over from Hales the task of informing the
English Ambassador of the synod's proceedings. He wrote
that

the question amongst us is whether the words of the Scripture,
which are likewise the words of our confession, ('Christ died for the

---

[38] Ibid., pp. 83–4, 129–30.   [39] Ibid., pp. 86–8.   [40] Ibid., pp. 90, 96–7.
[41] PRO, SP 84/88, fo. 155; Hales, *Golden Remains*, pp. 180–1.

whole human race, even for the sins of all the world'') be to be understood of all particular men, or only of the elect who consist of all sorts of men. Dr Davenant and Dr Ward are of Martinius of Breme his mind, that it is to be understood of all particular men. The other three [Balcanqual, George Carleton, and Goad] take the other exposition, which is of the writers of the Reformed Churches and namely of my late Lord of Sarisbury [Robert Abbot]. Both sides think they are right, and therefore cannot yield one unto another with a safe conscience.[42]

Balcanqual went on to suggest that discussion of this article be postponed until the end of the synod, and that in the meantime English Church leaders be consulted.

As a result of the information relayed by Balcanqual, Sir Dudley Carleton wrote to the British delegation advising them 'either to agreement among themselves or to write into Englande, which if they would not I tolde them I was bound to do. Hereupon they have written to your Grace [Archbishop Abbot], and I send their letters herewith.'[43] He also forwarded to England papers detailing the different points of view. The matter was thus referred to Abbot for decision, subject to royal approval, and his ruling of 20 February followed then current Calvinist orthodoxy. The British delegation were directed to conform themselves to the 'receaved distinction of "the sufficiency and efficacy of Christ's death", as likewise the restriction of those places which make Christ's suffering general to the world onely "to the world of the elect"*'. In this the Archbishop followed the published teaching of his brother, the late Bishop of Salisbury, and had the approbation of King James.[44]

Abbot's letter, however, was unduly delayed due to contrary winds over the North Sea, and during the interval the opposition group among the British delegation obtained the equivalent of a reversal of his ruling. This was made possible largely through the good offices of Dean Young of Winchester. For Young, whose influential position at this time has already been noticed, approached King James on behalf of Ward and the other hypothetical universalists. He argued, as instructed

[42] Hales, *Golden Remains*, p. 101.
[43] PRO, SP 84/88, fo. 155.
[44] PRO, SP 84/89, fo. 19; Hales, *Golden Remains*, p. 135.

by Ward, from the standpoint of a European Protestant reunion. Just such a scheme had recently been put forward by
the French Peter du Moulin, with the suggestion that
James should act as arbiter.[45] Now Young stressed the danger
of alienating the Lutherans, by 'to particulare and curious
a restraint' of redemptive grace when formulating the
doctrinal canons of Dort. This argument appealed to the
King, and Young was able to tell Ward that the synod would
be urged officially to use 'some general words as we find the
Scripture phrase often runneth', when drafting the relevant
canon.[46] It followed that the British delegates must frame their
combined judgement on this question in similarly 'general'
terms.

These new instructions arrived together with the conflicting
ones from Archbishop Abbot. Both, however, were too late to
influence the official British view concerning redemption,
which had already been read out to the synod. On its own
initiative the delegation had simply omitted all controversial
references, a decision which Balcanqual deemed in practice to
have fulfilled the new royal directive.[47] But now they were
further obliged to press their compromise on the synod as a
whole, in the actual framing of canons. The British delegation
were in a clear minority on this issue. Most of the other delegates wished to distinguish between the sufficiency and efficacy of Christ's death, and the canon as finally agreed
reflected the majority view. 'This death of the sonne of God is
. . . of infinite price and value, abundantly sufficient to expiate
the sinnes of the whole world.' Nevertheless 'God willed that
Christ, by the blood of his crosse, . . . should effectually
redeeme out of every people, tribe, nation, and language, all
them, and them only, who from eternity were elected unto salvation'.[48] On the other hand, Biblical references to *all* men
were not explicitly equated with the elect alone. As a consequence of this omission, Ward felt able to claim that the
Dort rulings had defined 'nothing . . . which might gainsay
the confession of the Church of England'.[49]

[45] Carleton, *Letters*, pp. 325–6.
[46] Bodleian, Tanner MS 74, fo. 196.
[47] Hales, *Golden Remains*, p. 135.
[48] Ibid., pp. 130–2; *The Judgement of the Synode holden at Dort* (1619), pp. 22, 24.
[49] Ussher, *Works*, xv. 145.

About the other three topics—the corruption of man's nature and the conversion and perseverance of the saints—there was no serious disagreement concerning Calvinist orthodoxy. When the synod came to an end in late April 1619, it was with 'common consent and subscription in publique'[50] to all the canons.

III

None of the British delegates at Dort, despite their doctrinal differences, can meaningfully be described as Arminian. In the 1620s both Davenant and Ward were to be found contending vigorously on the side of Calvinism against the English Arminians.[51] Similarly the sermons of Bishop Lake, Ward's mentor, contain hostile references to 'Arminian' teachings.[52] The doctrinal position of such theologians represents a genuine variant within Calvinism, rather than a transitional stage between it and Arminianism. Had illness not forced Joseph Hall to retire from Dort he would probably have sided with the hypothetical universalists. Certainly this is the thrust of an unpublished Calvinist work by him, dating from the mid-1620s.[53] Yet a tradition persists that one of the three stricter Calvinists among the British delegation, Thomas Goad, defected to the Arminians during the course of the synod.[54] This is not, however, borne out by the original records. Moreover, in the 1620s Goad both wrote and licensed books against Arminianism, the latter in his capacity as a chaplain to Archbishop Abbot.[55] The 'evidence' that his views changed derives from a posthumously published tract by him, *Stimulus*

[50] PRO, SP 84/89, fo. 196.
[51] Ward's anti-Arminian activities have been chronicled above, pp. 46–52. The surviving letters from Davenant to Ward, now among the Tanner manuscripts in the Bodleian Library, reveal him as an ardent religious supporter of the latter. The practical limits of hypothetical universalism emerge very clearly from Davenant's reply to Samuel Hoard and Henry Mason. John Davenant, *Animadversions upon a Treatise intitled God's Love to Mankind* (Cambridge, 1641), *passim*.
[52] Arthur Lake, *Sermons* (1629), i. 406–7, 424. I owe these references to Dr Fincham. This volume of sermons is dedicated to John Young, Dean of Winchester.
[53] Joseph Hall, *Works*, ed. P. Wynter (Oxford, 1863), ix. 490–2.
[54] R. L. Colie, *Light and Enlightenment* (Cambridge, 1957), p. 17.
[55] According to William Prynne, Goad was co-author with Daniel Featley of *Pelagius Redivivus* (1626). *Anti-Arminianisme*, p. 93. The same year Goad licensed Samuel Ward's *Gratia Discriminans*. Arber, iv. 122.

Orthodoxus, in the preface of which the editor speculated as to Goad's doctrinal position at Dort.[56] But the work in question, a discussion of the necessity and contingency of events, only indirectly concerns the Arminian controversy and is moreover compatible with a Calvinist stance on the points in question at Dort. Undeterred by these niceties, J. S. Brewer, in editing Thomas Fuller's *Church History*, wrote that Goad forfeited his chance of preferment, for services rendered at Dort, as 'having changed his opinions'.[57] This the author of the *DNB* article on Goad expanded as follows: 'At Dort, Goad, previously a Calvinist, went over to the Arminians. He is supposed to have lost in consequence a share in the high ecclesiastical preferments which were granted to his colleagues by James, and his name was omitted, accidentally perhaps, in the "acts" of the synod.'[58] Concerning the last point, the earliest Latin and English editions of the Dort canons both include Goad's name with those of the other delegates.[59]

Thus the theologians chosen to represent the Church of England, at the Synod of Dort, all took a definitely anti-Arminian stand, and in this they had the backing both of the supreme governor, King James, and of Archbishop Abbot.[60] At the same time, it is not being unduly cynical to conclude that the delegates sent to Dort were selected with an eye to their generally Calvinist views. One of the problems, however, in this connection, is to establish the degree to which English religious opinion was distorted by James's diplomacy. Secretary Lake, whose sympathies lay with the Dutch Arminians, had advised, in March 1618, against English support for their opponents on the grounds that 'if we were a popular state, as they are, it would make agitation here among divines.'[61] The previous November Bishop James Montagu, a Calvinist supporter, had confided to Sir Dudley Carleton 'I feare there will be found many in our countrey at home that are not farre from

[56] Thomas Goad, *Stimulus Orthodoxus sive Goadus Redivivus* (1661), sig. A.
[57] Fuller, *Church History*, v. 475.
[58] *DNB*, s.n. Goad, Thomas.
[59] *Judicium Synodi Nationalis . . . Dordrechti* (Dort, 1619), p. 44; *The Judgement of the Synode holden at Dort*, p. 76.
[60] Archbishop Matthew of York was kept informed of proceedings at Dort by Samuel Ward. Bodleian, Tanner MS 74, fos. 188, 217. For Matthew's Calvinism, see above, pp. 18–19.
[61] PRO, SP 84/83, fo. 37.

some of these [Arminian] opinions'.[62] But, as Lake said, government in England was not 'popular' and the expression of views hostile to it was never easy. Parliament, the most obvious platform for any opposition, had not sat since 1614 and from 1624 onwards the House of Commons was to be enlisted on the side of Calvinism.[63] Similarly when parliament was not sitting the clergy had no way of expressing a collective opinion, and in the event those who did so were a group of Calvinists in the lower house of convocation.[64] The medium of the press was state controlled, and a pamphlet war over English Arminianism only developed as a result of a split in the government ranks during the mid-1620s.[65] Hence the importance of the two universities as an index of changing religious attitudes, where developments often permit a year-by-year commentary; yet they, too, were far from being 'popular' institutions.

As we have seen the Calvinists at Oxford and Cambridge retained control of the Act and the Commencement, as well as the university presses, until the late 1620s. On the other hand, between 1595 and 1617 the two holders of the Cambridge Regius chair of divinity, Overall and Richardson, were both critics of Calvinist teaching, although they would seem to have come under growing pressure to conform with Calvinist orthodoxy and their views only circulated in manuscript. As late as 1616, however, it was still possible to air Arminian opinions at Cambridge without being overwhelmed in the attempt. But by the following year conditions had so deteriorated that Richardson apparently felt obliged to resign his professorship, as a supporter of the Arminians. At Oxford there was less of a tradition of dissent from Calvinism, and after 1613 Calvinists monopolized the divinity chairs. Clearly sensing a difference between the theology of the two universities, Archbishop Abbot, in 1619, compared the 'giddy parts' of a Samuel Ward from Cambridge with the 'better straine of iudgment' normally acquired at Oxford—a contrast which he

[62] PRO, SP 105/95, fo. 20ᵛ.
[63] See below, Chapter 6.
[64] Loe, *Sermon*, p. 25.
[65] Between 1624 and 1626 the Archbishop of Canterbury, George Abbot, and the Bishop of London, George Montaigne, who shared responsibility for licensing publications, were in effect pursuing rival policies.

felt to be epitomized by doctrinal disagreements among the British divines at Dort.[66] In general, the Dutch Arminian controversy served to erode the limited toleration previously extended to English anti-Calvinists.

During 1619 an English language edition of the Dort canons was produced by the royal printer. A preface sketches in the background to the calling of the synod and the Calvinist tenor of its conclusions is unmistakable. The opening paragraph of the first article runs that: 'Forasmuch as all men have sinned in Adam, and are become guiltie of the curse and eternall death, God had done wrong unto no man if it had pleased him to leave all mankind in sinne, and under the curse, and to condemne them for sinne.'[67] But the elect are chosen out of this corrupt mass by God, 'who bestoweth faith on some and not on others'. He 'graciously softens the hearts of the elect . . . and as for those that are not elect, he in just judgement leaveth them to their malice and hardnesse'.[68] This same year saw the publication of *A Meditation upon the Lord's Prayer*, by King James. In the course of the book he took occasion to refer to the errors of Arminianism, writing that

it sufficeth us to know that Adam by his fall lost his free will, both to himself and all his posterity. So as the best of us all hath not one good thought in him, except it come from God, who drawes by his effectuall grace, out of that attainted and corrupt masse, whom hee pleaseth for the worke of his mercie, leaving the rest to their owne wayes which all leade to perdition.[69]

Ominous perhaps for the future, however, was that James also referred, in this context, to the 'extremitie of some Puritans, who by consequent make God author of sinne'.[70]

Certainly by mid-1622 James seems to have had second thoughts about the condemnation of Arminianism. His directions to the clergy, issued that August, included a prohibition of all 'popular' preaching about 'predestination, reprobation, or of the universality, efficacy, resistibility or irrisistibility of God's grace'. Bishops and deans, however, were specifically

---

[66] PRO, SP 14/109, fo. 271.
[67] *The Judgement of the Synode holden at Dort*, p. 1.
[68] Ibid., p. 3.
[69] James I, *A Meditation*, p. 118.
[70] Ibid., p. 117.

exempted from the ban, as were 'learned men' in the universities, and in this respect it was less restrictive than similar pronouncement by Charles I in 1626 and 1628.[71] Furthermore these directions seem to have been largely inoperative.[72] But they clearly signify a change of mind and possibly of heart by King James. Officially explaining them in a Paul's Cross sermon, John Donne recalled Queen Elizabeth's 'inhibition' of the Lambeth Articles in 1595, 'that nothing not formerly declared to be so . . . be declared to be the tenet and doctrine of this Church'.[73] Probably among those whose views the King had taken into account when issuing his directions was Bishop Andrewes. Preaching before King James in April 1621, he referred in highly critical fashion to the five articles of Dort.

I pray God he be well-pleased with this licentious touching, nay tossing his decrees of late, this sounding the depths of his judgements with our line and lead, too much presumed upon by some in these days of ours . . . God's secret decrees they have them at their fingers' ends, and can tell you the number and the order of them just with 1, 2, 3, 4, 5.[74]

Moreover James continued to move in an Arminian direction, apparently underwriting the publication in 1624 of Richard Montagu's *A New Gagg for an Old Goose*. Montagu later claimed that his book was printed 'by King James's speciall warrant'.[75] If true, this represents a remarkable *volte-face* by James. For Montagu purported to correct Catholic misrepresentations of Church of England teaching. Such critics had assumed the English Church was Calvinist in doctrine. Montagu, however, now argued that this confused a Puritan gloss with the actual formularies of the Elizabethan religious settlement. None the less confusion, of the kind which Montagu suggests, can only have been increased by the presence of a British delegation at the Synod of Dort. Indeed the

[71] *Stuart Constitution*, ed. Kenyon, pp. 145–6, 154–5; *Constitutional Documents*, ed. Gardiner, pp. 75–6.

[72] I base this judgement on the surviving Paul's Cross sermons. By late 1624 Calvinist doctrine was being both preached at Paul's Cross, by ordinary clergymen, and licensed for the press. Robert Vase, *Jonah's Contestation about his Gourd* (1625), p. 46; William Proctor, *The Watchman Warning* (1625), pp. 51–2; Arber, IV. 91.

[73] John Donne, *Sermons*, ed. G. R. Potter and E. M. Simpson (Berkeley and Los Angeles, 1953–62), IV. 200–1. I owe this reference to Dr O. Kalu.

[74] Andrewes, *Works*, III. 32. This passage was pointed out to me by Dr Fincham.

[75] *Commons Debates, 1625*, p. 46.

Archbishop of Spalato, after his shortlived conversion to Pro-
testanism, had claimed, in 1623, that Dort finally convinced
him the Church of England was Calvinist in doctrine.[76]

Why King James should have supported Montagu at this
time is not entirely clear. One possible explanation, as has
been suggested in previous chapters, lies in the changing
international situation. Given that the centrepiece of James's
scheme for the recovery of the Palatinate was an Anglo-
Spanish marriage alliance, it made little sense for him to
countenance the Calvinist war party at home. In these circumstances he may have felt the need increasingly to
backtrack from his endorsement of Calvinism at Dort in 1619.
A way of doing this was to encourage the English anti-
Calvinists. Moreover the domestic situation in 1624 was especially complicated, because Prince Charles and the Duke of
Buckingham had recently been converted to a policy of war
with Spain. Was Richard Montagu then a pawn in the
developing power struggle between the King and his son?[77]
There is also the possibility that more personal religious considerations were at work on James's part, intimations of
mortality perhaps serving to erode an earlier intellectual com-
mitment to Calvinism.

The intention of Montagu's *A New Gagg* was almost certainly less innocent than outwardly it appeared. Whatever the
motives of the author, his clerical backers are likely to have
had more in mind than refuting Catholic libels. Published in
England and in English, *A New Gagg* had an obvious relevance
for a wider public than that of Catholic Englishmen. This fact
emerges from the petition to parliament against Montagu the
same year, which characterized his book as 'full fraught' with
'dangerous opinions of Arminius', and drew an analogy
between the English and Dutch situations.[78] Yet the petition
did not invoke the actual canons of the Synod of Dort, since,
despite English participation in their framing, they had never
been ratified for England. Montagu was quick to seize on this
de jure weakness of the Calvinist case. In his *Appello Caesarem* of

[76] M. Antonius De Dominis . . . declares the Cause of his Returne out of England (n.p.,
1623), pp. 69–70.
[77] K. Fincham and P. Lake, 'The Ecclesiastical Policy of King James I', *JBS*, 24
(1985), 202–6.
[78] Yates, *Ibis ad Caesarem*, iii. 46.

1625, he wrote of the Synod of Dort that 'I have nothing at all to doe with their conclusions, farther than they doe consent and agree to and with the conclusions and determinations of that Synod of London [the convocation of 1563], which established the doctrine of our Church, to which I am bound, and have subscribed'.[79]

Hence arose a number of attempts, by English Calvinists, to gain legal recognition for the Dort canons. Thus Bishop Carleton urged Archbishop Abbot, in early 1624, to have the canons adopted by convocation.[80] The stumbling block here, however, was the supreme governor of the English Church. Neither James nor, it transpired, Charles was willing to make the Dort canons binding for England. Furthermore it became increasingly clear after the accession of Charles that the monarchy now favoured a radical departure from Calvinist orthodoxy.

[79] Montagu, *Appello Caesarem*, pp. 69–70.
[80] PRO, SP 14/164, fo. 19ᵛ.

5

Bishop Neile and the Durham House Group

I

THE 1620s, taken as a whole, saw a dramatic shift in official Church of England teachings. Some idea of the extent of this change is conveyed by comparing the very different religious situations at the beginning and end of the decade. Bishop Carleton could write in July 1619 that 'in corners there is some muttering' against the condemnation of Arminianism at the Synod of Dort, 'but now I am sure that His Majestie's judgement putts all adversaries to silence, and nothing is heard but approbation of those thinges which His Majestie approves'.[1] Moreover, with the advancement of the Dort delegates Carleton and Davenant to the bishoprics of Chichester (1619) and Salisbury (1621), the maintenance of Calvinism seemed a safe avenue to promotion. By 1629, however, the leading ecclesiastical advisers of the government were being accused of Arminianism, and high office was said to be open only to those of their persuasion; 'some prelates, near the King, having gotten the chief administration of ecclesiastical affairs under His Majesty, have discountenanced and hindered the preferment of those that are orthodox, and favoured such as are contrary'.[2] This was the collective complaint of the House of Commons in February 1629. A year later Bishop Davenant himself was in serious trouble with the Privy Council, for having dared to maintain Calvinist views on predestination when preaching before King Charles.[3]

It can only be a matter for speculation what would have happened had King James not died in 1625. Nevertheless a very important element in the religious transition effected during this decade was the system of Arminian patronage and protection built up by Richard Neile, particularly as Bishop of

[1] PRO, SP 14/109, fo. 255.
[2] *Commons Debates for 1629*, p. 100.   [3] Bodleian, Tanner MS 290, fos. 86–7.

Durham. In an instructive passage, John Hacket later contrasted the role of Neile with that of his theologically like-minded seniors, who 'pleas'd all sides indifferently, because as touching opinions about predestination, converting grace, etc., they made no discrimination which or which propugners should be gratified in their advancements'.[4] Singlemindedness of religious purpose was indeed a characteristic of the clerical circle who came to be known by the sobriquet of Durham 'House' or 'College'—a reference to Neile's London residence from 1617 to 1628. Their influence was widely recognized. Davenant, for instance, wrote in June 1626, of the recent proclamation on the predestinarian controversy, 'how farr those of Durresme Howse will stretch the meaning thereof I know not'.[5] In his biography of Archbishop Laud, published after the Restoration, Peter Heylyn gives the following well-known sketch of the group.

That which gave him [Neile] most content was his palace of Durham House in the Strand, not only because it afforded him convenient room for his own retinue, but because it was large enough to allow sufficient quarters for Buckeridge, Bishop of Rochester, and Laud, Dean of Glocester, which he enjoyed when he was Bishop of St. Davids also. Some other quarters were reserved for his old servant Dr. Linsell and others for such learned men of his acquaintance as came from time to time to attend upon him, insomuch as it passed commonly by the name of Durham College.[6]

Neile went through more bishoprics than any of his contemporaries—Rochester, Coventry and Lichfield, Lincoln, Durham, Winchester, and York. Already by 1610, as Bishop of Rochester, he had become identified in the minds of Puritans as a bishop 'whom all the pious, as well private men as ministers', thought 'would do the most mischief'.[7] Four years later, a member of parliament could claim that Neile's 'disposition to Rome' was 'not well knowen', and request that he 'make his purgation'.[8] Neile had come to the attention of the House of Commons on this occasion because of his denial of

[4] John Hacket, *Scrinia Reserata* (1693), ii. 42.
[5] Bodleian, Tanner MS 72, fo. 135.
[6] Heylyn, *Cyprianus Anglicus*, p. 69. For a contemporary reference to Durham 'College', see Ussher, *Works*, xv. 356.
[7] Samuel Clarke, *Lives of Two and Twenty English Divines* (1660), p. 61.
[8] *Commons Debates, 1621*, ed. W. Notestein *et al.* (New Haven, 1935), vii. 648.

their right to discuss the crown's levy of impositions. This assertion of the royal prerogative elicited the comment that 'Scotland and Germany hath swept away greater myters than his', although the Commons were also urged 'not to tax the reverent degree of bishops by one man's error'.[9] Neile's earliest surviving visitation articles, for Lincoln diocese in 1614, are remarkably inquisitorial concerning Puritanism and evince hostility to combination lectures. As well as pursuing nonconformists, Neile wanted to know about attitudes towards convocation and its canons, and asked 'whether hath your minister presumed to appoint or hold any meetings for sermons, commonly tearmed by some prophecies or exercises, in market townes or other places'.[10]

As Bishop of Lincoln, between 1614 and 1617, Neile appointed his chaplain William Laud to the prebend of Buckden and the archdeaconry of Huntingdon. Neile had become Laud's 'patron' in 1608, on the recommendation of John Buckeridge, and in 1611 defended him at court against the Calvinist opposition to his becoming President of St John's College, Oxford.[11] It was Buckeridge perhaps who first introduced Neile to John Howson, by at latest 1612.[12] Howson and Laud became bishops in 1618 and 1621 respectively. With Buckeridge, they were in 1625 to certify the orthodoxy of the Arminian Richard Montagu.[13] At Lincoln Neile would have come into contact with Augustine Lindsell, his future chaplain, who had been appointed to a prebend by Bishop Barlow. Lindsell was later to help arrange for the publication of Montagu's *A New Gagg for an Old Goose*.[14] Probably from this Lincoln period also dates the association of Neile with Francis White, subsequently to license Montagu's *Appello Caesarem* and be rewarded with a bishopric in 1626. In 1617 White acknowledged Neile as 'my patron'.[15] Prior to his Durham appointment, however, the activities of Neile seem to have

[9] *Commons Journals*, I. 496, 498.
[10] Richard Neile, *Articles to be enquired of within the Diocese of Lincoln* (1614), sigs. B–B₂; P. Collinson, 'Lectures by Combination: Structures and Characteristics of Church Life in 17th Century England', *BIHR*, 48 (1975), pp. 204–5.
[11] Heylyn, *Cyprianus Anglicus*, pp. 55–6.
[12] PRO, SP 14/80, fo. 175.
[13] Laud, *Works*, VI. 244–6.
[14] *Commons Debates, 1625*, p. 46.
[15] Francis White, *The Orthodox Faith and Way* (1617), sig. ˝2ᵛ.

been fairly small scale, and, although an influence at court, he was an inadequate counterweight to the Calvinist triumvirate of George Abbot of Canterbury, John King of London, and James Montagu of Winchester.

II

The outline of Neile's own career is well known, but his religious views have remained something of an enigma. Information of a kind is provided by Peter Smart, one of the Durham prebendaries, in a highly prejudiced account of Neile written about the year 1640.

> Despairing to climbe to high preferment by learning and preaching, which he could not abide, hee [Neile] set his minde wholly upon advancing cathedrall pomp, and glorious ceremonies, easier a great deale to be performed and practised by an ignorant ideot, who hath onely the outside of a man, then the making of sermons or writing books.

Smart went on to say: 'I have known this man about sixty yeares, for we were schoole-fellowes in Westminster, when he was plaine Richard Neal and I Peter Smart, under Deane Goodman and Doctor Grant. Hee was then counted an heavy-headed lubber [and] put out of that schoole for a dunce and a droane.'[16] This picture of a prelatical ignoramus is, however, difficult to reconcile with Neile being chaplain in the households of both William and Robert Cecil, as well as Clerk of the Closet to King James. It reflects, perhaps more than anything else, the deep hostility with which the activities of Neile came to be viewed in 'godly' Calvinist circles. At the same time there appears to have been some truth in the allegation that Neile was no classical scholar, his 'barbarous' Latinity, for example, being commented on in 1613.[17] Yet poor grammar did not necessarily stand in the way of a good grasp of theology.

The main evidence for Neile's religious position comes from an extant speech, written for the House of Lords in 1629, but

---

[16] *The Acts of the High Commission Court within the Diocese of Durham*, ed. W. H. D. Longstaffe (Surtees Soc. 34, 1858), pp. 201–2.

[17] HMC Salisbury, VIII. 35 and XI. 358–9; PRO, SP 38/9 [fo. 15ᵛ]; *A Complete Collection of State Trials*, ed. T. B. and T. J. Howell (1816–28), II. 837.

not apparently delivered. In this speech, of which only a brief extract has ever been printed,[18] Neile sought to vindicate himself from the doctrinal and other charges made at this time by the House of Commons. Regarding his alleged 'Poperie', Neile described the 'Church of Rome' as 'a corrupt adulterated church, literally professinge the Catholike faith but in sundry particulars destroyinge the truth thereof'.[19] He proceeded to deny, among other things, the papal supremacy, transubstantiation, the invocation of saints, and purgatory.[20] Speaking of confession Neile said 'howsoever it is and may be of great use in God's Church, yet in the Church of Rome it is altogether abused'. This is because of 'the absolute necessitie they make thereof' and their requirement of an 'exact enumeration of all sins'.[21] He also claimed to be a frequent preacher.[22] As further evidence of his aversion to Catholicism Neile cited his doctoral theses, maintained at the Cambridge Commencement in 1600. These concerned 'the auricular confession of papists' and the idea of limbo, both of which Neile had refuted.[23]

   Interest attaches to Neile's Commencement theses on a number of counts. First, they are evidence of an ability to debate in Latin, which much reduces the force of Smart's and similar criticisms. Secondly, they reveal Neile as then aligned with the Cambridge Calvinists, against John Overall. Before the Commencement Overall had objected to the phrasing of Neile's theses.[24] At it he warned Neile against confusing the corruption of private confession, by Catholics, with the essential validity of the practice. While agreeing with him that limbo was a 'figment', Overall questioned whether 'the souls of the pious were in Heaven before the Ascension of Christ'*— as Neile had argued. The most that could be said with certainty, according to Overall, was that such souls were in some 'blessed place'*.[25] Neile replied that his remarks about confes-

---

[18] J. Le Neve, *The Lives and Characters . . . of All the Protestant Bishops of the Church of England since the Reformation* (1720), ii. 149–50.

[19] Durham Dean and Chapter Library, Hunter MS 67, no. 14, p.4.

[20] Ibid., pp. 4–6.

[21] Ibid., p. 7.

[22] Ibid., p. 8.

[23] Ibid., p. 9.

[24] HMC Salisbury, x. 210.

[25] A. Campbell, *The Doctrines of a Middle State between Death and the Resurrection* (1721), pp. 206–7.

sion were only meant of the popish sort, although he remained adamant about the souls of the pious. Overall was finally silenced by the moderator, Robert Some, who accused him of delivering erroneous doctrine.[26]

It seems reasonable to infer that by 1600 Neile's ideas were already in flux and that he was now in the process of emancipating himself from the consequences of ten years spent at St John's College, Cambridge, where the ultra-Protestant influences were notorious enough to be described later, by Archbishop Laud, as 'Johnnism'.[27] Moreover there are indications that Overall played a part in this transformation. Neile's visitation articles for Durham diocese, in 1624, contain a statement recommending private confession before receiving communion, which appears to be modelled on a similar passage in Overall's visitation articles for Norwich in 1619.[28] These are the two earliest known favourable notices of confession in any surviving set of visitation articles. Also in 1624, Neile's protégé Richard Montagu was to echo in print the views of Overall concerning the whereabouts of blessed souls before the Ascension.[29]

On the subject of 'Arminianisme' Neile claimed, in his draft speech of 1629, that he had 'ever carefully avoyded the reading into those questions, which I confesse I am not able to master'. The one exception to this generalization, so he said, was that during the 1590s William Cecil, Lord Burghley, had consulted him about the teaching of Peter Baro at Cambridge. Baro, under attack from the university authorities, had sent an exposition of his predestinarian views to Cecil as Chancellor. This document Cecil had passed on for comment to his chaplain, Neile. Now, more than thirty years later, Neile recalled that

I read it and finding him [Baro] to be of the opinion that God did elect 'on account of faith foreseen' I wrott about the quantitie of a sheet of paper against that opinion, and mayntained this that 'he who determined the end has disposed all the means conducing to it',

[26] Ibid., p. 208; Porter, *Reformation and Reaction*, pp. 403–4.
[27] Laud, *Works*, VII. 373.
[28] Durham Dean and Chapter Library, Hunter MS 67, no. 7, sig. A3ʳ⁻ᵛ; John Overall, *Articles to be enquired of in the Diocese of Norwich* (Cambridge, 1619), p. 8.
[29] Montagu, *A New Gagg*, pp. 277–9.

and that faith, repentance, obedience and whatsoever else were 'effects not causes of election'*".[30]

But he did not explain why, in 1624, his chaplains had judged this same opinion of Baro unobjectionable when expressed by Richard Montagu.[31]

Instead Neile provided 'a further account of my faith and conscience in the poynt of predestination'. By the 'powerfull operation of the Holye Spirit', man acquires the 'grace to obeye' which leads to salvation. Yet this working of the Holy Sprit is not 'as upon stocks and stones, coactive to some men whether they will or not'.[32] He went on to quote a sentence from 'the divines of Dortt' on the all-sufficiency of Christ's death.[33] Concerning the doctrine of 'perseverance', Neile said 'I never yet tooke upon me to determine of fallinge either finally or totallye. The elect of God may fall greevously, as holy David and St. Peter did [but] I dare not make any supposition had David had Peter dyed in impenitencye.'[34] 'Of reprobation', Neile concluded, 'I learne by our articles to be silent farther than with St. Augustine: "not to be elected is to be reprobated"* [and] the reward of sin is death.'[35]

Additional light is shed on Neile's religious evolution by one of the very few works which he is known to have licensed for the press.[36] This consists of two sermons preached in 1606 by Richard Meredeth, who like Neile had been a chaplain to Robert Cecil.[37] Christians may pray, says Meredeth in his second sermon, for 'remission of sinnes, grace, perseverance and glorie', and this *'without any limitation'* and *'without any determination'*. Such teaching remained only just within the bounds of the doctrinally permissible at this date. Meredeth also contrasts the 'holy exercise of prayer' with the opinion that 'all the chiefe parts and points of the Christian religion consisteth in the reading of scriptures, frequenting of lectures and hearing of sermons'. Prayer is the ordinary means of 'illuminating'

[30] Durham Dean and Chapter Library, Hunter MS 67, no. 14, pp. 12–13.
[31] Montagu, *A New Gagg*, pp. 179–81; *Commons Debates, 1625*, p. 46.
[32] Durham Dean and Chapter Library, Hunter MS 67, no. 14, pp. 13–14.
[33] Ibid., p. 14.
[34] Ibid., p. 14.
[35] Ibid., p. 15.
[36] Arber, III. 136. The possible significance of this work was drawn to my attention by Dr A. Foster.
[37] HMC Salisbury, IX. 400.

minds and 'rectifying' wills, whereas at sermons 'some beleeve, some doubt, some disdaine'.[38] It appears, therefore, that by 1606 Neile had severed his previous connections with Calvinism. But Neile's opening remarks about predestination in 1629 still afford the best direct evidence of the religious grounds which inclined him to support anti-Calvinist writers such as Richard Montagu and Thomas Jackson, during the 1620s, and earlier Meredeth.

I will not take upon me to open the mouth of the claye to dispute with the potter why hast thou made me thus, or to enter into the secrets of God's unreveled counsels, farther then in feare and reverence to apply the comfort of God's goodnes and generall promises of mercie to all penitent sinners layinge hold thereof by faith in Christ Jesus.[39]

Similarly in 1606 Meredeth had ended his sermon, subsequently licensed by Neile, with the assertion that 'the grace of God bringeth salvation unto all men'.[40]

III

As an Arminian patron Neile came into greatest prominence after his appointment to the bishopric of Durham in 1617. Yet to understand the full significance of his activities we must go forward six years, to 1623. Matthew Wren has left an account of a discussion which took place late that year between himself and Bishops Andrewes, Laud, and Neile. His version of this meeting, written many years after, is somewhat dramatized but furnishes valuable evidence of concerted thinking by the men who were to shape church policy in the next reign. During a London visit Wren received an early morning summons from his patron Andrewes to attend at Winchester House. On arrival he was admitted to the presence of the three bishops, and the doors were then locked. In the ensuing discussion, Neile revealed that they had been considering 'those things which we foresee and conceive will e're long come to pass'. They had decided to consult Wren, as a chaplain to Prince Charles, on 'how the Prince's heart stands to the Church of

[38] Richard Meredeth, *Two Sermons* (1606), pp. 27, 32, 40–1. My italics.
[39] Durham Dean and Chapter Library, Hunter MS 67, no. 14, p. 12.
[40] Meredeth, *Two Sermons*, p. 45.

England, that when God brings him to the crown we may know what to hope for'. Wren's answer provides illuminating comment, from an Arminian standpoint, on both past and future events. He replied that 'for upholding the doctrine and discipline, and the right estate of the Church, I have more confidence of him than of his father, in whom they say (better than I can) is so much inconstancy in some particular cases'.[41]

Among other things these remarks shed light on the religious standpoint of the future Charles I. Wren's particular knowledge derived from the fact that he had been with Prince Charles in Spain earlier that year, at a time when the latter was under pressure to turn Catholic. Probably as a result of this experience Charles had finally made up his own mind concerning the particular brand of Protestantism to which he subscribed. His Arminianism may, therefore, date approximately from this point. The cross-questioning of Wren in 1623 also suggests an element of long-term planning by a group of Arminians whose theology had tended to keep them from the highest ecclesiastical positions during the reign of King James. By themselves these clergy were unable to procure a general alteration in ecclesiastical affairs. But they could anticipate such an event following on the accession of a monarch more committed to their views, and prepare to exploit the new situation to the full. It is in this light that the activities of Bishop Neile and the Durham House circle assume their importance. For most of the religious *causes célèbres* in the 1620s were to be associated with members of this group, and it was they who came to set the pace of change.

The promotion of Neile to Durham in 1617 can be seen, in retrospect, to have struck a blow at the dominant position of Calvinism within the English Church, his advancement, with that of Lancelot Andrewes to Winchester in 1618 and George Montaigne to London in 1621,[42] involving a gradual shift in favour of Arminianism. It is unlikely that King James saw the appointment in this light, the desire to gratify an old servant most likely being his chief motive. Nevertheless Neile and his

[41] Christopher Wren, *Parentalia*, p. 46.
[42] It was a chaplain of Bishop Montaigne, Thomas Worrall, who licensed Richard Montagu's Arminian book *Appello Caesarem*. Arber, IV. 98; W. W. Greg, *Licensers for the Press, Etc. to 1640* (Oxford Bib. Soc., NS 10, 1962), pp. 100–1. Montaigne himself was another former chaplain of Robert Cecil. HMC Salisbury, XVIII. 421.

predecessor at Durham, Bishop William James, are fairly typical representatives of the two clerical groups who thenceforward came increasingly to vie for control. The Calvinism of Bishop James is plain from his will, made in May 1617, where he expressed the hope of being received into Christ's 'mercie seate with the rest of his electe and chosen Israell'.[43] Probably to be read in the same Calvinist light is his motto: 'By the grace of God I am what I am.'*[44] On the other hand it is misleading to call Bishop James a 'Puritan',[45] since in 1589 he can be found preaching at Paul's Cross in defence of bishops—'a calling begunne and continued from the Apostles' time unto this day'.[46]

Some idea of the Durham regime which had prevailed under Bishop James is conveyed by a sermon preached in his presence during 1608, less than two years after his appointment. The occasion was a diocesan synod and Thomas Oxley, 'preacher of God's word', took the opportunity to pass judgement on the parochial clergy.

How many blind seers may be seene here, foolish teachers, lame forerunners, negligent pastors, and dumbe cryers, shepheards indeed, but fitter to keepe sheepe than to care for soules . . . If you demaund further why blinde men are made seers, I must reply with Saint Bernard: the fault is in the overseers, 'bishops giving holy things to dogs and pearls to swine'*[47]

Drawing to a close Oxley had addressed the bishop directly. 'Take heede to yourselfe ['my honorable lord'], . . . and those evils which you could not stop in the beginning yet stay them in their proceeding.'[48] This sermon was published with a dedication to Oxley's patron, Archdeacon William Morton of Durham,[49] and seems to have accorded with the bishop's own sentiments. Thus in his visitation articles of 1613 the first question asked by Bishop James, of the churchwardens, was 'whether your parson, vicar, curate, or minister be a preacher

---

[43] PRO, PROB. 11/129, fo. 462.

[44] This is to be seen above a fireplace in the old Bishop's Palace at Durham.

[45] M. James, *Family, Lineage and Civil Society. A Study of Society, Politics and Mentality in the Durham Region, 1500–1640* (Oxford, 1974), p. 116.

[46] William James, *A Sermon preached at Paules Crosse* (1590), sig. A3.

[47] Thomas Oxley, *The Shepheard* (1609), sig. D3ᵛ.

[48] Ibid., sig. Eʳ⁻ᵛ.

[49] Ibid., sig. A2ʳ⁻ᵛ.

of God's word, and a maintainer and furtherer of religion?' Moreover it is assumed that such preaching involves 'sermons, lectures and other exercises'.[50] These articles also indicate that the bishop was keen to eradicate all 'memories of idolatrie'.[51] As regards the wearing of the surplice he only asked whether it was 'usually' worn,[52] which suggests a less than rigorous attitude to the enforcement of conformity. Bishop Neile's visitation articles of 1624 give a very different impression. They lack the previous stress on preaching and the hostility towards residual Catholicism. Furthermore the churchwardens are questioned whether the surplice is worn 'always and at every time'.[53] In addition these 1624 articles contain, as we have noted, one of the earliest such statements on the desirability of private confession before receiving communion.[54] This last connects with the English Arminian emphasis on sacramental grace and Neile in fact signalled his appointment to Durham, in 1617, by having the cathedral communion table moved back, from 'the midst of the quire'.[55] to the site of the pre-Reformation altar.

The main source of information about ceremonial changes in the cathedral during the episcopate of Neile is Peter Smart, who had been chaplain to Bishop James. The estrangement of Smart from his new colleagues seems to have been complete by 1628, the year in which he preached a notorious attack on the alterations of the past decade. Taking as his text part of the seventh verse of Psalm 31—'I hate them that hold of superstitious vanities'—Smart accused those responsible of committing 'spiritual fornication'.[56] He also spoke of

the presumptuous boldnesse of him, or them, which immediately after the death of our last learned bishop, before wee had another, about eleven years ago, took upon him, I know not by what authority, to alter the situation of the communion table, from the ould manner of standing which it had kept in all bishops times from the beginning of Queen Elizabeth's raigne.[57]

---

[50] Durham Dean and Chapter Library, Hunter MS 67, no. 6, sig. A2.
[51] Ibid., sig. B2.
[52] Ibid., sig. A2ᵛ.
[53] Durham Dean and Chapter Library, Hunter MS 67, no. 7, sig. A4.
[54] Ibid., sig. A3ʳ⁻ᵛ.
[55] Peter Smart, *A Sermon preached in the Cathedral Church of Durham* (Edinburgh, 1628), p. 33.   [56] Ibid., p. 26.   [57] Ibid., p. 35.

Smart was here referring in particular to Francis Burgoyne, installed as a prebendary in May 1617. Elsewhere he wrote of Burgoyne as 'the first corrupter of religion in our church', and that he 'was thrust in amongst us, by the Bishopp now of Winchester, then of Lincolne [Neile], about a 11 yeares agoe, to the great wrong of learned Mr. Alanson to whom the Bishop of Durham, Doctor James, had given that praebend under his seale'.[58] A graduate of Peterhouse, Cambridge, Burgoyne had been beneficed in the Durham area since 1595, but as a prebendary of Southwell perhaps came to know Neile at Lincoln which is only thirty miles away.

In moving the Durham Cathedral communion table back to an altarwise position in mid-1617, Burgoyne was performing an identical action to that of Laud, as Dean, at Gloucester Cathedral in January of the same year.[59] Given the mutual connection with Neile their activities are likely to have been closely linked. Laud's initiative, like that of Burgoyne, challenged a previously dominant Calvinism, and involved him in potential conflict with the Bishop of Gloucester, Miles Smith. The brand of religion to which Smith subscribed emerges most clearly from the sermon preached at his funeral in 1624 by the Sub-Dean, Thomas Prior, who recalled that 'some few dayes before his death . . . I heard him discourse sweetly of the certainty of salvation and of perseverance in grace, comfortable truths so much opposed by Papists, Arminians and carnall gospellers'.[60] In 1617 Prior himself had been suspected of secretly fomenting opposition to Laud, because of the ceremonial changes.[61] Laud justified his altering the position of the communion table on the grounds of cathedral practice elsewhere.[62] The latter certainly varied, but awareness of underlying theological differences seems to have made the issue a particularly sensitive one from 1617 onwards.

The prominent part played by Burgoyne at Durham was made possible by the fact that the Dean, Adam Newton, was a

[58] Bodleian, Rawlinson MS A.441, fos. 92, 98. 'Mr. Alanson' was probably John Allenson, Rector of Whickham, who edited the works of the Calvinist William Whitaker.
[59] Laud, *Works*, IV. 233.
[60] Miles Smith, *Sermons* (1632), pp. 303–4.
[61] PRO, SP 14/90, fo. 190.
[62] Laud, *Works*, IV. 233.

non-resident layman. Newton resigned in 1620, to be replaced
by Richard Hunt. As with Burgoyne earlier, Hunt's arrival
was marked by almost immediate change. According to Smart
'about *anno domini* 1620 the communion table was cast out of
the cathedrall churche at Durham, and an altar of marble
stones, set uppon columns, was placed in its steed, with many
cherubims thereuppon, and a carved screene curiously
painted and guilt set over the same'.[63] This stone altar still
exists, albeit denuded of its cherubims (plate 2). The previous
career of Hunt is obscure. He had matriculated at Trinity College, Cambridge, in 1582, the year after John Overall had
become a fellow, and both were to remain members of the
same college for the next sixteen years. It is possible that Neile
inherited Hunt, as he did John Cosin, from Bishop Overall
who died in 1619. The erection of this stone altar in 1620
seems to have produced the first recorded opposition from
among the Durham clergy. For the following year Robert
Hutton, a prebendary since 1589 and nephew of Archbishop
Hutton, was prosecuted in the High Commission Court for a
cathedral sermon 'reflecting' on bishop and ceremonies.[64]

It has been pointed out that Neile's episcopate 'saw more
deaths in the Durham dean and chapter than in any previous
decade since the Reformation'.[65] The two archdeaconries of
Northumberland and Durham also fell vacant between 1619
and 1621. As these deaths and resignations occurred, so the
posts were filled by men all of whom seem to have been Arminian sympathizers. For example, in 1619, Augustine Lindsell
was appointed to a prebend, the previous incumbent having
held it since 1580. Lindsell, a chaplain to Bishop Neile, was
later described by Peter Smart as 'the oracle of our Arminian
sectaryes'.[66] Given Lindsell's association with 'Dutch' Thomson, the description is probably not too far-fetched.[67] Francis
Burgoyne became Archdeacon of Northumberland in 1621
while John Cosin, another of Neile's chaplains, was made a
prebendary in 1624. Burgoyne, Cosin, and Lindsell were all

[63] Bodleian, Rawlinson MS D.821, fo. 4.

[64] R. Surtees, *The History and Antiquities of the County Palatine of Durham* (1816), I. 149.

[65] A. Foster, 'The Function of a Bishop: the Career of Richard Neile, 1562–1640', in
Continuity and Change, ed. R. O'Day and F. Heal, (Leicester, 1976), p. 45.

[66] Cosin, *Correspondence*, I. 175.

[67] *Sancti Gregorii Nazianzeni*, ed. Montagu, sig. ¶ 4ᵛ.

said, by Smart, to 'have tearmed the reformers of our Church ignorant and unlearned Calvinisticall bishops'.[68] Earlier, and via Bishop Overall, Cosin had developed links with Dutch Arminianism—corresponding with Grotius and owning some of Arminius' writings.[69]

That Cosin was an anti-Calvinist emerges clearly from two of his surviving manuscript sermons, which have been dated to 1625. They concern the perils of presumption. It is the Devil's work, says Cosin, 'to make us presume upon God's mercy, make us believe that we are the sons of God, and then that we may cast ourselves headlong into what sins we list, that we should be never a whit the worse for it, but as often as we fell down He and his angels would take us up again'.[70] He goes on to speak of 'a wild conceit of predestination, that God will work his work' and that men 'may jump into glorification without any more ado'. Our 'new masters' allege 'they have it from St. Paul that he who is once predestinated is sure enough for ever' and 'cannot fall'. Furthermore they teach 'that some men are forced and necessitated to sin'.[71] Cosin's *Collection of Private Devotions*, published in 1627, also contains a passage directed at the Calvinists. Offenders against the third of the Ten Commandments include, says Cosin, 'they that make curious and wanton questions concerning the nature, the actions, and the secret decrees of God, not contenting themselves with that which He hath revealed in his word'. This book carries the personal imprimatur of Bishop Montaigne of London.[72]

IV

As regards the more general intellectual outlook of the Durham Arminians, it has been claimed that they were 'saddled' with a sense of 'history as inevitable decline and "decay"' and turned to antiquity as a form of escapism. The evidence adduced is *The Legend of St. Cuthbert*, a manuscript work written in 1626 by Robert Hegge.[73] He was a Durham

---

[68] Cosin, *Correspondence*, I. 163.
[69] Grotius, *Briefwisseling*, II. 99–101; Cosin, *Correspondence*, I. 90.
[70] John Cosin, *Works*, ed. J. Sansom (Oxford, 1843–55), I. 58.
[71] Ibid., I. 66, 78–9.　　　　　　　　　　　　[72] Ibid., II. 84, 115.
[73] James, *Family, Lineage and Civil Society*, p. 135.

schoolboy who went on to Corpus Christi College, Oxford, becoming a fellow in 1624. In his *Legend*, which is also a history of Durham Cathedral, Hegge comments enthusiastically on the changes made by Bishop Neile, 'under whom the church of Durham seems to renew her age, and to take on a new lease of eternitie, who for the internal beauty of her high altar, cathedral music, and sacred laver and other ornaments, may challenge her sister churches for prioritie'.[74] Yet Hegge clearly believed that history was cyclical, writing of Durham Cathedral as 'growing' in the eleventh century to the 'hight of her glorie',[75] which was now being renewed in the early seventeenth century. Such is the concept of 'circular progress' as opposed to 'continual decline'.[76] Hegge, moreover, wrote a treatise on 'dialling', an activity which has been described as standard procedure for 'young mathematical practitioners'.[77] This interest of Hegge suggests a connection between Arminianism and science, which we have already encountered in the context of his Oxford college. Like some others who shared his religious standpoint, he also belongs in the camp of the moderns.[78]

Confirmation of Neile's own Arminian views comes from a letter by Oldenbarnevelt, Advocate of Holland and the chief lay supporter of Dutch Arminianism. Writing in May 1618 to the Dutch Ambassador in London, some two months before his own fall from power, he recommended that Bishops Buckeridge, Overall, and Neile be sent over to participate in resolving the Dutch religious crisis.[79] In the event, of course, divines of an opposite and Calvinist persuasion represented the English Church at the Synod of Dort, where they joined in condemning the Arminians. Nevertheless it is against this international background that we need to see Neile's patronage, in the 1620s, of the two leading English exponents of Arminianism—Richard Montagu and Thomas Jackson. Montagu like Lindsell had been an associate of 'Dutch'

[74] Robert Hegge, *The Legend of St Cuthbert*, ed. J. B. Taylor (Sunderland, 1816), p. 61.

[75] Ibid., p. 43.

[76] R. F. Jones, *Ancients and Moderns: a Study of the Rise of the Scientific Movement in Seventeenth Century England* (Berkeley, 1965), pp. 26, 30.

[77] E. G. R. Taylor, *The Mathematical Practitioners of Tudor and Stuart England 1485–1714* (Cambridge, 1970), pp. 335, 345.

[78] See below, pp. 140–5.   [79] Oldenbarnevelt, *Bescheiden*, III. 440.

Thomson,[80] and was perhaps introduced to Neile by Lindsell.
When Montagu began to publish his Arminian views in 1624,
it was with the approval of Neile. Indeed for a time he seemed
the sole bishop who did favour him, Montagu writing to Neile
in 1624 as 'the only true and reall frend the Church hath of
your rank'.[81] Neile's personal influence with King James was
crucial in the first stages of the Montagu controversy. His
encouragement of more open support for Montagu from like-
minded colleagues was also invaluable. Furthermore he
backed Montagu's claims to be promoted to the episcopate,
and in 1629 secured him a royal pardon.[82]

The other future Arminian controversialist to join the
Durham House circle in the 1620s was Thomas Jackson,
whom Neile preferred to the vicarage of St Nicholas Newcastle-upon-Tyne in 1623.[83] Jackson originated from Newcastle
and, as already remarked, was a member of the earliest group
at Oxford known to have had access to some of Arminius' own
writings. William Laud and John Howson had both been connected with its leader, Walter Browne, and one or the other
may have recommended Jackson to Neile. In two works published between 1625 and 1628 Jackson made his Arminian
beliefs increasingly plain. On the first occasion he attacked the
view that God 'doth predestinate most souls created by him to
an endless life more miserable than this mortal life'. None the
less his critique was still hedged about with qualifications,
Jackson 'not intending to prejudice the conclusions usually
received or well approved by learned reformers of religion'.[84]
By 1628 he had become much bolder, arguing that Church of
England teaching on the redemption was incompatible with
unconditional predestination.[85] This earned him the censure
of both Bishop Morton and the House of Commons.[86] The
same year, as we have seen, Jackson was Neile's candidate for
the Presidency of Corpus Christi College, Oxford.[87]

[80] *Sancti Gregorii Nazianzeni*, ed. Montagu, sig. ¶4ᵛ.
[81] Cosin, *Correspondence*, I. 84. Montagu dated his letters only by day and month, and
I disagree with many of the years suggested by Ornsby.
[82] Cosin, *Correspondence*, I. 79; *Commons Debates for 1629*, p. 50.
[83] Jackson, *Works*, VI. 303–4.
[84] Ibid., IV. 369, 371.
[85] Ibid., V. 178.
[86] Bodleian, Tanner MS 72, fo. 310; *Commons Debates, 1628*, ed. R. C. Johnson *et al.*
(New Haven, 1977–83), II. 86.   [87] Bodleian, Rawlinson MS D.47, fo. 16.

An indication of Neile's own thinking during the early 1620s may be contained in a work which he edited for publication in 1624. This is an account of the defection by Marcus Antonius de Dominis, former Archbishop of Spalato, from the Church of England which he had briefly joined in 1616. The immediate purpose of the book was to expose the 'shiftings in religion' of the Archbishop, and it consists mainly of a series of interviews with him in 1622. These had been conducted by Bishop Montaigne of London and Dean Young of Winchester, as well as Neile, whose additional task was to edit the material. The reported statements of de Dominis afforded a potentially safe medium for comment, by the editor, on the contemporary religious scene. While one cannot assert that they coincided with Neile's views, the reporting of a number of passages relevant to the Arminian controversy, without any overt editorial guidance, is suggestive. Speaking of the English hierarchy, de Dominis 'did say that some even of our owne bishops were over rigide Calvinists'.[88] While admitting his dissent on some doctrinal points, de Dominis added

> yet rather from some private men and teachers in the Church of England, then from the Church of England it selfe. As namely about free will and the eficacy of grace, and predestination and justification, and necessitie of workes and merits, and such like. Yet I professe that in these points I never dissented from the Articles of the Church of England, because I hold them all (understood in a right sense) to be true.[89]

This was the same attitude as adopted by Richard Montagu and, had the editor disagreed, one might have expected some adverse comment, or even omission of the offending passages.

What, however, particularly distinguished Neile at this time was the action he took in backing Richard Montagu, whereas his Arminian colleagues on the episcopal bench noticeably hung back. Thus, in October 1624, Montagu wrote of Laud 'I hope to see him one day where he will both do and say for the Church. Interim, if someways he concede, I blame him not.'[90] The following March 1625 he spoke of Buckeridge as 'ever wont to hold the reyns hard that I went not to quicke',[91] and in

---

[88] Richard Neile, *Marcus Antonius de Dominis . . . his Shiftings in Religion* (1624), p. 34.

[89] Ibid., pp. 40–1.

[90] Cosin, *Correspondence*, I. 24.   [91] Ibid., I. 66.

May he expressed the wish that Andrewes would 'open his mouth and speake out'.[92] By contrast Montagu described Neile in December 1624 as 'still like himself in his thorough courses for right, though alone and left alone'.[93] So far as the English Arminian movement had a leader among the bishops in these years, it was Neile. Similarly to the extent that there was an Arminian candidate for Canterbury, Neile was the man, for Andrewes was too old and Laud not yet sufficiently established.

Aside from the personal ambitions of Bishop Neile, the Durham House group provided the first organized opposition to English Calvinism. Its effectiveness derived from the blend of court influence and clerical patronage which he exercised. By 1624, more than any other bishop, Neile seems to have had the ear of King James. Some notion of the intimacy of the circle he built up is conveyed by his chaplain Lindsell's will, made in that same year. Neile headed the list of beneficiaries, described as one 'whose bountie hath beene extraordinarie in my preferment, and of whose favour and fatherlike indulgence towards me from time to time I have had most ample experience'.[94] Similarly remembered were Buckeridge, Cosin, and Laud, but the precedency of Neile reflects the then reality of power as well as personal allegiance to a patron. Two years later, however, the group was already starting to break up, as more conventional avenues to ecclesiastical influence became available and Laud overtook Neile in the race for leadership.[95] At work here was the combined favour of Buckingham and King Charles.[96]

The new-found confidence of the Durham House divines is apparent from the sermon preached by John Cosin at the consecration of Francis White, as Bishop of Carlisle, in December 1626. Durham House chapel provided the venue and the Duke of Buckingham's sister, the Countess of Denbigh, was in

[92] Ibid., i. 70.
[93] Ibid., i. 34.
[94] PRO, PROB. 11/166, fo. 365.
[95] Laud, *Works*, iii. 196.
[96] As early as October 1624 Richard Montagu urged that, when vacancies occurred on the episcopal bench, Laud should 'putt for the Church with the Duke [Buckingham], and use his greate creditt that we be not swallowed up with a Puritan bishopriqry'. Cosin, *Correspondence*, i. 22.

attendance. The consecration itself was 'executed' by Bishop Neile. In his sermon, Cosin roundly condemned the current state of the English Church.

We suffer scandal from them of the Church of Rome in many things, . . . that we have a service, but no servants at it; that we have churches, but keep them not like the houses of God; that we have the sacraments, but few to frequent them; confession, but few to practise it; finally, that we have all religious duties (for they cannot deny it), but seldom observed; all good laws and canons of the Church, but few or none kept; the people are made to do nothing; the old discipline is neglected, and men do what they list. *It should be otherwise, and our Church intends it otherwise.*

Cosin also spoke of those who now 'preach us all Gospel and put no law among it, *bishops* and priests that will tell the people all is well if they can but say their catechism and hear sermons [and] make them believe that there is nothing to be done more but to believe and so be saved'.[97] Blending doctrine with practice, this indictment also involved a programme of action for the future. As the Arminian policy of Durham House became that of the English Church, however, so Neile's organization lost much of its *raison d'être*. Nevertheless, in a period of transition, it had provided a rallying point for those clergy who finally came to power during the 1630s.

---

[97] Cosin, *Works*, I. 96–7. My italics. Dr Fincham alerted me to this sermon.

6

Richard Montagu, the House of Commons, and Arminianism

I

CALVINISM clearly had the capacity to arouse lay as well as clerical passions, both for and against. Thus during the 1590s, in the aftermath of the Lambeth Articles, Archbishop Hutton can be found lamenting 'that the court should boil at the doctrine of predestination'.[1] Direct evidence, however, of lay attitudes is relatively hard to find. Hence the importance of the debates of the 1620s, in the House of Commons, provoked by the anti-Calvinist writings of Richard Montagu. Beginning with a petition to parliament in 1624, the Montagu case involved the educated laity with these questions as never before.[2] In every subsequent parliamentary session of this decade Arminianism was discussed, and laymen now wrote about it for the enlightenment of their fellows.[3] Throughout these debates Montagu's books were the chief concern, although his opponents increasingly linked them with a wider conspiracy to subvert the established teachings of the English Church.

The parliamentary case against Montagu centred on two of his works, published successively in 1624 and 1625. The first, *A New Gagg for an Old Goose*, was written in answer to a Catholic tract by John Heigham of St Omer,[4] which had been cited by some friars operating in Montagu's parish of Stanford Rivers in Essex. Therefore Montagu, in replying, countered both local missionary activity and the latest Catholic apologetic. His second book, *Appello Caesarem*, was an attempt to

---

[1] BL, Harleian MS 7029, fo. 51ᵛ.
[2] The Lambeth Articles were mentioned during the parliamentary session of 1604, although no recorded discussion ensued. *Commons Journals*, I. 199.
[3] For example William Prynne, *The Perpetuitie of a Regenerate Man's Estate* (1626).
[4] *The Gagge of the Reformed Gospel* (Douai, 1623). For the authorship of this tract see A. F. Allison, 'John Heigham of St Omer c.1568–1632', *Recusant History*, 4 (1957–8), 237–8.

vindicate himself from subsequent attacks by fellow Protestants who considered *A New Gagg* to contain, among other things, Arminian teaching. As regards *A New Gagg*, it does not appear that Montagu was aiming primarily at Calvinism. His answer, however, to Heigham's criticisms of various Protestant doctrines, including absolute predestination, was not to justify by explanation but to dissociate the Church of England from them. 'Against [English] Protestants your *Gag* is directed, not Puritans, and yet all your addresses, well-neer, are against Puritan positions, malitiously imputed to Protestants.'[5] The points at issue between England and Rome, as listed by Heigham, were thus dramatically reduced from forty-seven to eight. Probably it was the dismissal of Calvinism as Puritanism that particularly struck those who read Montagu's manuscript and produced additional pressure to publish, if possible with royal approval. A committee of the House of Commons later recorded that his 'first booke was printed by King James's speciall warrant, procured without his privity, as it should seeme, by Dr Lincy [Augustine Lindsell] and Mr. Cosins [John Cosin] the Bishoppe of Dorrham [Richard Neile]'s chaplaynes, to whom he sent the booke'.[6]

Montagu had sent the manuscript of *A New Gagg* to Cosin, in December 1623, with the instruction 'read it over privately, or att most with Austen [Lindsell], and get it licensed, but of no Puritan'.[7] Although Cosin was chaplain to Bishop Neile of Durham, Montagu wrote to him as a friend based in London rather than as a fellow-client of Neile. Only as a consequence of the publication of *A New Gagg* did Montagu become clearly identified with Neile's group; thus by January 1625 he can be found writing that 'I give Duresme House "right"* and leave to use me as they will',[8] and his *Appello Caesarem* published the same year has been described as the product of a 'literary partnership'[9] with Cosin. The association, however, of Neile's chaplains with *A New Gagg* helps put in perspective the fact that not until May 1625 did Montagu begin reading

---

[5] Montagu, *A New Gagg*, pp. 323–4.
[6] *Commons Debates, 1625*, p. 46.
[7] Cosin, *Correspondence*, I. 33.
[8] Ibid., I. 9.
[9] Ibid., I. p. xiii.

Arminius.[10] Prior to 1619 Cosin had been secretary and librarian to Bishop Overall, and as such had held a key position in the household of apparently the only English bishop who dared to defend the Dutch Arminians on the eve of the Synod of Dort.[11] Augustine Lindsell, Neile's other chaplain, was to be described by Peter Smart in 1630 as 'a profest disciple of that arch-heretick, and enemy of God, Arminius, and a ringleader of that cursed sect in England'.[12] Certainly during the first decade of the seventeenth century Lindsell had been a contemporary at Clare College, Cambridge, of 'Dutch' Thomson, who knew Arminius personally and approved of his teachings. But Montagu himself had moved in the same circle; in the preface to his first book, published in 1610, he acknowledged the help of both Lindsell and Thomson.[13] Moreover, some time prior to 1610, Montagu had been 'appointed' by the Provost of King's, his own Cambridge college, to copy out the Lambeth Articles, which may mean that his anti-Calvinist views had already emerged.[14]

There can be little doubt that, by the beginning of the 1620s, Montagu knew where he stood in relation to Arminianism. Indeed, as a consequence of the Synod of Dort, it would have been difficult for any member of the English intelligentsia to plead complete ignorance of the subject. Furthermore the Dort canons had been published in English translation, and laymen would also have become aware of the predestinarian controversy from attending the annual Cambridge Commencements and Oxford Acts, where Arminianism was subjected to attack.[15] In addition, the trial and execution of Oldenbarnevelt gave rise in England to a considerable literature. Much of this was translated from the Dutch and helped to popularize the term 'Arminian'.[16] When the case was raised in the Commons, in 1624, John Pym

---

[10] Ibid., 1. 68, 90.

[11] Ibid., 1. 5; PRO, SP 14/99, fo. 160.

[12] Cosin, *Correspondence*, 1. 165.

[13] *Sancti Gregorii Nazianzeni*, ed. Montagu, sig. ¶4ᵛ. Overall also is mentioned in the notes. *Notae*, sig. a.3.

[14] Cosin, *Correspondence*, 1. 56.

[15] See above pp. 46, 72–4.

[16] The outstanding example is *Barnevel's Apology* (1618), where the term Arminian is used more than thirty times.

described *A New Gagg* as containing 'dangerous opinions of Arminius, quite contrary to the articles established, in five several points'.[17] The reference to *five* points appears to be to the canons of Dort. Again, in 1625, one of the charges against Montagu was that 'he labors so much to uphold the opinion of Arminianesme, which the Kinge [James I] labored so much to suppresse'.[18] The same definition of Arminianism, in terms of the doctrine condemned by the Synod of Dort, recurs during the parliamentary debates of 1626 and 1628–9.[19]

Throughout the four parliaments between 1624 and 1629 there was probably a Calvinist majority in the Commons. Although there is no direct evidence for 1624 or 1625, since the question was not put to the vote, Pym's statement for 1625 that 'the waight both of number and reasons were on the other [Calvinist] side'[20] and the recorded votes of 1626 and 1629 seem sufficient testimony. On 29 April 1626 it was resolved, by question, that 'Mountague is guiltie of publishinge doc- tryne contrarie to the Articles of the Religion established in the Churche of England'. This contrary doctrine included falling from grace.[21] There was a similar resolution on 29 January 1629, that

we the Commons now in Parliament assembled do claim, profess, and avow for truth, the sense of the Articles of Religion which were established in parliament in the 13th. year of Queen Elizabeth, which by the public acts of the Church of England, and by the gen- eral and current exposition of the writers of our Church, hath been delivered unto us. And we reject the sense of the Jesuits and the Arminians, wherein they do differ from us.[22]

The report drawn up by the committee for religion, on 23 Feb- ruary 1629, illustrated 'the general and current exposition' of the Thirty-nine Articles by citing the Lambeth Articles of 1595 and the judgement of the British divines at Dort.[23]

According to S. R. Gardiner, the opinions of Montagu 'had

[17] *Commons Journals*, i. 788.
[18] *Commons Debates, 1625*, p. 48.
[19] Ibid., p. 183; *Commons Debates for 1629*, p. 99. Cf. H. Schwartz, 'Arminianism and the English Parliament, 1624–1629', *JBS* 12/2 (1973), 46–57.
[20] *Commons Debates, 1625*, p. 52.
[21] PRO, SP 16/25, fos. 10ᵛ, 115.
[22] *Commons Debates for 1629*, p. 23.
[23] Ibid., p. 99.

made but little way amongst the lawyers and country gentlemen—the two most conservative classes in the nation—of
whom the House was mainly composed'.[24] This, however,
could be taken to point a sharper contrast between clergy and
laity than Gardiner intended, for he added elsewhere that
Montagu's views 'were those of a minority among the clergy,
and of a still smaller minority among the laity'.[25] There are
indeed grounds for thinking that at this date the majority
viewpoint of the Commons was fairly representative of the
clergy as a whole.[26] Such difference as there was in the relative
support that Arminianism received from clergy and laity is
probably to be explained by the higher proportion of university graduates among the former. In the 1624 House of
Commons, out of the 485 members for English and Welsh
constituencies 269 are known to have attended university, of
whom the large majority had been at Oxford.[27] Of these 269
Commons members whose names occur in the university
records, 88 had proceeded to a degree and there the predomi-
nance of Oxford was even more marked than in the total
attendance figures.[28] Two facts call for comment. The first is
that, whereas in the 1620s well over half of the clergy in England and Wales possessed a first degree,[29] only a sixth of the
MPs for English and Welsh constituencies in 1624 were so
qualified. Secondly, the dominance of Oxford may be important, given that its ethos appears to have been more uniformly
Calvinist than that of Cambridge. Less tangible but also
important is the question of curriculum emphasis while at university, for presumably students who intended to become
clergymen would be more alive to theological questions than
those planning other careers.

Clearly the MP who had sat in successive parliaments, from
1624 to 1629, would be in a better position to know the facts of

[24] S. R. Gardiner, *History of England, 1603–1642* (1896), v. 355.
[25] *DNB*, s.n. Laud, William.
[26] The doctrinal issues raised by Montagu's writings were never allowed to come to
a vote in convocation. But as late as February 1629 Bishop Davenant was convinced
that a majority would support the doctrines of unconditional predestination and final
perseverance, against Montagu. Bodleian, MS Tanner 72, fo. 310.
[27] 166 Oxford and 103 Cambridge students.
[28] 58 Oxford and 30 Cambridge BAs.
[29] M. H. Curtis, 'The Alienated Intellectuals of Early Stuart England', *Past and
Present*, 23 (1962), 32–3.

the Montagu case than one arriving at Westminster for the first time. Of the 485 members who sat in 1624, 136 were to be returned to the three following parliaments in 1625, 1626, and 1628.[30] While it is not possible to give a precise answer to the question of just how well-informed MPs in general were concerning Arminianism, we can distinguish a small group of anti-Arminian or Calvinist activists in the discussions on doctrinal matters. Their advocacy was apparently sufficient to secure a majority. Between 1624 and 1629, thirty-two such MPs are traceable. The number would no doubt be considerably larger if more record of discussions in committee had survived. Twenty-two of these activists had attended an English university, and thirteen had first degrees. This last figure, representing over a third, contrasts with the sixth of all MPs in 1624 who were university graduates. The difference, however, may merely indicate that graduates were more articulate than others. Again those with an Oxford attendance record predominated,[31] although the Cambridge minority consisted entirely of graduates. Perhaps more significant is that fourteen of the twenty-two had either graduated or left university before 1600, whereas out of all university-educated MPs in 1624 only some two-fifths are in this category.[32] It suggests that there may have been a difference of university generations between the anti-Arminians and the rest, with Elizabethans tending to defend a Calvinist interpretation of the Thirty-nine Articles during the 1620s. But the small numbers involved make it unwise to press this conclusion too far.

II

John Pym and Thomas Wentworth are the only Calvinist activists recorded for the 1624 parliament. If any one man can be said to have headed the anti-Arminian group from the start, it was Pym. His report from committee on 13 May 1624

---

[30] The figures in this and the previous paragraph were calculated from the following sources: *Return of Members of Parliament* (1878–91), pt. i. England, 1213–1702; Venn, *Alumni Cantabrigienses*, and Foster, *Alumni Oxonienses*. Where a by-election occurred, I have only included the new member in my analysis of the 1624 House of Commons.

[31] There were seventeen Oxonians, of whom at least seven were graduates.

[32] 107 out of 269.

was a conflation of the petition and accompanying doctrinal articles against Montagu.[33] During the three ensuing parliaments he was to chair committees, deliver reports to the Commons and draft charges for presentation to the House of Lords, all concerned with the Montagu case. Pym had matriculated from Broadgates Hall, Oxford, in 1599 and first entered parliament in 1621. His religious expertise probably owed something to the fact that his stepbrother, and fellow-MP from 1626 onwards, was Francis Rous, a theological writer and opponent of Arminianism.[34] Wentworth, in the wake of Pym's 1624 report, urged strong action against Montagu, and he further 'alleged that one that had preached the like . . . was made to recant'.[35] He most likely had in mind the recantation of Arminianism by Gabriel Bridges at Oxford the previous year,[36] which he would have known about as member and Recorder for the City of Oxford. Wentworth had matriculated from University College, Oxford, in 1584 and represented Oxford City in all the parliaments between 1604 and 1626.

From the 1625 parliament come the names of a further five Calvinist activists: Sir Heneage Finch, Laurence Whitaker, Francis Drake, Sir George and Sir Robert More. It was Finch who, on 7 July, presented to the Commons the first full committee report on Montagu's writings.[37] A lawyer, he had graduated from Trinity College, Cambridge, in 1596 and initially entered parliament in 1607 as the result of a by-election. He sat in each save the last parliament of the 1620s, and in 1626 was Speaker. His father's chaplain, Edward Simpson, had been accused of Arminianism in 1617 and ordered to preach a recantation sermon.[38] Finch was an undergraduate at the time of the Cambridge predestinarian disputes of the 1590s, which makes it all the more interesting that during the discussion of his 1625 report Laurence Whitaker 'remembered' the case of William Barrett, and his recantation at Cambridge, in 1595, of views similar to those of Montagu.[39]

[33] *Commons Journals*, i. 788.
[34] See below, pp. 134–5.
[35] BL Add MS 18597, fo. 182.
[36] OU Arch., Reg. N.23, fos. 157ᵛ–8.   [37] *Commons Debates, 1625*, pp. 47–51.
[38] See above, pp. 42–3 and *DNB*, s.n. Simpson, Edward.
[39] *Commons Debates, 1625*, p. 52.

Whitaker had also been a Cambridge contemporary, and graduated from St John's College in 1597.[40] The parliament of 1624 had been his first, and he was returned again in 1626 and 1628. During the second session of the 1625 parliament, on 2 August, Francis Drake described Arminianism as 'contrary [to] the Articles of the Church of England', and also invoked the Calvinist synods of Dort and Charenton.[41] On the same occasion, Sir George More, helped out by a theological exposition on grace from his son, Sir Robert, was listed as 'accordant' with Drake.[42] This was Drake's second parliament; he had sat the previous year, and probably matriculated from New College, Oxford in 1593. Drake was elected again in 1626 and in 1628. Sir George More, who had graduated from Corpus Christi College, Oxford, in 1572, was a member as early as 1584; Sir Robert had graduated from University College, Oxford, in 1598 and first entered parliament in 1601. Both Mores had sat in the 1624 parliament, but that of 1625 was Sir Robert's last and his father was only elected once more, in 1626.

Three new opponents of Arminiansm in the 1626 parliament were Henry Sherfield, Christoper Sherland, and Sir Thomas Fanshaw. Sherfield claimed that Montagu's books dishonoured the memory of King James, whose representatives had condemned Arminianism at the Synod of Dort, and that they were furthermore 'seditious as tending to bring the King [Charles] in dislike with his best subjects'. At the same committee meeting on 6 March, Sherland quoted a discussion he had had with Bishop Morton of Coventry and Lichfield, who told him 'he would sooner dye than hold some of his [Montagu's] opinions'.[43] Sherfield and Sherland were both lawyers and neither had been to university. Sherfield sat in all the parliaments of the 1620s and Sherland in all from 1624. Fanshaw's speech in 1626 dates from a few days before the

[40] I have identified 'Mr Whitaker' as Laurence rather than William, also an MP, because of his acquaintance with the Barrett case of thirty years earlier.

[41] *Commons Debates, 1625*, p. 71.

[42] *Commons Journals*, I. 810; *Commons Debates, 1625*, p. 71. S. R. Gardiner assumed that Sir Robert was an Arminian, but there is no sign of a clash of opinion with his father, and if the speech had been understood as a defence of Montagu it would certainly have called forth comment. Gardiner, *History*, v. 400. Details of Sir George More's university career have been supplied by Dr A. Davidson. Clark, *Register*, p. 14 and *HMC Seventh Report*, pp. 622b, 625a.   [43] CUL MS D.d. 12/20. fos. 19–20.

dissolution of parliament, and was made on 12 June. 'Our religion is att stake', he said, and 'I am glad to heare that the Arminians shall be by proclamation cried downe.'[44] That events turned out differently need not detract from the genuineness of his sentiments. Fanshaw had graduated from Queens' College, Cambridge, in 1596, and sat in parliament as early as 1601. He was elected to all the parliaments of the 1620s.

Most names of Calvinist activists, however, derive from the parliament of 1628–9. During the 1628 session eight speakers are now known explicitly to have condemned Arminianism. These were Sir Nathaniel Rich, Sir Robert Harley, Sir Henry Mildmay, Sir Edward Giles, Sir William Beecher, Richard Knightley, Walter Long, and Sir John Jackson. Thus, on 24 March, Rich, Harley, and Mildmay between them extended the attack from Montagu to Thomas Jackson and other suspected Arminians. 'The complaints against Montagu, let them be brought in,' said Rich; 'three parliaments have condemned his books.' Harley wanted to 'add another to Montagu, no less dangerous. 'Tis one Doctor Jackson.' Mildmay complained generally of 'a new faction' of Montaguists.[45] Both Rich and Mildmay had been at Emmanuel College, Cambridge, Rich graduating in 1605 and Mildmay in 1612. Rich sat in all the parliaments from 1614 to 1629, and Mildmay throughout the parliaments of the 1620s save that of 1626. Harley had graduated from Oriel College, Oxford, in 1599, and first entered parliament in 1604. He was not elected again until 1624, and sat thereafter in 1626 and 1628–9. As early as 1617, however, Harley had corresponded with the future Lord Herbert of Cherbury about questions of free will and predestination. He had been shocked by the anti-Calvinist stance of Herbert, who had communicated to him some of the views later reiterated in his book *De Veritate*.[46]

Towards the end of the 1628 session, on 3 June, Sir Edward Giles can be found exclaiming that 'the honor of God is now at he stake. Good men, how they are disrespected! And

[44] CUL MS D.d. 12/22, fo. 52ᵛ.   [45] *Commons Debates, 1628*, II. 85–6, 93.
[46] HMC Portland, III. 8–10; Lord Herbert of Cherbury, *De Veritate*, tr. M. H. Carré (Bristol, 1937), pp. 136–7, 164, 299–300. This book was first published at Paris in 1624. An English edition appeared in 1633.

Arminians, in what respect are they?'[47] He had matriculated from Exeter College, Oxford, in 1583. Giles was first elected in 1597 and sat in all the parliaments of the 1620s except for 1626. Three days later, Sir William Beecher and Richard Knightley added their voices to the anti-Arminian chorus. Beecher wanted an investigation of 'growing Arminianism', by 'some unsuspected provincial synod', and Knightly complained that 'none but Arminians can be preferred'.[48] Beecher is probably to be identified with his namesake who graduated from Corpus Christi College, Oxford, in 1597. He sat in parliament as early as 1614 and was a member throughout the 1620s. Knightley, who had not been to university, sat in all the parliaments of the 1620s save that of 1626. Then on 14 June 1628, Walter Long successfully moved that in their Remonstrance the Commons should name Bishops Neile and Laud as 'Arminians'. Among those speaking in support of this was Sir John Jackson, who said that as Bishop of Durham Neile had 'poisoned the whole see' with Arminian appointments.[49] Long had sat in the two previous parliaments, but had not attended university. Jackson had graduated from Magdalen Hall, Oxford, in 1615, and had sat in all the parliaments since 1624.

In the course of the 1629 session of parliament fourteen more anti-Arminians can be identified: Francis Rous, Edward Kirton, Sir Robert Phelips, Sir Walter Earle, Sir Benjamin Rudyerd, Sir John Eliot, William Coryton, Sir Thomas Hoby, Sir Francis Seymour, Sir James Perrott, Sir Dudley Digges, Henry Waller, Sir Miles Fleetwood, and Sir Richard Grosvenor. On 26 January Rous inaugurated the attack on Arminianism with a remarkable harangue. Referring to alleged infringements of the Petition of Right, he said

there is a right of an higher nature, that preserves for us far greater things, eternal life, our souls, yea our God himself; a right of religion

---

[47] *Commons Debates, 1628*, IV. 66. Giles is an addition to the list of anti-Arminian speakers in C. Russell, *Parliaments and English Politics, 1621–1625* (Oxford, 1979), p. 435.

[48] *Commons Debates, 1628*, IV. 157, 169. The ascription of this speech to Beecher, rather than to Sir Francis Annesley, corrects the list in Russell, *Parliaments*, p. 435. By 1640 Beecher was a suspected Roman Catholic. G. E. Aylmer, *The King's Servants. The Civil Service of Charles I, 1625–1642* (1961), p. 232.

[49] *Commons Debates, 1628*, IV. 320–1. Jackson is also an addition to the list in Russell, *Parliaments*, p. 435.

derived to us from the King of Kings, conferred upon us by the King of this Kingdom, enacted by laws in this place, streaming down to us in the book of the martyrs, and witnessed from Heaven by miracles, even by miraculous deliverances.

Appealing here to memories of the Armada and Gunpowder Plot, he described Arminianism as 'this Trojan horse' which threatened to overthrow both religion and liberty.[50] Rous had graduated from Broadgates Hall, Oxford, in 1597 and thereafter spent some time at Leiden University.[51] This Dutch period may have sparked off his longstanding hostility to Arminian teachings. He first entered parliament in 1626, and the same year published his treatise *Testis Veritatis*, which sought to demonstrate the Calvinism of King James, the English Church, and true Christianity in general. His oration of January 1629 was a distillation of the earlier book. Rous was followed by a number of speakers in the same vein. Edward Kirton explained Arminianism in terms of crypto-papist clerical ambition—'the highest dignity that they can attain unto here in England is an archbishopric, but a cardinal's cap is not here to be had'[52]—while Sir Robert Phelips blamed it for driving God out of England. 'I desire therefore', Phelips concluded, 'that we may humble ourselves before God by fasting and prayer, that we may bring him again into England . . . to go before our armies, that God may crown our actions and bless our counsels.'[53] Neither Kirton nor Phelips had been to university. Kirton sat in all the parliaments of the 1620s and Phelips in every parliament from 1604 onwards, apart from that of 1626.

Discussion about Arminianism was reopened on 27 January 1629 by Sir Walter Earle, arguing that religion should take precedency over all other matters. He spoke of 'Popery and Arminianism, joining hand in hand', and the 'truths established by laws, confirmed by synods national and provincial, [which] have been called in question'.[54] Two days later Sir Benjamin Rudyerd suggested that the Lambeth Articles be

[50] *Commons Debates for 1629*, pp. 12–13.
[51] E. Peacock, *Index to English Speaking Students who have graduated at Leiden University* (1883), p. 85.
[52] *Commons Debates for 1629*, p. 15.
[53] Ibid., p. 16.
[54] Ibid., pp. 18–19.

used as a test of orthodoxy,[55] and Sir John Eliot elaborated on the need for such a yardstick to be established by parliament.[56] All three men had matriculated at Oxford University, Rudyerd from St John's College in 1588, Earle from Queen's College in 1602 and Eliot from Exeter College in 1607. Rudyerd and Earle sat in all the parliaments of the 1620s and Eliot in those from 1624 onwards. Both Earle and Eliot had first sat in 1614.

The definition of orthodoxy was again considered on 3 February, and the Arminians were accused of misinterpreting the Church of England's teaching. William Coryton complained that 'the truth' enshrined in doctrinal statements like the Lambeth Articles had been suppressed.[57] Sir Thomas Hoby singled out Richard Montagu, now a bishop, as an arch offender in this matter of religious misinterpretation, and Sir Francis Seymour recommended that Montagu's book *Appello Caesarem* be burnt as an earnest of royal intentions.[58] Sir James Perrott reported the words of one of Bishop Laud's chaplains as being 'what the Arminians hold and write, this I will maintain and do believe',[59] and Sir Dudley Digges wanted such heterodox teachers brought to justice.[60] Neither Coryton nor Seymour had been to university, and both sat in four out of the five parliaments in the 1620s. The others had been at Oxford University, Hoby matriculating in 1574 from Trinity College, Perrott matriculating in 1586 from Jesus College, and Digges graduating in 1601 from University College. Hoby had first been an MP in 1589, and sat in all the parliaments of the 1620s. So did Digges, who initially was returned at a by-election in 1610. Between 1604 and 1629, Perrott sat in all the parliaments save that of 1625.

Two additional names of Calvinist activists derive from the record of discussion of 11 February. Henry Waller, an MP for London, presented a petition on behalf of the booksellers and printers, about the 'restraint of books written against Popery

---

[55] Ibid., p. 116.
[56] Ibid., pp. 24–8.
[57] Ibid., pp. 34–5, 121–2.
[58] Ibid., p. 122.
[59] Ibid., p. 35. The chaplain in question was said to be 'one Bayliff'. Ibid., p. 122. The most likely candidate is Richard Baylie. See below, p. 183.
[60] *Commons Debates for 1629*, p. 122.

and Arminianism, and the contrary allowed of by the only means of the Bishop of London [Laud]'.[61] On the same occasion Sir Miles Fleetwood rehearsed the charges against Richard Montagu chief of the 'Arminian sectaryes'.[62] Lastly, Sir Richard Grosvenor made a long speech about religious grievances on 13 February. He deplored the promotion of Arminians, like Montagu, to the episcopate, 'as if the ready way to obtain a bishopric now were to undermine religion, and to set the Church in combustion'.[63]This was Waller's only parliament and he had not been to university. Fleetwood, who had not attended university either, sat in all the parliaments from 1614 to 1628–9. Grosvenor graduated from Queen's College, Oxford, in 1602 and was elected to the parliaments of 1621, 1626, and 1628–9.

III

Of these thirty-two anti-Arminians at least eight were office-holders,[64] which is consistent with the view that Calvinism had been establishment orthodoxy but was now under threat. Given, however, the equation, by Richard Montagu, of Calvinism with Puritanism it is pertinent to ask whether such a religious correlation existed. Probably the most accurate indication, at this date, of whether or not an MP was a Puritan is his attitude towards clerical subscription. In the three parliaments of 1625, 1626, and 1628–9 bills were introduced which sought to limit the subscription required of the clergy, to those of the Thirty-nine Articles 'which only concerned the confession of the true Christian faith and the doctrine of the sacraments'.[65] Similar attempts had been made before the 1620s, and the proposed measure catered for those clergy with scruples either about the Prayer Book or the actual institution of episcopacy. A very full record of the debates on this topic survives for 1628. Out of the twenty-seven known opponents

---

[61] Ibid., p. 58.
[62] Ibid., p. 193.
[63] Ibid., p. 68.
[64] Aylmer, *King's Servants*, pp. 352–4. These eight are William Coryton, Sir Thomas Fanshaw, Sir Miles Fleetwood, Sir Robert Harley, Sir Henry Mildmay, John Pym, Sir Benjamin Rudyard, and Laurence Whitaker.
[65] Russell, *Parliaments*, pp. 231, 307; *Commons Debates, 1628*, III. 459.

of Arminianism present during the session, no less than eight spoke in favour of some modification of clerical subscription.[66] This was out of a total of twelve recorded favourers of the bill, and it certainly lends plausibility to the Arminian notion of 'doctrinal' Puritanism. On the other hand, shared Calvinist views had not in the past prevented bishops prosecuting Puritan nonconformists. Here it is significant that of the office-holders only one, John Pym, is known to have supported modifying the form of clerical subscription. The novelty of the situation during the 1620s was the retreat from Calvinism by the ecclesiastical hierarchy and the concomitant vogue for labelling these views as Puritan. Hence the anguished comment in 1628 by Bishop Davenant. Writing to Samuel Ward, like him a former delegate to the Synod of Dort, he exclaimed

> why that should now be esteemed Puritane doctrine, which those held who have done our church the greatest service in beating down Puritanisme, or why men should bee restrained from teaching that doctrine hereafter, which hitherto has been generally and publiquely maintained, wiser men perhaps may but I cannot understand.[67]

The overlapping, however, between Calvinism and Puritanism in the parliaments of the 1620s serves to emphasize the importance of religious motivation among lay opponents of Arminianism. Some of the ideas at work here can be discovered from the contemporary published writings of Francis Rous. For Rous, who was intellectually close to his stepbrother Pym, has some claim to be regarded as an ideological spokesman, at this time, for the Calvinist gentry. The younger son of a Cornish knight and originally intended for a legal career, he had experienced a religious conversion when, as he put it, 'a storm from heaven chased me away to the study of eternity'.[68] The fruits of that study began to appear in print from 1616 onwards. His first book, *Meditations*, was characteristically dedicated to 'the right noble, the sons of the most high, his blessed brethren by the best, that is the sec-

---

[66] Ibid., III. 513–22. These eight are Sir Walter Earle, Sir Thomas Hoby, Walter Long, Sir James Perrott, John Pym, Sir Nathaniel Rich, Francis Rous, and Christopher Sherland.

[67] Bodleian, Tanner MS 72, fo. 298.

[68] Francis Rous, *Treatises and Meditations* (1657) [sig. A4ᵛ]. The general preface to this collected edition speaks of Pym and Rous as being 'enter-woven' by 'many bands of alliance, coeducation and intimate conversation' [sig. A3ᵛ].

ond birth'.[69] This and his second book, *The Art of Happiness*, published in 1619, are written from the standpoint of someone who has forsworn worldly ambition. Careerism is criticized by him as a stumbling-block to salvation, and he complains that nowadays the 'true saint is called a Puritan'.[70] Rous, however, was no advocate of monastic withdrawal. 'Contemplation must not end in itself, but it must proceed, and the due proceeding of it is to end in action.'[71]

In Rous's case action took the form of greater public involvement during the 1620s, first in his writing and then by entering parliament. His *Diseases of the Time* was published in 1622 with a dedication to Sir Benjamin Rudyerd, an intimate of the third Earl of Pembroke. Next year came *Oyl of Scorpions*. Rous now sees his role as 'interpreter to the people' of the 'miseries of these times'.[72] Sin, in his view, is the root cause of contemporary disasters; plague, poverty, harvest failure, and trade recession, all are divine punishments. Collective repentance is the only cure. Four years later, in 1627, and via a treatise on predestination, appeared his pamphlet *The Only Remedy*. God's wrath is still unassuaged, domestic sores continue to fester and the Protestant cause in Europe goes from bad to worse. The explanation which increasingly suggested itself to Rous was that of national apostasy; by way of Arminianism, England was selling out to 'Romish tyranny and Spanish monarchy'. Thus Rous urged his fellow-MPs in January 1629 to 'consider the times past, how we flourished in honour and abundance, but as religion decayed so the honour and strength of this nation decayed; when the soul of a commonwealth is dead, the body cannot long overlive it'.[73] Many of his colleagues were by then voicing similar sentiments, on the eve of a decade when both parliament and Calvinism would be in abeyance.

IV

While at least the Calvinist leaders in the House of Commons can be identified, the minority support for Arminianism is

---

[69] Ibid., p. 489.   [70] Ibid., p. 572.
[71] Ibid., p. 147.   [72] Ibid. [p. 217].
[73] *Commons Debates for 1629*, p. 13; Francis Rous, *Testis Veritatis* (1626), pp. 106–7.

more elusive. Such supporters, who are again best studied in the context of the Montagu controversy, consisted of some Buckinghamites, genuine Arminians, and those with Catholic leanings. The behaviour of the first group reflected the policy of the Duke of Buckingham. In February 1626 Buckingham had emerged as Richard Montagu's defender at the York House Conference.[74] By March, however, the Duke, now threatened with impeachment proceedings by the Commons, was eager to dissociate himself from the Arminians. At this time a member of the committee for religion wrote to Montagu that Buckingham 'hath by his friends disavowed you and your books and doctrine in open parlement'.[75] This implies the existence of religious chameleons ready to change colour with their patron. The only traceable name in the 1626 parliament is that of Sir Miles Fleetwood, who reported Buckingham's abhorrence of Arminianism.[76] Yet Fleetwood can be found personally attacking Montagu's doctrines in 1629, some months after the death of the Duke, which suggests that his Calvinist sentiments were genuine.[77] Similarly Sir John Finch who defended Buckingham's religious orthodoxy in 1628 seems to have been a convinced Calvinist.[78]

Indeed the line between policy and belief in the rightness or wrongness of the Arminian cause was probably often unclear. Richard Dyott, who sat in all the parliaments of the 1620s, was, for instance, both a supporter of Buckingham and an Arminian. A lawyer, he had graduated from Corpus Christi College, Oxford, in 1607. On 7 July 1625, as member for Lichfield, he defended Montagu's doctrine as 'populer and most common and not yet condemned by the Church of England'.[79] During the next parliament, on 9 May 1626, he was 'sequestered' from the Commons for criticizing their proceedings against Buckingham.[80] Although Dyott also sat in the 1628–9 parliament, there is no record of a further defence by him of Arminianism. But in the privacy of a notebook he confided the view that 'there be doctrinal Puritans, as well as disciplinarians'.[81] This was precisely the argument of the

[74] Cosin, *Works*, II. 22.　　　　　　　　　　[75] Cosin, *Correspondence*, I. 89.
[76] CUL MS D.d. 12/20, fo. 85.　　　[77] *Commons Debates for 1629*, pp. 193–4.
[78] *Commons Debates, 1628*, IV. 256, VI. 136.　　　[79] *Commons Debates, 1625*, p. 52.
[80] *Commons Journals*, I. 858; CUL MS D.d. 12/20, fos. 178ᵛ, 183ᵛ.
[81] Staffs. RO, MS D. 661/11/1/7, p. 86.

Arminian Richard Montagu and his clerical adherents, who
redefined Puritanism so as to include Calvinist teachings on
predestination and thus discredit their opponents.

Thanks to the survival of a Dyott family archive,[82] we can
answer a number of questions about the socio-economic
background of this particular representative of lay
Arminianism. Richard Dyott's grandfather John, Bailiff of
Lichfield, had been granted arms in 1563,[83] and the family
wealth derived from a combination of the legal profession and
farming. Anthony Dyott, father of Richard, was a practising
barrister, but it is clear from an estate valuation that he was
also a farmer who produced grain, meat, and wool, some at
least for the market. He believed, moreover, in agricultural
improvement 'by inclosure and lymyng', and 'mucke a good
deal'.[84] Regarding more general economic attitudes, his son
Richard noted that, although 'tillage sett many on worke, and
2 or 3 shepheards will keepe numbers of sheep, yet it is to be
considered wooll [also] sets many on worke, as spinner, car-
der, weaver, clothier, carryer, merchant etc., for many depend
on wooll'.[85] Such arguments, it has been said, 'involved a
'revolution' in thinking, whereby 'the ploughman was
dethroned'.[86] Richard Dyott became head of the family on his
father's death in 1622 and concentrated thereafter on a legal
career.[87] During the 1630s he was appointed to the Council of
the North, and in 1635 was knighted.[88] By this date he had
leased out most of his land.[89] All three generations chose to
reside in Lichfield.[90]

Richard Dyott's religious opinions were most likely
acquired while at Corpus Christi College, Oxford. He had

[82] I am very grateful for their help to the present Dyott family and to the staff of the
Staffordshire Record Office, where the archive is now deposited.
[83] Staffs. RO, MS D. 661/1, no. 124; *Erdeswick's Survey of Staffordshire* ed. T. Har-
wood (1844), p. 306.
[84] Staffs. RO, MS D. 661/1, no. 44. For the agricultural importance of lime see Mr
Havinden's essay in *Rural Change and Urban Growth 1500–1800*, ed. C. W. Chalklin and
M. A. Havinden (1974), pp. 104–34.   [85] Staffs. RO, MS D. 661/11/1/7 [p. 9].
[86] J. Thirsk, *Economic Policy and Projects* (Oxford, 1978), pp. 147–8.
[87] For the date of Anthony Dyott's death, I follow the late Major R. A. Dyott. Family Bible, Freeford Manor, Lichfield.
[88] R. R. Reid, *The King's Council in the North* (1921), p. 253; Foster, *Alumni Oxonienses*,
i. 439.
[89] Staffs. RO, MS D. 661/1, no. 139.
[90] *Erdeswick's Survey*, p. 306.

been an undergraduate at a time when at least one of the college fellows, Thomas Jackson, was beginning to formulate anti-Calvinist views, and his notebook contains a passage on free will which may well derive from Jackson. The entry concerns the maltreatment of the Israelities by Pharaoh and God's vengeance, as related in the book of Exodus, which was a favourite illustration with Jackson when discussing the predestinarian question. Dyott notes that

God is said to have hardened Pharaoh's heart (Exodus 7) and Pharaoh himself is said to have hardened it (Exodus 8) . . . God by withholding, in justice, his grace from Pharoah, whoe had offended him by contempt of his divine majestie and oppression of his people, in despight of his commandment (Exodus 5); Pharaoh by reiteration and continuance of his sin, until his heart was obdurate. See what plagues God sent, and at the prayer of Moses removed, and yet [Pharaoh] relapsed or persisted.[91]

Richard Dyott also records an anecdote concerning John Overall, Bishop of Coventry and Lichfield from 1614 to 1618, who 'when Calvin's *Institutions* were cited in disputation before him would say "why cite you Calvin? I have studied divinity more yeares than he was yeares of age when he wrote his *Institutions*"'.[92] As for Dyott's politics, these have to be inferred from his actions. We have already noticed his intervention in 1626 on behalf of Buckingham, and when it came to the Civil War in 1642 Dyott helped to organize the defence of Lichfield for King Charles. It was his deaf-mute brother John—'Dumb Dyott'—sniping from the cathedral spire, who shot dead the Puritan Lord Brooke during the subsequent siege.[93] Sir Richard Dyott lived on until 1660, but in reduced financial circumstances due to war losses and sequestration.[94] A modern to the last, he bequeathed thirty pounds to the bailiffs of Lichfield to buy 'a brasse engine for the quenching of houses that are on fire'.[95]

[91] Staffs. RO, MS D. 661/11/1/7 [p. 236].

[92] Ibid., p. 85.

[93] *The Heraldic Visitations of Staffordshire in 1614 and 1663–4*, ed. H. S. Grazebrooke (William Salt Archaeological Society 5/2, 1885), p. 118; S. Shaw, *The History and Antiquities of Staffordshire* (1798–1801), i. 237–8.

[94] Staffs. RO, MS D. 661/1, no. 33.

[95] A copy of Sir Richard Dyott's will is preserved at the Lichfield Joint Record Office, P/C/11, 16 April 1663.

Not until 1628 can another member of the House of Commons be found clearly speaking out in favour of Arminianism. This was Richard Spencer, second surviving son of the first Baron Spencer of Wormleighton and thus a scion of the most famous grazier family in England; in the course of the sixteenth century the Spencers had risen almost entirely on profits made from sheep-farming, and only in the 1630s did they 'reduce their flocks and lease out some of the pastures'.[96] An intervention by Richard Spencer, during a debate in the Commons on 14 June 1628, elicited the response from Sir Nathaniel Rich that he was 'sorry . . . any man here should speak in defence of Arminianism'.[97] Spencer had asked for proof that Bishops Neile and Laud were Arminians. Furthermore in the second session, on 29 January 1629, he claimed that the Lambeth Articles had been suppressed by authority and with them the Cambridge recantation of William Barrett. This had been one of Montagu's arguments in his book *Appello Caesarem*.[98] Spencer also said, in reply to the naming of Montagu and Jackson as Arminian authors, 'I desire and think it fit when any man is accused to name particulars in what part of his book he doth not conform himself to our reformed religion, for I think there be some that oppose that seek to bring in novel opinions'.[99] Like Dyott, Spencer was a graduate of Corpus Christi College, Oxford, although he had apparently stayed on for another two years to take his master's degree in 1614. We have already remarked the probable influence of Thomas Jackson on Dyott. In the case of Spencer probability becomes a virtual certainty, because Jackson was his tutor and actually dedicated a sermon about predestination to him and his brother Edward.[100] This dedication is dated 1619, although Jackson noted elsewhere that the sermon had been composed originally about the year 1612.[101] He begins his dedicatory remarks with the statement that 'there is no argument in divinity, wherein every soul that earnestly seeks salvation (or the avoidance of damnation) ought in reason to be

[96] M. E. Finch, *The Wealth of Five Northamptonshire Families, 1540–1640* (Northamptonshire Record Society, 19, 1956), p. 48.

[97] *Commons Debates, 1628*, IV. 321.

[98] *Commons Debates for 1629*, p. 117; Montagu, *Appello Caesarem*, p. 71.

[99] HMC Thirteenth Report, VII. 66.

[100] Jackson, *Works*, I. xlii, IX. 504–8.   [101] Ibid., VIII. 256.

more desirous of satisfaction, than in the point of eternal election and reprobation'. Jackson compares himself to those astronomers who seek a 'middle way' between Ptolemy and Copernicus.[102] Most of the sermon is taken up with Pharaoh's case and rebutting the idea of absolute reprobation; 'during all this progress from bad to worse, the immediate object of God's immutable and irresistible will was mutability in Pharaoh. But this progress, which was not necessary by any eternal decree or law, being *de facto* once accomplished his destruction was inevitable'.[103] The Arminians Spencer and Dyott also opposed any modification of clerical subscription, out of a total of seven speakers to this effect in 1628.[104]

Richard Spencer sat in all the parliaments of the 1620s for Northampton. His fellow-MP for this borough from 1624 onwards was Christopher Sherland, a leading opponent of Arminianism. In June 1626 Spencer had argued in favour of political moderation, urging that the subsidy bill take precedence over any declaration against Buckingham.[105] The previous month it was reported that the 'Lord Spencer's second son [Richard] has byn lately sworne of the Bed Chamber which has drawn a party to the Duke's side in both Houses'.[106] In July 1628 Richard Spencer was nominated as Ambassador to the United Provinces, but for reasons which are unclear never took up the appointment.[107] On the eve of the Civil War he featured prominently among royalists in Kent, and subsequently helped raise two regiments of horse on behalf of King Charles.[108] Spencer's Kentish connections derived from his marrying in 1628 Mary Sandys, daughter of Sir Edwin Sandys, and he thereafter resided at Orpington.[109] By this marriage Spencer allied himself to one of the prominent figures in England's early colonial trade.[110] The same year saw the publication of some verses commemorating his recently

---

[102] Ibid., IX. 504–5.   [103] Ibid., IX. 486.

[104] *Commons Debates, 1628*, III. 455, 521.

[105] CUL, MS D.d. 12/22, fo. 53.

[106] National Library of Wales, Wynn Papers, no. 1414. I owe this reference to Lady de Villiers.

[107] PRO, SP 38/14, fo. 167ᵛ.

[108] A. Everitt, *The Community of Kent and the Great Rebellion, 1640–60* (Leicester, 1966), pp. 95, 98–9; PRO, SP 29/13, fo. 23.

[109] Finch, *Five Northamptonshire Families*, pp. 58–9.

[110] T. K. Rabb, *Enterprize and Empire* (Cambridge, Mass., 1967), pp. 5–7.

deceased father, Baron Spencer. These verses conclude with an attack on the idea of the decay of nature and on those who praise the past at the expense of the present.

> Unthankfull world, which still imput'st the crimes
> Of thine owne folly to these latter times,
> As if all things were worse, and Nature's strength
> Were wasted so, that shee must sinke at length.
> If learned Hackewell have not chaung'd this thought,
> And prov'd 'tis not the time, but thou art nought.
> See an Heroicke, who I dare presage,
> Our sonnes will say, liv'd in a golden age.[111]

In 1627 George Hakewill, to whom the poet here refers, had published his *Apologie*, which comprised 'the first significant defence of modernity in England'.[112] Thus Richard Spencer and Richard Dyott, the two most thoroughgoing Arminians in the House of Commons during the 1620s, both turn out to have close capitalist and modernist links.[113]

Like his son-in-law Spencer, Sir Edwin Sandys was a graduate of Corpus Christi College, Oxford. In 1605 Sandys expressed in print views similar to those later called Arminian, referring to 'the rigor of certaine speculative opinions, especially touching the eternall decrees of God', which had 'exceedingly scandalized all other churches'. He wrote also of 'that doctrine, touching the eternall counsels of God, which Calvine (as some conceive) first reveiled or rather introduced into the world'.[114] Twenty years later, on 7 July 1625, he opposed the majority vote of the Commons that Montagu was guilty of 'contempt' for having published his book *Appello Caesarem*.[115] Sandys sat once more, in 1626, and his legalistic approach resembles that of John Selden, whom Montagu asked in 1626 to act as 'arbitrator'[116] between him and his parliamentary accusers. Selden had matriculated in 1600 from

[111] R. Parre, *The Ende of the Perfect Man* (Oxford, 1628), sig. E2. This sermon is dedicated to Richard Spencer's elder brother William.

[112] Jones, *Ancients and Moderns*, p. 29.

[113] I particularly have in mind here, by way of contrast, the school of thought epitomized by the writings of Dr C. Hill.

[114] Sir Edwin Sandys, *A Relation of the State of Religion* (1605), sigs. T1ᵛ–T2, Y4ᵛ. This work was suppressed at the time, for reasons that are unclear. T. K. Rabb, 'The Editions of Sir Edwin Sandys's Relation of the State of Religion', *Huntington Library Quarterly*, 26, (1962–3), 323–6.

[115] *Commons Journals*, 1. 805.

[116] Cosin, *Correspondence*, 1. 93.

Hart Hall, Oxford. He sat, for the first time, in the parliament of 1624 but missed that of 1625. From his posthumously published *Table Talk*, Selden seems to have been very critical of predestinarian teaching, speaking there, for example, of 'the Puritans who will allow noe free will, but God does all'.[117] During the 1629 debates Selden denied the binding force of the articles of Lambeth and Dort, as lacking in 'publique authority'.[118] He was to side against King Charles in the Civil War and his case is a reminder that Arminianism and royalism were not inseparable.

Other probable parliamentary supporters of Arminianism in the 1620s were Sir Robert Killigrew, Sir Thomas Lake, Nicholas Ferrar, Edward Dowse, and Christopher Brooke. Killigrew had been a patron of 'Dutch' Thomson, while Lake had opposed the holding of the Synod of Dort. Killigrew sat in all the parliaments of the 1620s and Lake in those of 1625 and 1626. In September 1625 Killigrew, like Richard Spencer three years later, was nominated Ambassador to the United Provinces,[119] which perhaps indicates pressure for a new Arminian orientation in foreign as well as domestic policy during these years. He had matriculated from Christ Church, Oxford, in 1591. Lake, by contrast, is not known to have attended university. Nicolas Ferrar had been the pupil of the Arminian Augustine Lindsell at Clare College, Cambridge, from which he graduated in 1610. He was also a great admirer of the works of the Arminian Thomas Jackson.[120] The parliament of 1624 is the only one in which he sat. Edward Dowse was a member of the Earl of Northumberland's household and personally acquainted with Montagu, who wrote of him in 1625 as 'one that will speake if need be'.[121] The parliament of 1625 was both his first and last during the 1620s. He had graduated in 1601 from Hart Hall, Oxford. Christopher Brooke was brother of the Arminian Samuel Brooke and on 7 July 1625 moved that a petition from Montagu be read in the Commons.[122] He sat in all the parliaments of the 1620s, except

---

[117] *Table Talk of John Selden*, ed. F. Pollock (1927), p. 49.

[118] *Commons Debates for 1629*, pp. 119–20.

[119] PRO, SP 38/13, fo. 132.

[120] *DNB*, s.n. Ferrar, Nicholas; Jackson, *Works*, i. pp. xxviii–xxix.

[121] Cosin, *Correspondence*, i. 73.

[122] *Commons Journals*, i. 805. Christopher Brooke was also on very close terms with

that of 1628–9, but had not apparently attended university. Some of these men are likely to have been among those whom Pym described, in July 1625, as 'insinuatinge, so farr as they durst, a defence of Mr. Mountague's doctrine'.[123]

A final source of possible support for Arminianism was the small group of Catholic sympathizers in the Commons. These members seem best comprehended under the contemporary title of Church Papist. They had to be outwardly conformist, and as such bad Catholics, even to contemplate standing for parliament. Their names are hard to come by, because of the necessarily clandestine nature of their beliefs. While it has been calculated that in the Long Parliament a maximum of fifteen members 'inclined towards Roman Catholicism',[124] for the 1620s no figure is available. It may be that members of this group would support Arminianism as less aggressively Protestant, and in the hope of long-term religious toleration for Catholicism. One case which suggests such a connection is that of Sir Thomas Riddell. He sat for Newcastle-upon-Tyne in 1621, 1625, and 1628–9, but had not attended an English university. In 1623 a trunk addressed to Riddell was intercepted at Dover and was reported to contain 'certen prohibited Jesuiticall smale bokes'.[125] Two years later his wife and eldest son are recorded as known recusants, although shortly thereafter the son converted to Protestantism.[126] Riddell senior's parliamentary candidature for Newcastle in 1624, on that occasion unsuccessful, had the support of the Arminian Bishop Neile but was opposed by local Calvinists.[127]

V

The original petition against Montagu, which Pym reported to the House of Commons from committee on 13 May 1624, has not survived. But a copy was published in 1626 by John

the Arminian John Donne. R. C. Bald, *John Donne: a life* (Oxford, 1970), pp. 500–1. For Donne, see below, pp. 182, 261.

[123] *Commons Debates, 1625*, p. 52.
[124] M. F. Keeler, *The Long Parliament, 1640–41* (Philadelphia, 1954), p. 13.
[125] PRO, SP 14/146, fo. 125.
[126] *Memoirs of . . . Ambrose Barnes*, ed. W. H. D. Longstaffe (Surtees Soc., 50, 1867), p. 310; A. Foster, 'A Biography of Archbishop Richard Neale, 1562–1640', Oxford D.Phil. thesis, 1978, p. 79.   [127] Bodleian, Tanner MS 73, fo. 437.

Yates, now lecturer at Norwich and one of the signatories. The petition runs as follows:

It is apparent unto the world how the erroneous and dangerous opinions of Arminius and his sectaries have infested, and had brought into great perill the states of the United Provinces, if the King's Majesty by his gracious care, power, piety and providence, had not helped to quench that fire. Notwithstanding, this dangerous doctrine and other erroneous opinions hath of late been hatched, and now begins to be more boldly maintained by some divines of this our kingdom, especially by one Mr. Richard Mountagu, who hath published a booke with shew of license by authority, full fraught with these opinions, tending to the great danger and disturbance of the true religion professed and established within this realme.

May it therefore please this most honourable assembly, out of their zeale to God's truth and care of the peace and welfare of the Church and Commonwealth, to take into their grave and godly considerations the representing unto His Majesty these greatly growing evils, that through his princely authority these sparkles of erroneous doctrine may timely be put out, and such order be taken with the authors that their infectious and corrupt doctrine may spread it selfe no further, and we may be freed from the perill that in other places they have produced.[128]

At approximately the same time as this petition was handed in to the Commons, so was a list or 'information' of twenty-one articles, detailing Montagu's supposed doctrinal errors. The information was distinct from the petition, and Yates subsequently denied all responsibility. Indeed, if Yates's recollections some fifteen years later are to be trusted, he first set eyes on the petition itself at a parliamentary committee, having been summoned as a witness in a case against Bishop Harsnett of Norwich.[129] A clue to the possible source of both petition and articles is provided by Montagu. Relating the events of 1624, he wrote that Thomas Goad and Daniel Featley were 'as apt as with Dr Hall of W[orcester] and Dr Prideaux, att first to informe or attend informations against

---

[128] Yates, *Ibis ad Caesarem*, iii. 45–6.

[129] BL Add MS 25278, fos. 127ᵛ, 136, 138ʳ⁻ᵛ. I owe this information to Dr K. Shipps, who has also pointed out that Yates's fellow-signatory to the petition was Nathaniel Ward and not Samuel Ward as is usually said. For evidence on this last point see PRO, SP 14/166, fo. 199.

me att parlement'.[130] This was an influential quartet number-
ing Archbishop Abbot's two chaplains, the Dean of Worcester
and the Oxford Regius Professor of Divinity. Their reported
behaviour suggests powerful clerical backing, even instiga-
tion, for the attack by the Commons on Montagu, and that *A
New Gagg* was clearly recognized by the Calvinists as a challenge to their hegemony.

No copy of the original articles against Montagu seems to
have survived, but they can be deduced from his second book,
Appello Caesarem, in which he answered his 'unjust informers'.
The charges were divided into the two categories of
Arminianism and Popery. As regards Montagu's
Arminianism, the evidence derived from his remarks in *A New
Gagg* concerning the doctrines of predestination and persever-
ance. He had there stated that the Church of England was
'opposed' to the teaching of 'some Protestants' that

> Peter was saved because that God would have him saved absolutely,
> and resolved to save him necessarily because hee would so and no
> further; that Judas was damned as necessarily because that God, as
> absolute to decree as omnipotent to effect, did primarily so resolve
> concerning him and so determine touching him, without respect of
> anything but his owne will. Insomuch that Peter could not perish
> though he would nor Judas be saved doo what he could.[131]

Montagu also claimed 'the learnedst in the Church of England' taught that justifying faith 'may be lost totally and
finally'.[132] His Popery consisted in such contentions as that
Rome was a true church and the Pope not demonstrably
Antichrist.[133] These articles, and the petition against Montagu, provided the basis of Pym's report on 13 May. The
Commons, however, 'after much debate and dislike of the
booke beinge soe offensive to the state, yet not willinge to
become judges in soe deepe points of religion', decided to refer
the matter to Archbishop Abbot.[134] This decision may well
have been part of a pre-arranged manœuvre, aimed at
strengthening the hand of the Archbishop against the newly

[130] Cosin, *Correspondence*, I. 50.
[131] Montagu, *A New Gagg*, p. 179.
[132] Ibid., p. 158.
[133] Ibid., pp. 50, 74–5.
[134] BL Harleian MS 159, fo. 120ʳ.

powerful Arminian faction at court—a case of Lambeth Palace versus Durham House. Certainly it looks significant that two of the five-man delegation sent to Abbot, by the Commons, had close connections with him. These were Sir Dudley Digges and Sir Robert Hatton, an intimate friend and his 'servant' respectively.[135] The delegation reported back on 19 May that Abbot 'returns great thanks to this House, for their great care, and will take such order in it as shall give this House satisfaction'.[136]

But by June 1625, when a new parliament met, the Archbishop had apparently done nothing and Montagu meanwhile had published a further book in his own defence. Probably it was envisaged originally that Abbot would make representations to King James about *A New Gagg*, and secure either its suppression or at least a more acceptable second edition. 'Amongst us at this day', wrote a contemporary pamphleteer, 'do we not all know that Arminianism would have much more prevailed and infected farther than yet it doth, if the King's Majesty were either for it or not against it?'[137] By 1625, however, such assumptions were less easily made. Montagu, in his second book, *Appello Caesarem*, claimed to have had King James's approval for his views.[138] Summoned before a Commons committee in July 1625, he asserted that both his books had been printed by the 'Kinge's warrant'.[139] Montagu sought to explain this apparent change of front by James in terms of *raison d'état*; it was not that the King's opinions had altered, but that political circumstances in 1618 had led him to support the Dutch Calvinists.[140] This was an over-simplification, as even those who agreed with Montagu's doctrines admitted. Writing at the Restoration, the Arminian Peter Heylyn saw the death of Bishop James Montagu of Winchester in 1618 as the removal of an important Calvinist influence

---

[135] John Rushworth, *Historical Collections* (1659–1701), i. 450–1; Bodleian, Rawlinson MS A.346, fo. 226. I owe these references to Dr A. Davidson and Professor C. Russell respectively. During the 1625 debates on subscription, both Digges and Hatton opposed any concessions to nonconformists. *Commons Debates, 1625*, p. 28.

[136] *Commons Journals*, i. 790.

[137] Thomas Bedford, *Luther's Predecessours* (1624), p. 27. I owe this reference to Professor Russell.

[138] Montagu, *Appello Caesarem*, sig. a3ʳ⁻ᵛ.

[139] *Commons Debates, 1625*, p. 46.

[140] Montagu, *Appello Caesarem*, pp. 41–2.

on King James.[141] For a time this role was partly filled by the Scottish John Young, Dean of Winchester, whose theology was of a similar brand to that of his late diocesan.[142] Nevertheless in the early 1620s other views came increasingly to bear on the King, especially those of Bishop Neile of Durham.

During 1624 Neile was entrusted by King James with handling the Montagu affair.[143] Francis White, Dean of Carlisle and a protégé of Neile, was assigned the task of reading *Appello Caesarem* in manuscript and his formal approbation appeared in the printed version.[144] The death of King James, however, occurred in March 1625, before the knowledge of his having patronized Montagu became generally available. Because of this posthumous element in Montagu's claim to have had royal approval, many of those concerned chose to believe that James had never ceased supporting the Calvinists. Daniel Featley, for instance, reported that a few months before his death the King was still equating Arminianism with Pelagian heresy, and the Commons in July 1625 accused Montagu of 'dishonouring' James's memory by contradicting his utterances and actions in connection with Arminianism.[145] But in private a more realistic attitude was adopted, especially as a result of Archbishop Abbot's inability to discipline Montagu. While the Archbishop was personally willing to take action against him, no effective royal backing had been forthcoming. He merely received permission to interview Montagu, and could do no more than 'advise' him to rewrite his book.[146] 'Remisness . . . by command' was how Sir John Eliot characterized Abbot's inertia.[147]

It was this failure to secure redress concerning Montagu, by reference to Archbishop Abbot, that seemingly led the Commons in 1625 to embark on judicial proceedings. Yet they still considered a further approach to Abbot worth making, while announcing, on 7 July, that they would proceed against Montagu by conference with the Lords during the next parliamentary session. The Archbishop was asked 'to take some such

---

[141] Heylyn, *Historia Quinqu-Articularis*, iii. 106.

[142] Hacket, *Scrinia Reserata*, i. 225.   [143] Cosin, *Correspondence*, i. 83–4.

[144] Montagu, *Appello Caesarem*, sig. A4ᵛ.

[145] Daniel Featley, *Cygnea Cantio* (1629), p. 32; *Commons Debates, 1625*, pp. 48–9.

[146] *Commons Debates, 1625*, pp. 34–5.

[147] Sir John Eliot, *An Apology for Socrates*, ed. A. B. Grosart (1881), i. 79.

course, as in his judgment he shall think fit, for the suppression of these books and preventing the danger that may grow
by the divulging thereof'.[148] At the same time the Commons
claimed the right themselves to punish Montagu for 'contempt' of their privileges, in that he had published a defence,
Appello Caesarem, when his case was still being considered by
parliament. As Sir Edward Coke put it, at the start of the second session, 'we meddle with him only for his contempt to this
House, whereof we have jurisdiction. We will not meddle ourselves alone with adjudging his tenets. Yet we may inform the
Lords, where the bishops are, and they are to judge it.'[149]
Much of this short-lived August meeting was in fact taken up
with debating the government request for a second subsidy,[150]
and the projected conference with the Lords, about the Montagu case, failed to materialize. The session did, however, see
an attempt to embody the canons promulgated by the Synod
of Dort in a parliamentary statute. A bill was apparently
introduced into the Commons entitled 'for the repressing and
preventing of haeresies and false doctrines'. The most likely
sponsor was Francis Drake.[151] Framed in the form of a petition
to King Charles, it sought to enact that the

determinations of the said Synode [of Dort], consisting of seventeene
articles positive and nine rejective or opposite, may stand and bee
likewise annexed, received, ratified and established within this your
said Kingdome, as part of the doctrine of the Church of England.
Against which it shall not, or may not bee, lawfull for any to preach,
write or print anything. But that such as shall so doe may bee censured as the impugners of the Church of England and disturbers of
the peace thereof.[152]

How this bill was received by the Commons in general is not
recorded, but it does not seem to have been reintroduced into
subsequent parliaments. The implication is that most members regarded the bill as an impractical measure. They were

[148] *Commons Journals*, 1. 805–6.
[149] Ibid., p. 809.
[150] Russell, *Parliaments*, pp. 238–59.
[151] *Commons Debates, 1625*, p. 71.
[152] *Anti-Montacutum: An Appeale or Remonstrance of the Orthodox Ministers of the Church of England against Richard Montagu* (1629), pp. 5–6. This is a collection of otherwise mainly familiar material against Montagu. It purports to be printed at Edinburgh, but is in fact a London production.

furthermore distracted in 1625 from dealing with Arminianism due to widespread fears of a general toleration of Catholicism,[153] in the wake of the Anglo-French marriage alliance.

When a new parliament assembled in February 1626, the issue which rapidly came to take precedence over all others was the attempted impeachment of the Duke of Buckingham.[154] Although a committee for religion was appointed on the fourth day of the meeting, this did not report the charges against Montagu until 17 April and claimed, somewhat disingenuously, to handle his teaching only so far as it tended to 'disturbe the peace of the Church and Commonwealth' (*sic*).[155] As regards Montagu's Arminianism, the committee fastened on the doctrine of perseverance. 'Whereas the article of the Church of England denieth the falleing from grace, Mr Mountigue affirmeth that men after grace received maie fall and rise againe.'[156] Perseverance was in many ways the Calvinist heart of the matter. As Bishop Carleton, who was Montagu's diocesan, commented, 'the question is whether they that are according to God's purpose predestinated, called and justified, may loose these graces of their predestination, calling and justification'. Carleton went on to say that 'these things are not, as this man [Montagu] in scorne calleth them, scholastical speculations. *They are the grounds of our salvation.*'[157] Parallel with the charge of Arminianism was the distinct but related one of Popery. Particular exception was taken to Montagu's claim that Rome was a true, although unsound, church.[158] Calvinists, by contrast, tended to define the true church in terms of the elect.[159]

On 17 April, after some debate, the Commons decided that Montagu should be given an opportunity to answer on his own behalf, and that members be allowed time to familiarize themselves with his works. Meanwhile Charles, like Buckingham, gave the impression at this time of relinquishing the

[153] Russell, *Parliaments*, pp. 206–8, 229–33, 248.
[154] Ibid., pp. 260–322.
[155] *Commons Journals*, I. 817; *Commons Debates, 1625*, p. 179.
[156] Ibid., p. 181.
[157] Carleton, *An Examination*, pp. 43, 117. My italics.
[158] *Commons Debates, 1625*, p. 180.
[159] For example George Abbot, *A Treatise of the Perpetuall Visibilitie and Succession of the True Church in All Ages* (1624), pp. 1–3, 20–2, 93–6.

Arminian cause. Having informed the Commons in July 1625 that Montagu was his 'servant', he now 'signified his dislike of Mr Mountagew his writings' and stated that he would refer them to convocation.[160] This did not, however, deflect the Commons from their course. On 29 April, Montagu having failed to appear, the House voted him guilty of publishing matter contrary to the doctrine of the Church of England. Discussion then ensued as to how the case was to be presented to the Lords. The committee for religion had recommended that five MPs handle the case, in five separate parts, by way of a conference. It was voted, however, that the complaint of the Commons should be delivered as a message at the bar of the Lords, 'beinge said to be the greatest busines that hath come into the House since *primo* Elizabeth'. John Pym was chosen as sole messenger, on the grounds that he was best informed about the case. He was given till 1 May to 'consider upon his notes, that he maie then signifie to the House when he can be readie'.[161] Over a month later, on 3 June, the message to the Lords was still being prepared by a sub-committee.[162] Only on 14 June were the articles against Montagu engrossed and even at this date, the day before the dissolution, the sub-committee had still to draw up 'proofs against Mountagew'.[163]

During these same last days of the 1626 parliament, an attempt was again made to deal with the problem of Arminianism in general, by way of legislation, when on 13 and 14 June a bill was read 'for the better continuing of peace and unity in the Church and Commonwealth'.[164] It was also a Calvinist riposte to the royal proclamation, dated 14 June, for the 'peace and quiet of the Church of England',[165] which in effect had opened the door to Arminianism. The bill, which was reintroduced into the 1628 parliament, aimed at giving joint statutory authority to the Thirty-nine Articles of 1563 and the Irish Articles of 1615. 'Whereas articles were made in Queene Elizabeth's time, and King James his time and sent into Ireland, now it is enacted that if any person or persons shall, by

---

[160] *Commons Journals*, i. 807, 847.
[161] PRO, SP 16/25, fos. 115^{r-v}.
[162] *Commons Journals*, i. 866.
[163] Ibid., p. 871.
[164] Ibid., pp. 870, 871.
[165] *Stuart Constitution*, ed. Kenyon, pp. 154–5.

1. The 'Good Shepherd' chalice, c.1615, St John's College, Oxford

2. Dean Hunt's altar, c.1620, Durham Cathedral

3. The Crucifixion, by Baptista Sutton, *c.* 1621, originally at Easton Lodge, Essex

The text within the stained glass reads:

The tr[u]th here of is historicall deuine and not su[pers]tiffious : · : Anno Domini · 1629 · ✱

4. The Deposition, by Abraham van Linge, 1629, originally at Hampton Court, Herefordshire

printing or preaching, set forth and mainteyne any doctrine contrary to the said articles they shall be in danger of a *praemunire*.'[166] Had this bill passed, the position of Montagu and the other English Arminians would have become untenable, since the Irish Articles incorporated the Calvinist Lambeth Articles of 1595.[167] According to the original printed edition, these Irish Articles had the assent of the Irish Convocation meeting at Dublin.[168] In 1625 the Commons claimed that they had been 'sent into Ireland, under the great seale of Englande',[169] and this was the assumption of the bills for 'peace and unity' in 1626 and 1628. It remains a mystery both what part King James played in framing the Irish Articles and how he subsequently regarded them. By 1626, however, King Charles was ignoring them when, in his proclamation for 'peace and quiet', he made the Thirty-nine Articles the only yardstick for orthodoxy in both England and Ireland.[170]

In the course of the 1626 parliament at least five books were published attacking Richard Montagu as an Arminian.[171] Aimed at an educated English readership, they all define Arminianism in terms of the doctrines condemned by the Synod of Dort. Most authoritative was the reply by Bishop Carleton, who had headed the British delegation at Dort. According to Carleton, Montagu 'hath with confidence delivered the doctrines of the Pelagians and Arminians for the doctrines of the Church of England'. First, 'in the doctrine of predestination he attempteth to bring in a decree respective' claiming 'that God's will heerein is directed by somewhat fore-seene in men'.[172] Secondly, Montagu maintains 'that a justified man may fall away totally and finally'.[173] Carleton also denies the historical accuracy of Montagu's use of the

---

[166] *Commons Debates, 1628*, II. 324.

[167] The making of the Irish Articles is traditionally ascribed to Archbishop Ussher. R. B. Knox, *James Ussher, Archbishop of Armagh* (Cardiff, 1967), pp. 16–18. The 1629 edition of the Irish Articles indicates those in which 'are comprehended, almost word for word, the nine articles agreed on at Lambeth the 20th of November Anno 1595'. sig. A2ᵛ.

[168] *Articles of Religion agreed upon . . . in the Convocation holden at Dublin.*

[169] *Commons Debates, 1625*, p. 48.

[170] *Stuart Constitution*, ed. Kenyon, p. 155.

[171] BL Harleian MS 390, fo. 83.

[172] Carleton, *An Examination*, sig. A3ᵛ, pp. 1, 14.

[173] Ibid., p. 95.

term Puritan. Questions of doctrine had not in the past distinguished the church hierarchy from its nonconformist or presbyterian critics.[174] His remarks are dedicated to Charles I. 'When the Church is in danger to whom may we flie unto for helpe, next under God, but only to your Majestie, whom God hath set a nursing father of his Church here.'[175]

Two other opponents of Montagu, Henry Burton and John Yates, also dedicated their books to Charles as supreme governor of the English Church. Burton accuses Montagu of holding that

universall grace [is] equally offered to all, to receive if they will [and] when a man hath received grace that hee may fall away totally, yea finally, from the grace of God and justification [and] that God hath predestinated none to glory but those whom he foresaw would both by their freewill receive grace and would or could of themselves persevere to the end.[176]

Montagu, says Yates, 'fights against' the Church of England 'under the ensigne of Arminius',[177] in his teaching on predestination and perseverance. Both Yates and Burton explicitly reject Montagu's imputation of Puritanism, claiming not only to be conformists themselves but to have persuaded others to conform.[178] Daniel Featley, in his 'writ of error sued against the Appealer', writes that 'if Arminius or Bertius be the voice, the Appealer is the eccho; if the Appealer be the voice, Arminius or Bertius is the eccho'.[179] Featley then goes on to parallel the doctrines of the Dutch Arminians on predestination and falling from grace with those of Montagu. He ends by referring Montagu, if he persists in his errors, 'to the examination and censure of the most learned, religious and judicious house of convocation now sitting, to whom under his Majesty the cognizance of doctrinall differences properly belong'.[180]

Featley himself had licensed for the press William Prynne's

[174] Ibid., pp. 5, 78.
[175] Ibid., sig. A3ᵛ.
[176] Henry Burton, *A Plea to an Appeale* (1626), sigs. aᵛ–a2.
[177] Yates, *Ibis ad Caesarem*, sig. B2.
[178] Ibid., iii. 43–4; Burton, *A Plea*, p. 8.
[179] Featley, *A Second Parallel*, sigs. B3ᵛ–B4.
[180] Ibid., pp. 95–6.

The Perpetuitie of a Regenerate Man's Estate,[181] which includes an attack on Montagu. Prynne chose to dedicate his book to Archbishop Abbot, as being in 'the highest place of rule and dignitie in this our Church'. He urges him to 'take heart and courage for the truth', for 'you have the votes and prayers of all true hearted Christians', and to 'execute, stirre up and act that place and power, which God and man have given to you'.[182] According to Prynne, Montagu was both an Arminian and a plagiarist. 'I finde all Mr Mountague's quotations [on the subject of perseverance], one only excepted . . . recorded verbatim by that famous Arminian Bertius in his booke *De Apostasia Sanctorum*; neither are they to be found in any man's works but his.'[183] Some of the theological arguments used by Prynne on this occasion were subsequently to be stigmatized as 'Brownist' by Archbishop Laud.[184] Lastly Anthony Wotton dedicated his refutation of Montagu to parliament, asking them to 'take this cause into your consideration'.[185] As for Montagu's claim never to have read Arminius, 'it is community in his faith (not his writings) that procures that [Arminian] title'.[186]

VI

After the dissolution of June 1626, parliament was not called again for nearly two years and in the intervening period divisions within the ranks of the English political nation grew deeper. Further military defeats abroad were subsidized at home by unparliamentary taxation, in the form of a forced loan and tonnage and poundage. Meanwhile Calvinism was proscribed,[187] on the basis of the 1626 proclamation, and Arminianism established as the highway to ecclesiastical preferment. In the minds of some MPs, these developments increasingly came to be regarded as different aspects of the same deep laid plot. Their mood was articulated by Henry

---

[181] Arber, IV. 118. Prynne's book was entered in the Stationers' Register on 7 April. It may not have been published until after the dissolution of parliament. Cosin, *Correspondence*, I. 102.

[182] Prynne, *The Perpetuitie*, sigs. ¶2–¶4.   [183] Ibid., p. 192.

[184] Ibid., pp. 339–42; Laud, *Works*, VI. 132–3.

[185] Anthony Wotton, *A Dangerous Plot Discovered* (1626), sig.)(2ᵛ.

[186] Ibid., p. 2.   [187] BL Harleian MS 390, fo. 83.

Burton in his pamphlet *Israel's Fast*, which he dedicated to the new parliament in 1628. Burton, Rector of St Matthew's Friday Street, drew an analogy between Old Testament Israel in the days of Joshua and England under Charles I. Now as then the land is troubled, the King at variance with his people and the nation's foes triumphant. Today the troublers include the Arminians, those Popish fellow-travellers with 'their syren-songs', who divide ruler from subject and England from God. 'Their theames and theorems are that kings are partakers of God's owne omnipotency though this be a divine attribute incommunicable to any creature.' Similarly by asserting the free will of man they go about to overturn the 'whole essence' of God. Arminians and their allies are traitors twiceover, 'betraying us into our enemies' hands, by making God our enemy'.[188] Such men must be rooted out, if England is not to be overwhelmed.

Other clerical commentators in 1628 offered a similar diagnosis of events to that of Burton, who already two years earlier had described Montagu's *Appello Caesarem* as 'a disastrous comet [which] portendeth universal ruine both to Church and State',[189] Thus Jeremiah Dyke, Vicar of Epping, preaching before parliament on 5 April 1628, spoke of the necessity for an ark, both of Noah and of the covenant, 'to save us from the rage of the mercilesse waters'.[190] God's warnings of imminent judgement have been delivered to the English. 'The common complaint is that Popery spreads, that Arminianisme spreads. As these come in, so God will goe out.' Catastrophe could only be avoided by holding fast to the 'old God' and the 'old truth'.[191] The views of Burton and Dyke clearly chimed in with those of Francis Rous and other Calvinist laymen. But it was agreed by most MPs in 1628 that the future of parliament as an institution was now at stake, and that this 'crisis' had to be resolved first of all.[192] For, if the right of parliament to grant or

---

[188] Henry Burton, *Israel's Fast* (1628), sigs. B2ᵛ–B4.

[189] Burton, *A Plea*, sig. ¶3ᵛ.

[190] Jeremiah Dyke, *A Sermon preached at the Publicke Fast* (1628), p. 37.

[191] Ibid., p. 43. I am grateful to Lady de Villiers for drawing my attention to the role of Burton and Dyke. William Prynne also addressed parliament at this time in similar vein. *A Briefe Survay and Censure of Mr Cozens his Couzening Devotions* (1628), sigs. A2ᵛ–A4ᵛ.

[192] *Commons Debates, 1628*, ii. 58.

withhold taxation was not vindicated, then the only compelling reason for a king to summon one would disappear.

Just as in 1626 the attempt by the Commons to impeach Buckingham had dominated their proceedings, so the first session of the next parliament, which began in March 1628, was primarily concerned with the Petition of Right.[193] In the background, however, Arminianism loomed more threateningly than it had before. On 24 March, seven days after the opening of parliament, Sir Nathaniel Rich asked that the charges against Montagu be brought into the House. 'We see now those men that profess these opinions are advanced and preferred . . . and, under authority and a monarchy, will undermine authority and will preach we have no property.'[194] The case was old but the conclusions drawn were new. Thus this speech is both the first clear indication that members of the Commons were conscious of an Arminian party and the first recorded identification by an MP of Arminianism with the absolutist attack on property rights. One ecclesiastical promotion that Rich must have had in mind especially was that of Francis White to Carlisle in December 1626. At White's consecration a placard had appeared with the inscription 'Is an Arminian now made Bishop?'[195]—an allusion to his role as licenser of *Appello Caesarem*. As to the alleged link between Arminianism and unparliamentary taxation, there was no necessary connection. Nor in fact does there appear any direct evidence that Robert Sibthorpe and Roger Mainwaring, the two notorious clerical propagandists of the forced loan, were Arminians in religion. What they shared with the Arminian Montagu was royal patronage, but this was now sufficient to brand both as parts of a single sinister design.

On the other hand, members of the Commons were correct at this time in linking the name of Thomas Jackson with that of Richard Montagu. As we have seen, Jackson had privately rejected Calvinism in about 1605 and like Montagu had acquired Neile as a patron during the early 1620s. The book for which he came under attack in 1628 was the first part of his *The Divine Essence and Attributes*, published the same year.

[193] Russell, *Parliaments*, pp. 343–89.
[194] *Commons Debates, 1628*, II. 85.
[195] BL Harleian MS 390, fo. 168ᵛ.

Jackson compounded his offence by dedicating the work to the third Earl of Pembroke, whom he says will 'be thought to patronise Arminianism'[196] as a consequence. In *The Divine Essence* Jackson writes that

the Church of England . . . doth not in her public and authorized doctrine come short of any church this day extant in the extent of God's unspeakabble love to mankind. No national council, though assembled for that purpose, could fit their doctrine more expressly to meet with all the late restrictions of God's love than the church our mother, even from the beginning of reformation, hath done.[197]

He went on to argue that, 'whilst God of a loving father becomes a severe judge, there is no change or alteration at all in God but only in men and in their actions'.[198]

Jackson's case was raised by Sir Robert Harley, who went on to explore the theme of Arminianism as a threat to religious unity and consequently to national security. 'Dissolution is the daughter of division. When there's buzzing among bees their king is gone away, and so the King of Heaven will go from us.'[199] His solution was not a moratorium on all controversy, as proclaimed by the King, but the establishment of Calvinist orthodoxy. With this in mind, the bill 'for the better continuing of peace and unity in Church and Commonwealth' was reintroduced on 3 April.[200] After a second reading, on 7 April,[201] the bill disappeared into a committee from which it failed to re-emerge. Not until 11 June did the committee for religion report the charges against Montagu.[202] This was four days after the final royal assent to the Petition of Right. As in 1626, Pym was chosen to present the Montagu case to the Lords, the Commons claiming only to defend religious truth 'that is clear' and not to determine matters in doubt.[203] Once more, however, time was running short. On 13 June a subcommittee was appointed to help Pym in preparing the charge against Montagu,[204] and on 26 June the House was prorogued.

Parliament reassembled on 20 January 1629 and Arminianism soon emerged as an overriding concern of the Commons. The new tone was set by Francis Rous in his speech of 26 January about 'right of religion'. Rous and the

[196] Jackson, *Works*, v. 4.   [197] Ibid., pp. 148–9.   [198] Ibid., p. 188.
[199] *Commons Debates, 1628*, ii. 86.   [200] Ibid., p. 275.   [201] Ibid., p. 323.
[202] Ibid., iv. 236–7.   [203] Ibid., p. 238.   [204] Ibid., p. 291.

speakers who succeeded him, on this and the following day,
now took up in earnest the cry of Burton and Dyke ten months
earlier that Arminianism was the origin of all England's troubles.[205] To understand this change of emphasis we need to
recall the mounting political passions and physical violence of
the previous year. On at least one occasion, towards the end of
the 1628 parliamentary session, the Commons had suc-
cumbed to collective hysteria when forbidden to discuss government policies, 'some weeping, some expostulating, some
propheciing of the fatall ruine of our kingdome, some playing
the divines in confessing their owne and their countrie's sins
which drew these judgements upon us'. The focus of this
passionate recrimination, on 5 June, had been the Duke of
Buckingham, 'the cause and author of all their miserie'.[206]
Shortly afterwards a servant of the Duke, Dr Lambe, while
walking in the London streets, fell victim to the 'rage of the
people', who 'cryed moreover, whilest they were killing him,
that if his master were there they would give him as much'.[207]
When Buckingham himself was assassinated, on 23 August,
his murderer was hymned in many quarters as a national
hero.[208] It rapidly became clear, however, that Buckingham's
death solved nothing and in this impasse many MPs switched
their main attack to the Arminians.

   The religious emotion shown by the House of Commons in
early 1629 was thus in part born of intense political frustra-
tion, whereby Arminianism and its clerical leadership became
something of a scapegoat. Yet this is far from being the whole
story. For recent months had seen a crop of Arminian episcopal promotions, of which Richard Montagu's consecration
as Bishop of Chichester in August 1628 was only the most
flagrant example.[209] The suppression by proclamation of Montagu's book *Appello Caesarem*, three days before parliament
reconvened, far from being a gesture of conciliation merely
made impracticable further attempts to prosecute him.

[205] *Commons Debates for 1629*, pp. 12–16, 18–21.
[206] BL Harleian MS 390, fo. 410.
[207] Ibid., fo. 412.
[208] *The Diary of John Rous*, ed. M. A. E. Green (Camden Soc., 66, 1856), pp. 29–30.
[209] William Laud, Samuel Harsnett, John Howson, and Francis White were all
translated, to London, York, Durham, and Norwich respectively, while among other
newly made bishops was Richard Corbett of Oxford.

Moreover the Montagu case paled into insignificance beside the growing body of evidence that a general Arminianization of the English Church was in process. The Commons claimed that the Arminians had gained a monopoly of ecclesiastical preferment, and asked that for the future bishops be chosen on the advice of the Privy Council.[210] Some members suggested taking a religious covenant, which should be defended if necessary to the death, and the House as a whole attempted to place on record a Calvinist statement of faith.[211] At the same time there were complaints of a creeping ceremonialism, particularly associated with the activities of Bishop Neile at Durham and Winchester, and of a growing toleration of Roman Catholicism.[212] Initially Rous's apocalyptic views swept all before them, but thereafter more secular voices were again heard—notably as regards the levying of tonnage and poundage without the consent of parliament. None the less Arminianism remained a leading issue to the end of the session.[213]

No member of parliament publicly argued that the rise of Arminianism discredited bishops as such, although according to Alexander Leighton some had begun to do so in private.[214] Leighton argued, in his book *Sion's Plea*, for the root and branch extirpation of episcopacy. Printed abroad and, according to the title page, in 'the year and moneth wherein Rochell was lost', the book arrived too late for presentation to the 1629 session of parliament.[215] The fall of La Rochelle in October 1628, English forces having failed to relieve the Calvinist garrison, seemed to symbolize the nadir of Protestant fortunes in Europe and the vulnerability of England to invasion. Against this backdrop, Leighton elaborated a comprehensive indictment of the episcopal order. He claimed that bishops were essentially evil and Arminianism was merely old Popery in new guise. Nothing short of abolition would content God.[216] In

---

[210] *Commons Debate, 1629*, p. 100.

[211] Ibid., pp. 14, 19, 23, 99.   [212] Ibid., pp. 50–1, 97.

[213] C. Thompson, 'The Divided Leadership of the House of Commons in 1629', in *Faction and Parliament*, ed. K. Sharpe (Oxford, 1978), pp. 245–84; Russell, *Parliaments*, pp. 404–16.

[214] Alexander Leighton, *An Epitome or Briefe Discoverie* (1646), pp. 1–2.

[215] Ibid., p. 2.

[216] Alexander Leighton, *An Appeal to the Parliament, or Sion's Plea against the Prelacie* (Amsterdam, 1628), pp. 23, 86, 234–5 and *passim*.

the event the House of Commons was forcibly dispersed on 2 March, and eleven years of personal rule by King Charles ensued. During the interim, however, Leighton's approach increasingly recommended itself to those alienated by the turn of religious events.

7

The York House Conference

I

THE House of Commons failed in their attempt to prosecute Richard Montagu before the House of Lords. This did not mean, however, that the upper house remained completely uninvolved with the Arminian controversy. Thus, during May 1624, when the Commons referred the Montagu case to Archbishop Abbot, they also forwarded to the Lords a complaint against Bishop Harsnett of Norwich. Although not accused of Arminianism, Harsnett, in his reply of 19 May, chose to defend himself against any such imputation, wondering 'why he should be thought a Papist. He thought it might be owing to his disputations and his sermon at Paul's Crosse, of predestination negative, unadvisedly preached by him, for which he was checked by the Lord Archbishop Whitguifte and commanded to preach no more of it, and he never did . . .'[1] The sermon to which he referred had been preached forty years before, in 1584, and his 'disputations' on the same subject probably date from that period. Both survive and together they constitute a complete rebuttal of Calvinist teaching, Harsnett portraying himself at the time as a lone David challenging the 'Goliah' of predestination.[2]

While Harsnett does not appear ever to have preached again on these questions, after being 'checked' by Archbishop Whitgift, he did take an active interest in the Cambridge predestinarian disputes of the 1590s and made contact with Dutch Arminianism by at latest 1622.[3] Moreover, the religious charges against him in 1624 are significant of his continuing theological convictions. Harsnett was said to have inhibited

[1] *Lords Journals*, III. 389.
[2] Samuel Harsnett, *A Fourth Sermon*, appended to Richard Steward, *Three Sermons* (1656), p. 134; BL Harleian MS 3142, fos. 54–61ᵛ. Harsnett had also referred to the views which he attacked as 'Puritan'. *A Fourth Sermon*, p. 165.
[3] BL Harleian MS 7029, fo. 49; Grotius, *Briefwisseling*, II. 240–1.

sermons and to have countenanced the setting up of religious images, including a 'dove on the font'.[4] His actions symbolize the replacement of the grace of predestination, conveyed by preaching, with that grace received via the sacraments, which was now becoming a stock English Arminian response to Calvinist determinism. He also provides a living link across the years with the Arminians before Arminius. Yet Harsnett remained somewhat aloof from the Arminian movement of the 1620s, his source of patronage being the Earl of Arundel as opposed to the Duke of Buckingham.[5]

Arminianism was also brought to the attention of the House of Lords during the 1625 and 1626 parliaments. On 30 June 1625 Bishop Morton delivered a message from Archbishop Abbot, suffering from gout, 'that the Commons had sent a former booke of Mr Montague's and desired his answer . . . Hee [now] desires your Lordship's direccion'.[6] Presumably Abbot hoped that the Lords would instruct him to proceed against Montagu, although their answer is not recorded. In 1626, on 10 May, Christopher Sherland described Buckingham, at a conference with the Lords, as 'the principal patron and supporter of the Semi-Pelagian[s] . . . whose tenets are liberty of free will, though somewhat mollified'. Buckingham paraphrased this as accusing him of being 'a patron of heresy, the Pelagian heresye, which opynion I never herde of before'.[7] On none of these occasions did any debate about Arminianism apparently ensue. Some peers did, however, attend a conference in early 1626, under the chairmanship of Buckingham and during the second session of which Richard Montagu was present. These meetings occurred on 11 and 17 February 1626 at Buckingham's residence, York House in the Strand. Their subject was the published views of Montagu,

[4] *Commons Journals*, I. 784.
[5] K. Sharpe, 'The Earl of Arundel, His Circle and the Opposition to the Duke of Buckingham, 1618–28', in *Faction and Parliament*, ed. Sharpe, pp. 231, 236–7, 240. It may be significant that Harsnett was not among the bishops who wrote to Buckingham in support of Richard Montagu. Laud, *Works*, VI. 246, 249.
[6] *Notes of the Debates in the House of Lords . . . 1621, 1625, 1628*, ed. F. H. Relf (Camden, 3rd ser., 42, 1929), p. 57.
[7] Rushworth, *Historical Collections*, I. 337; *Notes of Debates in the House of Lords . . . 1624 and 1626*, ed. S. R. Gardiner (Camden Soc., 2nd ser., 24, 1879), pp. 193–4. C. G. C. Tite, *Impeachment and Parliamentary Judicature in Early Stuart England* (1974), p. 199.

and according to Buckingham the conference had been arranged at the request of the Earl of Warwick.[8]

King Charles's second parliament had assembled five days earlier, on 6 February, and the decision that Montagu should face his accusers was seemingly an attempt by the crown to conciliate some of its critics. Nevertheless, when opening the conference Buckingham affirmed his 'good opinion' of Montagu, whose 'soundness in religion' had been certified by 'divers learned prelates'.[9] Although he gave no names, the bishops involved were Andrewes, Buckeridge, Laud, Montaigne, and Neile, Arminian sympathizers to a man.[10] The Duke also stressed the private nature of the conference to which the King and he had agreed, and in fact no account of it was published at the time. Among the nine laymen who attended only one, Secretary Sir John Coke, was not a member of the House of Lords, and it appears that the York House Conference was designed among other things to defeat Montagu's prosecution by the House of Commons. If a sufficiently influential body of peers could be convinced in advance of his innocence, or at least come to doubt his guilt, then there was a good chance of the case against Montagu failing in the Lords. More than this Buckingham may already have been anticipating the subsequent attack by the Commons on the whole of his own recent administration, and in clearing Montagu from the aspersion of heresy he perhaps hoped to prevent any charges of a religious nature being preferred against himself.

But the York House Conference also needs to be seen in the wider context of church policy. For the accession of Charles I in March 1625 had seen an acceleration of changes already evident during the last years of his father. Continuity was provided by Buckingham who as early as 1622 was linked with Arminianism, through the person of his chaplain William Lucy, although he remained a patron of the Calvinist John Preston until mid-1626.[11] In December 1624, however, Laud,

---

[8] Cosin, *Works*, II. 21–2. Cosin entitled his account the 'Sum and Substance of the Conference lately had at York House', probably in conscious imitation of William Barlow's *Summe and Substance* of the Hampton Court Conference in 1604. This is a further example of the Arminian tendency to equate Calvinism with Puritanism.

[9] Cosin, *Works*, II. 22.   [10] Laud, *Works*, VI. 249.

[11] BL Harleian MS 389, fo. 213; Thomas Ball, *The Life of the Renowned Doctor Preston*,

now Bishop of St David's, drew up for Buckingham a 'tract about Doctrinal Puritanism', which apparently defined Calvinist teaching on predestination as Puritan.[12] From about this date he seems to have been more in the Duke's religious confidence than was Preston. Within ten days of King James's death Laud had submitted to Buckingham a schedule of leading clergy, tabulated on the basis of 'O[rthodox]' and 'P[uritan]', for perusal by the new monarch.[13] The information contained in this list probably lies behind the virtual exclusion of the Calvinist element from various episcopal committees appointed in the succeeding months.[14] In April 1625 Laud was directed to consult Bishop Andrewes concerning the 'Five Articles', that is to say Arminianism, as to 'what he would have done'.[15] (It is worth remembering that some years earlier King James had silenced Andrewes on precisely this subject.)[16] That July Charles intervened in parliament on behalf of Montagu, and in February 1626 the Arminian Cosin was able to close his account of the York House Conference with the statement that the King 'swears his perpetual patronage of our cause'.[17]

During June 1626 the recommendations of the 'learned prelates', to whom Buckingham had referred during the York House Conference, were embodied in the proclamation for 'the peace and quiet of the Church of England'.[18] As understood by Arminians, this meant the banning of Calvinism from press and pulpit. In July 1627 Charles sequestered the Calvinist Archbishop Abbot from his ecclesiastical jurisdiction, which was then vested in a commission composed of Arminian bishops.[19] The occasion of Abbot's disgrace was his refusal to license a sermon in defence of the forced loan. Throughout the previous year, however, Abbot had had little effective say in church affairs.[20] By contrast, Laud was

---

ed. E. W. Harcourt (1885), pp. 66–9, 84–5, 89, 98, 100–1, 103–4, 106, 108–9, 114, 117–18, 122–3, 141–6.

[12] Laud, *Works*, III. 155–6; Heylyn, *Cyprianus Anglicus*, p. 119.
[13] Laud, *Works*, p. 159.   [14] Ibid., pp. 166, 178–9.   [15] Ibid., pp. 160.
[16] Winwood, *Memorials*, III. 459.
[17] Cosin, *Works*, II. 74.
[18] Laud, *Works*, VI. 249; *Stuart Constitution*, ed. Kenyon, pp. 154–5.
[19] Laud, *Works*, III. 205–6.
[20] Rushworth, *Historical Collections*, I. 431–47.

appointed to preach at the opening of parliament in 1625 and 1626, and in October 1626 was promised the succession to Canterbury.[21] The following April he was made a privy councillor, together with Bishop Neile. According to the Venetian Ambassador, these two new councillors were 'strongly opposed to the Archbishop of Canterbury' and 'Protestants rather than Puritans'.[22]

II

There was one factor, however, which tended to modify the pattern of religious development. This was the presence of certain Calvinist laymen among Charles's privy councillors, most important being the third Earl of Pembroke. He took an active part in the York House Conference, and may have been responsible for the appointment of the Calvinist Joseph Hall to the bishopric of Exeter in 1627.[23] As already remarked Pembroke, as Chancellor of Oxford, secured for the university a respite from enforcing the 1626 proclamation, which under Buckingham at Cambridge had been used immediately to silence Calvinism. Among the richest of the English nobility, Pembroke was the chief rival of Buckingham at court and his clients in the House of Commons were to play a leading part in the 1626 attempt to impeach Buckingham.[24] It is possible that Charles and Buckingham, by agreeing to a confrontation of Arminians by Calvinists at York House, hoped to drive a religious wedge between Pembroke and other more politically radical peers such as Warwick and his ally Viscount Saye. Both the latter had inherited from their fathers a tradition of Protestant extremism. The Elizabethan household of Robert Rich, first Earl of Warwick, has been described as constituting a system of 'presbytery in episcopacy', while a similar type of church government was apparently supported in the Bermudas, from 1617, by his son the second Earl.[25] Baron Saye had been a prominent critic of the established church, and his

[21] Laud, *Works*, III. 165, 182, 196.

[22] *Cal. SP Venetian, 1626–28*, p. 218.

[23] Hall, *Works*, v. 174. Another of Hall's patrons was the Earl of Norwich. Ibid., p. 425.   [24] Russell, *Parliaments*, pp. 289–90.

[25] Collinson, *Elizabethan Puritan Movement*, pp. 343–4; HMC Eighth Report, II, nos. 209–10, 264.

son Viscount Saye showed inclinations to religious separatism as early as 1608.[26] At York House Warwick and Saye made abundantly clear their hostility to the teachings of Richard Montagu, and Puritan seems an appropriate term by which to describe them. They were also, later the same year, to be among the refusers of the forced loan.[27]

Another privy councillor sympathetic to Calvinism and present at the York House Conference was the Earl of Carlisle. In July 1625 Carlisle had encouraged the publication of a Calvinist sermon, preached at court by Henry Leslie, in which conversion is defined as 'God's power overcoming all resistance in the will of man'.[28] Two years later Leslie was to publish a further statement of his Calvinist views, this time with the support of the Earl of Montgomery, brother to Pembroke and also a privy councillor. On this second occasion Leslie taught that the regenerate man 'sinneth not totally, with full purpose and resolution, nor finally for, though he fall, he recovereth himselfe againe by repentance, being kept by the power of God unto salvation'.[29] None the less the religious views expressed at York House by Pembroke and Carlisle were, according to Arminian sources, hostile towards Calvinism, particularly as regards the doctrine of perseverance in grace.[30] Allowing for bias, and in the light of stronger contrary evidence, Pembroke's position is best understood as moderate Calvinist. For in July 1626 he endorsed publicly the stand taken against Arminianism by Prideaux at Oxford, and immediately after the conference was reported as saying that 'none returned Arminians thence save such who repaired thither with the same opinions'.[31] Carlisle probably falls into the same religious category as Pembroke, since his father-in-law, the Earl of Norwich, can be found writing to him in September 1628 that 'pietie may goe begg in rages if addorned with never so sound learninge, eather in church or commonwealthe, unless policie and Arminionisme put on the rochet

[26] *Proceedings in Parliament, 1610*, ed. Foster, I. 224–5; HMC Salisbury, XX. 48.
[27] PRO, SP 16/41, fo. 3.
[28] Henry Leslie, *A Sermon preached before His Majesty at Windsore* (Oxford, 1625), sig. A2ʳ⁻ᵛ, p. 8.
[29] Henry Leslie, *A Sermon preached before His Majesty at Wokin* (1627), sig. A2ʳ⁻ᵛ, p. 15.
[30] Cosin, *Works*, II. 58–9.
[31] OU Arch., Reg. N.23, fos. 226ᵛ–7; Fuller, *Church History*, VI. 34.

and the robe'.[32] In political terms Pembroke and Carlisle seem to have belonged to a middle group among the peers.[33] A privy councillor, by contrast, whose Calvinism is in no doubt was Secretary Coke, since at the conference he proposed that the Church of England ratify the rulings of the Synod of Dort. Evidently a man of strong religious convictions, Coke was also an old friend of Bishop Morton who led the attack on Montagu at the York House Conference.[34]

Of the three other peers at the conference, Edmund Sheffield, Earl of Mulgrave, had been dismissed as Lord President of the Council of the North, in 1619, partly on account of his hard line policy towards Catholic priests.[35] Since his dismissal he had held no important office, but was created an earl little more than a week before the conference. Mulgrave is not recorded as siding with Warwick and Saye at York House nor did he join them, the following November, in their resistance to the forced loan. The Earls of Bridgewater and Dorset appear, in retrospect, to have attended at York House as Buckingham's henchmen, because only a few months later they were described respectively as 'a dependent' and 'a friend' of the Duke.[36] Since, however, they were not appointed privy councillors until July and August 1626, it may be that as late as February their position on the religious question was still in some doubt. Certainly Bridgewater was said by his eldest daughter, Lady Frances, to have been responsible for 'seasoning her against Arminian principles'.[37] After parliament was dissolved in June 1626 Dorset emerged as a leading advocate of the forced loan, arguing that 'war must be maintained with the property of the subject, all being bound to contribute when it [the cause] is just'.[38] Bridgewater, although as a privy councillor obliged to support the forced loan, was more circumspect.

Such were the laity who assembled at York House to hear

[32] PRO, SP 16/116, fo. 16.

[33] *Notes of Debates in the House of Lords . . . 1624 and 1626*, ed. Gardiner, pp. 206, 211, 214, 231–2; *Letters of John Holles, 1587–1635*, ed. P. R. Seddon (Thoroton Soc., 35, 1983), II. 331.

[34] Cosin, *Works*, II. 38, 63; HMC Twelfth Report, I. 66, 68, 444.

[35] Reid, *Council in the North*, pp. 387–8.

[36] *Cal. SP Venetian, 1625–6*, pp. 495, 500.

[37] John Collinges, *Par Nobile* (1669), p. 4. I owe this reference to Professor Russell.

[38] *Cal. SP Venetian, 1625–6*, p. 528.

the teachings of Richard Montagu disputed between Calvinist and Arminian clergy. The Calvinists were represented by Bishop Morton of Coventry and Lichfield and John Preston, a client of Viscount Saye as well as of Buckingham.[39] Morton was in many ways a typical example of the kind of churchmanship common during King James' reign. He had acquired his theology at Cambridge in the 1580s, under William Whitaker of St John's College, and condemned Dutch Arminianism as early as 1609.[40] As a bishop he was known for his tolerance of Puritans.[41] In 1625 he acted as Archbishop Abbot's parliamentary spokesman on the Montagu controversy, and his stand at York House almost certainly had the primate's tacit approval. John Preston is often dubbed a Puritan, but there is no evidence of his ever being a nonconformist. On the other hand, Preston's patrons included Bishop Davenant of Salisbury, with whom he had recently discussed Montagu's teachings.[42] Bishops like Davenant and Morton, however, now found themselves being forced into religious opposition.

Morton's episcopal counterpart at York House was the Arminian Bishop Buckeridge of Rochester. The assistants of Buckeridge on the first day were Francis White, Dean of Carlisle, and John Cosin, both of whom had been involved with the licensing of Montagu's books. At the second session the author himself was present. So far as age went there was little difference between the clergy on either side. Buckeridge, Morton, and White had all been born in the early 1560s, Montagu in 1577, Preston in 1584, and Cosin in 1594. Buckeridge, the only Oxford cleric attending, had avoided declaring his views during the predestinarian disputes of the 1590s; but his early influence on William Laud at Oxford suggests that no major alteration had occurred in his thinking.[43] Moreover, there were other elements in his theology at variance with Morton which indicate that each belonged to different traditions.[44] By

[39] Preston's will, dated July 1618, describes Saye as his 'honourable and faithful friend' and appoints him executor. PRO, PROB. 11/154, fo. 102ᵛ.
[40] Richard Baddiley, *The Life of Dr Thomas Morton* (York, 1669), pp. 33–4.
[41] J. E. B. Mayor, 'Materials for the Life of Thomas Morton, Bishop of Durham', *Cambridge Antiquarian Soc.*, 3 (1865), 12–13.
[42] Ball, *Life of Preston*, p. 114.
[43] Heylyn, *Cyprianus Anglicus*, pp. 44–5.   [44] See below, pp. 175–6.

comparison the position of White had undergone considerable change, his opponents being able to embarrass him with earlier utterances.[45] Richard Montagu, during the first decade of the century, had as we have seen moved in Cambridge circles connected with Dutch Arminianism, while apparently resisting attempts by his college head to guide him in the paths of doctrinal Calvinism. The youngest of this Arminian quartet was Cosin, who at the outset of his clerical career had become involved in the cause of continental Arminianism through his being secretary to Bishop Overall,[46] and all four belonged to the Durham House group.

III

The record of the actual discussions at York House survives in no one single version, but in various overlapping accounts from the rival camps. The Arminian versions mainly cover the first session as the Calvinist ones do the second. This difference in treatment may derive from a propagandist wish to show each party in action at the meeting during which it fared the better. Arminianism was only discussed at the tail end of the first session, on 11 February, Morton concentrating on the points described as 'Popish' by Montagu's critics. Initially he attempted to exploit a disagreement believed to exist between White and other backers of Montagu, over the licensing of *Appello Caesarem*. The book as printed was allegedly different from the version licensed by White, in the section which discussed the identity of Antichrist.[47] 'Authority', said Morton, 'had been abused.' White, however, refused to rise to the bait, claiming that it was 'a matter of no moment'. Furthermore his colleague Buckeridge challenged Morton 'to shew where the Church of England had either one way or [the] other determined that controversy'.[48] Morton declined the invitation, although later in the proceedings he was apparently to cite the authority of King James for the view that the Pope was Antichrist.[49]

[45] Ball, *Life of Preston*, p. 126; Prynne, *The Perpetuitie*, p. 220.
[46] Cosin, *Correspondence*, I. 5; PRO, SP 14/99, fo. 160.
[47] Cosin, *Correspondence*, I. 196.
[48] Cosin, *Works*, II. 22–3.
[49] Ibid., pp. 21, 23, 80–1.

For the present Morton turned instead to various doctrinal positions supposedly held by Montagu contrary to the Thirty-nine Articles. The first concerned his opinion that general councils could not err 'in fundamentals'. At issue here were rival definitions both of general councils and of fundamentals, Morton using the terms in a more inclusive sense than Montagu.[50] Morton's view seems to have approximated to that of Bishop Jewel, the Elizabethan apologist for the Church of England, who had claimed that 'God is able not only without councils, but also will the councils nill the councils, to maintain and advance his own kingdom'.[51] One consequence of the restrictive definition of fundamentals, favoured by Montagu and his supporters, was to reduce the distance separating Protestant from Catholic, while another was to open the way for treating Arminianism as at least on a par with Calvinism. Indeed Morton subsequently returned to this question, in relation to the Church of Rome and Montagu's distinction between 'matters of faith' and fundamentals. Rome, claimed Montagu, only erred as regards the former. Like Morton, the Calvinist Bishop Carleton also claimed that the post-Tridentine Catholic Church was guilty of 'fundamentall' errors.[52]

The next two charges related to the doctrine of justification. Montagu, in allowing good works a role in justification, had departed from the solifidian view still current in the universities. 'All his discourse about justification tends to the justifying of the popish doctrine and to the making of good works a part of our justification, or an access unto the very act of it at least,'[53] said Morton. (This particular controversy received a much wider airing at the Cambridge Commencement in 1633, when the new view was maintained by one of Archbishop Neile's chaplains.)[54] Morton then moved on to the definition of royal supremacy in the Church of England, expounding this in the sense of the monarch as supreme in all causes, spiritual and temporal, rather than as over all persons in all causes,

[50] Ibid., pp. 23–8.

[51] John Jewel, *Works*, ed. J. Ayre (Parker Soc., Cambridge, 1845–50), III. 102.

[52] Cosin, *Works*, II. 33–4; George Carleton, *Directions to know the True Church* (1615), pp. 79, 84.

[53] Cosin, *Works*, II. 29.

[54] See above, p. 54.

which Montagu taught.[55] On this point it is instructive to recall the admiring description by Toby Matthew, the future archbishop, of King James at the Hampton Court Conference, in 1604, as playing the part of 'kyng and prieste in one person'.[56] Bishop Jewel similarly countenanced monarchs handling 'mysteries of religion',[57] and the question had now become particularly urgent with Calvinists invoking the views of the late King.

According to Cosin's account, Morton fared worse in all the foregoing exchanges. Finally, after an argument about the number of sacraments admitted by the English Church, Morton used the absence of Montagu as an excuse to move an adjournment. His failure to handle the predestinarian question probably reflects an original agreement whereby Preston was to concentrate on that aspect of the case. But the latter did not appear until the conference was about to break up. Then, in an apparent effort to save the day, Saye raised 'the chiefest matter', the Arminian charges, and recommended that Preston be heard.[58] This was agreed, and a discussion opened on the doctrine of perseverance in grace as handled by Montagu. Could a truly justified man fall from grace as a result of sin? White cited the Biblical case of David, once justified yet living in adultery, saying that he could not be in a state of saving grace until he forsook his sin. Morton replied that this did not affect his election which was unalterable. White countered with a quotation from Aquinas that 'predestination implants nothing in the predestined'*. He further elaborated that if 'it be God's predestination that always makes a man to be in a state of justification, then was St Paul a justified man when he was knocking out St Stephen's brains, and all the while that he continued to blaspheme and persecute the church'. White concluded that such teaching—what Buckeridge called 'a most licentious, a sensual and a dangerous doctrine'—could only encourage immorality. It was this consequence, the setting up of 'a school of sin', which Pembroke and Carlisle allegedly deplored.[59] Preston then restated

[55] Cosin, *Works*, ii. 32–3.
[56] Cardwell, *Conferences*, p. 166.
[57] Jewel, *Works*, iii. 97.
[58] Cosin, *Works*, ii. 56; Ball, *Life of Preston*, pp. 119–20; BL Burney MS 362, fo. 86.
[59] Cosin, *Works*, ii. 56–9.

the case saying that, although a justified man sinning was subject to God's wrath, there remained in him the 'seed of God'
which 'would repaire him, as in water there remains a principle of cold, even when it boyleth over, that will undoubtedly
reduce it when the heate and fire is removed, as in Peter,
David, Sampson and others'. God 'did not disinherit them
and blot their names out of the Book of Life'. For 'if one cease
to be a sonne because he commits a sin that doth deserve eternall death . . . we should be always out of sonshipp, and have
neither certeinty nor comfort in our estate'.[60]

Morton also argued that 'a godly man might goe farr and
yet retorne, by the instance of the prodigal [son]. But Doctor
White exclaimed against any that should think the prodigall,
in acts of drunkenness and whoredome, not to be fallen from
grace.' They 'that doe such thinges are worthy of death'.
Preston

answered that those sins indeed made a forfeiture of their interest
into the hands of God and he might take the seysure if he pleased,
yet did not unto those that were his children and in covenant with
him—as two tenants, not paying of their rent or [not] keeping
covenants, forfeited their leases, yet the Lord might seize the one
and not the other as he pleased.[61]

The question now arose as to how Morton and Preston reconciled their teaching on perseverance with the grace indiscrimi-
nately bestowed in baptism, since not all the baptized were
saved. This elicited from Morton the reply that, in his view,
the references to regeneration in the Prayer Book baptismal
service referred to a future event, which it was charitably
assumed would come to pass. His position emerges as identical to that of Saye, both of them denying that sacraments conferred grace. On the other side, Buckingham and Carlisle said
that Morton 'disparaged his own ministry' and did 'debase'
the sacrament of baptism.[62]

Both Buckeridge and Morton, ranged against one another
in 1626, had previously committed themselves to printed
statements on baptism which, in the light of the York House
Conference, were clearly divergent. Buckeridge had written of

[60] Ibid., p. 59; Ball, *Life of Preston*, pp. 121–2.
[61] Ibid., pp. 120–1.
[62] Cosin, *Works*, II. 61–2.

sacraments generally as 'chanels and conduits, wherein God's mercies and graces doe runne', and quoted favourably Optatus' opinion that the 'baptisme of Christians, given in the name of the Trinity, conferreth grace'.[63] In a work published the same year, 1618, Morton described baptism as a 'signe of regeneration, that is . . . of grace conferred by the spirit of God'.[64] For him election was a prerequisite of sacramental efficacy, whereas Buckeridge believed that 'sacraments (as much as in them is) cannot be without their own vertue'.[65] Bishop Carleton adopted a similar position to Morton on baptism, when replying to Montagu's *Appello Caesarem*: 'the sacrament is good to them to whom it is a seale of the righteousness of faith, but it is not a seale in all that receyve the sacrament for many receyve the signe which have not the thing.' Carleton also wrote that it was a judgement of 'charity' that all baptized infants were truly regenerate, and quoted St Augustine to this effect.[66] That Morton and Carleton should hold the doctrine of absolute predestination, with its emphasis on prevenient grace, and also have a limited expectation of the sacraments, goes far to explain the ceremonial changes of the 1630s when their brand of churchmanship went into eclipse. It was no accident that during the Arminian ascendancy altars and fonts came to dominate church interiors, for the two were logically connected, sacramental grace replacing the grace of predestination.

The first day's session at York House concluded with a motion by Saye and Coke that, to end all controversy, the rulings of the Synod of Dort should be established as authoritative in England. Here Buckingham, as chairman, again quoted the Arminian advice given him 'by divers grave and learned prelates' against such a course, and White proceeded to attack Dort teaching on the redemption. 'The Dortists . . . have denied that Christ died for all men.' On such a basis 'how could we say to all communicants whatsoever "The

[63] John Buckeridge, *A Discourse concerning Kneeling at the Communion* (1618), pp. 29, 31. Nevertheless, Buckeridge also quoted Calvin's words that 'the sacraments doe effect that which they figure onely in the elect'. Ibid., p. 32.
[64] Thomas Morton, *A Defence of the Innocencie of the Three Ceremonies of the Church of England* (1618), p. 229.
[65] Buckeridge, *A Discourse*, p. 31.
[66] Carleton, *An Examination*, pp. 96–8.

Body of our Lord which was given for thee", as we are bound to say? Let the opinion of the Dortists be admitted, and the tenth person in the Church shall not have been redeemed.'[67] As when discussing baptism, White based his arguments on the Catechism and the Prayer Book and pilloried Morton's position as an untenable gloss on these documents. Moreover, if Cosin is to be believed, Pembroke and Carlisle also argued against the reception of the Dort canons, saying that 'in England we have a rule of our own'.[68] This apparent willingness to bide by the Thirty-nine Articles, despite their lack of precision as regards predestinarian teaching, underlines the moderate stance of Pembroke and Carlisle at this time.

IV

The second and final session of the York House Conference took place on 17 February. Montagu was in attendance, as well as the five original clerics. Among the laity Buckingham, Pembroke, Carlisle, Warwick, Saye, and Coke were reinforced by Mulgrave, Bridgewater, and Dorset. Apparently Morton covered much the same ground as on the previous occasion, with Montagu being given an opportunity to reply in person to the various accusations against him.[69] Preston then took over from Morton. He began by questioning Montagu's placing 'traditions' on the same level as 'written instructions' for establishing Christian doctrine and practice, saying that this was based on a forged passage in St Basil. Montagu, in reply, 'confessed it was suspected by some of the preciser cut, but Dr. Preston told him that Bishop Bilson was none of them yet he did judge it supposititious'.[70] Although Preston did not make the point, one implication of Montagu's teaching was that religious ceremonies ceased to be a matter of 'indifference' and became instead obligatory by divine law. Indeed Buckeridge had earlier implied as much, writing of kneeling at communion that 'I dispute not whether it be a duetie of necessitie or a ceremonie of indifferencie'.[71] Again this has significance for developments during the 1630s, when conformity was more rigorously enforced.

[67] Cosin, *Works*, ii. 63–4.   [68] Ibid., p. 64.   [69] Ibid., pp. 73–4.
[70] Ball, *Life of Preston*, p. 124.   [71] Buckeridge, *A Discourse*, p. 243.

From the question of traditions Preston then returned to Arminianism, citing a number of passages from *A New Gagg* and *Appello Caesarem* where Montagu maintained 'election out of foresight, or to be a respective condicionall decree'.[72] In *A New Gagg*, Montagu had written that the English Church 'opposed' the teaching that St Peter 'was saved because that God would have him saved absolutely and resolved to save him necessarily'.[73] Similarly in *Appello Caesarem* Montagu had argued that 'there must needs first be a disproportion before there can bee conceived election or dereliction', and that all mankind being in a state of perdition God 'drew them out that took hold of mercy'.[74] Also in the *Appello*, Montagu had again denied an 'absolute, necessarie, determined, irresistable, irrespective decree of God, to call, save and glorifie St. Peter, for instance, infallibly, without any consideration had of, or regard unto, his faith, obedience [and] repentance'.[75] Back in 1618, at the Cambridge Commencement, White had determined against election being 'on account of works forseen'".[76] Aware of this, Preston now challenged him to defend Montagu's teaching. At this point White 'gave in and affermed that against that exception he had nothing to say, but left Mr Montagu to himsealfe to defende it'.[77] In the words of Preston's contemporary biographer, Thomas Ball, Montagu—bereft 'of his animating champion Dr White'—was

greatly troubled and cavilled at the words awhile, but the booke [*A New Gagg*] adjudging it for Dr Preston he said that the Church of England had not declared any thinge against it. Dr Preston alledged the 17TH article [of the Thirty-nine Articles and in support of unconditional election].[78]

Montagu was reduced to promising that 'he would write a booke to the contrary to explain himselfe better'.[79]

White's retreat as regards the question of conditional election is the more understandable given the ambiguous terms in

[72] BL Harleian MS 6866, fo. 77ʳ⁻ᵛ.
[73] Montagu, *A New Gagg*, p. 179.
[74] Montagu, *Appello Caesarem*, p. 64.
[75] Ibid., p. 58.
[76] See above, p. 44.
[77] BL Burney MS 362, fo. 92.
[78] Ball, *Life of Preston*, pp. 126, 129–30.
[79] BL Harleian MS 6866, fo. 78.

which he had earlier endorsed the teaching of Montagu on this subject. Explaining his reasons for licensing *Appello Caesarem*, in a memorandum addressed to Bishop Andrewes, White wrote of the relevant passages:

[Montagu's] meaning is that God all good, provoked by noe exter- nall cause, of his meere mercy, decreed to deliver all them from per- dition, and appointed them only to heavenly blisse, whom he did forsee that they would in tyme (being prompted and assisted by his grace) beleeve in Christ and embrace his mercy.[80]

White, however, had gone on to distinguish between election to grace and election to glory. The former is 'without respect to faith and repentance, and in causality precedeth them'.[81] Furthermore White had confessed that 'it is a matter very difficult, and peradventure imposible in this life, exactly and distinctly to declare the whole manner and order of divine election, and how the same being one aeternall and simulta- neous act in God is to be conceaved according to severall acts in our apprehension'.[82] At the York House Conference, as Pre- ston put it, White 'disclamed' and Montagu 'retracted' the doctrine of predestination from faith forseen.[83]

This first success scored by the Calvinist critics of Montagu was followed by a renewed request that the rulings of the Synod of Dort be given confessional status in England. Again it was urged by some of the laity present, and much stress was laid on the fact that 'there was nothing there [at Dort] deter- mined but what our delegates approved'.[84] White once more took his stand on the question of the redemption, objecting that the Dort canons denied Christ had died for all mankind. He 'affirmed earnestly that Christ dyed for all alike in God's intention and decree, for Cain as well as Abel, for Saul as well as David, for Judas as well as Peter, for the reprobate and damned in Hell as well as for the elect and saints in Heaven'.[85] To which Preston replied:

if Christ bee given alike to elect and reprobate in God's intention and decree then the greatest love that God ever shewed to mankind, and the best gifte that ever he gave, is like intended to the saints in

---

[80] Bodleian, Rawlinson MS C. 573, fo. 36.　　[81] Ibid., fo. 36ᵛ.
[82] Ibid., fo. 37.　　[83] BL Burney MS 362, fo. 93.
[84] Ball, *Life of Preston*, p. 130.　　[85] Ibid., p. 132.

Heaven and to the damned in Hell, but this is contrary to the Scriptures which are frequent in setting forth God's peculiar grace.[86]

White countered that 'the worst men had grace enough to keepe corruption and the evil of their nature downe, but the elect such as would do it easily'.[87] He also challenged Preston to say whether Christ had died 'for all or not'.[88] In reply Preston resorted to the conventional Calvinist distinction between the sufficiency of Christ's death for all and its efficacy to the elect alone, adding that 'the Arminians saie that no man can repent and beeleve without God's grace, but this grace he may take or refuse as he will'. Thus, on Arminian grounds, 'it is not God that maketh the difference beetwixt Peter and Judas but there owne freewill'.[89]

This second session of the York House Conference appears to have ended on an inconclusive note, and Montagu's promise to write a further book remained unfulfilled. What, then, did the conference achieve? The Montagu case never came before the House of Lords, and therefore the reactions of Pembroke and Carlisle were not put directly to the test. Certainly the conference failed to prevent Pembroke playing a part in the subsequent attempt to impeach Buckingham, although it is true that religion was a negligible element in the charges. As for Warwick and Saye, by late 1626 they were clearly in opposition to the crown. Yet in retrospect the York House Conference can be seen as poised between two worlds. Calvinist England was soon to be transformed into a country of overtly competing sects and churches and Calvinist bishops were about to be overtaken by the fate of prehistoric animals, unable to survive in a changed climate. If in the long term such a development was inevitable, the York House meeting hastened the process. The conference also marked the approximate point at which the circle of clerics patronized by Bishop Neile of Durham emerged as the effective spokesmen of the English Church.

---

[86] BL Harleian MS 6866, fo. 79.
[87] Ball, *Life of Preston*, p. 134.
[88] BL Harleian MS 6866, fo. 79ᵛ.
[89] Ibid., fos. 80–1.

8

Arminianism during the Personal Rule and after

I

THE decision of Charles I to dispense with parliament in 1629 ushered in a decade when, as Heylyn writes, 'the anti-Calvinist party became considerable both for power and number'.[1] At the beginning of Charles's reign, the Arminian Richard Montagu promised him 'defend me with the sword and I will defend you with the pen'', while the Calvinist George Carleton countered 'defend the truth and faith, whereof God hath made you the defender, and God (who only is able) will not faile to defend you'.[2] The King had decided against those who claimed to be on God's side, favouring instead a clerical group prepared to preach up monarchical authority in defence of its beliefs. Until 1628, however, both English archbishoprics continued to be held by Calvinists. That year the long-lived Archbishop Matthew of York died, to be replaced in rapid succession by three Arminians: Montaigne (1628), Harsnett (1628–31), and Neile (1632–40). Only in 1633 did the death of Archbishop Abbot make way for Laud at Canterbury. Via their episcopal lieutenants Laud and Neile actively sought to enforce Charles's religious declaration of 1628, throughout the dioceses of England and Wales, which meant in effect the proscription of Calvinism.[3] Because of royal support, Laud and Neile were now increasingly able to implement ideas which they had held for many years.

The new policy was clearly biting in London diocese as early as 1629. There a petition had begun to circulate among the clergy of the capital, until intercepted by Laud. Referring

---

[1] Heylyn, *Historia Quinqu-Articularis*, iii. 110.
[2] Montagu, *Appello Caesarem*, p. 322; Carleton, *An Examination*, sig. A3.
[3] Laud, *Works*, v. 312, 328; PRO, SP 16/259, fo. 167^{r-v}; R. A. Marchant, *The Puritans and the Church Courts in the Diocese of York, 1560–1642* (1960), pp. 82–3.

to the royal rulings of 1626 and 1628, against controverting the Arminian question, the authors complained that the

said edicts are so interpreted, and pressed upon us, as we are not a little discouraged and deterred from preaching those saving doctrines of God's free grace in election and predestination, which greatly confirme our faith of eternal salvation and fervently kindle our love to God, as the 17th article expressly mentioneth. So as we are brought into a great strayt either of incurring God's heavy displeasure, if we do not faithfully discharge our embassage in declaring the whole councell of God, or the danger of being censured for violators of your Majestie's said acts, if we preach these constant doctrines of our Church and confute the opposite Pelagian and Arminian heresies [which are] both preached and printed boldly without feare of censure. As if the saving doctrines of Christ were prohibited and these impious heresies priviledged.[4]

An example of such Arminian preaching is provided by the remarks of John Donne at Paul's Cross that November. His words almost certainly had the approval of higher authority, for we know that Laud, as Bishop of London, required to see copies of Paul's Cross sermons before they were preached.[5]

Donne, the Dean of St Paul's, referred on this occasion to those who

in an over-valuation of their own purity despise others as men whom nothing can save [and] will abridge and contract the large mercies of God in Christ, and elude and frustrate in a great part the generall promises of God. Men that are loth that God should speak so loud as to say 'He would have all men saved', and loth that Christ should spread his armies or shed his blood in such a compasse as might fall upon all. Men that think no sinne can hurt them because they are elect and that every sin makes every other man a reprobate. But with the Lord there is *copiosa redemptio*, plentifull redemption, and an overflowing cup of mercy.[6]

In the margin of the printed version of this sermon, and presumably also in Donne's original manuscript, is the word 'Cathari'—that is to say Puritans in Latin. The following January 1630 it was reported that Archbishop Harsnett of York had banned the sale, 'within his province', of the works

[4] Prynne, *Canterburies Doome*, p. 165; PRO, SP 16/408, fos. 322–4.
[5] M. MacLure, *The Paul's Cross Sermons, 1534–1642* (Toronto, 1958) p. 13.
[6] Donne, *Sermons*, IX. 119.

of William Perkins and Zacharias Ursinus.[7] This was certainly a way of cutting Calvinism off at source, albeit involving a very broad interpretation of Charles's declaration on the
predestinarian question. At about this time also Richard
Baylie, in his capacity as Archdeacon of Nottingham, wrote to
the ministers of his 'jurisdiction' that they were not to dispute of moderne divines amongst the reformed churches,
wharby you will rather teach than confute what you suppose
error'. Instead they were to preach 'Jesus Christ and him
crucified' as well as 'obedience to authority, even for conscience'.[8] Baylie himself succeeded Juxon as President of St
John's College, Oxford, in 1633 and was to be executor of
Laud's will.

Two London clerics bold enough to continue teaching Calvinist doctrine from the pulpit were Meredith Madey and
Daniel Votier. Madey preached that 'election is not universall
and common, but speciall and peculiar', saying Christ 'died
not for all, not for Cain, Esau, Judas [or] Julian'. For,
although God 'calls all' it is 'with limitation': 'of all nations
some, of all degrees some and of all kindes some.' Madey also
maintained 'the principall and efficient cause' of election to be
'the will of God' without 'any merit of man', concluding 'with
that reverend councell of Dort' that 'God does not elect for
good workes or faith foreseene, but to good workes and faith'.[9]
Similarly Votier taught 'that some are elect, some reprobate'
and 'that Christ died only for the elect'.[10] Both men were suspended by Laud, although such doctrine had been normal
until recently. By contrast in 1633, on the eve of Laud being
promoted to Canterbury, a new edition of the standard Latin–
English dictionary was dedicated to him, which contained for
the first time the term 'praedestinatiani'. They were defined
as 'a kinde of heretiques that held fatall predestination of
every particular matter, person or action, and that all things
came to passe and fell out necessarily, especially touching the
salvation and damnation of particular men'.[11] Within two

[7] BL Add MS 35, 331, fo. 36ᵛ. For Perkins and Ursinus, see above, pp. 29, 35.
[8] Bodleian, Rawlinson MS C.421, fo. 27.
[9] PRO, SP 16/186, fos. 49, 104.
[10] PRO, SP 16/499, fo. 147.
[11] Francis Holyoke, *Dictionarium Etymologicarum Latinum* (1633), sigs. [A2], Bbbbbʳ⁻ᵛ.

years this definition was being used against Calvinists by Arminians.[12]

Indeed, the most obvious index of religious change at this time is provided by the publications of the London and university presses. Before 1624 these were almost exclusively Calvinist. Thereafter an alteration in licensing policy occurred, with the consequent appearance of a series of Arminian works. Calvinist teaching, on the other hand, was subject to a growing censorship.[13] By 1635 the publishing situation had been transformed. At least nine books printed in this year contained favourable notices of Arminian doctrine. The most forthright was a second edition of *God's Love to Mankind* manifested, according to the subtitle, 'by disprooving his Absolute Decree for their Damnation'. Ascribed jointly to Samuel Hoard, Rector of Moreton in Essex, and Henry Mason, now Rector of St Andrew Undershaft in London, the work was unlicensed. Nevertheless, there seems to have been little attempt at suppressing either edition.[14] Of works licensed this year, we have already cited the hostile references to the Synod of Dort by Bishop Andrewes, first published in 1629 and now appearing in a third edition of his sermons, as well as the Arminian views of Thomas Laurence and Robert Shelford, published at Oxford and Cambridge respectively.[15] Edward Boughen, former chaplain to Bishop Howson, also aired his Arminian sympathies in print at this time, referring to those who make Christ 'a saviour but of a little flock' and 'cannot endure to receive God's promises in such wise as they bee generally set forth to us in Holy Scripture'.[16] Similarly Thomas Chown, a layman and leading member of the Sussex gentry, in his *Collectiones Theologicarum* posits the universal offer of salvation to fallen man which can be accepted or rejected, while opposing belief in what he calls 'stoical necessity''. He dedicated his remarks to Archbishop Laud.[17] Chown and Boughen

---

[12] Edmund Reeve, *The Communion Booke Catechism Expounded* (1635), p. 67.

[13] Prynne, *Canterburies Doome*, pp. 171, 279–88, 303–7, 309–12, 313, 331–2, 334–5, 343–5.

[14] Twisse, *The Riches of God's Love*, ii. sig. Aaa2 and *passim*.

[15] See above, pp. 45, 53, 83, 103.

[16] Edward Boughen, *Two Sermons* (1635), ii. 49. Boughen describes himself as chaplain to Bishop Howson in the dedication of his *A Sermon of Confirmation* (1620), sig. A2ᵛ.

[17] Thomas Chown, *Collectiones Theologicarum* (1635), sigs. A3–A4, pp. 7, 12–21.

had both been at Christ Church, Oxford, in the first years of the seventeenth century.[18] James Conyers, in a Paul's Cross sermon both preached and printed in 1635, attacked those who think themselves 'cleare of all tincture of sinne'. No one, he indicated, could be sure of final perseverance.[19] Meanwhile Thomas Jackson continued to criticize Calvinist teaching, in his *The Humiliation of the Son of God*. He writes there, for example, of the 'preposterous presumption' of authors who set forth 'maps or systems of God's decrees before all times'.[20] Lastly Edmund Reeve incorporated the whole gamut of Arminian doctrine in his *Communion Booke Catechism*, teaching conditional predestination, universal grace and that 'the elect' might perish.[21]

The consequences of this rise of Arminianism were particularly serious for contemporary Puritanism, altering as it did the doctrinal basis of English Church membership. As late as January 1633, Archbishop Abbot could report that 'there is not in the Church of England left any inconformable minister which appeareth', save two or three 'whom no time can tame, nor instruction conquer'. These, wrote the Archbishop, had now been deprived.[22] Two years earlier a similar picture had come from the Puritan side. Humphrey Fenn, a presbyterian agitator from Elizabethan days, complained in the preamble to his will of 'this time wherein, through the defection of many, others thinke the cause forsaken'. Since the accession of King James, he continued, 'our cause hath lost many lovers by death' and 'many famous ministers and others' by desertion.[23] Clearly Puritanism had not ceased to exist, and Abbot's claim particularly is liable to strike a modern reader as extremely optimistic. But after the initial drive against Puritan nonconformity, following the Hampton Court Conference, a *modus vivendi* seems to have been reached. Only 'occasional conformity' was now required of those clergy who subscribed to the legality of Prayer Book and bishops. This, it has been

---

[18] Foster, *Alumni Oxonienses*, pp. 154, 275.
[19] James Conyers, *Christ's Love and Saints' Sacrifice* (1635), pp. 12–13.
[20] Jackson, *Works*, VII. 416.
[21] Reeve, *Communion Booke Catechism*, pp. 47–9, 61–7.
[22] Laud, *Works*, V. 310.
[23] *The Last Will and Testament, with the Profession of Faith of Humfrey Fen, sometimes Pastor of one of the Churches of Coventry* (1641), sigs. A3, A4; PRO, SP 16/260, fos. 166–7.

argued, was royal policy and considerably antedated the promotion of Abbot to Canterbury in 1611.[24] Underlying such an accommodation was the much more long-standing assumption that in matters of doctrine Puritans and their opponents were in fundamental agreement.

To some extent Puritanism has always existed in the eye of the beholder. Certainly the religious perceptions of Laud and Neile were very different from those of their archiepiscopal predecessors. As we have seen, English Arminians extended the definition of puritanism so as to include Calvinist doctrine. They also objected to some of the most characteristic features of the Jacobean Church, notably the stress on preaching and anti-Catholic polemic. Both of these themes had found expression in the dedication to King James, in 1611, of the authorized translation of the Bible—itself the brainchild of the Puritan John Reynolds. James was there congratulated on his encouragement of preaching, 'that inestimable treasure which excelleth all the riches of the earth', and his writing against the Pope, 'that man of sin'. Indeed the pulpit has some claim to be regarded as the icon of Jacobean religious life. The Arminians' dislike of excessive preaching is most clearly manifested in their attempts to suppress lectureships, the purpose of which was the provision of sermons.[25] It was also a familiar refrain in the mouth of Lancelot Andrewes.[26] As regards the Arminian attitude towards Catholicism, in 1629 a doctor of divinity told the House of Commons that Neile said 'he had oftentimes heard him preach before King James and that he used to preach against Popery, which he said was well liked of then but now (said he) you must not do so'.[27] At the same time Arminians placed great emphasis on the sacraments, underlining this by a novel ceremonialism.

During the 1630s awareness that Calvinism was no longer the orthodoxy of the English Church contributed to the growth of nonconformity and even separatism. An early instance is that of John Davenport. In the 1620s Davenport conformed, taking the attitude that it is 'better to unite our

[24] K. Fincham, 'Pastoral Roles of the Jacobean Episcopate in Canterbury Province', London Ph.D. thesis, 1985, pp. 276–313.
[25] Collinson, 'Lectures by Combination', pp. 203–9.
[26] Andrewes, *Works*, I. 421–3, III. 318, IV. 376–7, V. 186–8, 202.
[27] *Commons Debates for 1629*, p. 50.

forces against those who oppose us in fundamentalls then to be divided amongst our selves about ceremonialls'. For Davenport one such fundamental was 'Arminianisme', believing as he did that 'God hath . . . before the foundation of the world chosen some in Jesus Christ to eternall life, to the praise and glory of his grace, and rejected or reprobated others to the praise of his justice'. Such teaching was central to his profession of faith. But as it became increasingly clear that the Arminians had permanently 'stolne in and taken possession of the house', this reason for conforming ceased to operate. Davenport's growing disenchantment with the Church of England coincided with the rise to power of Laud, culminating in his own withdrawal to Amsterdam in 1633.[28]

Another well-documented case is that of Henry Burton. One of his earliest published works was a reply in 1626 to Richard Montagu's *Appello Caesarem*. Answering the allegation that Calvinists were Puritans, Burton had provided the following thinly disguised sketch of himself in the role of *Orthodoxus*.

In one sense he is no Puritan, for he is conformable [and] none of the refractories, but doth both practise himselfe and preach upon occasion in the defence of ecclesiasticall ceremonies, and that very earnestly insomuch as I have seene him sometimes put backe from the communion those which would not receive it kneeling.[29]

Three years later Burton can be found asking rhetorically 'why should the world, O Lord, complaine and cry where is the spirit of those ancient bishops and martyrs, and learned champions of thy truth, as of Cranmer, Ridley, Latimer, Hooper, Bucer, Peter Martyr, Jewel, and other faithfull witnesses . . .?'[30] In the autobiography which Burton subsequently wrote, he recalled that during the mid-1630s 'I began in my practice, as in my judgement, to fall off from ceremonies', because of the rise of a 'prelaticall party' which 'laboured to undermine and overthrow the true Protestant religion'.[31] True Protestantism, according to Burton, involved

---

[28] John Davenport, *Letters*, ed. I. M. Calder (Yale, 1937), pp. 3, 13–14, 23–4, 39, 69.
[29] Burton, *A Plea*, pp. 8, 91.
[30] Henry Burton, *Truth's Triumph over Trent* (1629), sig. *4.
[31] Henry Burton, *A Narration* (1643), pp. 8–9.

such 'fundamentalls as praedestination, election, freewill, justification, faith, perseverance in saving grace, certainty of salvation and the like'.[32] By 1640 he was advocating the total abolition of episcopacy.[33]

For Calvinists the death of William Herbert, third Earl of Pembroke, had special significance. To Thomas Chafin, preaching at his funeral in April 1630, it seemed to presage a dark and fearful future. Taking as his text Isaiah 57:1, he elaborated on the theme that Pembroke had been spared the possible evils to come. 'Should the abomination of desolation, the idoll of the masse, bee set up againe in the holy place . . . should we see in our owne land, and of our owne country-men, ensigne borne against ensigne, and crosse against crosse . . . happy he his eyes should behold none of al this.' Meanwhile Pembroke, the 'just man', is 'now taken up into the company of the faithfull saints departed . . . felled to make timber for the triumphant church in heaven'.[34] There is perhaps a danger of reading too much prophetic insight into these remarks, particularly since Chafin subsequently changed his tune.[35] Moreover at this time he held out the hope that Pembroke's brother and heir, Philip Herbert, would imitate his predecessor in 'the couragious prosecution of all good causes for God's glory and the church'.[36] Nevertheless, the mood of apprehension was real enough.

II

Evidence in microcosm of the actual complexity of the English religious situation, at the start of Charles I's personal rule, survives for the county of Essex. It consists of two petitions, each addressed to Laud as Bishop of London in November 1629. The first is signed by forty-nine clergy, styling themselves as 'obedient to his Majestie's ecclesiasticall lawes', while the second is signed by forty-one clergy who claim to be

---

[32] Burton, *A Plea*, sig. ¶3.

[33] Henry Burton, *Lord Bishops none of the Lord's Bishops* (1640); W. Lamont, 'Prynne, Burton and the Puritan Triumph', *Huntington Library Quarterly*, 27 (1963–4), 103–13.

[34] Thomas Chafin, *The Just Man's Memoriall* (1630), pp. 13–14, 22, 24, 33–4. I owe my knowledge of this sermon to Professor D. Hirst.

[35] A. G. Matthews, *Walker Revised* (Oxford, 1948), p. 371.

[36] Chafin, *Just Man's Memoriall*, sig. A3.

'of the conformable part'. Both petitions have reference to the intended prosecution for nonconformity of Thomas Hooker, lecturer at Chelmsford, whom the forty-nine clergy describe as 'for his disposition peaceable, no wayes turbulent or factious'. The forty-one 'conformable' clergy, by contrast, complain of widespread 'irregularities' in London diocese, 'most men doing what seemeth good in their owne eyes, and fewe regarding the authoritie of the Church or their owne duetie'; they ask Laud 'to enforce those irregulars to conforme'.[37] Each group consisted predominantly of Cambridge graduates and there was little difference in age. The supporters of Hooker, however, included seven former members of Emmanuel College,[38] where he had been a fellow, compared with only one among his opponents.[39] Similarly six at least of Hooker's supporters held livings in the gift of the Earl of Warwick, whose county residence was at Felsted, and his patronage was confined to them.[40] (Warwick subsequently emerged as a protector of Hooker.[41]) There is also a geographical division, approximately along the line of the road from London to Colchester, with the forty-one 'conformable' clergy beneficed mainly in the south-east of the county.[42] This may indirectly reflect the more advanced Protestantism of those engaged in the cloth industry, which was located in north Essex. It also suggests a considerable potential following for the policies being pursued by Laud. But the comparative fluidity of the situation is indicated by the fact that three clergy felt able to sign both petitions.[43]

The initiative in prosecuting Hooker almost certainly came from Laud, who was translated to the bishopric of London in July 1628, although a local lobby to the same effect soon

[37] PRO, SP 16/151, fo. 65^{r-v} and SP 16/152, fo. 4^{r-v}.
[38] Giles Allen, Theodore Herring, Isaac Joyner junior, Stephen Marshall, William Pease, Nehemiah Rogers, and Nathaniel Ward.
[39] William Eyre.
[40] John Beadle, Samuel Collins, Daniel Duckfield, Samuel Hoard, Christopher Scott, and Samuel Wharton.
[41] Thomas Hooker, *Writings*, ed. G. H. Williams *et al.* (Cambridge, Mass., 1975), p. 23. Warwick had himself attended Emmanuel College, and probably overlapped with Hooker there.
[42] See map. One of Hooker's supporters, Mark Mott, gives no parish of residence. This may be the Rector of Little Raine. Alternatively it could be his namesake who was curate at Stisted by 1634. Venn, *Alumni Cantabrigienses*, III. 222.
[43] Tobias Hewett, Nicholas Padmore, and Robert Paley.

emerged. In the summer of 1629 the air was said to be 'filled with the obstreperous clamours of his [Hooker's] followers against my lord of London, as a man indeavouring to suppres good preaching and advance Popery'. The same informant

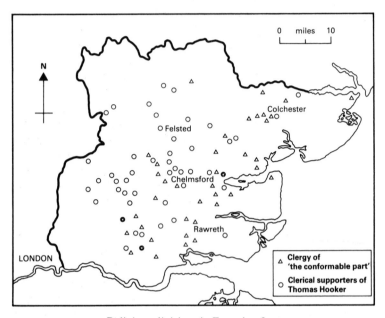

Religious divisions in Essex in 1629

wrote of Laud as going 'to take the wolf by the ears'*[44] Clerical opposition to Hooker within the county appears to have been led by John Browning, Rector of Rawreth. Browning had been chaplain to the Arminian Bishop Andrewes, of whom he wrote to Laud on 3 November 1629 in terms of 'that duty I shall ever owne to the ever-blessed and never dynge memory of my most holy, learned and religious lord and patron'. According to him, Andrewes had silenced Hooker previously in Winchester diocese, and 'I doubt not of your lordship's treadinge in the same steps of that most religious prelate'. More generally he complained of 'our labours overturned, our studyes as water spilt, our persons traduced, our selves even in those

[44] PRO, SP 16/142, fo. 161 and SP 16/144, fo. 65.

highest businesses of our callings . . . utterly slighted and con-
temned', by Hooker and his like.[45]

 Browning's co-petitioners included Joshua Mapletoft, Vicar
of Margaretting and nephew of the Arminian Nicholas Ferrar.
When Mapletoft came to make his will in 1634 he requested
that his wife and children join the Ferrars in retreat at Little
Gidding, there to 'spend their tyme in the . . . constant service
of God Almighty'.[46] Yet on the same side was Thomas Oxley,
now Rector of Chignal St James, who twenty years earlier
can be found inveighing against the dumb dogs of Durham
diocese.[47] While among Hooker's supporters Nathaniel Ward,
who had petitioned parliament against Arminianism in
1624,[48] was joined by Samuel Hoard soon to be notorious for
his Arminian views. Someone, however, who signed neither
petition was John Eaton, Rector of South Hanningfield since
1598. Whether or not this absenteeism was intentional, Eaton
writes of himself in his will of 1638 as 'confidently and steed-
fastly beleeving . . . to be one of the elected and chosen people
from the begining of the world' and, he goes on, 'I renounce
and detest all doctrine of religion not agreable to the doctrine
preached and professed in the Church of England in the dayes
of our famous princes Queen Elizabeth and King Jeames'.[49]
Such was the authentic voice of the Calvinist old guard.

 Between them these two petitions indicate that something of
a *laissez-faire* attitude towards nonconformity had prevailed
among Laud's predecessors in London diocese. They also
point to the reputation which the new bishop had already
established. From 1604 to 1621 a succession of committed
Calvinists had held the bishopric of London.[50] These were followed by George Montaigne, an Arminian but an easygoing
one who did not try to enforce complete conformity. Indeed
Hooker was *persona grata* enough with Montaigne apparently

[45] PRO, SP 16/151, fo. 19ʳ⁻ᵛ.
[46] PRO, PROB. 11/169, fo. 26ᵛ.
[47] See above, p. 115.
[48] See above, pp. 148, n. 129.
[49] Greater London Record Office, DL/C/362, fo. 369.
[50] Richard Vaughan (1604–7), Thomas Ravis (1607–9), George Abbot (1610–11),
and John King (1611–21). For Abbot, King, and Ravis, see above, pp. 21–2, 62–3.
Among other evidence of Vaughan's Calvinism is the fact that he helped draw up the
Lambeth Articles. Fuller, *Church History*, v. 219.

to have preached before him at Chelmsford during the 1620s.[51] The replacement of Montaigne by Laud in 1628, however, is characteristic of the general alteration by then under way in the leadership of the English Church. At the same time the Essex petitions of November 1629 foreshadow the religious polarization of the 1630s. Hooker and at least two of his supporters, Nathaniel Ward and Thomas Weld, were shortly to sail for New England exile. 'God is going', said Hooker, in his farewell sermon.[52] The Chelmsford stipendiary lectureship was converted in February 1630 into a combination served by local clergy such as Browning.[53] Henceforward the evangel formerly preached by Hooker, berating 'the carnall cavills of gracelesse persons' who 'hate the minister that brings the word with any power to their souls',[54] was replaced by sermons both extolling the virtues of conformity and Arminian in doctrinal tone. For example, in March 1630 Browning spoke of 'that old condemned heresie . . . that no man can depart from grace after baptisme', and asked his auditory 'if a church, a congregation, a number of faithfull men is not, what one (though for the present faithfull and believing) can be secure?'[55]

By 1634 Browning had acquired as a patron Lord Maynard, who in August of the following year became joint Lord-Lieutenant of Essex with the Earl of Warwick.[56] Maynard succeeded the Earl of Portland in the joint lieutenancy, and it looks as if his appointment represents not only a continuing wish to counterbalance Warwick politically but also the growing power of Archbishop Laud at court. As early as 1621 Maynard had build a private chapel at his family home, Easton Lodge. The outstanding feature of this chapel, long since demolished, was the painted glass which included a

[51] A. Clark, 'Dr Plume's Pocket-Book', *Essex Review*, 14 (1905), 67.

[52] Thomas Hooker, *Writings*, p. 245.

[53] Collinson, 'Lectures by Combination', p. 207; PRO, SP 16/160, fo. 131 and SP 16/161, fo. 74.

[54] Thomas Hooker, *The Soules Preparation for Christ* (1632), pp. 49, 68.

[55] PRO, SP 16/163, fo. 65; John Browning, *Concerning Publike Prayer and the Fasts of the Church* (1636), pp. 164–5. These sermons are dedicated to Lord Maynard, whom Browning describes as 'a chief auditor at the preaching of some of them' and 'my most noble, free and bountifull patron'. Ibid., sigs. A3–A4ᵛ.

[56] Newcourt, *Repertorium*, II. 238; J. C. Sainty, *Lieutenants of Counties, 1585–1642* (1970), p. 20.

picture of Christ's crucifixion. This glass survives and is among the first of its kind in an English Protestant context (plate 3).[57] Laud's arbitration of a tithe dispute involving Maynard perhaps first brought the two men together in 1630.[58] Eight years later Maynard, when making his will, asked that Laud be appointed, with Lady Anne Maynard, guardian of his son. He also referred there to his own chapel-building activities both at Easton Lodge and at Waltons, his other Essex residence where a private chapel had been consecrated in 1636. 'Since the consecration of which said chappells', he notes, 'I have evidently perceaved the favour and blessing of Almighty God to have increased towards me.' This revived doctrine of good works was accompanied by an elaborate statement of religious faith. Maynard speaks of 'not knowinge when the master of the house cometh' but 'that the Lord hath pronounced those servants blessed whome when he cometh hee shall finde watching', and he goes on to invoke Christ's 'generall promises unto all men penitent synners'.[59]

A first generation peer, whose father had been one of Burghley's secretaries, Maynard was among those involved in London property development.[60] He had probably acquired his religious views during the first decade of the century whilst resident at St John's College, Cambridge. In the aftermath of the Calvinist rule of William Whitaker, as Master, a different theology had gained ground fairly rapidly in the college.[61] The best-known among these early anti-Calvinists was Valentine Carey, future Bishop of Exeter. Maynard can be found in 1620 writing with affection of Carey 'and the rest of our good friends of St. John's'.[62] The Arminian Richard Montagu described Carey in 1625 as 'doctrinally sound' and 'one of the firmest against our [Puritan] faction'.[63] Maynard kept in close

---

[57] M. Archer, '17th Century Painted Glass at Little Easton', *Essex Journal*, 12 (1977), 3–10. I am most grateful to Mr Archer for his advice both in this particular and as regards the painted glass of the period generally. At an earlier stage of my inquiries Miss M. Tomlinson of Little Easton was also very helpful.

[58] Newcourt, *Repertorium*, ii. 580–1.

[59] PRO, PROB. 11/185, fos. 185, 190ᵛ, 194ʳ⁻ᵛ.

[60] Stone, *Crisis of the Aristocracy*, p. 362.

[61] Thomas Baker, *History of the College of St. John the Evangelist, Cambridge*, ed. J. E. B. Mayor (Cambridge, 1869), i. 196.

[62] *The Eagle*, 36 (1914–15), 30.

[63] Cosin, *Correspondence*, i. 60.

touch with his former college, among other things retaining a 'chamber' there, and on more than one occasion invited his 'good friends of St. John's' to stay at Easton Lodge. When recommending candidates to the college for election to fellow-ships during the early 1620s, he also tended to emphasize their freedom from 'Puritanisme'.[64] In the circumstances Maynard was likely to have been finely attuned to the predestinarian controversy.

During the 1630s Maynard's former Cambridge college, St John's, emerged as second to none in the lavishness of its new chapel furnishings. William Beale, who became Master in 1634, seems to have been mainly responsible, although he was abetted by the senior fellow—John Price. The latter appa-rently secured the removal of the communion table to an altarwise position before the appointment of Beale. Neverthe-less, it was under Beale's mastership that the chapel was 'dressed up after a new fashion'. The changes included a new altar frontal depicting Christ 'taken from the cross and pre-pared for his sepulchre'. On the back of the altar was 'a large crucifix' and above this was a canopy painted with angels, while over the altar was a 'sunne with great light beames and a dove in the middest'. Around the walls were large gilt-framed pictures, portraying the life of Christ 'from his concep-tion to his ascension'.[65] Beale was also chiefly responsible, as Vice-Chancellor, for the publication at Cambridge in 1635 of Robert Shelford's Arminian discourses.[66] Only Peterhouse chapel, under the mastership of the Arminian John Cosin, can challenge comparison with that of St John's.[67] Both, moreover, illustrate the link between Arminianism and the 'beauty of holiness'.[68]

Lord Maynard himself is a reminder that Arminianism had genuine lay support. Clerical attitudes, however, are easier to discover, and there survive some interesting accounts of

[64] *The Eagle*, 23 (1901–2), 18–19 and 36 (1914–15), 30, 135. I am grateful to Dr R. Cust and Dr M. Underwood for their help concerning Lord Maynard's connections with St John's College, Cambridge.

[65] BL, Harleian MS 7019, fo. 74.

[66] Ibid., fo. 68.

[67] Ibid., fo. 71.

[68] Among many examples of such a link, one of the clearest is provided by the writ-ings of Shelford himself. See above, pp. 53–6.

Arminianism among the English parish clergy. The records of
the Earl of Manchester's committees for scandalous ministers,
covering the counties of the Eastern Association, are one
source. Also a number of petitions or informations were presented to the Long Parliament in its early days complaining
about the doctrine and life of individual incumbents. In addition the occasional contemporary comment survives. Such
evidence cannot be used for statistical purposes, among other
reasons because of the unwillingness of witnesses to come forward. Many parishioners, wrote Manchester, were 'enimyes
to that blessed reformacion so much desired by the parliament
and lorth to come under a powerfull minesry'. Others, he
complained, had been bribed by the parson waiving demands
for tithes.[69] The accused on their part stressed the doubtful
character of many of those who informed against them.
Moreover, the political loyalties of the clergy soon became an
overriding consideration, while the religious issues of the
1630s were replaced by more immediate ones like the Solemn
League and Covenant. There is a further question of the general level of religious awareness. Would the average
parishioner know whether he or she were hearing an Arminian sermon? Alternatively they may have thought such
teachings to be in accord with true Christianity. What we
have here then are a number of illustrative cases.

Twenty-five instances are currently known to me, where
local clergy were accused of Arminianism. They come from
the City of London and nine English counties. There were six
doctors of divinity among them.[70] Four of the twenty-five had
been at university during the 1590s,[71] although a majority had
attended either Oxford or Cambridge in the second decade of
the seventeenth century.[72] No particular college clearly stands
out, the biggest single group being four former members of
Christ's College, Cambridge.[73] Seven such accusations survive

[69] A. Everitt, *Suffolk and the Great Rebellion* (1961), pp. 64–5.
[70] Nicholas Andrewes, William Brough, Robert Cottisford, John Gifford, John Mountford, and Thomas Vane.
[71] John Gifford, William Mervin, John Mountford, and Robert Sacker.
[72] Nicholas Andrewes, Theodore Beale, William Brough, James Buck, Edward Cherry, Robert Cottisford, Henry Meriton, Christopher Newsteade, Jeremiah Ravens, and Thomas Vane.
[73] William Brough, Edward Cherry, Robert Pory, and Thomas Vane.

from Huntingdonshire, although no details are given. John Clement, Rector of Chesterton and Woodston, and Henry Salmon, Vicar of Stanground, were both 'defamed for Arminianisme'. Henry Meriton, Rector of Stilton, was reported as 'leaning to the Arminian side'. John Reynolds, Vicar of St Ives, his unnamed curate, and William Sampson, curate of Waresly, were all said to be 'superstitious Arminianes'. Finally Robert Sacker, curate of Upwood, was described as being 'a light vaine Arminiane'.[74] Elsewhere specific Arminian teachings are usually mentioned.

Thus of the four Suffolk allegations of Arminianism, Theodore Beale, Vicar of Ash Bocking, argued 'that Christ must save the greatest parte of people otherwise he can be no saviour, and that by the rule of logicke. For if two captaynes go into the feild to fight he that loseth the greatest part of men how cann he be said to be a saviour?'[75] James Buck, Vicar of Stradbroke, maintained 'universal grace',[76] while Robert Cottisford, Rector of Hadleigh, taught that 'men have by nature free will to all good'.[77] Jeremiah Ravens, Rector of Chattisham, was 'an Arminian teaching that today a man may be a child of God and tomorrow a child of the Devil'.[78] Three Essex clergy were similarly charged. Edward Cherry, Vicar of Much-Holland, preached that 'baptisme washeth away originall sinne, and that all men may be saved if they will and have free will thereunto'.[79] Christopher Newsteade, Rector of Stisted, asserted that 'Christ died for all, proving it by the catechisme in the Common Prayer Book', against his curate's distinction between the sufficiency and efficiency of Christ's death.[80] At Mount Bures a kinsman of the Vicar, who was John Simpson, defended 'finall falling from grace'.[81] The three London cases are especially detailed. William Brough, Rector of St Michael Cornhill, taught 'the errors of Arminianism, of universal grace and free-will in man fallen, and the apostacy of the saints'.[82] John Gifford, Rector of St Michael Bassishaw,

---

[74] Bodleian, Carte MS 103, fos. 64, 65. I owe this reference to Professor Russell.
[75] Lincoln City Library, MS 5458, fo. 15.
[76] John White, *The First Century of Scandalous, Malignant Priests* (1643), p. 43.
[77] Ibid., p. 8.
[78] Bodleian, John Walker MS C.6, fo. 26.
[79] White, *First Century*, p. 3.
[80] BL Add MS 5829, fo. 19.
[81] Ibid., fo. 15.
[82] *Lords Journals*, v. 664.

'endeavoured by his preaching to corrupt his people with the leaven of Arminianism . . . pressing upon them to believe election in faith forseen, universal grace, free-will in man fallen and falling away from grace'.[83] The Rector of St Margaret New Fish Street, Robert Pory, preached the 'Arminian doctrine that there is no divine decree of particular actions or persons, nor love of God to particular persons, but that Christ died for all and the ground of our election to be in ourselves'.[84]

From Kent Edward Boughen, Rector of Woodchurch, was cited for 'obscure handling of such places of Scripture as seeme to implye generall salvation' and 'the doctrine of beleevers' assurance',[85] while Thomas Vane, Rector of Crayford, had apparently determined 'against predestinacion and for free will, to the great discomforte, trouble and greife of many of the auditors'.[86] Of the two Lincolnshire accusations, Hugh Barcroft, Rector of Wyberton, urged on his first Sunday in the parish 'this Popishe Arminion and false point of doctrine that noe man canne bee assured of his salvaccion in this life, or as much in effect'.[87] Thomas Gibson, Vicar of Horncastle in the same county, maintained 'that a man sinninge is reprobate and repenting is elect, and sinninge again the same elect is reprobate, and that neither eleccion nor reprobacion are from eternity, and speakinge against eleccion said that Calvin went aboute to disthrone God'.[88] In Hertfordshire John Mountford, Rector of Anstey, reportedly 'endeavoured to leaven his people with the doctrines of Arminianisme'. He also taught that 'God was alwayes present at the altar by the presence of his grace'.[89] In Surrey Nicholas Andrewes, Rector of Guildford, 'in his sermons', so it was said, 'greatly exclaimes against that doctrin which teacheth that the greatest part of the world should be damned'.[90] In Wiltshire William Mervin, Rector of Fonthill Gifford, was named as one 'suspected to be an Arminion'.[91] Lastly in Somerset, during 1632, Walter

[83] Ibid., p. 635.   [84] Ibid., p. 665.

[85] *Proceedings . . . in the County of Kent*, ed. L. B. Larking (Camden Soc., 1st Ser. 80, 1862), p. 123.

[86] Ibid., p. 118. This petition did not emanate from Vane's own parish, but from Dartford where he had also preached.

[87] J. W. F. Hill, 'The Royalist Clergy of Lincolnshire', *Lincoln Architectural and Archaeological Society*, 2 (1938), 47.

[88] Ibid., p. 59.   [89] White, *First Century*, p. 13.

[90] Ibid., p. 9.   [91] BL Add MS 22084, fo. 134.

Travers, Vicar of Pitminster, was defamed as 'a heretic and an Arminian'.[92]

As regards two of these twenty-five clergy, their alleged views can be tested against published work. Both Boughen's sermons of the 1630s and Buck's *Treatise of the Beatitudes*, published in 1637, go far towards confirming the later charges. Boughen alluded in 1635 to the Arminian controversy and criticized members of the episcopate who still supported Calvinism, 'for truth would oppose if falshood did displease, and every bishop would readily prevent such contagious doctrine if he were really offended with it'.[93] We have already quoted Boughen's advocacy of universal grace. Buck likewise referred to a division of opinion among the hierarchy, and argued that their majority decision must be accepted. The 'faith of England is not in the sole dead letter of our Articles, and Church booke etc., but in the living spirit and consent of the fathers of the Church, as proper judges in spiritualities, determining the sense of the Articles and declaring to us the opinion of our mother the holy Church of England'. On these grounds he endorsed current religious changes, ignoring the potentially all-important role of the royal supremacy. Buck also said harsh things about lecturers who 'suck up the fat of the earth'.[94] Two years before he had been involved in a tithe dispute with his parishioners, which the Privy Council adjudicated in his favour.[95] This may well have left a legacy of hostility.

Such charges of Arminianism in the early 1640s are found associated with others complaining of a novel emphasis on the sacraments, especially that of communion. Pictures of the crucifixion had appeared in the east windows of chancels and elaborate bowings were employed in approaching newly devised altars, sometimes accompanied with singing part of the 43rd Psalm—'Then will I go unto the altar of God'.[96] This last seems to have been modelled on the Sarum Missal.[97] Con-

---

[92] T. H. Peake, 'The Somerset Clergy and the Church Courts in the Diocese of Bath and Wells, 1625–42', Bristol M.Litt. thesis, 1978, p. 36.

[93] Boughen, *Two Sermons*, i. 3.

[94] James Buck, *A Treatise of the Beatitudes* (1637), pp. 283–4, 332.

[95] PRO, SP 16/304, fo. 61.

[96] White, *First Century*, p. 13; J. W. F. Hill, 'Royalist Clergy', p. 58.

[97] *The Sarum Missal*, ed. and tr. A. H. Pearson (1884), p. 291.

fession was also urged and doctrines of the eucharist which approximated to transubstantiation had apparently been broached.[98] Moreover, on occasion, 'the picture of a flying dove', symbolizing the grace of 'the Holy Ghost', was placed over the font.[99] As early as July 1629 the Hertfordshire grand jury had complained at the assizes of 'the exceedinge increase of Poperye and Arminianisme'. The previous March Thomas Rayment, Rector of Ashwell, was presented for removing 'the auncient communion table from the middest of the chaunsell wheare it hath stoode before, ever since the beginninge of Queen Elizabeth her raigne'. Instead he had installed a new one, 'close to the walle at the east end of the chauncell'.[100] The theory behind these practices is exemplified by Edmund Reeve's *Communion Booke Catechism* of 1635. With the baptismal 'laver of regeneration' all infants are 'received into the number of the children of God', for 'God is mercifull to universall man-kinde'. Similarly Reeve cites the words of the communion service, concerning the body and blood of Christ, in order to refute the idea that anyone is 'absolutely reprobated'.[101]

III

During the 1630s the interiors of many English parish churches were transformed more radically than at any time since the Elizabethan settlement of religion. This chiefly involved the conversion of communion tables into altars, permanently railed in at the east ends of chancels. The individual initiatives of clergy such as Thomas Rayment, or the more famous Vicar of Grantham, Peter Titley,[102] now became official government policy. According to Heylyn, the precedent for change was established by King Charles's judgement, on 3 November 1633, concerning the position of the communion table at St Gregory's Church, which adjoined St Paul's

[98] White, *First Century*, pp. 8, 43; *Proceedings . . . in the County of Kent*, ed. Larking, p. 118.

[99] White, *First Century*, p. 39. The clergyman concerned in this particular case, Thomas Bailey, was not directly accused of Arminianism.

[100] PRO, ASSI. 35/71/4, fo. 6 and ASSI. 35/71/5, fo. 10. I owe these references to Mrs J. Calnan.

[101] Reeve, *Communion Booke Catechism*, pp. 2, 20, 66–7.

[102] It was Titley's dispute with some of his parishioners, about the placing of the communion table, which led to the initial intervention of Bishop Williams in 1627.

Cathedral in London.[103] Charles had found in favour of the cathedral authorities, who wanted the St Gregory's communion table to be placed 'altarwise'. He also laid it down that parish practice should be 'guided' by that of the 'cathedral mother church'.[104] In this sense Charles was indeed the author of the new policy. Nevertheless, some sixteen years earlier Laud and Neile had both been involved, at the cathedral level, with the conversion of communion tables into altars.[105] As Bishop of Winchester, in 1628, Neile was reported to have complained of communion tables 'standing in the middle of the quire' saying he would have them 'stand att the upper end'.[106] Moreover in 1632 there had been two cases before the London Court of High Commission about the placing of seats in relation to communion tables. Laud and Neile had each objected, in the strongest terms, to arrangements whereby worshippers sat 'above', that is to say eastward of, communion tables. Sitting 'above God Almighty' was how they described it.[107] Finally, in the course of 1633, Neile, as Archbishop of York, can be found, prior to the St Gregory's ruling, removing parish communion tables to an eastward position.[108] Both Laud and Neile, in their capacity as privy councillors, were present when Charles delivered his judgement on the St Gregory's case. It is difficult to resist the conclusion that they were the prime instigators, not least because by this date Charles had been king for eight years and Laud archbishop for only three months.

The Elizabethan injunctions of 1559 had ordered that 'the holy table in every church' should be

set in the place where the altar stood . . . saving when the communion of the sacrament is to be distributed; at which time the same shall be so placed in good sort within the chancel, as whereby the minister may be more conveniently heard of the communicants in

[103] Peter Heylyn, *A Coale from the Altar* (1636), pp. 63–6.

[104] *Constitutional Documents*, ed. Gardiner, pp. 103–5.

[105] See above, pp. 116–17.

[106] *Commons Debates for 1629*, pp. 64, 133.

[107] *Reports of Cases in the Courts of Star Chamber and High Commission*, ed. S. R. Gardiner (Camden Soc., NS 39, 1886), pp. 282, 302. Dr A. Foster drew my attention to these references.

[108] Borthwick Institute, York Chancery Act Book 1633–34/5, fos. 10, 125–39. Again I am indebted for this very important information to Dr Foster, whose own study of York diocese during the 1630s is forthcoming.

his prayer and ministration, and the communicants also more conveniently, and in more number communicate with the said minister.
And after the communion done, from time to time the same holy
table to be placed where it stood before.[109]

The ecclesiastical canons of 1604 largely incorporate this particular injunction, although the place where the table ought to
stand when communion was not being administered is left
unspecified. Also the canon speaks of the table being placed,
for the communion service, in 'church or chancel'.[110] In the
event, however, the peripatetic practice envisaged by both
injunction and canon seems to have been largely abandoned,
with parishes opting instead for a communion table permanently positioned in the middle of the chancel. Such was the
situation which Laud and like-minded bishops, enthusiastically backed by King Charles, now set out to change.

Laud's own view as regards the positioning of the communion table is stated most fully in his speech at the trial of
Bastwick, Burton, and Prynne in June 1637. He was adamant
that the Elizabethan injunction was still in force, and that correctly interpreted this meant all communion tables should be
placed 'at the upper end of the choir, north and south or altarwise'. He went on to say that 'to set it otherwise is to set it
cross the place not "in" the place where the altar stood', as the
injunction requires.[111] By his own subsequent admission,
Laud had similarly argued, at the time of the St Gregory's
judgement, against the parishioners who objected to the placing of the communion table altarwise.[112] As he said in 1637, 'it
may stand so (if authority please) in any church', and it was
only 'reasonable' that 'parish churches should be made conformable to the cathedral and mother churches'. But Laud
also stated that the placing of the communion table was itself
a matter of 'indifferency' and that nothing had been done to
date 'by violence or command'.[113] The altarwise position was

[109] E. Cardwell, *Documentary Annals of the Reformed Church of England* (Oxford, 1844),
I. 234.
[110] E. Cardwell, *Synodalia* (Oxford, 1842), I. 293.   [111] Laud, *Works*, VI. 59–60.
[112] Ibid., IV. 225–6. According to another version of Laud's trial, the archbishop
had written to Sir Nathaniel Brent in September 1635 directing him 'to remove the
communion table to the end of the chancell, close to the wall, east and west or north
and south', HMC, House of Lords, NS 11. 398. Even if correctly reported the context
of this letter is unclear, and Laud did not argue at his trial that this had in fact been
his policy.   [113] Laud, *Works*, IV. 59–60.

indifferent presumably in the sense that, like other ceremonies, it was not a divine prescript. What Laud meant by his
reference to the actual implementation of the new policy is
however less clear. He perhaps alluded to the fact that up
until now enforcement had been sporadic. Thus, for example,
in Canterbury diocese it was only from late 1637 that churchwardens found themselves regularly before the church courts
for failing to move the communion table.[114] Nevertheless individual parishes had certainly been ordered to resite their communion tables during the preceding three years.

Official explanations of the change emphasized the need for
decency and order. Yet clearly more was involved. Laud himself acknowledged this in his speech of 1637. 'The altar', he
said, is 'the greatest place of God's residence upon earth. I say
the greatest, yea greater than the pulpit, for there 'tis *Hoc est
corpus meum*, "This is My body", but in the pulpit 'tis at most
but *Hoc est verbum meum*, "This is My word." '[115] When Laud
came to make his will, in 1644, he requested that his body
should be buried in the chapel of St John's College, Oxford,
'under the altar'.[116] His predecessor at Canterbury, George
Abbot, had by contrast expressed the hope that he might die
in the pulpit[117]—a sentiment voiced earlier by Bishop Jewel.[118]
At issue here are rival views of the Christian religion, the one
built around the sacraments and the other focused on the sermon. The latter, according to Calvinists, was the means
'whereby the foreknown of God from all eternity, and the predestinated to life of God's pure favour, are effectually called
from the state of servitude to liberty'.[119]

As already remarked, Archbishop Neile started converting
communion tables, at the parish level, in 1633. The first
recorded case dates from January and concerns the church of
St John's Beverley. Further cases followed in October.[120]
Events, however, moved more slowly in the southern province. Despite the decision in the St Gregory's case,

[114] Canterbury Cathedral Archives, Z.4.6., fos. 73–227ᵛ.
[115] Laud, *Works*, VI. 57.
[116] Laud, *Works*, IV. 442.
[117] *Proceedings in Parliament, 1610*, ed. Foster, I. 78.
[118] Jewel, *Works*, IV. p.xxi.
[119] Sebastian Benfield, *A Sermon preached at Wotton Under Edge* appended to *A Commentarie or Exposition upon Amos* (Oxford, 1613), p. 269.
[120] Borthwick Institute, York Chancery Act Book 1633–34/5, fos. 10, 125–39.

Archbishop Laud did not begin to apply this policy generally until the late spring or early summer of 1634. He conveyed his wishes in a letter to his Vicar General, Sir Nathaniel Brent, who was already conducting a metropolitical visitation. This general instruction took its immediate origin from the case of All Saints Maidstone, in Kent.[121] There the curate, Robert Barrell, had come into conflict with some of his parishioners for 'causing the communion table to be sett up to the wall at the east end of the chancel'.[122] Brent, by his own account, referred the matter to Laud who both supported the curate's action and ordered that 'the like you are required to doe in all churches, in all other places where you are to visit metropoliti-cally'.[123] As Archbishop of Canterbury, Laud was also Rector of All Saints Maidstone and this fact perhaps finally decided him to take action.[124] The period of delay, however, may indi-cate some uncertainty on Laud's part as to the precise legal situation.

A number of bishops in the southern province anticipated Laud's general direction concerning communion tables, as conveyed by his visitors. Probably first in the field was Wil-liam Piers, Bishop of Bath and Wells, who by March 1634 had drawn up a schedule of 'reasons why the communion table in every church should be sett close under the east-window or wall, with the ends north and south, and railed in'. The seventh and final reason, listed by Piers, echoes the royal judgement in the St Gregory's case. 'Daughters should be like their mother, the parochiall churches should be like the cathedrall churches, that soe there may be an uniformity in this respect in every church.'[125] At this time Piers's officials were involved in a parish dispute about the position of the communion table.[126] His action is the more striking given his

---

[121] Prynne, *Canterburies Doome*, p. 89; Lambeth Palace Library, Archbishop Laud's Register I, fo. 82ᵛ. Laud's register provides the date by which the visitation of Canter-bury diocese was officially completed, namely 28 June 1634.

[122] *Proceedings . . . in the County of Kent*, ed. Larking, p. 204.

[123] Prynne, *Canterburies Doome*, p. 89.

[124] Another possibility is that there was some prior collusion between Laud and Barrell.

[125] Lambeth Palace Library, Lambeth MS 943, pp. 475–8.

[126] M. F. Stieg, *Laud's Laboratory: the Diocese of Bath and Wells in the Early Seventeenth Century* (Lewisburg, 1982) p. 297. The parish concerned at this stage appears to have been that of Mells.

role ten years earlier at Oxford when, as Vice Chancellor he had presided over the condemnation of the Arminian Gabriel Bridges.[127] In the changed climate of the 1630s this must have been an embarrassing episode to recall, and it may be that Bishop Piers was keen to demonstrate his zeal for the religious regime of King Charles.

Whether by now Piers was himself an Arminian in doctrine is not known. Certainly this cannot simply be inferred from his predilection for altars, although the two did tend to go hand in hand. It is, however, legitimate to use Bath and Wells diocese as a measure of the ease with which parish communion tables were converted into altars in the southern province. For in this diocese events are likely to have moved fastest. Yet by January 1636, according to Bishop Piers himself, only 140 out of 469 parishes had converted their communion tables.[128] A failure rate of 70 per cent, at this date, indicates that the proposed change had encountered widespread resistance. While the expenditure involved was clearly one factor, so also was religious motivation. Many parishes in Bath and Wells diocese were probably awaiting the outcome of the Beckington, Somerset, case, in which the churchwardens had appealed to the Court of Arches against Bishop Piers. (Their appeal was rejected in January 1636.) Such a resort to law was costly in financial terms. Moreover, the arguments used by the Beckington churchwardens were religious as well as legal. They challenged Piers's interpretation of both the Elizabethan injunction and Jacobean canon, and claimed that 'all the orthodox bishopps [and] governors of the Church upon the reformacion of Kinge Edward's tyme, of blessed memory, have either writen or preached against alteringe the communion table'.[129]

Francis Dee, Bishop of Peterborough, included in his printed 1634 visitation articles a provision that the communion table be 'placed conveniently at the east end of the chancel' and 'cancelled in'.[130] This was the year before the

---

[127] See above, p. 75.

[128] Prynne, *Canterburies Doome*, p. 98.

[129] Lambeth Palace Library, Lambeth MS 943, p. 481.

[130] Francis Dee, *Articles to be enquired of throughout the Whole Diocese of Peterborough* (1634), pp. 2–3. I owe this reference to Mr J. Fielding and Mr R. Norris. Dee's attitude to Arminianism has not been ascertained.

metropolitical visitation of Peterborough diocese, and appears
to be the earliest example of its kind. Nevertheless not until
August 1637 was there a major drive in Peterborough diocese
to enforce the new requirement concerning communion
tables.[131] Another bishop who similarly took action in advance
of the metropolitical visitation was the Arminian Matthew
Wren. His Hereford visitation articles for 1635 ask, apropos
the communion tale, 'ordinarily doth it stand up at the east
end of the chancell, where the altar in former times stood, the
end[s] thereof being placed north and south?'[132] Elsewhere
much might depend, at least initially, on the attitude of the
bishop or his subordinates. The metropolitical visitation took
three years to complete and in consequence some dioceses in
the southern province received no archiepiscopal instructions
about communion tables until early 1637. Uncooperative
churchwardens were also a general problem. But once such an
order had been issued it was difficult thereafter completely to
disregard it.

In Chichester diocese, during the episcopate of the Arminian Richard Montagu, the metropolitical visitation of mid-
1635 was energetically followed up.[133] On that occasion
churchwardens were ordered by Brent to model their communion tables on St Thomas-in-the-Cliffe, Lewes. 'Henceforth the communion table in every parish church shall be
decently placed at the upper end of chancell, and shall stand
north and south, and . . . be rayled in.'[134] Defaulters, however,
were still being reported as late as March 1639. The strongest
resistance was encountered at St. Michael's, Lewes, in mid-
1637, where one of the churchwardens moved the communion
table back to its position in the middle of the chancel.[135] At the
Michaelmas quarter sessions in 1639 Anthony Stapley, a
member of the bench, attacked the placing of 'the communion

---

[131] New College, Oxford, Diary of Robert Woodford, MS 9502, fo. 11. I owe my
knowledge of this manuscript to Mr Fielding, who tells me that Woodford's statement
is borne out by the Peterborough diocesan court records.

[132] Matthew Wren, *Articles to be inquired of within the Diocese of Hereford* (1635), sigs.
A2ᵛ–A3.

[133] A. Fletcher, *A County Community in Peace and War: Sussex 1600–1660* (1975),
pp. 85–7, 91–2.

[134] W. C. Renshaw, 'Notes from the Act Books of the Archdeaconry Court of
Lewes', *Sussex Archaeological Collections*, 49 (1906), 64.

[135] Fletcher, *County Community*, pp. 91–2.

table altarwise' as 'an innovation detracting from God's glory'. He went on to say that 'some prelates in this kingdom did not approve of it'.[136]

Montagu's own visitation articles for Chichester diocese, and those of his successor Brian Duppa, have been aptly described as 'the authentic voice of Arminianism'.[137] From 1628 onwards Montagu can be found asking if the font is positioned near the church door, 'signifying that baptism is our entry into the church of God', and whether ministers 'exhort' prospective communicants to make their confessions.[138] Dee's and Wren's articles similarly ask about confession.[139] In 1631 Montagu added a question concerning the enforcement of the royal declaration silencing religious controversy. 'Doth your minister preach or teach anything contrary to his Majestie's late injunctions, about predestination, falling from grace etc., to trouble men's minds with those deep and darke points, which of late have so distracted and engarboyled the world?'[140] Not until 1638, however, did Montagu, now Bishop of Norwich, ask if 'the communion table' was 'fixedly set . . . at the east end of the chancell, close unto the wall, upon an ascent'. By this date he also envisaged the possibility that the 'communion table or altar' might be made 'of stone', describing it as the place 'whereat a manifold sacrifice is offered to God'.[141] His successor, Duppa, was almost equally forthright in the same year. 'Is your communion table or altar . . . set according to the practise of the ancient church, upon an ascent at the east end of the chancell, with the ends of it north and south?'[142]

Furthermore Montagu in 1638 expanded his remarks about baptism, asking whether anyone in the parish maintained that

---

[136] Ibid., pp. 76, 93.

[137] Ibid., pp. 80–1.

[138] Richard Montagu, *Articles to be enquired of throughout the Whole Diocese of Chichester* (1628), sigs. A3, B[v], and *Articles to be enquired of throughout the whole Diocese of Chichester* (1637), sigs. A3, B[v].

[139] Dee, *Peterborough* (1634), p. 7; Wren, *Hereford* (1635), sig. B1.

[140] Richard Montagu, *Articles to be enquired of throughout the Whole Diocese of Chichester* (1631), sig. A4[v].

[141] Richard Montagu, *Articles of Enquiry and Direction for the Diocese of Norwich* (Cambridge, 1638), sigs. A3[v], B4.

[142] Brian Duppa, *Articles to be inquired of throughout the Diocese of Chichester* (1638), sig. B2[v].

'the sacrament of baptisme is not of absolute and indispensable necessity unto salvation' and 'eternall election sufficeth'.[143] Similarly Duppa wanted to know if either minister or member of the laity held that baptism 'is not the doore that lets us into the Church'.[144] Both bishops exhibit a shared belief in the need for confession, although Montagu wanted it on a more regular basis.[145] Apropos the royal declaration, Duppa asked whether the minister preached 'Christ and him crucified, abstaining from those high points of speculation which have in severall ages rais'd combustion in Christian Churches'.[146] Montagu, however, was by now much more expansive. Does the minister

in his popular sermons fall upon those much disputed and little understood doctrines of God's eternall predestination, of election antecedaneous, of reprobation irrespective, without sinne foreseene, of freewill, of perseverance, and not falling from grace, points obscure, unsoldable [sic], unfoordable, untraceable, at which that great apostle [St Paul] stood at gaze?[147]

Matthew Wren, Montagu's predecessor at Norwich, repeated for Norwich in 1636 the clause about communion tables from his Hereford visitation articles of 1635, again asking whether they 'ordinarily' stood 'at the east end'. Any possible ambiguity was ruled out by an accompanying set of orders. These survive in manuscript and specify that 'the communion table in every church do *alwayes* stand close under the wall of the chancell'.[148] But the reluctance of bishops to say such things in print remains a puzzle. As late as 1636 Bishop Piers, for example, had nothing to say in his printed visitation articles about placing communion tables at the east end of chancels.[149] Were they still uncertain of their legal ground? Certainly the relevant canon, passed by convocation in 1640,

[143] Montagu, *Norwich* (Cambridge, 1638), sig. B2.
[144] Duppa, *Chichester* (1638), sig. A4.
[145] Montagu, *Chichester* (1628), sig. B^v; Duppa, *Chichester* (1638), sig. B.
[146] Duppa, *Chichester* (1638), sig. A3^v.
[147] Montagu, *Norwich* (1638), sig. B2.
[148] Matthew Wren, *Articles to be inquired of within the Dioces of Norwich* (1636), sig. A3. These manuscript orders are bound up with the British Library copy of the articles and the passage quoted is from folio 1. The italics are mine.
[149] Information kindly supplied by the staff of Archbishop Marsh's Library, Dublin, where the unique copy of these articles is located.

can be read as a retrospective endorsement of past practice during the 1630s; according to Heylyn, Laud's aim then was the 'countenancing and confirming his former actings'.[150] King Charles, in his preface to the canons, speaks of the 'want of an express rule', while the canon itself says that the long-continued altarwise position of the communion table in the royal chapels, 'most' cathedrals and 'some' parish churches, 'doth sufficiently acquit the manner of placing the said tables from any illegality'. Nevertheless, the canon goes on to enact that 'all churches and chapels do conform themselves in this particular to the example of the cathedral or mother churches'.[151]

Wren made a deep impression on Norwich diocese, and his changing the position of the communion table was to be one of the charges against him in 1641.[152] In London diocese, under Bishop William Juxon, the conversion of communion tables into altars seems initially to have proceeded smoothly, and moreover in advance of the metropolitical visitation. But in June 1636 Robert Aylett, Juxon's commissary, reported that, in parts of Essex, his work was being undone by ministers and parishioners who sought to exploit the silence of Laud's metropolitical visitation articles on this question.[153] The latter merely enquired whether the communion table was 'placed in such convenient sort within the chancel or church, as that the minister may be best heard in his prayer and administration, and that the greatest number may communicate'.[154] Juxon also, the previous year, required from the 'ministers and lecturers in and about London' assent unto a series of religious propositions. These began with the statement that 'every one that is baptised is regenerated'.[155] Like the Cambridge Commencement thesis of 1629—'All baptised infants are undoubtedly justified'*—this was apparently aimed at the Calvinist doctrine of perseverance.[156]

Some of the fiercest opposition anywhere in England to the

---

[150] Heylyn, *Cyprianus Anglicus*, p. 397.
[151] Laud, *Works*, v. 610, 625.
[152] Rushworth, *Historical Collections*, iii/i. 351–2.
[153] PRO, SP 16/327, fo. 187.
[154] Laud, *Works*, v. 421.
[155] PRO, SP 16/308, fo. 87.
[156] See above, p. 52.

placing of communion tables 'altarwise' seems to have been encountered in Peterborough diocese. There at All Saints, Northampton, between August 1637 and June 1638, the communion table was repeatedly moved back and forth, by the churchwardens in opposition to the visitors. Much of the detail is recorded by Robert Woodford, Steward of Northampton, who also writes in his diary at this time how he 'prayed against wicked bishops and their hierarchy'.[157] A comparable tug-of-war over the communion table occurred at Pattishall in the same county.[158] A more usual tactic, however, on the part of churchwardens was simply to stonewall, as at Davington and Whitstable, in Canterbury diocese, where they were still refusing to remove the communion table to the 'upper end of the chancell' in July 1640.[159]

IV

But what of those bishops who, to quote Anthony Stapley, 'did not approve' of the new altar policy? The most famous opponent was Bishop John Williams of Lincoln. He engaged in a long-running battle on this issue, culminating with the publication in 1637 of his *The Holy Table, Name and Thing*. Williams argued that the Elizabethan injunction correctly interpreted meant that parish communion tables should be aligned east and west, not altarwise, at the end of chancels, and that it was permissible to move them for the celebration of communion.[160] He was also a Calvinist in doctrine, as emerges from his sermon preached before the House of Lords in February 1629. Entitling his remarks *Perseverantia Sanctorum*, Williams referred to 'this perseverance unto the end, which some late divines had rather fasten with a rope of sands to the libertie of our will, then with a chaine of adamant to God's steddie and immoveable grace and goodnesse'.[161] Only in 1638, after he

---

[157] New College, Oxford, MS 9502, fos. 11–12, 27, 32, 47ᵛ, 52, 58ᵛ, 77; PRO, SP 16/393, fo. 28.

[158] PRO, SP 16/395, fo. 143.

[159] Canterbury Cathedral Archives, Y.6.4. fos. 391ᵛ, 398.

[160] John Williams, *The Holy Table, Name and Thing* (1637), pp. 14–20, 44–5.

[161] John Williams, *Perseverantia Sanctorum* (1628/9), p. 37. John Hacket, the contemporary and biographer of Williams, confirms that he was indeed a Calvinist. *Scrinia Reserata*, i. 16.

had been imprisoned on a variety of charges, including the subornation of witnesses in Star Chamber, were communion tables apparently converted on a large scale in Lincoln diocese.[162]

Yet Williams was clearly not a lone figure. For Charles I, in his preface to the canons of 1640, stated that the currently controverted 'rites and ceremonies', including 'the standing of the communion table sideways under the east window of every chancel', are 'now insisted upon but only in some dioceses and are not generally revived in all places'.[163] If the connection between doctrine and ceremony holds broadly true, then those most likely alluded to here are the other surviving Calvinist bishops. Here one case which has been generally misunderstood is that of Bishop John Davenant of Salisbury. Thus Laud, in his Star Chamber speech of 1637, quoted the Calvinist Davenant as a supporter of placing the communion table altarwise.[164] He did so on the basis of an 'order' by Davenant, dated 17 May 1637, sent to the parish of Aldbourne in Wiltshire. This order does indeed 'inhibit you the churchwardens, and all other persons whatsoever, to meddle with the bringing downe of the communion table or with altering the place thereof at such times as the Holy Supper is to be administered'.[165] There are, however, a number of peculiarities about Davenant's order which point to a different conclusion from that drawn by Laud.

First, and most important, Davenant writes that King Charles 'hath beene lately informed that some men factiously disposed have taken upon themselves to place and remove the communion table', in Aldbourne church, 'and thereupon his highness hath required me to take present order therin'. Therefore the initiative in this matter appears to be that of the King not the Bishop, the latter being told by higher authority what to do in his own diocese. Davenant goes on to say that

because some doe ignorantly suppose that the standing of the communion table where altars stood in times of superstition has some

[162] Beddow, 'The Church in Lincolnshire', p. 293; C. Holmes, *Seventeenth-Century Lincolnshire* (Lincoln, 1980), p. 121.
[163] Laud, *Works*, v. 611.
[164] Ibid., vi. 61–2.
[165] Ibid., vi. 61.

relish of Popery, and some perchance may as erroniously conceive that the placing thereof otherwise when the holy communion is administered savours of irreverence, I would have you take notice . . . that the placing of it higher or lower in the chancell, or in the church, is by the judgment of the Church of England a thing indifferent and to be ordered and guided by the only rule of convenience.[166]

This remains closer to the spirit of the Elizabethan injunction than does Laud's pronouncement of the same year, both in expressly retaining the peripatetic principle and ignoring the notion that cathedrals should be the models for parish churches.[167]

The suspicion, moreover, that Davenant was not a free agent in the Aldbourne affair is strengthened by the knowledge that the Vicar of the parish was Richard Steward, recently appointed Clerk of the Closet to King Charles and an Arminian.[168] Steward was the most likely informant of Laud and Charles. But why go over the head of Davenant, if he was of the same persuasion? A contemporary in no doubt as to the real facts of the situation was a silenced minister called Shepherd. After hearing Laud refer to Davenant in his Star Chamber speech, Shepherd is reported to have said that 'I din'd with one the other day who was of the same towne and told mee how it was. He [Laud] useth the King, labors with the King, to have his letters mandatory that it should bee done.'[169] What however clinches the argument that Davenant was not in sympathy with the ceremonial changes of the 1630s is a surviving letter from him to Samuel Ward, of October 1639. He writes that 'I wish wee could all content our selfs with that doctrine and those rites which our predecessors have left unto us. I can see nothing altered, or augmented, for the better.'[170] Since Davenant links doctrinal with ritual change, he must be referring to officially inspired alterations during the 1630s. For he can be found complaining earlier about the prohibition of predestinarian doctrine 'hitherto . . . generally

[166] Ibid., vi. 61.

[167] See above, p. 201.

[168] *VCH Wiltshire*, xii. 83. In 1626 Steward reportedly commented in highly unfavourable terms on the Calvinist teaching of Samuel Ward, as contained in his sermon *Gratia Discriminans*. Bodleian, Tanner MS 72, fo. 150.

[169] PRO, SP 16/361, fo. 249.

[170] Bodleian, Tanner MS 67, fo. 147.

and publiquely maintained', but now slandered by the name of 'Puritane'.[171]

The attitude of another Calvinist bishop, Thomas Morton of Durham, has similarly been misconstrued by later commentators. In 1631 appeared the first edition of Morton's *Institution of the Sacrament*. The book was an attack on the Roman Catholic doctrine of the mass, and Morton had noted in passing that 'the table of the Lord . . . anciently stood in the middest of the chancell'.[172] This also served to describe the situation then obtaining generally in English parish churches. By 1635, however, when a second edition of Morton's *Institution* was published, a policy to convert communion tables into altars was under way. Morton chose to retain this reference, but added that 'you are not to thinke that wee do hereby oppugne . . . the now situation thereof in our Church, for use as convenient and for order more decent'.[173] Genuine apologists denied, by contrast, what Morton still claimed was 'ancient' practice.[174] Furthermore Prynne states that some three months before the publication of this second edition Morton had written to Daniel Featley declaring 'his judgement both against altars and placing of Lord's tables altar wise'.[175] We do not know whether pressure was exerted on Morton, who had Archbishop Neile as his metropolitan, but it is worth recalling that even Bishop Williams was induced in 1638 to recant the views expressed in *The Holy Table, Name and Thing*.[176]

As regards Joseph Hall, Bishop of Exeter, two autobiographical accounts survive of his activities during the 1630s.[177] Hall was unusual among his fellow-Calvinists in wanting to give the benefit of the doubt to Richard Montagu, on the subject of Arminianism.[178] Nevertheless Hall's own Calvinism is beyond serious dispute. Thus in 1629 he went on

[171] See above, p. 138.
[172] Thomas Morton, *Of the Institution of the Sacrament* (1631), p. 306.
[173] Thomas Morton, *The Institution of the Sacrament* (1635), p. 462.
[174] Heylyn, *A Coale from the Altar*, pp. 53–7; John Pocklington, *Altare Christianum* (1637), pp. 92–119.
[175] William Prynne, *A Quench-Coale* (Amsterdam, 1637), p. 289.
[176] H. T. Blethen, 'Bishop Williams, the Altar Controversy and the Royal Supremacy, 1627–41', *Welsh History Review*, 9 (1978–9), 152–3.
[177] Hall, *Works*, I. pp. xix–lii.
[178] Ibid., pp. xliii–xliv.

public record in defence of the doctrine maintained at the
Synod of Dort. 'I . . . shall live and die in the suffrage of that
reverend synod, and do confidently avow that those other
opposed opinions cannot stand with the doctrine of the
Church of England.'[179] Hall also claimed to have refuted
Arminianism regularly from the pulpit, and there are a
number of such passages in his extant writings. For example,
he can be found attacking 'these new disciples of Leyden' who
'teach that a true, solid, radicated saving faith may be totally,
finally lost'. On the contrary, says Hall, 'the regenerate' never
became apostates. 'He that hath ordained we shall be saved,
hath ordained our perseverance.' Against 'these doubtmon-
gers', Hall posits the 'sure anchor of our undeceivable hope'.[180]

Bishop Hall, by his own account, 'was never guilty of urging
any new impositions' and only enforced 'the anciently
received orders'. Likewise, Hall refers to his 'disliking all
novel devices'.[181] Given the context, he must be referring,
among other things, to the new altars. On his appointment to
Exeter, Hall says that finding 'some factious spirits very busy
in that diocese I used all fair and gentle means to win them to
good order, and therein so happily prevailed that saving two
of that numerous clergy . . . they were all perfectly reclaimed'.
At the same time he proved a friend to the local lecturers, and
his rule recalls the more harmonious days of the Jacobean
Church. But this won Hall no bouquets from higher authority.
Quite the reverse, 'for some that sat at the stern of the Church
had me in great jealousy for too much favour of Puritanism'.
He was complained against at court and 'was three several
times upon my knee to his Majesty to answer these great
criminations'. Things got so bad that 'I plainly told the Lord
Archbishop of Canterbury [Laud] that rather than I would be
obnoxious to those slanderous tongues of his misinformers I
would cast up my rochet'.[182] This distrust, of which Hall complains, was also the common lot of Davenant and Morton.[183]

---

[179] Ibid., viii. 740.
[180] Ibid., i. 1, v. 237, ix. 520–4.
[181] Ibid., i. p. xlvi, 1.
[182] Ibid., p. xlvi.
[183] PRO, SP 16/233, fo. 175 and SP 16/442, fos. 84^{r-v}, 273^{r-v}. The extent to which
ceremonial change was actually enforced in Durham, Exeter, and Salisbury dioceses
must await the detailed local studies on which Mr J. Davies is currently engaged.

Integral to the altar campaign was the idea of the cathedral
as exemplar—the mother on which the daughter churches
should model themselves. Therefore, it was very important
that cathedrals did in fact set the correct example. As we
have seen, Laud and Neile were involved as early as 1617
in moving the communion tables at Gloucester and Durham
cathedrals.[184] At Durham, however, opposition did not
finally come to a head until 1628 when one of the prebendaries, Peter Smart, launched a sermon attack on the
religious developments of the past decade. His special target
was 'superstitious ceremonies', and he described the setting
up of altars as an act of 'Anti-christian presumption'.
Preaching in the cathedral, Smart told the assembled congregation for the future to 'stay at home, in the name of God,
till things be amended and reduced to the state and forme they
were in our lesse ceremonious, and more preaching, bishop's
time'.[185] This was a reference to Neile's predecessor, Bishop
James, and to dismiss Smart as a Puritan is much too simple.
By his own lights he was in the mainstream of English Protestantism and apparently had the private support of the Calvinist Archbishop Abbot, to whom the following couplet is
ascribed:

Peter preach downe vaine rights with flagrant harte
They guerdon shall be great, though heare thou Smart[186]

The same year as Smart's sermon, Neile, now Bishop of Winchester, ordered that the cathedral communion table in his
new diocese be 'removed to the upper end of the quyre to
stand like an altar'.[187] In a sermon dedication of five years
earlier, Abraham Browne, a prebendary of Winchester since
1581, had referred to the communion table standing 'in the
middest of the church as our Common Prayer Book alloweth,
that it may be farther from an altar'.[188] Another Winchester
prebendary, Robert More, reported Neile's order to the House

[184] See above, pp. 116–17.
[185] Smart, *A Sermon*, pp. 8–9, 26.
[186] G. W. Kitchin, *Seven Sages of Durham* (1911), illustration facing p. 99.
[187] *Commons Debates for 1629*, p. 144.
[188] Abraham Browne, *A Sermon preached at the Assizes . . . at Winchester* (1623), sig. A4.
The Prayer Book rubric reads 'The table having at the communion time a fair white
linen cloth upon it, shall stand in the body of the church or in the chancel . . .'

of Commons in 1629. More was already in trouble with Neile and resigned his cathedral post in 1632. The Dean of Winchester, John Young, laconically noted on this occasion that 'Dr. Moure preached upon the text 2 Kings 4, "I dwell amongst my owne people"', and 'came oup without surplice because of his resignation'.[189] As Archbishop of York Neile, in 1633, had the communion table in Chester Cathedral moved back to an eastward position. In 1634, however, he was still trying to enforce the same change in Carlisle Cathedral.[190] According to Prynne, whose ideological antiquarianism makes him a valuable source for the discriminating user, the communion tables also at Bristol, Exeter, Salisbury, and Worcester cathedrals were placed altarwise relatively late. Writing in 1637, Prynne says the changes there had occurred 'within these few years'.[191]

It may well be that at Bristol, Exeter, Salisbury, and Worcester cathedrals the communion tables were only moved in the wake of Laud's metropolitical instruction of 1634. Certainly at Exeter Matthew Sutcliffe, Dean for over forty years until his death in 1629, is unlikely to have supported any such innovation. In his will of November 1628 he writes that 'I hate as apostates from the faith and traitors to God's true church' those 'amonge us that palliate Popish heresies and under the name of Arminius seek to bringe in Poperie, and endeavour with all theire little skill to reconcile darkeness to light, Antichrist to Christ, heresie to the true Catholike faith'.[192] Two years earlier Sutcliffe's reply to the Arminian Montagu had been seized in the press.[193] Yet it is worth remembering that during the 1590s Sutcliffe had been one of the earliest English exponents of *jure divino* episcopacy.[194] Probably Sutcliffe's successor as Dean, William Peterson, was responsible for purchasing the new communion table and rail which is mentioned in a petition at the Restoration in 1660.[195] At Worcester

---

[189] *Commons Debates for 1629*, p. 144; *The Diary of John Young*, ed. F. R. Goodman (1928), p. 97.

[190] PRO, SP 16/259, fo. 168ᵛ.

[191] Prynne, *A Quench-Coale*, p. 161.

[192] PRO, PROB. 11/156, fo. 271.

[193] Prynne, *Canterburies Doome*, p. 159.

[194] Matthew Sutcliffe, *A Treatise of Ecclesiasticall Discipline* (1591), pp. 43–53.

[195] W. J. Harte, 'Ecclesiastical and Religious Affairs in Exeter, 1640–62', *Transactions of the Devonshire Association*, 69 (1937), 51.

Roger Mainwaring, appointed Dean in 1633, can be found
boasting soon after that he had erected 'an altare stone of marble . . . sett uppon fower columnes'.[196] But what happened at
Bristol and Salisbury remains unclear.

V

Arminianism, especially in its ceremonial aspects, provoked
widespread hostility. Nevertheless we should not make the
mistake of assuming that the movement was without a significant following in the wider community. Clearly there was a
growing body of clerical supporters, and Arminians, like Calvinists, needed lay patronage. Of particular interest here is a
group of four surviving Paul's Cross sermons, preached during the 1630s by James Conyers, John Gore, and Oliver
Whitbie. All betray Arminian sympathies. Three are dedicated to prominent members of the gentry and one to a Lord
Mayor of London. The earliest is by John Gore. Preached in
May 1632, the printed version of the same year is dedicated to
Sir John Mede of Wendon Lofts, in Essex, where Gore was
Rector. Mede was at the time High Sheriff of Essex and Gore
describes himself as Mede's 'chaplain'. Entitled *The Way to
Prosper*, this sermon is in reality an Arminian gloss on the doc-
trine of perseverance. Gore took as his subject the case of King
Uzziah in the Old Testament, who began in a state of grace
but afterwards fell away.

Such is the case betwixt a man and his God. As long as a man
holds in good termes with God and hath his conversation in
Heaven, and sets his affections on things above, so long God
will cast his favour upon him and he shall shine as a light in the
midst of a crooked and perverse generation. But if he once decline
from that pitch, and fall downe from a godly conversation, into
any earthly, base, ungodly disposition, tis a venture but his
prosperity will vanish away and his latter end prove worse than
his beginning.

The duty of man is 'to seek to please God, to seek to get into
favour with God, to seek to get God's good will', whereas
'God's mercy is to prosper them that seeke him'. But if

<hr />

[196] PRO, SP 16/298, fo. 84.

instead, like Uzziah, we turn to 'wickednesse and sinne' the 'spring of grace' will become 'stopt up'.[197]

Gore preached a further Paul's Cross sermon in December 1635. Printed the following year, under the title *The Oracle of God*, this was dedicated to Christopher Clitherow, then Lord Mayor of London and soon to be knighted. Gore's theme on this occasion was the universality of grace. God in 'Christ is no niggard of his grace . . . but doth graciously impart it, and mercifully bestow it, so much upon everyone as he seeth in his wisdome to be enough and sufficient for him'. Again Gore argues that 'the way to keepe God's favour and good will is to please God', whereas 'God for his part is so gracious that he denyes his grace to none but offers it and (I may say) gives it to every one that will but aske and accept it'. None the less 'though God offer his grace to men, hee will not force it upon them against their will; he will have them sue for it, hee will have them desire it, or they may thanke themselves if they goe to Hell without it'. Moreover, grace once received can subsequently be lost. For 'if wee take God's candles and hold them downwards, turne them the wrong way up, and apply and abuse them to sinne, it is much to bee feared the light of God will goe out and thou shalt be left at length in a place of utter darkenesse'.[198]

These two sermons by Gore were licensed respectively by chaplains of Laud and Juxon.[199] Gore was a regular preacher at Paul's Cross, with four such sermons extant, and also preached on occasion before the royal household.[200] Yet nothing seems discoverable about his background. There appears to be no record of him at either Cambridge or Oxford, although it is highly unlikely that he was not a graduate. Indeed his sermons are replete with Greek as well as Latin quotations. Via Sir John Mede, Gore came into contact with John Penruddock of Compton Chamberlain in Wiltshire.

[197] John Gore, *The Way to Prosper* (1632), sig. A2^{r-v}, pp. 1–3, 34.

[198] John Gore, *The Oracle of God* (1636), sig. A2^{r-v}, pp. 2, 9, 14, 19–20, 24.

[199] William Bray and Thomas Weekes. Arber, IV. 245, 327; Greg, *Licensers for the Press*, pp. 12–13, 101–6. The imprimatur by Weekes describes him as 'chaplain" to Bishop Juxon. Gore, *The Oracle of God*, sig. A1^v.

[200] MacLure, *Paul's Cross Sermons*, pp. 252–4; John Gore, *The Man for Heaven. A Sermon preached at the Court . . .* (1639). Another of Gore's sermons is concerned with the necessity of good works. John Gore, *The Way to Well-doing* (1635), pp. 14–28.

Penruddock was a local justice of the peace and Mede's brother-in-law. One of Gore's other Paul's Cross sermons, *The Way to be Content*, is dedicated to Penruddock. While not directly Arminian in doctrine, Gore links this sermon to its predecessor—*The Way to Prosper*.[201] Mede himself had matriculated from St John's College, Cambridge, in 1608, thus overlapping with his fellow Essex landowner Lord Maynard, whose Arminianism we have analysed above.

James Conyers preached at Paul's Cross in August 1635. Like Gore, he raised the possibility that 'wee' may, by sinning, run on the 'rockes and so sinke barke and goods'. He also attacked the 'self-beseeming pure generation', saying 'for my own part with the leper I confesse I am uncleane and with the wings of devotion, faith and prayer, hie me to the mercy-seat, and in the publican's posture crie "Lord be mercifull to me a sinner"'. Conyers was curate at St Mary's, Stratford-le-Bow, having graduated from Sidney Sussex, Cambridge, in 1613. His sermon, printed in 1635, is dedicated to Sir Roger North of Milden Hall, in Suffolk, and to his sons Henry and Dudley North.[202] It was licensed by one of Bishop Juxon's chaplains.[203] A third Paul's Cross preacher to sound a recognizably Arminian note was Oliver Whitbie, in January 1638. He chose as his subject 'the egresse and regresse of prodigall children', and asked 'can a man returne when he will? Hath hee power, as to sinne, so to convert himselfe from it? Are not the hearts of men in the hands of God, who turnes them like the rivers of water?' Both propositions, says Whitbie, are true. 'God drawes every man, yet not violently'—rather with 'sweet and gracious perswasions'. But 'some men resist to their owne damnation'. A 'willing contract', not a 'fatall decree' is involved. For 'in our conversion there is . . . no absolute irresistable power'. Whitbie was Rector of St Nicholas Olave, in London, and graduated from Trinity College, Oxford, in the early 1620s. His sermon, printed in early 1638, is dedicated to John Pulteney, of Langley in Buckinghamshire and Misterton in Leicestershire. During the plague of the previous summer, Whitbie had taken refuge with Pulteney and remarks approv-

---

[201] John Gore, *The Way to be Content* (1635), sig. A2^{r-v}, p. 1; *The Visitations of Essex*, ed. W. C. Metcalfe (Harleian Soc., 13, 1878), p. 448.

[202] Conyers, *Christ's Love*, sigs. A2–A3, pp. 12, 14.

[203] Samuel Baker. Arber, IV. 322; Greg, *Licensers for the Press*, p. 8.

ingly of the 'reverent conformity in your private chapel'.[204] Pulteney himself matriculated from Exeter College, Oxford, in 1627.

That Clitherow, Mede, North, and Pulteney approved of the anti-Calvinist doctrines contained in the sermons dedicated to them is not inherently unlikely. We have already encountered advocates of Arminianism among the gentry— notably Thomas Chown, Richard Dyott, and Richard Spencer.[205] The reference by Whitbie to Pulteney's 'private chapel' is furthermore suggestive of Arminian proclivities, especially in the light of Lord Maynard's chapel-building. More famous is the case of Viscount Scudamore who rebuilt Abbey Dore church in Herefordshire during the 1630s. Scudamore was very close to Laud and is usually remembered for his restoration of impropriated tithes, although he was also an agricultural improver.[206] The religious painted glass commissioned by Scudamore is still *in situ* at Abbey Dore, and includes a picture of Christ's ascension.[207] His fellow Herefordshire landowner Fitzwilliam Coningsby, of Hampton Court, seems to have been responsible for one of the most remarkable pieces of religious glass to survive from this period; dated 1629, and signed by Abraham van Linge, it shows Christ being taken down from the cross. An inscription reads: 'the truth hereof is historicall devine and not superstissious' (plate 4).[208] Laud later recalled how Coningsby sought his help over a friend who was tempted to turn Roman Catholic, and that he successfully prevented it.[209] There is also Lady Alice Dudley who, in the late 1630s, presented gothic revival chalices to four Warwickshire churches. Her daughter, Lady Frances Kniveton, presented similar chalices to five

---

[204] Oliver Whitbie, *London's Returne* (1637/8), sigs. A3–A4ᵛ, 2, 8–9. There is no record of this sermon in the Stationers Register; *The Visitation of the County of Buckingham*, ed. W. H. Rylands (Harleian Soc., 58, 1909), p. 102.

[205] See above, pp. 140, 143, 184.

[206] Trevor-Roper, *Archbishop Laud*, pp. 450–3; C. Hill, *Economic Problems of the Church* (Oxford, 1956), pp. 271–2; M. Gibson, *A View of the Ancient and Present State of the Churches of Door, Home-Lacy and Hempsted* (1727), pp. 70–1.

[207] *Herefordshire*, Royal Commission on Historical Monuments (1931–4), I. 17.

[208] This is now to be found in the Victoria and Albert Museum (C.62–1927), and I owe my knowledge of it to Mr M. Archer. See his article 'English Painted Glass in the Seventeenth Century: the Early Work of Abraham van Linge', *Apollo*, 101 (1975), 30.

[209] Laud, *Works*, III. 413.

Derbyshire churches in 1640.[210] While we cannot automatically deduce doctrine from practice, a connection probably existed.

Evidence moreover survives of prominent townsmen who were opposed to Calvinism. At Boston, in Lincolnshire, the spirit of Peter Baro, the Elizabethan Arminian *avant la lettre*, lived on in the person of his alderman son and namesake. According to the Puritan John Cotton, who arrived at Boston in 1612, Baro junior had 'leavened many of the chief men of the town with Arminianism'. Although a physician by profession, Baro 'spent the greatest strength of his studies in clearing and promoting the Arminian tenents'. As a consequence, 'in all the great feasts of the town the chiefest discourse at table did ordinarily fall upon Arminian points, to the great offence of the godly ministers both in Boston and neighbour towns'. As regards this last allegation, it is worth recalling that the Arminian cleric William Williams, who had fallen foul of local Calvinists in the late 1590s, was beneficed only some thirteen miles from Boston.[211] Cotton's riposte to Baro was, by preaching and conference,

to defend the doctrine of God's eternall election before all foresight of good or evil in the creature, and the redemption 'by grace" only of the elect, the effectuall vocation of a sinner 'through the irresistible power of grace", without all respects of the preparations of free will, and finally the impossibility of the fal of a sincere beleever either totally or finally from the estate of grace.[212]

Cotton says that Baro then retreated into silence, but he and his circle are unlikely to have abandoned their religious beliefs. (Baro died in 1630.) At Coventry, that 'second Geneva' as Richard Montagu called it in the mid-1620s,[213] Arminianism seems to have made serious inroads among the city governors by 1638. That November, Robert Woodford, Steward of Northampton, attended a dinner at Coventry 'counsell house', after the swearing in of the new mayor. He

---

[210] Oman, *English Church Plate*, pp. 147–8, 206. The paten-covers of the Dudley chalices are engraved on the inside with a crucifix. Ibid., p. 225. For the significance of gothic revival chalices, see above, p. 71.

[211] See above, p. 33, n. 19.

[212] John Cotton, *The Way of Congregational Churches Cleared* (1648), pp. 33–4.

[213] Cosin, *Correspondence*, i. 66.

records that 'one Mr Nayler, an Arminian, and I had much dispute about predestinacion. The Lord much moved my hart to defend his truth, but I found few there that favoured it.'[214] Christopher Clitherow, therefore, was probably part of a similar London group of Arminian sympathizers. These latter perhaps included the two aldermen remembered in his will— Anthony Abdy and Henry Garway.[215]

Lay support for Arminianism, however, involves a paradox, because there was undoubtedly a sacerdotal element to the movement. Thus the Arminian Thomas Laurence taught that the duty of the laity required 'an humble distance from God', while the privilege of the clergy involved the 'immediatenesse of their acesse'. That part of the church nearest the altar was 'the inviolablest sanctuary of all', where only a priest could partake of the eucharist.[216] The same position was argued in more extravagant language by Jasper Fisher, who during 1636 was in trouble with Bishop Williams for erecting a stone altar.[217] Fisher referred to the 'twice-dipt purple of the priesthood', who were a class sent as ambassadors 'from Heaven by the Lord of Hosts, about a peace between God the father and sinfull mankind'. A priest is a 'ghostly father' and laymen must not turn him into a 'fellow speaker'. He also reminded his fellow-clergy 'thou art elevated above this wicked world, and indued with a heavenly power'.[218] At the episcopal level Archbishop Harsnett asked to be depicted on his memorial brass in full vestments.[219] This resurgent clericalism was potentially offensive to all those confident of their own spiritual standing with God and for whom a once-for-all act of faith was the pathway to salvation. But for someone unable to make this mental leap a priestly intercessor had obvious attractions. Here the revived practice of confession is especially significant. Private confession to a clergyman was increasingly urged in visitation articles, while some preachers now maintained that it was a 'necessity'.

[214] New College, Oxford, MS 9502, fo. 139.

[215] PRO, PROB. 11/187, fo. 279ʳ⁻ᵛ.

[216] Thomas Laurence, *Two Sermons*, i. 3, and *A Sermon preached before the King's Majestie at Whitehall* (1637), pp. 9–10.

[217] Laud, *Works*, v. 342.

[218] Jasper Fisher, *The Priest's Duty and Dignity* (1635), pp. 9, 34, 42, 46.

[219] PRO, PROB. 11/160, fo. 74. The brass still survives in the parish church of Chigwell, Essex.

Two sermons advocating confession were preached at Cambridge University in 1637, by Sylvester Adams and Anthony Sparrow. That by Sparrow was printed the same year at London. He taught that sin must be confessed in order to obtain remission. Sinning itself is an act of free will and consequently avoidable. 'At all times man may sinne or not sinne if he will.' The power of absolution belongs to the priesthood, who are 'God's vicegerents here on earth'. After our confession, God 'will purge us from all iniquity by the infusion of his grace'. No sin apparently is unforgivable, for even Judas could have been forgiven if he had confessed to Jesus. Although Sparrow admits that confession can be public as well as private and that the latter is 'out of use', it is clear that both he and Adams had auricular confession primarily in mind.[220] Thus Adams was accused by the Vice-Chancellor of Cambridge, the Calvinist Ralph Brownrig, of saying that 'a speciall confession unto a priest . . . is necessary unto salvation'.[221]

Given that Arminianism had some lay appeal, the question remains how far down the social scale this extended. During the 1630s a correlation emerged between the Arminian doctrine of the regime and a more relaxed attitude towards Sunday observance. While the Jacobean Declaration of Sports had remained a dead letter, its reissue in 1633 was followed by general enforcement. Moreover, the two most prominent defenders of Caroline policy, as regards Sunday pastimes, were the Arminians Peter Heylyn and Francis White.[222] On Sunday, says White, Christians celebrate 'the benefit of redemption' which 'by the antecedent will of Christ is intended to all . . . and none are excluded from it but only they which by their owne demerit have made themselves unworthy'. The reprobate are those among the 'redeemed' who either reject outright the offer of salvation, or having accepted it 'returne againe into bondage'. Sunday duties themselves ought to be 'possible' of fulfilment by ordinary mortals and not too oner-

[220] Anthony Sparrow, *A Sermon concerning Confession of Sinnes and the Power of Absolution* (1637), pp. 2, 6, 8, 14, 16, 18–19.

[221] G. B. Tatham, *The Puritans in Power* (Cambridge, 1913), p. 269.

[222] Peter Heylyn, *The History of the Sabbath* (1636); Francis White, *A Treatise of the Sabbath-Day* (1635). White's Arminianism has been discussed above (pp. 174–80). That of Heylyn emerges most fully from his history of Arminianism published at the Restoration. *Historia Quinqu-Articularis, passim.*

ous, the 'actuall performance of religious offices' being balanced by time for recreation.[223] The Arminian Sunday, which reversed a long-standing trend towards the imposition of strict sabbatarianism, was undoubtedly popular.

VI

But the rise of English Arminianism, and its associated sacramentalism, also meant an erosion of the shared Calvinist middle ground which had previously existed between Puritans and members of the ecclesiastical hierarchy. The experience of John Ley, Vicar of Great Budworth in Cheshire, was perhaps fairly typical of many a future presbyterian minister. A graduate of Christ Church, Oxford, he had held a college living since 1616, becoming a prebendary of Chester in 1627 and Sub-Dean. Ley gave no signs of serious religious disaffection until 1635. In June of that year he wrote a letter to Bishop Bridgeman, on the subject of an alleged stone altar newly erected in the cathedral. (Two years earlier the communion table had been moved back to an eastward position, on the orders of Archbishop Neile.) Ley describes the setting up of an altar as 'schismaticall', and warns that in consequence Puritans 'will be more stiffe in standing out against conformity . . . and we that are conformable shall be lesse strong to contest with them'. He goes on to ask 'can there by anything in that heap of stones which may serve to repaire the ruines which an altar may make?' Nevertheless the letter is couched in generally respectful terms and Ley quotes the opinion of Aquinas that 'an inferior clerke may sometimes admonish a prelate'. He also refers to the 'great moderation', for which Bridgeman is renowned, and as late as 1641 recalled how they had been preachers together in the Warrington exercise.[224] By this latter date, however, Ley regarded men like his diocesan as exceptions to the general run of bishops, and was himself moving steadily in a presbyterian direction. Two years later he subscribed the Solemn League and Covenant, thus committing himself to the 'extirpation' of episcopacy.[225]

[223] White, *Sabbath-Day*, pp. 82–3, 256, 266.
[224] John Ley, *A Letter against the Erection of an Altar* (1641), pp. 15, 16–18, 21, and *Defensive Doubts, Hopes and Reasons for the Refusall of the Oath* (1641), sig. a4.
[225] John Ley, *Sunday a Sabbath* (1641), sigs. a2–c2; *DNB*, s.n. Ley, John.

At the same time, during the 1630s, the earlier Jacobean policy of occasional conformity was abandoned. Nonconformists were now harried with a new intensity and those suspected of such inclinations were assumed to be guilty until they proved their innocence. The county of Essex felt the full brunt of this soon after Laud became Bishop of London. We have already mentioned the silencing of Thomas Hooker, but there was a crop of similar cases. Best documented is that of Thomas Shepherd, lecturer at Earls Colne, who by his own account was not a resolute nonconformist when the wrath of Laud fell upon him in 1630. Despite having a 'license to officiate the cure' from Laud's predecessor, Shepherd was forbidden to 'exercise any ministerial function' in London diocese. According to Shepherd, in his autobiography, it was only sometime after this episode that 'the Lord let me see into the evil of the English ceremonies, cross, surplice and kneeling'. Doubts about 'church government' by bishops soon followed.[226] During the episcopal visitation of the following year, 1631, a revealing exchange is recorded as having taken place between Laud and Stephen Marshall, Vicar of Finchingfield. Marshall and a group of fellow-ministers had denied being nonconformists. 'Do you conform always?', Laud asked, to which Marshall replied 'sometimes but not always'. Marshall was ordered to mend his ways although he remained under suspicion, Sir Nathaniel Brent reporting six years later that 'no man doubteth but he hath an inconformable heart but externally he observeth all'.[227]

When Marshall himself came to preach before the Long Parliament, in November 1640, he presented a five point religious indictment of the Caroline regime. First, he instanced the 'miserable defection' in doctrine, and asked 'what one article of faith controverted betwixt us and the Church of Rome is there that our pulpits and presses, and university acts, have not been bold withall, as if we were weary of the truth which God hath committed to us'. Secondly, he said, 'there hath not been in all the Christian world such high affronts offered to the Lord's day, as of late hath been in Eng-

---

[226] Thomas Shepherd, *My Birth and Life*, in A. Young, *Chronicles of the First Planters of . . . Massachusetts Bay* (Boston, Mass., 1846), pp. 516–28.
[227] H. Smith, *The Ecclesiastical History of Essex* (Colchester, 1932), pp. 44, 53.

land'. Thirdly, 'the preaching of the word', that 'chariot upon which life and salvation come riding', has been suppressed. Fourthly, 'God's worship' is newly corrupted by 'idolatry and superstition'. Only his fifth and final point, where he deplored the indiscriminate admission of all parishioners to 'the holy sacrament of the Lord's supper', suggests a Puritan at heart.[228] Moreover, in so far as Marshall mentioned bishops at all, it was as potential reformers, and he did not emerge as a thoroughgoing opponent of episcopacy until 1641.[229]

Someone whose growing alienation from the established church can be dated with unusual precision is the lawyer William Prynne. Between 1626 and 1629 he produced three books against Arminianism—*The Perpetuitie of a Regenerate Man's Estate, God no Imposter nor Deluder*, and *The Church of England's Old Antithesis to New Arminianisme*. During the same period he denounced Cosin's *Collection of Private Devotions* as 'meerely Popish'.[230] By the mid-1630s Prynne had turned his attention to the profanation of the sabbath and the moving of communion tables to an altarwise position. His general stance was that of a defender of traditional Church of England teachings and practices, against what he deemed to be recent innovations. He still distinguished between 'godly bishops' and the rest, writing that 'all of you are not alike culpable, but some more, some lesse, and some of you (perchance) altogether innocent'. Now, however, he had also developed a critique of what he called 'lordly prelacy'.[231] Indeed the germ of this was already present in 1629, when he urged the English bishops collectively, 'the master overseers of Christ's most precious flock', to stem the advance of Arminianism.

Arise and shine forth before us, by humility, by purity of life [and] of doctrine, as the lampes—the splendor of our church . . . You are our

---

[228] Stephen Marshall, *A Sermon preached before the Honourable House of Commons . . . November 17, 1640* (1641), pp. 32–5.

[229] Ibid., pp. 20–1, 46–7; Stephen Marshall *et al.*, *An Answer to a Book entitled an Humble Remonstrance* (1641), *passim*.

[230] William Prynne, *The Perpetuitie* (1626), *A Briefe Survay and Censure of Mr. Cozens his Couzening Devotions* (1628), *God no Imposter nor Deluder* (1629), and *The Church of England's Old Antithesis to New Arminianisme* (1629). The second and much enlarged edition of this book, published in 1630, is entitled *Anti-Arminianisme*.

[231] William Prynne, *A Looking-Glasse for all Lordly Prelates* (1636), sig. a2, pp. 18–19, 23, *The Unbishoping of Timothy and Titus* (Amsterdam, 1636), pp. 23–8, and *A Quench-Coale*, pp. 48, 63 and *passim*.

shepheards. You eat [and] we yeeld our milke. O nourish, o feed [and] instruct us for it, with the wholesome, the soule-saving word and bread of life. You reape our temporall. O sow, o give unto us spirituall things. You are our master-heardsmen. Your wages, yea your flockes are great. O then be vigilant, diligent, carefull and laborious for them, resident and present with them.[232]

In 1629 Prynne addressed his remarks to 'the right reverend fathers in God, the archbishops and bishops of the Church of England', whereas by 1636 these had become 'the pontificiall lordly prelates of England', apostates from the faith and 'fallen from the pietie, holinesse, humility, poverty, zeale, meekenesse, laboriousnesse, heavenly mindedness, charity and equality with other ministers, that was in the true Christian bishops of the primitive church'.[233] Lordly prelates are both 'dumbe themselves, very seldome or never preaching in their diocesse[s]' and deaf to the cries of the 'many godly, faithfull, painfull ministers and people' whom they oppress. They are in fact the opposite of the ideal held up earlier.[234] In his *A Looking-Glasse for all Lordly Prelates*, published in 1636, Prynne catalogued the recent religious changes, portraying them as the logical consequence of lordly prelacy. Moreover his *The Unbishoping of Timothy and Titus*, of the same year, verges on an outright demand that bishops be abolished. He begins by inviting Laud and Neile to resign their archbishoprics, having 'long since given over the maine part of your episcopall function [which is] preaching', and ends with a general call to 'all our lordly prelates' to 'lay downe their bishopricks'. The only qualification occurs in the preface where Prynne prophesies the imminent 'fall' of the bishops, 'unless with speed they wholly quit these false [*jure divino*] foundations and bottom their prelacy and jurisdiction onely on his Majestie's princely favour'.[235] Not until 1641 did Prynne advocate in print the 'utter extirpation' of episcopacy, but his almost total disillusionment with the institution is already apparent in 1636.[236]

---

[232] Prynne, *The Church of England's Old Antithesis*, sigs. ¶¶2, ¶¶4.
[233] Ibid., sig. ¶; Prynne, *A Looking-Glasse*, sig. a2, p. 2.
[234] Prynne, *A Looking-Glasse*, p. 4.
[235] Prynne, *The Unbishoping*, pp. 6, 10–21, 165.
[236] William Prynne, *The Antipathie of the English Lordly Prelacie both to Regall Monarchy*

Just as religious developments during the personal rule of Charles I profoundly alarmed some Protestants, concomitantly the hopes of members of the English Catholic community were raised. If not actual reunion with Rome, then at least a general toleration of Catholicism seemed a distinct possibility. Particularly significant here was the appearance in 1634 of a book entitled *Deus, Natura, Gratia*. Written by the Franciscan Christopher Davenport, and dedicated to King Charles, it sought to reconcile the doctrinal teachings of the English Church with those of Roman Catholicism. Much of the work was concerned with questions at issue in the Arminian controversy and the views of Richard Montagu are cited with enthusiasm. Davenport also refers approvingly to a Cambridge Commencement thesis, by Eleazer Duncon, on the subject of justification by faith and works.[237] The second edition, published the next year, has a preface in which Davenport makes even plainer his purpose in writing. As the Church of England sloughs off 'the old Calvinist man'*, so its disagreements with Rome will diminish and even disappear.[238] That there was an element of wishful thinking here is not the point. These same years saw Catholicism becoming increasingly prominent at the royal court, under the protection of Queen Henrietta Maria, while the numbers both of lay recusants and missionary priests in England continued to rise.[239]

This is the context of the contemporary burgeoning of Popish plot theory. The rise of English Arminianism had been explained by Henry Burton effectively in terms of a Popish plot as early as 1628,[240] although subsequent developments gave the theory a new impetus. It was again most fully articulated by Burton, in two sermons preached on 5 November 1636. Yet, according to the charges subsequently made against him in the Court of High Commission, he had for at least five years been similarly 'insinuatinge' the existence of

and Civill Unity (1641), sig. ¶¶. This reassessment of Prynne builds on the pioneering work of Professor William Lamont in his *Marginal Prynne, 1600–1669* (1963).

[237] Christopher Davenport, *Deus, Natura, Gratia* (Lyons, 1634), pp. 7, 159, 211. He was a brother of the Puritan John Davenport.

[238] Christopher Davenport, *Deus, Natura, Gratia* (Lyons, 1635), sigs. A6, B6^{r–v}.

[239] C. Hibbard, *Charles I and the Popish Plot* (Chapel Hill, 1983), ch. 3; J. Bossy, *The English Catholic Community, 1570–1850* (1975), p. 422.

[240] See above, pp. 157–8.

'some plott or practice . . . for the suppressing of the true religion here established [and] for the bringing in of Popery'.[241] In
his most recent sermons Burton had argued that, since Gunpowder Plot, there was 'another broode risen up amongst us',
likewise aiming to overthrow church and state but by different
means. 'And to bringe this about they first prohibite ministers
from meddlinge with matters of controversy, especially with
Arminian heresyes which doe combine with Popery.' Here he
condemned 'to the pitt of Hell the error of the Arminians who
hold that a child of God may fall away from grace'. The present 'plotters' bring in 'newe lawes, new rites, newe ceremonies into the Church of God'. Thus 'whole dioces can tell
you howe tables are turned into altars and those altars sett at
the end of every chancell'. Meanwhile 'the mouthes . . . of
faithful ministers are stopt for preachinge the doctrine of grace
and salvation'.[242]

VII

Granted that a Popish plot in the strict sense was largely the
product of overheated Protestant imaginations, the reality of
Arminianism on the other hand is underlined by the efforts of
King Charles and Archbishop Laud to export it to Ireland
and Scotland. Both the Irish Church and the Scottish Church
had, during the second decade of the seventeenth century, put
on record statements of Calvinist faith. Indeed the Irish Articles of 1615 and the Scottish Confession of 1616, when taken
together with British participation in framing the canons of
Dort, between 1618 and 1619, indicate the religious gulf
between the Jacobean and Caroline periods. The Irish Articles incorporated almost verbatim the Lambeth Articles of
1595, and in so far as they differ the Calvinism of the former is
even stricter. Thus the thirty-eighth Irish article states that a
'true, lively, justifying faith and the sanctifying spirit of God is
not extinguished nor vanisheth away in the regenerate, either
finally or totally', substituting 'the regenerate' for 'the elect' as

---

[241] PRO, SP 16/335, fo. 147. I owe my knowledge of this document to Professor
Russell. The printed version of these sermons differs somewhat. Burton, *For God and
the King*.
[242] PRO, SP 16/335, fos. 148–9ᵛ.

the fifth Lambeth article has it.[243] This rules out any possible doubt about the fate of the non-elect. According to the Scottish Confession, 'albeit all mankind be fallen in Adam yit onlie these who are elected before all tyme are in tyme redeemed, restored, raised and quickened againe; not of themselfs or of their works . . . but onlie of the mercie of God'. The elect 'albeit they offend through infirmitie and through the entisements thereof sinne greivouslie, to the great offence of God, yit they cannot altogether fall from grace'.[244]

The royal proclamation of 1626 concerning the Arminian controversy effectively ignored the Irish Articles, by making the Thirty-nine Articles binding in Ireland as well as England. Nothing was said, however, about Scotland. The subsequent declaration prefacing the Thirty-nine Articles only named England. Nevertheless it was apparently on the basis of this declaration that in 1631 King Charles ordered the suppression of a Calvinist work recently published at Dublin. Written by Bishop George Downham of Derry and entitled *The Covenant of Grace*, the author had appended to it a treatise specifically defending the thirty-eighth Irish article concerning perseverance. The book is dedicated jointly to the Lord Chancellor of Ireland, Viscount Loftus, and the Earl of Cork.[245] Three years later Laud secured the replacement of the Irish Articles by the Thirty-nine Articles. The change was embodied in the new Irish canons of 1635, which also ordered that communion tables 'be placed at the east end of the church or chancel'.[246] A chief agent in these alterations was John Bramhall, chaplain to Lord Deputy Wentworth and who succeeded Downham as Bishop of Derry in 1634. Bramhall's own Arminianism was to emerge most clearly in his later controversy with the philosopher Thomas Hobbes.[247]

---

[243] *Articles of Religion agreed upon . . . in the Convocation holden at Dublin*, sig. C2. For the text of the Lambeth Articles, see above, pp. 30–1.

[244] Calderwood, *History of the Kirk in Scotland*, VII. 234, 238.

[245] Prynne, *Canterburies Doome*, pp. 171–2; George Downham, *The Covenant of Grace* (Dublin, 1631) [sig. A2], pp. 233–414. Downham is sometimes called a 'Puritan', but by 1608 he was also an advocate of *jure divino* episcopacy. George Downham, *A Sermon defending the Honourable Function of Bishops* (1608).

[246] Laud, *Works*, VII. 66; Strafford, *Letters*, ed. W. Knowler (1739), I. 298, 329, 342–4, 378; *Constitutions and Canons Ecclesiastical . . . of Ireland* (Dublin, 1664), pp. 7–8, 90.

[247] John Bramhall, *Works* (Oxford, 1842–5), I. pp. lxxix-lxxxi, IV. 67–82, 104–7, 228–49.

As in England so in Ireland the demise of Calvinism was associated with an attack on Protestant nonconformity. Up until the 1630s the Scottish clergy in Ulster, although ordained into the Church of Ireland, had been left largely to their own religious devices. Such apparently was the conscious policy of the Calvinist Archbishop Ussher, and many of them, moreover, had influential aristocratic patrons, such as Viscount Clandeboye.[248] This toleration ended with the arrival of Wentworth and his clerical adviser Bramhall, the latter personally reporting to Laud in December 1634 on the extent of Ulster nonconformity.[249] By this date a number of leading nonconformists had already been silenced. The following year an Irish Court of High Commission was set up and further deprivations followed. They were carried out by Henry Leslie, as Bishop of Down and Connor, whose Calvinist sermons during the later 1620s we have quoted above. Clearly, therefore, one should not exaggerate the congruence between Calvinism and a willingness to tolerate nonconformity. Ironically some of these deprived ministers returned in 1637 to Scotland, where they helped foment the Prayer Book rebellion.[250]

The rise of English Arminianism had elicited a hostile Scottish response as early as 1627, with the publication of *Vindiciae Theologicae pro Perseverantia Sanctorum in Gratia Salvifica* by William Leslie. Dedicated to Bishop Patrick Forbes of Aberdeen, who was also a Scottish privy councillor, this comprised part of Leslie's exercise for the degree of bachelor of divinity at King's College, Aberdeen.[251] By 1631, however, there was said to be much 'corrupt preaching' in Edinburgh 'for universall grace—Christ dieing for all—[and] the saints not persevereing'. A key figure seems to have been William Forbes, who was consecrated in February 1634 as Bishop of the newly created diocese of Edinburgh. Ten years before he had been accused by members of his Edinburgh congregation of utter-

---

[248] Robert Blair, *The Life*, ed. T. M'Crie (Edinburgh, 1848), pp. 58–9, 80–1, 98–9.

[249] PRO, SP 63/254, fo. 498.

[250] M. Perceval-Maxwell, 'Strafford, the Ulster-Scots and the Covenanters', *Irish Historical Studies*, 28 (1972–3), 524–51.

[251] William Leslie, *Vindiciae Theologicae pro Perseverantia Sanctorum in Gratia Salvifica* (Aberdeen, 1627), sig. A1ᵛ and *passim*. It was also claimed in 1629 that the 'academies' of St Andrews, Edinburgh, and Glasgow had all 'condemned' Richard Montagu's books. *Anti-Montacutum*, p. 34.

ing 'some poynts smelling of Arminianisme'. William Forbes had subsequently removed to Aberdeen, but among the other Edinburgh ministers Thomas Sydserf was perhaps closest to him theologically. Sydserf later edited the posthumously published *Considerationes Modestae et Pacificae* by Forbes, who died within a few months of becoming a bishop.[252]

Preaching before King Charles at Edinburgh in June 1633, during the royal visit to Scotland, William Forbes had described 'predestination' and 'the manner in which grace operates' as topics on which it was dangerous to make any 'positive determinations'*.[253] This was also the spirit in which his *Considerationes* were written. One consequence is that the views of Forbes remain somewhat elusive. He writes, for example, concerning the question of the certainty of salvation, 'that the elect cannot finally fall away is agreed by all who describe election either *a priori*, i.e. from a certain absolute decree of God, or *a posteriori*, i.e. from a final perseverance in faith and grace, about which matter there have always been in the Church opinions dissentient'. Nevertheless, Forbes urges all parties to accept that 'not only the elect truly believe and are justified, but many reprobate also', who 'afterwards altogether and for ever fall away'. Moreover, he describes the views of the British divines at the Synod of Dort, concerning the sins of the justified, as 'altogether frivolous'. In fact most of his criticisms are reserved for those he calls the 'rigid' Protestants.[254]

Members of the William Forbes circle, especially John Maxwell, played a leading part in the production of a new Scottish liturgy based on the English Prayer Book. Forbes himself, in his sermon preached before King Charles, had advocated a common liturgy and catechism, as well as a common confession of faith.[255] The same year a section of the Scottish nobility claimed, in a supplication to Charles, that 'there

---

[252] John Row, *The History of the Kirk of Scotland*, ed. D. Laing (Edinburgh, 1842), pp. 336, 354, 371–2. William Forbes, *Considerationes Modestae et Pacificae*, ed. and tr. G. Forbes (Oxford, 1850–6), II. 4, 9–12. The importance of Scottish Arminianism was first brought home to me by reading M. Kitshoff, 'Aspects of Arminianism in Scotland', St Andrews M.Th. thesis, 1968.

[253] John Forbes, *Opera Omnia* (Amsterdam, 1703), I/i. 293.

[254] William Forbes, *Considerationes*, I. 287, 292–5.

[255] G. Donaldson, *The Making of the Scottish Prayer Book of 1637* (Edinburgh, 1954), pp. 40–5, 47–8, 50, 57–8; John Forbes, *Opera*, I/i. 293.

is now a generall feare of some innovation intended in essentiall poynts of religion, and that this apprehension is much
increased by the reports of an allowance given in Ingland for
printing of books full of Poperie and Arminianisme, and by
preaching of Arminianisme in this countrey without censure'.[256] The next four years, culminating in the imposition of
a Scottish Prayer Book, saw the further erosion of Calvinist
orthodoxy. Here the case of Samuel Rutherford is particularly
significant. Rutherford was a nonconformist who had ministered undisturbed at Anwoth in Kirkcudbright, until the
appointment of Sydserf as Bishop of Galloway. He was
silenced in mid-1636 and banished to Aberdeen. According to
Rutherford, the occasion of his prosecution was the publication by him of a book 'against the Arminians'.[257] Printed at
Amsterdam and dedicated to the young Viscount Kenmure,
the work attacked among others the English Arminian
Thomas Jackson.[258] Once arrived in Aberdeen, Rutherford
soon found himself in dispute 'about Arminian controversies'
with Robert Barron, Professor of Divinity at Marischal College.[259]

   Some idea of the centrality of the religious ideas at stake is
conveyed by the diary of Archibald Johnston of Wariston. He
records there, for instance, a private meditation of September
1638.

I thought of the Lord's creating, praeserving, ruling all, and ten
thousand alls mor if thair wer, only and soly from his auin will and
pleasure . . . Then I thought of his wonderful wysdome in ordeaning
man's fall [and] the infinit love of God in redeeming som of lost
mankynd, quhilk proceeded from his freie underserved election of
som vessels to honor, as uthers to dishonor wer left in the corrupt
masse of mankind. Heir my heart failed me and my apprehension
fell schort quhen I thought of the freiedom of this electing and prae-
veining love, having mercie on quhom he will haive mercie, and
hardning quhom he wil harden.[260]

   [256] Row, *History of the Kirk of Scotland*, pp. 377–8.
   [257] Samuel Rutherford, *Letters*, ed. A. A. Bonar (Edinburgh, 1894), p. 141.
   [258] Samuel Rutherford, *Exercitationes Apologeticae pro Divina Gratia* (Amsterdam,
1636), sigs. ∴2–∴6ᵛ, pp. 351–5.
   [259] Rutherford, *Letters*, p. 239.
   [260] *Diary of Sir Archibald Johnston of Wariston, 1632–9*, ed. G. M. Paul (Scottish History Society, 61, 1911), p. 386.

Johnston is remembered as one of the architects of the Scottish national covenant, yet in the early 1630s he can be found happily attending the church services of ministers subsequently deprived by the Glasgow Assembly of 1638.[261] Part of the explanation is that a revolution, imposed from above, had occurred during the interim. For the new Scottish Prayer Book of 1637 marked a radical departure from its predecessor, Knox's Book of Common Order. The difference between the two baptismal services is particularly striking, Knox's Book being adamant that baptism is unnecessary to salvation. Nor should one believe any

virtue or power to be included in the visible water, or outward action, for many have been baptised and yet never inwardly purged, but that our saviour Christ, who commanded baptism to be ministered, will, by the power of his Holy Spirit, effectually work in the hearts of his elect, in time convenient, all that is meant and signified by the same. *And this the Scripture calleth our regeneration.*[262]

By contrast the new Scottish Prayer Book, like its English counterpart, calls all baptized infants 'regenerate'. In addition a novel Scottish rubric requires the minister to say, each time the water in the font is changed, 'Sanctify this fountain of baptism, thou which art the sanctifier of all things'. It is also prescribed that the communion table 'stand at the uppermost part of the chancel or church'.[263] This last change had already been incorporated in the new Scottish canons of 1636, which also enjoined all preachers to teach 'the necessity of good works'.[264]

The preface to the Scottish Prayer Book echoes William Forbes's sermon of 1633, in saying that

it were to be wished that the whole Church of Christ were one, as well in form of public worship as in doctrine, and that as it hath but one Lord and one faith so it had but one heart and one mouth. This would prevent many schisms and divisions, and serve much to the preserving of unity. But since that cannot be hoped for in the whole Catholic Christian Church, yet at least in the Churches that are

---

[261] Ibid., pp. xvii–xviii.

[262] *The Book of Common Order of the Church of Scotland*, ed. G. W. Sprott (Edinburgh, 1901), pp. 135–6. My italics.

[263] Donaldson, *Scottish Prayer Book*, pp. 183, 206, 210.

[264] Laud, *Works*, v. 590, 600.

under the protection of one sovereign prince the same ought to be endeavoured.

Hence the provision for Scotland of a prayer book 'like unto that which is received in the Churches of England and Ireland'.[265] Probably the long-term intention was to make the English Thirty-nine Articles, as glossed by King Charles, authoritative in Scotland as well. The doctrinal ambience of the Scottish Prayer Book helps explain the preoccupation of the Glasgow Assembly with 'Arminianism', when it met in November 1638. By this date the new Scottish liturgy had been firmly rejected and the covenanters had gone on to demand further changes both in religious worship and church government. During the assembly episcopacy was to be abolished. Nevertheless, the continuing concern about Arminianism is also evident.

Early on in the proceedings the Scottish bishops, who refused to recognize the jurisdiction of the Glasgow Assembly, were likened to the Dutch Remonstrants at the Synod of Dort. The first bishop to be accused by name was Thomas Sydserf, of whom it was said that 'both in publicke and private he defended Arminianism'.[266] During the first week in December three members of the assembly delivered formal refutations of the 'five articles' of Arminianism. First was David Dickson, who like Rutherford had been silenced by the new Scottish High Commission. Dickson was followed by Andrew Ramsay and Robert Baillie. It is clear from the surviving accounts that these speakers based themselves upon the canons of the Synod of Dort.[267] Three other bishops were explicitly accused of Arminianism at this time. They were Bishop James Fairlie of Argyll, Bishop John Maxwell of Ross, and Bishop James Wedderburn of Dunblane. Of Fairlie it was claimed he 'had preached Arminianisme, specially universall grace, illustrating it by the simile of a pilot in a storme, who intends to save all within the shipp but is hindered by the violence of the storme [and] not by the will of the maister of the shippe'.[268]

---

[265] Donaldson, *Scottish Prayer Book*, p. 101.
[266] James Gordon, *History of Scots Affairs*, ed. J. Robertson and G. Grub (Aberdeen, 1841), I. 176, II. 29.
[267] Ibid., II. 46–7, 49.
[268] Ibid., II. 141–2.

Maxwell was reported to have defended 'all the heterodoxies of the Arminians, publickly both by himself and his associatts', while Wedderburn, as Professor of Divinity at St Andrews, had allegedly 'recommended' Arminian authors 'above all others' and thereby infected 'his hearers'.[269] Significantly Maxwell and Wedderburn had been the two Scottish bishops most closely involved in the production of the new Prayer Book.[270]

Scotland in fact provides an analogue for England, with Arminianism in both countries featuring prominently as part of the indictment against episcopacy. Thus the English root and branch petition of December 1640, calling for the abolition of bishops, gives as the second reason for such a course of action 'the faint-heartedness of ministers to preach the truth of God, lest they should displease the prelates, as namely the doctrine of predestination, of free-grace, of perseverence, of original sin remaining after baptism [or] against universal grace, election for faith foreseen [and] free will'.[271] This recalls the London petition of 1629.[272] Moreover the Scottish national covenant of February 1638 anticipates similar pronouncements by the Long Parliament, in alluding to a Popish plot aimed at the subversion of 'the true religion'. Recent religious 'innovations' are all said 'sensibly [to] tend to the reestablishing of the Popish religion and tyranny'.[273] At the same time the note of extremism that increasingly characterized Scottish demands in the late 1630s found an answering call among Archbishop Laud's own circle of intimates. Viscount Scudamore, writing to Laud in January 1639 about the Scottish rebellion, says that

it joyes mee, in the midst of my bounden compassion and anxietie, to see that you continue unmov'd and resolute to stand the storme to the uttermost, and so to rush through your martyrdome (for such it is) to the crowne of glory which is lay'd up for you . . . [As] for those that oppose may their conceptions bee chaff, and their fruite stubble, and the fire of their own breath their devourer, if they will not returne and seeke the Churche's peace.[274]

[269] Ibid., II. 134–7.
[270] For Wedderburn see Donaldson, *Scottish Prayer Book*, pp. 49–55, 81–2.
[271] *Stuart Constitution*, ed. Kenyon, p. 172.   [272] See above, pp. 181–2.
[273] W. C. Dickinson *et al.*, *A Source Book of Scottish History* (1958), III. 101–2.
[274] Gibson, *Churches of Door, Home-Lacy and Hempsted*, pp. 92–3.

The attitude of the King towards his Scottish opponents appears to have been equally intransigent.[275]

VIII

Successful military resistance by the Scots forced King Charles to summon an English parliament, in order to pay for their suppression. Religion, it has been calculated, was the most important single national issue in the ensuing elections.[276] But there was seemingly no recognition on Charles's part that the parliament might provide a platform for the English critics of his religious policies. Certainly no gestures of conciliation are discernible. On the contrary, the convocation of clergy, which accompanied the parliament, proceeded to underwrite the most controversial innovations in worship while rejecting a call from Bishop Davenant to ban Arminian books.[277] Members of the Short Parliament, which met in April 1640, consciously sought to pick up the threads of debate from where they had been forcibly dropped in March 1629.[278] As on that earlier occasion, it was Francis Rous who now most clearly articulated the religious frame of reference, which was to become a hallmark of the parliamentary opposition in the early 1640s. Speaking on 17 April, Rous claimed that 'the roote of all o[u]r grievances' is 'an intended union betwixt us and Roome'. He elaborated that 'for the setling of this worke the word Puritan is an essentiall engine', meaning 'in the mouth of an Arminian an orthodox man, in the mouth of a Papist a Protestant, and so it is spoke to shame a man out of all religion if a man will bee ashamed to bee saved'.[279]

Pym's more famous keynote speech immediately followed that of his stepbrother Rous, and is logically connected. 'Religion', he said, 'is in truth the greatest grievance to bee lookt into.' He went on to speak of a 'plot' to 'reduce our land to the

[275] D. Stevenson, *The Scottish Revolution, 1637–44* (Newton Abbot, 1973), pp. 72, 81, 85, 95–7, 133.

[276] J. K. Gruenfelder, 'The Election to the Short Parliament, 1640', in *Early Stuart Studies*, ed. H. S. Reinmuth (Minneapolis, 1970), p. 219.

[277] *Proceedings of the Short Parliament of 1640*, ed. E. S. Cope and W. H. Coates (Camden, 4th ser., 19, 1977), p. 111.

[278] Ibid., p. 212.

[279] Ibid., pp. 146–7.

Pope', listing the 'innovations to prepare us to Poperie'. These included the printing and preaching of 'many Popish poynts', as well as their maintenance in university disputations, and 'the introducion of Popish ceremonyes' such as 'setting up altars'.[280] Pym distinguished these ceremonies from those which 'the reformed religion continued unto us', while complaining, as did Rous, about the persecution of 'conscionable' clergy.[281] Although more than half of Pym's speech is taken up with secular grievances, concerning 'property in goods and priviledges of parlement', the underlying religious assumptions are much the same as those evinced by Rous. Furthermore, Pym was chosen to handle the subject of 'religion' at a proposed conference with the Lords on grievances. King Charles described this as putting 'the cart before the horse', whereas he required parliament to vote supply first.[282] Members of the Commons, especially Pym, also questioned the rights and wrongs of the war with Scotland and cast doubt on official explanations which denied that religion had any bearing on the matter.[283] The resulting deadlock was only broken by the dissolution of parliament on 5 May.

This was followed by violent demonstrations in London. Archbishop Laud in particular was singled out and a mob marched on Lambeth Palace, calling for the blood of 'William the fox'.[284] Motives are always difficult to disentangle, but placards were displayed with the wording 'Come now and help us that we may destroy this subtle fox and hunt this ravening wolf out of his den, which daily plotteth mischief and seeks to bring this whole land to distruction by his Popish inventions'.[285] Order was restored in the capital with some difficulty, and during the following months the newly erected altar rails became the target of mutinous soldiers levied for the Scottish war. The county of Essex seems to have been the centre of these disturbances, the Arminian Lord Maynard writing to the Privy Council in July that the soldiers have

---

[280] Ibid., pp. 149, 151, 217.

[281] Ibid., pp. 147, 151.

[282] Ibid., pp. 70, 181.

[283] Ibid., pp. 190, 191, 195–6; *Stuart Royal Proclamations*, ed. J. F. Larkin and P. L. Hughes (Oxford, 1973–83), II. 662–7.

[284] Laud, *Works*, III. 284.

[285] *Stuart Royal Proclamations*, ed. Larkin and Hughes, II. 711.

'taken uppon them to reforme churches, and even in the tyme of divine service to pull downe the rayles about the communion tables'.[286] Four weeks later Maynard reported that Scottish printed propaganda was circulating among these same soldiers. The broadside in question survives and seeks to make common cause with 'all the true English', against 'the wicked counsels of Papists, prelats and other fire-brands their adherents'.[287] A subsequent Scottish pamphlet, of October, described the common enemy as a 'Canterburian faction of Papists, Atheists, Arminians [and] prelats, the misleaders of the King's Majesty'.[288]

The war with Scotland was unpopular at all levels of society, but as regards the attitudes of the governing class the decision by King Charles to press ahead with a new book of canons for the English Church proved especially divisive. By custom, the convocation should have terminated with the parliament on 5 May. Nevertheless, after consulting with some of the judges, Charles authorized the convocation to continue in being.[289] The 1640 canons, as printed, are prefaced by a fairly lengthy explanation, in the name of King Charles, as to why they were deemed necessary. This preface indicates that a major concern was to buttress the ceremonial changes of the 1630s. 'Our subjects', it says, 'being misled against the rites and ceremonies now used in the Church of England have lately taken offence at the same, upon an unjust supposal that they are not only contrary to our laws but also introductive unto popish superstitions.' The preface claims that 'the said rites and ceremonies' were Edwardian in origin and 'also again taken up' under Elizabeth, being 'ordinarily practised for a great part of her reign, within the memory of divers yet living, as that it could not then be imagined that there would need any rule or law for the observation of the same'. Thereafter, however, 'for want of an express rule', they 'began to fall into disuse' and instead 'other foreign and unfitting usages by

---

[286] PRO, SP 16/461, fo. 38. On 24 June 1640 Maynard had added a codicil to his will lest he should 'come to an untymely end', attempting to suppress mutineers in Cambridgeshire where he was also Lord-Lieutenant. PRO, PROB. 11/185, fo. 195ᵛ.

[287] PRO, SP 16/464, fo. 182; *Notes of the Treaty carried on at Ripon . . . 1640*, ed. J. Bruce (Camden Soc., 100, 1869), pp. 70–1.

[288] Ibid., p. 75.

[289] Laud, *Works*, III. 285–6.

little and little to creep in'. Canon number seven reveals that the rites and ceremonies in question concerned 'the situation of the communion table and the approaches thereunto'. The canon goes on to underwrite the altarwise position and railing of communion tables.[290]

As we have seen, this involved a dubious reading of the relevant Elizabethan injunction, and by the King's own admission meant putting the clock back half a century. Moreover, the seventh canon also recommends genuflexion on entering and leaving church, 'according to the most ancient custom of the primitive Church in the purest times'.[291] The importance of this appeal to antiquity is highlighted by the terms in which the Arminian Bishop Montagu had addressed King Charles in 1636, describing him as responsible for 'bringing back, renewing, restoring, repairing, protecting and preserving the ancient rites, the ceremonies of our forefathers, the apostolical and ecclesiastical traditions'*. This comprised part of a full page dedication to Charles, by Montagu, of *De Originibus Ecclesiasticis*. Both book and dedication were re-issued in 1640.[292] Clearly, then, more was involved than simply a return to the supposed mid-sixteenth-century model of the English Church. At issue, in addition, was the practice of the first Christian centuries. Whether one dubs the changes made on this basis renovations or innovations, their novelty in the eyes of most English people alive in the early seventeenth century is indisputable.

Apart from the seventh canon, numbers one and six were also highly controversial. The first, 'concerning the regal power', includes the statement that 'tribute and custom, and aid and subsidy, and all manner of necessary support and supply be respectively due to kings from their subjects by the law of God, nature and nations, for the public defence, care and protection of them'.[293] No mention is made of the role of parliament and the language was all too reminiscent of that used by Roger Mainwaring and Robert Sibthorpe, in defence of the force loan in 1627, and which had led to the identification of

---

[290] Ibid., v. 609–10, 624–5.
[291] Ibid., v. 625–6.
[292] Richard Montagu, *De Originibus Ecclesiasticis Commentationem* (1636) [sig. A2].
[293] Laud, *Works*, v. 613–14.

Arminianism with the attack on property rights.[294] Canon
number six embodies an oath to be taken by all clergymen
that 'the doctrine and discipline' of the Church of England
contains 'all things necessary to salvation', and promising
never to 'consent to alter the government of this church by
archbishops, bishops, deans and archdeacons *etcetera*, as it
stands now established and as by right it ought to stand'.[295]
Among other things, this seemed to involve a blanket endorsement of the new Arminian status quo.

In fact a vigorous rearguard action was fought against these
canons by a minority group of Calvinists in the lower house of
convocation itself. This opposition was led by three
archdeacons, namely Ralph Brownrig, John Hacket, and
Richard Holdsworth.[296] Archbishop Laud anticipated such a
difference of opinion to the extent that the sermon preached at
the opening of convocation, by his chaplain Thomas Turner,
concluded with a reference to bishops who were 'too easy and
remiss' in administering church discipline and 'sought to gain
to themselves the popular praise of meekness and mildness'.
Turner had 'advised them all with equal strictness to urge an
universal conformity'.[297] How far Calvinist bishops like
Davenant and Hall dared to speak out in the upper house of
convocation is not known. But after the dissolution of parliament thirty-six members of the lower house protested against
the continuance of the convocation. Having failed to termi-
nate it they then sought, according to Thomas Fuller who was
among them, 'to moderate proceedings with their presence'.[298]

The Arminian Peter Heylyn, who was also a member of this
convocation, provides much of the detail regarding the Calvinist opposition, although he plays down its extent. Apropos
the provision of the first canon concerning the basis of taxation, 'some thought fitter to leave [this] at large according to
the laws of several countries than to entitle it to the law of

[294] See above, pp. 157–9.
[295] Laud, *Works*, v. 623.
[296] Fuller, *Church History*, VI. 163; Lambeth Palace Library, Lambeth MS 943,
pp. 599–600. For the Calvinism of these three, see above, pp. 45–6, 54, n. 120 and John
Hacket, *A Century of Sermons* (1675), pp. xliii–xliv.
[297] Fuller, *Church History*, VI. 161–2.
[298] Ibid., pp. 164, 167. Fuller's own Calvinism emerges most clearly in his treatment of the Lambeth Articles. Ibid., v. 227.

God, nature and nations'.[299] Presumably the aim of this amendment was to protect the rights of the English parliament. While Heylyn records no serious questioning of the new oath, as proposed by the sixth canon, another account by Thomas Warmstry, one of the clerks for Worcester diocese, indicates that far-reaching objections were raised. Thus Warmstry claimed that the reference to doctrine in the oath was 'ambiguous', because the Thirty-nine Articles 'have been diversly interpreted to serve the turnes of Arminians and those that have been disaffected to the true sense of them'. In addition he challenged the concept that the discipline of the English Church was 'unalterable'.[300] On the other hand, Heylyn does note the disagreement in committee about 'placing the Lord's table where the altar stood, the drawing near unto it to receive the sacrament, and the making of due reverences at the entering into the church and going out of it'. In this connection he mentions a vitriolic exchange between the Prolocutor of the lower house, who was the Arminian Richard Steward, and Richard Holdsworth, the Archdeacon of Huntingdon.[301] Nevertheless Holdsworth's followers were outvoted both in committee and full convocation.

At the conclusion of the convocation members of both houses all subscribed the new canons, 'suffering ourselves', as Fuller puts it, 'to be all concluded by the majority of votes though some of us in the committee privately dissenting in the passing of many particulars'.[302] The consequence of this unanimous subscription was further to destroy belief in an uncorrupted body of Calvinist episcopalians, distinct from the reigning 'Canterburian faction'. Calvinist bishops especially were revealed as broken reeds. Yet the ecclesiastical ideal of Warmstry and his convocation colleagues remained close to that voiced by William Prynne ten years earlier.[303] Addressing the convocation summoned at the time of the Long Parliament, in November 1640, Warmstry spoke of the qualities

[299] Heylyn, *Cyprianus Anglicus*, p. 405.

[300] Thomas Warmstry, *A Convocation Speech* (1641), pp. 16–17. This speech was delivered in the convocation which was summoned at the time of the Long Parliament, but Warmstry indicates that he had argued similarly during the previous convocation. Ibid., p. 2.

[301] Heylyn, *Cyprianus Anglicus*, p. 407.

[302] Fuller, *Church History*, VI. 173.

[303] See above, pp. 225–6.

required of church governors. 'I desire that their authoritie may be supported by those pillars of learning, zeale, holinesse, industrie, meeknesse, courage and humilitie.' Bishops should be 'fatherly, not despoticall, much less tyrannicall [and] not as lords over God's heritage, but as stewards of the manifold graces of God'. A bishop is 'more splendid, and more like an apostle, in a pulpit than upon a throne'. Reviewing the changes of the 1630s, Warmstry attacked the new 'altars' and 'images', complaining that 'preaching of the word is discouraged' and 'pictures brought in'. Similarly he referred to 'candles in the day time', as the 'embleme of a fruitless prelacy or clergy in the church'.[304]

The autumn of 1640 saw widespread resistance to the *etcetera* oath,[305] as it came to be known, while in London on the eve of the Long Parliament a large and angry crowd burst into St Paul's Cathedral, where they 'broke down the altar and tore to pieces the books containing the new canons'.[306] Once again the unresolved Scottish problem forced King Charles to summon a parliament. When it met the Commons rapidly turned their attention to the canons. On 7 November, five days after the start of the session, the subject was raised both in a speech by Harbottle Grimston and in a petition from Hertfordshire. Grimston referred to the authors of the oath as 'Arminians and Popish affected persons' and said that bishops 'have overthrowne . . . religion'.[307] Speaking in the same debate, Pym took as his basic premiss that there existed 'a designe to alter the kingdome both in religion and government'.[308] The following Monday, 9 November, Sir John Holland enumerated as the first of a list of grievances the 'usurping of the prelates', while a petition was presented on behalf of Alexander Leighton who had been eleven years in prison for writing 'a booke against prelacie'.[309] Two days later Oliver St John gave as one reason why the bishops should not vote in the trial of Lord Deputy Wentworth, now Earl of Strafford, their being 'generally charged with innovations of religion'.[310]

While pressing ahead with the impeachment of Strafford, as

---

[304] Warmstry, *Convocation Speech*, pp. 2, 5–6, 10, 13–15.
[305] PRO, SP 16/467, fo. 113ʳ⁻ᵛ, 131–2 and SP 16/468, fo. 188.
[306] *Cal. SP Venetian, 1640–42*, p. 93.
[307] *Sir Simonds D'Ewes, Journal*, ed. W. Notestein (New Haven, 1923), pp. 5–6.
[308] Ibid., p. 8.   [309] Ibid., pp. 15, 17.   [310] Ibid., p. 29.

a subverter of fundamental law and an introducer of tyranny,
the Commons none the less found time to investigate the legality of the canons. The latter were condemned as illegal by a
series of votes on 15 and 16 December, and a committee was
appointed 'to take into consideration the offence of the mak-
ers' as well as 'to enquire whether the Archbishop of Canter-
burie ought not to bee charged with high treason'.[311] Laud was
so charged on 18 December, Harbottle Grimston describing
him as 'the roote and ground of all our miseries and
calamities'.[312] The guilt or innocence, however, of the convocation members generally was still undecided in March 1641,
by which date there had emerged the much more controversial question of episcopacy as such. This debate was conducted between those who distinguished bishops into good
and bad and those who wished to abolish them outright.[313]
Sympathizers with the Arminian programme of the 1630s
understandably kept a low profile, but it would be naive to
suppose that there were none left.[314] At the same time the convenient fiction that Laud and a few others were solely responsible was difficult to maintain in face of the many petitions
complaining about the activities of local parish clergy.[315]
There was also the further question of the relationship of the
King to his so-called 'evil councillors', whether Strafford or
Laud.

The unwillingness of Charles unambiguously to repudiate
the policies which he and his advisers had been pursuing since
the late 1620s is central to the failure to reach a settlement in
the years 1640 to 1642. Instead distrust deepened and fears
intensified. Myth and reality mingled in the idea of a Popish
plot, which substituted for political thought more convention-
ally defined. The terms Arminianism and Popery were now

[311] Ibid., pp. 157, 162.
[312] Ibid., p. 169. The charges against Laud were both secular and religious, in
roughly equal proportions. Common to the religious charges is the theme of Popery.
Rushworth, *Historical Collections*, III/i. 196–9.
[313] *D'Ewes, Journal*, pp. 335–8, 425–8.
[314] Thus the subsequent Surrey petition to parliament, in defence of episcopacy,
went so far as to endorse the Caroline proscription of Calvinist teaching. A. Fletcher,
The Outbreak of the English Civil War (1981), p. 287.
[315] J. Morrill, 'The Attack on the Church of England in the Long Parliament,
1640–42', in *History, Society and the Churches*, ed. D. Beales and G. Best (Cambridge,
1985), pp. 107–8, 111.

used virtually interchangeably and had secular as well as religious connotations—signifiying absolutism in addition to heresy and idolatry. Many opponents of the Caroline regime professed to believe that the attack on property rights and parliamentary privileges was a means 'to bring in Popery'.[316] Hence the protestation oath, imposed nationally by parliament in May 1641. This linked defence of 'the true reformed Protestant religion, expressed in the doctrine of the Church of England', with that of 'the power and priviledge of parliaments' and 'the lawful rights and liberties of the subjects'.[317] The Grand Remonstrance of December 1641 was even blunter, in blaming all the ills of the kingdom on a 'Popish party' which included the 'Arminians'.[318]

[316] Both Sir Benjamin Rudyard and Francis Rous so argued. Rushworth, *Historical Collections*, III/i. 24, 210.

[317] *Constitutional Documents*, ed. Gardiner, p. 156.

[318] Ibid., pp. 204, 207.

Conclusion

THE signs are that religion was a major contributory cause of
the English Civil War. To say this, however, is not to belittle
the importance of other issues. Clearly there was a long-term
financial problem facing any English government of the day.
At root this was how to harness the wealth of the nation more
effectively to the growing revenue needs of the state. The first
decade of the seventeenth century had seen an abortive
attempt at a parliamentary solution. Thereafter royal finance
ministers sought, albeit intermittently, to exploit the fiscal
potential of the royal prerogative. Almost inevitably this led to
periodic confrontations, over impositions, monopolies, forced
loans, and latterly ship-money. Nevertheless, it would be misleading to see these measures as part of a consistent drive
towards monarchical absolutism. By comparison, Caroline
religious policy was much more coherent and marked a clear
break with both the Jacobean and Elizabethan past. As such it
provided a relatively early and continuous focus for opposition
which was largely absent in the secular sphere.

The religious fears voiced in the late 1620s were given
increasing substance by events during the 1630s. Of the various terms which can be used to describe the thrust of religious
change at this time Arminian is the least misleading. It does
not mean that the Dutch theologian Jacobus Arminius was
normally the source of the ideas so labelled. Rather Arminian
denotes a coherent body of anti-Calvinist religious thought,
which was gaining ground in various regions of early seventeenth-century Europe. Arminianism itself can plausibly be
understood as part of a more widespread philosophical scepti-
cism, engendered by way of reaction to the dogmatic certain-
ties of the sixteenth-century Reformation.[1] Calvinism was also
attacked as being 'unreasonable'. Yet in a world where toleration of diversity of belief was a rarity, anti-Calvinists or

---

[1] H. R. Trevor-Roper, *Religion, the Reformation and Social Change* (1967), pp. 193–
236; N. Tyacke, 'Arminianism and English Culture', in *Britain and the Netherlands*, ed.
A. C. Duke and C. A. Tamse, VII (1981), 105–17.

Arminians had to struggle for survival. English Arminians vilified their Calvinist opponents as theocrats and in consequence disloyal subjects to the crown. They were correct to the extent that Calvinists believed in a church of the elect, the individual members of which could be assured in this life of their godly status. More generally Calvinists adopted a tone of moral censoriousness, which monarchs tended to find especially irksome.

Against the incipient egalitarianism of Calvinism, Arminians stressed the hierarchical nature of both church and state in which the office not the holder was what counted. This difference of emphasis probably predisposed hereditary rulers to look benevolently on anti-Calvinists. Some such calculation may have informed the decision of Charles I to support the English Arminian movement, on becoming King in 1625. At the same time Arminians claimed to purvey a gospel of hope, in which salvation was the potential lot of everyone. But the English Arminian mode, as it emerged during the 1630s, was that of communal and ritualized worship rather than an individual response to preaching or Bible reading. The basis was provided by the English Prayer Book, itself a unique survivor in a Calvinist context. Building on the Prayer Book, English Arminians elaborated a scenic apparatus in which the sacrament of holy communion had a key role. The altar, railed in at the east end of churches and often set on a dais, became the focal point of worship. Theorists of the movement both glossed away Calvinist expositions of the Prayer Book and provided a new liturgical dimension. As Archbishop Laud put it, 'in all ages of the Church the touchstone of religion was not to hear the word preached but to communicate'.[2]

Arminians, therefore, not only rejected Calvinist orthodoxy—they also transformed the issue of Protestant nonconformity. Not surprisingly, with their reinterpretation of the Prayer Book and imposition of new ceremonies, Arminians became the *bête noire* of Puritans. Traditionally Puritans had appealed to parliament against the persecuting activities of bishops, themselves the instruments of the royal supremacy in ecclesiastical affairs. The English Arminians chose to appeal to the crown, but their favourable reception did not appear

[2] Laud, *Works*, IV. 284.

inevitable to contemporaries. Thus one of the Calvinist replies to the Arminian Montagu's *Appello Caesarem* was entitled *Ibis ad Caesarem*,[3] with the clear implication that the royal judgement might go against the Arminians. Nevertheless, whatever his public statements, King Charles in practice consistently favoured the Arminians from the outset of his reign. One result was that church patronage at the higher levels became a mainly Arminian preserve and hence the famous quip about Arminians holding all the best bishoprics and deaneries.[4] There was also a revived attempt to improve the financial position of the clergy more generally,[5] while the sacramental dimension of English Arminianism involved an enhancement of priestly status. Such advantages, however, were expected to be paid for by an unswerving loyalty to the monarchy. This last would have been fairly innocuous had the secular policies of the government not now come into increasing conflict with traditional property rights.

More fundamentally the rise of English Arminianism challenged the Calvinist world picture, which envisaged the forces of good and evil as locked in a struggle that would only end with the final overthrow of Antichrist. This view is epitomized by the Calvinist Bishop Carleton's *A Thankfull Remembrance of God's Mercy*, first published in 1624 and subtitled 'an historicall collection of the great and mercifull deliverances of the Church and State of England, since the gospell began here to flourish'. Future prosperity was conditional on holding fast to 'the oracles of God committed to us' and having no truck with the Papists.[6] Yet it was precisely these conditions which, in Calvinist eyes, were ceasing to be met by the end of the 1620s, with the triumph of a different and Arminian set of assumptions.

[3] Yates, *Ibis ad Caesarem*.
[4] Edward Hyde, Earl of Clarendon, *The Life* (Oxford, 1827), I. 56.
[5] C. Hill, *Economic Problems*, pp. 245–337.
[6] George Carleton, *A Thankfull Remembrance of God's Mercy* (1624), p. 175.

APPENDIX I

From Calvinist to Arminian: the doctrinal tenor of the Paul's Cross sermons, 1570–1638

It has been more commonly asserted than demonstrated that Calvinist teaching on predestination predominated in the Church of England, during the Elizabeth and Jacobean periods. Nevertheless, from the seventeenth century onwards, historians of various religious persuasions have agreed that this was the actual situation.[1] Recently, however, a series of counter-assertions have been made, to the effect that Calvinism never achieved more than a position of equality in the English Church with other contrary doctrine.[2] Thus there is now an especially pressing need to settle the question, if possible, once and for all. Among the tests which can be applied, the most cogent involves a systematic sampling of the religious output of the English printing presses. Thanks to the work of Millar MacLure, such a sample exists in the Paul's Cross sermons printed between 1570 and 1638. While MacLure's listing is incomplete, the omissions are random and do not detract from its representative character.[3] Paul's Cross was the most public pulpit in the land, the preachers selected by the Bishop of London, and those sermons which ended up in print normally did so with the blessing of authority.[4]

From 1570 onwards a series of Paul's Cross sermons survive, and MacLure lists fifty-one which were first printed in the reign of

[1] Among seventeenth-century historians, the Calvinist Fuller and the Arminian Heylyn both indicate that anti-Calvinists were very much in a minority by the late sixteenth century. Fuller, *Church History*, v. 227; Heylyn, *Historia Quinqu-Articularis*, iii. 77–93. Twentieth-century historians who take a similar line included W. H. Frere, *The English Church in the Reigns of Elizabeth and James I* (1904), pp. 282–4, 382–3, E. W. Watson, *The Church of England* (1914), p. 164, H. O. Wakeman, *An Introduction to the History of the Church of England* (1927), pp. 322–3, 349, N. Sykes, *The English Religious Tradition* (1953), pp. 37–8, H. R. McAdoo, *The Spirit of Anglicanism* (1965), pp. 28–9.

[2] Porter, *Reformation and Reaction*, p. 287; K. Sharpe, 'Archbishop Laud', *History Today*, 34 (1984), 57; P. White, 'The Rise of Arminianism Reconsidered', *Past and Present*, 101 (1983), 35.

[3] MacLure, *The Paul's Cross Sermons*, pp. 206–7. Professor MacLure confirms in correspondence that he compiled his list from Pollard and Redgrave's *Short-Title Catalogue*, supplementing this by means of personal visits to a number of English, especially London, libraries.

[4] The licensing of religious works was largely controlled by the Archbishop of Canterbury and the Bishop of London, although a deputy usually undertook the task of authorization.

Elizabeth. A further ninety-eight Paul's Cross sermons were printed
during the Jacobean period. Finally there were thirty-five new
Caroline printings up to and including the year 1638.[5] Less than a
third of these sermons mentioned the predestinarian question, but,
of those fifty-five which did, all took an orthodox Calvinist line
before the 1630s.[6] Not until 1632 did an Arminian sermon preached
at Paul's Cross appear in print.[7] Conversely Calvinist sermons
ceased to be printed after July 1628, the same year and very month
in which William Laud was translated to the bishopric of London.[8]
Monopoly by Calvinists, rather than simply dominance, best
describes the situation between 1570 and mid-1628.

I

There were thirteen Calvinist sermons printed in the Elizabethan
period, three of them being almost entirely devoted to the subject of
predestination. Two of these latter were preached by future
bishops—John Bridges and Gervase Babington. The earliest of the
thirteen Elizabethan sermons is one by the martyrologist John Foxe,
both preached and printed in 1570. According to Foxe, 'the favour of
God is perpetual to them whom he receaveth to reconciliation'.
These are 'the elect' whose names are written in 'the booke of God's
reconcilement'. The 'wrath of God for synne toward his elect con-
tinueth but a tyme'. He 'that beleveth that God hath hys election
from the begynyng, and so persuadeth himselfe to bee one of the
same elect and predestinate, hath a good belief and is well persuaded'.[9]

John Bridges' sermon was preached and printed the following
year, 1571. At the time he was a prebendary of Winchester. Taking
as his text John 3: 16—'God so loved the world, that he gave his only
begotten son'—Bridges defined the world in terms of 'the elect of
God'. He similarly argued that gospel references to the salvation of
'all men', as in 1 Timothy 2: 4, meant 'not every man but men
of every sort'. Bridges quoted St Augustine as his authority for this

[5] These figures are adjusted to take account of earlier editions not known to Mac-
Lure. No sermons apparently were printed in 1639, and I have omitted the year 1640
from my calculations because of the unusual conditions obtaining at that time.
[6] Seventeen out of fifty Calvinist sermons are unrecorded in the Stationers' Register, but there is no reason to think that any of them were clandestine publications.
[7] Gore, *The Way to Prosper*. For a discussion of this sermon, see above, pp. 216–17.
[8] Le Neve, *Fasti*, ii. 303; Robert Sanderson, *Two Sermons preached at Paules-Crosse*
(1628). The dedication of this sermon, to Thomas Harrington of Boothby Pagnell, is
dated 1 July 1628. Ibid., sig. A3. For the doctrinal content of these sermons, see
below, p. 263.
[9] John Foxe, *A Sermon of Christ Crucified* (1570), fos. 19ᵛ–20, 24, 62.

interpretation, and noted that he was almost the only church father untainted by Pelagianism.[10] The 'wil of God is not that all in general shuld be saved, but those whom he hath chosen'. Here Bridges attacked as 'blasphemie' the 'Papist' distinction between the antecedent and the consequent will of God. It is not true that 'God by his former will woulde have all men without any choice saved, and gyveth every man freedom of will and grace alike'. Conversely the elect cannot fall from grace and they are endowed with 'a full assured confidence' in their salvation. Furthermore, the doctrine of predestination is a proper subject for the pulpit, and does not breed 'desperation or presumption'.[11]

Two sermons printed in 1578 contain briefer references to predestination. By way of conclusion Thomas White, perhaps the Vicar of St Dunstan, Fleet Street, had said that 'God predestinating us before tyme, doth yet call us in due tyme' and 'he never leaveth us untyll he hath drawne us up unto himselfe'.[12] John Walsall, Rector of Eastling in Kent, likewise preached that, 'before the foundations of the worlde were laide', God 'did in his exceeding ritch mercie electe and chuse unto salvation a certaine number of mankinde'. God's means are the Bible and preaching, whereby his will is 'manifested and made known both to the elect, for their calling unto Christ, and also to the reprobate for their juster condemnation'.[13] In a sermon printed the following year, 1579, John Stockwood, Master of Tonbridge Grammar School, took occasion to explain 1 Timothy 2: 4 in the same sense as Bridges earlier. 'Who is so mad as heere to take "all" for every particular person of the world . . . but rather for every kind of man?'[14]

Also in a printed sermon of 1579, John Knewstubb, Rector of Cockfield, Suffolk, claimed that the 'ungodly' only ascribe to God 'a general kind of goodnesse, which they take to be indifferently cast downe among men'. This is also the view of 'the Papistes' as regards 'God's grace'. The case, however, is different with the servants of God. They acknowledge 'Christ Jesus gave himselfe for us, to purge us, that we might be a peculiar people unto himselfe, zealous of good workes'.[15] Next year, 1580, saw the printing of a sermon by Laurence Chaderton, then lecturer at St Clements in Cambridge, who taught

---

[10] John Bridges, *A Sermon preached at Paules Crosse* (1571), pp. 15–16, 22–3, Bridges probably had in mind here St Augustine's *Enchiridion ad Laurentium*, ch. 103.

[11] Bridges, *A Sermon*, pp. 27–9, 34, 69, 147–8. This sermon is dedicated to Lord Burghley. Ibid., sigs. Aii–Aiii^v.

[12] Thomas White, *A Sermon preached at Pawles Crosse* (1578), pp. 61–2.

[13] John Walsall, *A Sermon preached at Pauls Cross* [1578], sig. BV^{r-v}.

[14] John Stockwood, *A very Fruitefull Sermon preched at Paule's Crosse* (1579), fo. 63^v.

[15] John Knewstubb, *A Sermon preached at Paulles Cross* (1579), sigs. P6^v, Q2, S2. This sermon is appended to *A Confutation of Monstrous and Horrible Heresies* (1579).

that 'it is the gift of the Holy Ghost which maketh God's children carefull and studious not onely to do the father's will, for that may be after some sort in the reprobate and castawayes, but to doe it with . . . assurance of faith'.[16] William Fisher, of St Edmund Hall, Oxford, argued similarly in a sermon printed the same year. 'The callyng of Christ is of two sortes: the one is common wherewith we are in deed stirred up after a sort, but not effectually bound and brought to the purpose.' This is the benefit of 'reprobate' and 'elect' alike. 'Now the other is a convenient and mighty calling, whereby the minds of sinners are touched and thorowly changed.' As for these latter, 'faith' is planted 'so fast in them that nothing can drawe them from Christ'.[17]

Among a collection of sermons by Archbishop Edwin Sandys of York, published in 1585, is one preached at Paul's Cross which includes a passage on predestination. This sermon is concerned with the 'signs' of the approaching end of the world. 'Men's minds shall be troubled, their faith shall wither and waste away as an untimely plant. They shall utterly fall from God and all hope of salvation. Yea, the very elect shall quake and tremble.' There will arise 'false prophets . . . so forcible in persuasion that they might deceive, if it were possible, even the elect of God'.[18] Passages from Gervase Babington's predestinarian sermon, printed in 1591, have already been quoted above. It is prefaced by a list of 'things touched on in this sermon'. These include 'the doctrine of our election', the 'dislikers of it' and 'reasons why it ought to be taught', the 'evidence of the doctrine', the 'causes of election', its 'stabilitie' and 'the number certaine', the 'knowledge of it in ourselves', the 'use and comfort of it', the 'certainty of our salvation', and 'yet how a child of God may be shaken'.[19] Babington himself was promoted to the episcopate this same year.

Elaborating these points, Babington taught that 'to come to Christ by faith proceedeth as an effect from the father's giving of us to Christ by election' and 'they onely beleeve which are ordayned'. By contrast 'the most part of men are not [so ordained and] therefore they beleeve not'. The doctrine of election 'in no case is to be avoyded, but both spoken and heard of as occasion shall serve'. Indeed 'there is no one thing more plainely and fully testified in the word then this is'. Only 'ignorant minds' object to it. 'Two sorts there are in this counsell of God, [of whom] one must rise and the other must fall being so appointed.' Christ is to the 'cursed

[16] Laurence Chaderton, *An Excellent and Godly Sermon* (1580), sig. E1.
[17] William Fisher, *A Sermon preached at Paules Crosse* (1580), sig. E4ʳ⁻ᵛ.
[18] Edwin Sandys, *Sermons*, ed. J. Ayre (Parker Soc., Cambridge, 1842), pp. 364–5.
[19] Babington, *A Sermon*, sig. A IV.

castawaies . . . a stone to stumble at and a rock of offence, they being disobedient and even ordeigned to this thing'. Yet 'to the godly, which are pure, all things are pure'. The 'elect cannot finally be cast away', for 'their names are written in the booke of life'. They will feel a 'sweete assurance' of their election. As for 'the reprobate they sinne necessarely in respect of God's decree, but yet they sinne not constreynedlie'. Nevertheless, 'if a man be appoynted unto death and a reprobate it is never possible that his deeds should be good in respect of himselfe but alwaies there wil be some poyson in them'.[20]

This distinction between reprobate and elect was again mentioned in a Paul's Cross sermon by Richard Lewes, Rector of Kelmarsh in Northamptonshire, and printed at Oxford in 1594. 'The wicked have a glauncing glimpses, a sodden lightning, a momentary motion, even a small tast of the things that are heavenly and eternal, but in the hearts of the godly they are sealed with God's spirit, confirmed with his promises and written with a pen of yron and with the point of a diamond, yea ingraven in the table of their souls.'[21] The sermon by John Dove, printed and preached in 1597, like those of Bridges and Babington is largely taken up with predestination. Dove was Rector of St Mary Aldermary, London, and, as we have previously noted, his sermon has reference to contemporary disputes at Cambridge University. It may also be a conscious refutation of a notorious anti-Calvinist sermon preached at Paul's Cross in 1584 by Samuel Harsnett. (Harsnett had as a consequence been silenced on the subject by Archbishop Whitgift, and his sermon did not appear in print until 1656.)[22] Certainly the text chosen by Dove was the same as Harsnett's—'As I live, saith the Lord God, I have no pleasure in the death of the wicked' (Ezekiel 33: 11).

'In so great a clowde of witnesses of God's mercie, which is extended to all, and that hee delighteth not in the death of a sinner how', asked Dove, 'can it be that many are called and few are chosen?' Dove rejected the argument that 'the cause is in themselves . . . as though the wil of God could be crossed by the wil of men'. Citing St Augustine, as we have seen, he expounded the salvation of 'all men' as meaning 'of all sortes some'.[23] Election and reprobation stem from 'the absolute will of God'. Thus 'Jacob and Esau were both, as we all are, by nature the children of wrath'. It is God's purpose which makes the difference between them. The 'children of God can never revolt and start back from the faith and their state of

[20] Ibid., pp. 2–3, 5–6, 8–9, 14–15, 27, 29–30.

[21] Richard Lewes, *A Sermon preached at Paules Crosse* (Oxford, 1594), sig. A8ᵛ.

[22] *Lords Journals*, III. 389; Harsnett, *A Fourth Sermon*.

[23] Dove, *A Sermon*, pp. 13, 15, 17–19. Dove gives as his reference St Augustine's *Enchiridion ad Laurentium*.

salvation'. Dove concluded by vindicating Calvin from the charge that to teach 'Christ dyed not to save all, but onelie those which in his will hee had predestinated, were plaine Mahometisme'.[24]

Bishop Thomas Bilson of Winchester completes the roll-call of authors of Calvinist Paul's Cross sermons, printed in the Elizabethan period. He taught that 'the gifts and calling of God are without repentance, and therefore it is utterlie impossible that God's election should alter or that hee should not love his owne unto the end'.[25] At least three of these thirteen Calvinist preachers—Chaderton, Foxe, and Knewstubb—can meaningfully be called Puritan. But they also include four bishops, or future bishops, namely Babington, Bilson, Bridges, and Sandys. Nor were the Puritans the most extreme advocates of Calvinist theology. Moreover, Babington's sermon, which must rank among the harshest of Elizabethan statements on predestination, was personally licensed for the press by Archbishop Whitgift.[26] There is only one clear case in the Elizabeth period of anti-Calvinist views being preached at Paul's Cross.[27] This was by Harsnett, and we know from his own account that he got into trouble as a result.[28] It is also clear from the surviving text of the sermon that Harsnett realized at the time just how unfashionable his views were.[29]

II

Of the Paul's Cross sermons printed during the reign of James I, twenty-seven contain Calvinist teaching on predestination. This Jacobean series was inaugurated by John Hayward, Rector of St Mary Woolchurch, London, preaching almost immediately after the death of Queen Elizabeth. He took the opportunity to enrol the late Elizabeth among the saints who cannot fall from grace, for 'true comfort indureth perpetually in the elect [and] if it beginneth at any

[24] Dove, *A Sermon*, pp. 14, 34, 71, 74.

[25] Thomas Bilson, *The Effecte of Certaine Sermons touching the Full Redemption of Mankind by the Death and Blood of Jesus Christ* (1599), pp. 131–2.

[26] Arber, II. 279.

[27] Richard Hooker's sermon of about 1581 is a possible further case. If Isaak Walton is to be believed, Hooker then maintained views concerning the antecedent and consequent will of God which, as we have seen, Bridges had attacked as 'blasphemie' in 1571. Hooker, *Works*, I 16–17. Certainly Hooker made what appears a similar distinction in some of his extant writings. Richard Hooker, *Of the Laws of Ecclesiastical Polity* (Cambridge, Mass., 1977–82), II. 204, IV. 143, 146.

[28] *Lords Journals*, III. 389.

[29] 'This opinion is growne huge and monstrous (like a Goliah) and men doe shake and tremble at it; yet never a man reacheth to David's sling to cast it down.' Harsnett, *A Fourth Sermon*, p. 134.

time to faint it is restored by the Holy Ghost '. Hayward also taught that 'a choice number there is bearing the marke of the foundation'. They 'are distinguished from the rest . . . by the benefit of redemption' and 'the foundation of God abideth sure'. These God 'inricheth with gifts [and] graces of his spirit in this world . . . making them by beleeving the sonnes of God'.[30]

This was followed two years later, in 1605, by an extended Calvinist exposition from Samuel Gardiner, Rector of Great Dunham, Norfolk. The 'booke of life is a register or role in the Lord's right hand of the names of such as are predestinated to everlasting life'. Gardiner went on to say that

heare we are to open the vaine of the livelyest and sweetest question in the Bible. Whether hee whose name is once entered into the booke of life may ever be blotted out, that is whether an elect childe of God can ever be a reprobate? Our answere is negative that he cannot, and the affirmative part is most detestable and divelish.

For 'as God could not be stopped by the foreseene sinnes of his saints from making entrie of their names into the Lambe's booke of life, so when sin hath done the extent of his spight it shall never separate his love towards us, wherein it thus pleaseth him at the first to enrole us'. Because 'wee are written unto life by God wee shall not sinne contumaciouslie and stubbornely, or continue in it as the wicked doe'. Even though our faith 'may bee as the last sparke of a fire readye to goe out . . . yet shall it kindle and recover again'. Indeed 'our salvation is cock-sure as being wholye in God', whose 'decree of our election is unmooveable'.[31]

We have already discussed above the Calvinist sentiments of Samuel Collins, a fellow of King's College, Cambridge, the printed version of his sermon being dedicated to Archbishop Bancroft in 1607.[32] William Loe, a prebendary of Gloucester. whose sermon was printed in 1609, dedicated his remarks to Bishop Thomas Ravis of London. Prayers for the salvation of all men, he taught, are not to be 'understood "collectively" but "distributively"', as Master Perkins consenteth'. The word 'all' refers to 'some of every kind'*.[33] Another Paul's Cross sermon printed in 1609 was that by Lancelot Dawes, Vicar of Barton Kirk in Westmoreland. It is dedicated to Bishop Henry Robinson of Carlisle. 'God made all men', says Dawes, 'so

[30] John Hayward, *God's Universal Right proclaimed* (1603), sigs. A3–A4, D5.

[31] Samuel Gardiner, *A Sermon preached at Paules Crosse* (1605), sigs. E2ᵛ, G3ʳ⁻ᵛ, Hᵛ, H2ʳ⁻ᵛ.

[32] See above, p. 44.

[33] William Loe, *The Joy of Jerusalem and Woe of the Worldlings* (1609), sigs. ¶–¶2ᵛ, Eᵛ. Loe is alluding to *An Exposition of the Lord's Prayer* by William Perkins. Perkins, *Workes*, I. 347–8.

that they are all his sonnes by creation, but hee ordained not all to life, so that there is but a remnant which are his sonnes by adoption.' For Adam 'by transgressing God's commandment . . . lost his birth-right'. and 'all his children were made uncapable of their father's inheritance'. But 'God . . . as he purposed to shew his justice in punishing the greater part of such as so greevously incurred his displeasure, so on the contrary side it was his good pleasure to shew his mercy in saving some though they deserved as great a degree of punishment as the other'. Therefore 'before all times it was enacted' that Christ should 'suffer for our transgressions and gather a certaine number out of that masse of corruption, wherein all mankind lay'.[34]

A third sermon printed in 1609 was that by Robert Johnson, chaplain to Bishop William Barlow of Lincoln. This is particularly interesting since it is dedicated to Barlow, whose personal sympathies lay with the anti-Calvinists. While less strident than most of the foregoing preachers, Johnson none the less took an orthodox Calvinist line. He distinguished God's grace into a number of constituent parts. There is 'a grace going before that worketh in us . . . regener-ation', which is neither given nor received in vain. 'Even as the raine falling on the earth mollifieth the same and both worke to bring forth fruits, so the grace of God being distilled into the will and minde of man worke both together to the bringing forth of the fruites of righteousnesse.' Moreover 'God doth prevent his children from sinne', and his 'subsequenting grace . . . shall follow'.[35] William Sclater, Vicar of Pitminster in Somerset, in a sermon printed in 1610, attacked those who taught that 'God's children, chosen to salvation [and] called according to his purpose, may (at least for a time) fall from the state of grace'.[36]

A second sermon by Samuel Gardiner was printed in 1611. By this date he was chaplain to Archbishop Abbot, and his remarks are entirely taken up with predestination. The 'state of our salvation is sure, as seated upon the decree of God'. It is impossible that the elect can be seduced 'totally and finally'. But 'the schoole of Rome would teach us otherwise'. to the effect that 'predestination is chaungeable' and 'he that is predestinated is contingently or casu-ally predestinated'. Nevertheless 'they come to Christ who are given by predestination, by the Father, unto Christ'. Election and reproba-tion are both 'eternal', and Judas, for example, was 'preordinated to be lost'. Predestination 'is not onely of the ende but also of the meanes that make to that ende'. Faith and works are effects of election, and

[34] Lancelot Dawes, *God's Mercie and Jerusalem's Miseries* (1609), sigs. A2–A3ᵛ, C6ᵛ–C7.
[35] Robert Johnson, *David's Teacher* (1609), sigs. [A2], F4ʳ⁻ᵛ.
[36] William Sclater, *A Threefold Preservative* (1610), sig. Bᵛ.

among the elect the spirit of God can never become 'quite extinct'.[37] John Denison's sermon, also of 1611, is dedicated to Bishop John King of London. 'Whosoever is borne of God . . . sinneth not totally and finally.' While 'God's dearest children may commit very haynous sinnes, yet they do it of infirmitie and not maliciously'. Such was the case of David when committing adultery or of St Peter in denying Christ. Christ's prayer for Peter that his 'faith faile not' is 'effectuall for all God's children', who can never be 'wholly eclipsed'.[38] Denison was Vicar of St Laurence, Reading.

Perseverance was likewise a theme of sermons by William Pemberton in 1613 and Miles Mosse in 1614, the latter printed at Cambridge. Pemberton, Rector of High Ongar in Essex, maintained that 'those precious gifts and lovely graces of the sanctifying spirit of God' cannot be lost. 'The same God that gave them will still maintain them, and second his kindnes with a supply of new grace.' 'Temptation may obscure the outward glosse, but cannot hurt the inward substance. Some leaves may fall and some fruit may fade but the seede and roote of grace shal still remaine, [because] in the highest heavens is no mutability.'[39] According to Mosse, Rector of Combes in Suffolk, 'if at any time mistrustfull or carnall feare doe take hold upon the saints yet it is neither totall nor finall, as it is in the devills, for the regenerate partie will ever cleave to God's mercie by faith and the spirit of adoption will at length get the victorie'. In Mosse's terminology 'devills' are synonymous with 'reprobates'.[40] Henry Greenwood, Vicar of Great Samford in Essex, in his sermon of 1615 referred to predestination, both double and absolute. Following on from Adam's fall, God 'vouchsafed in his sonne to shew mercy upon some by election to salvation, as to shew justice upon other some by reprobation to damnation'. Heaven and Hell are prepared according to this 'irrevocable decree'. He also appended a prayer, which includes the petition 'give us that we may clearely see our names written in the booke of life'.[41]

In another sermon of 1615 John White, a royal chaplain, returned to the question of prayer for all men.

We do not pray that all men generally, including the reprobate, may be saved . . . Yet for the temporall good of reprobates . . . we may both pray

---

[37] Samuel Gardiner, *The Foundation of the Faythfull* (1611), sigs. A2ᵛ–A5, A7ʳ⁻ᵛ, B3ᵛ, Cᵛ. Gardiner describes himself as chaplain to Archbishop Abbot in the dedication prefacing *The Scourge of Sacriledge* (1611), sig. A4.

[38] John Denison, *The Sinne against the Holy Ghost plainely described* (1611), sigs. A3ʳ⁻ᵛ, pp. 22, 27–8.   [39] William Pemberton, *The Godly Merchant* (1613), pp. 12, 91.

[40] Miles Mosse, *Justifying and Saving Faith distinguished from the Faith of the Devils* (Cambridge, 1614), pp. 27, 30.

[41] Henry Greenwood, *Tormenting Tophet* (1615), p. 3, sig. G3ʳ⁻ᵛ.

and give thankes. The reason is for God gives such temporall things to the reprobate and for his churches good, to glorifie his name, magnifie his liberality, make them without excuse and benefite his children. Which being ends belonging to the sanctification of God's name in the wicked, we justly pray for all that which may advance them.[42]

William Jackson, lecturer at Whittington College in London, dedicated his sermon of 1616 to Bishop King. It 'doth not followe', he claimed, 'because we can doe nothing without grace that therefore God is bound to give it'. Indeed 'we are bound to serve him, but he is not bound to bestow his grace upon us'. The difference between the sins of the godly and others is that the former 'sinne not with an intent'. In this life, 'the childe of God can speake with confidence of assurance of glory'.[43]

There were two further Calvinist sermons printed in 1616, by Sampson Price and Charles Richardson. Price, of Exeter College, Oxford, taught that 'there may be an eclipse of God's graces in the best, but hee can never fall away finally or totally from faith'. For the child of God 'is built upon the immoveable rocke of Christ Jesus'.[44] Like William Jackson, Richardson, 'preacher' at St Katherine's by the Tower, London, discussed the nature of sin in the godly who 'although they have in them the seedes of all sinne yet they doe not commit all sinne, but by the mercy of God they are kept from falling into many sinnes. The seede of grace and regeneration is in them and that preserveth them that they cannot sinne as the wicked doe.' When the godly do sin 'it is sore against their wils', while 'the wicked they sinne willingly, voluntarily and of their owne accord'. The 'godly though they fall seaven times a day . . . yet they rise again'.[45]

Samuel Ward's sermon of 1617 is the first recorded at Paul's Cross to mention Arminianism as such. The author was lecturer at Ipswich. 'Wee Christians know our selves sure of Heaven,' said Ward.

Without which certainety Christians were of all men most miserable. Popery and nature, and the old leven of Pelagius newly worse sowered by Arminius, never having had experience of this plerophorie, serve Christians when they boast of this their confidence as Ananias did Paul—strike them on the face with the terms of pride and presumption.[46]

A second Calvinist sermon by Charles Richardson also appeared in

---

[42] John White, *Two Sermons* (1615), p. 15.
[43] William Jackson, *The Celestiall Husbandrie* (1616), sigs. ¶2–¶4ᵛ, pp. 17, 19, 129.
[44] Sampson Price, *Ephesus Warning before her Woe* (1616), p. 20.
[45] Charles Richardson, *A Sermon concerning the Punishing of Malefactors* (1616), pp. 34, 36–7.
[46] Samuel Ward, *Balme from Gilead* (1617), p. 59.

1617. He quoted Beza as his authority for limiting Christ's atonement to 'the elect alone'. When 'it is saide that our Saviour Christ died for all wee may safely understand it that he died for men of all sorts and conditions, whether they be high or low, rich or poor, bond or free'. There

is a world of them that shall be saved. For them Christ was given. And there is a world of them that shall be damned. For them Christ doth not pray. I doe not deny but that the death of Christ is sufficient to save al men, for his blood . . . is of infinit value. But it is not effectuall to save all . . .

Richardson went on to state that 'there are vessels of wrath prepared to destruction, as well as vessels of mercy prepared unto glory', and some 'were appointed to bee damned before ever they were borne'.[47]

In a sermon of 1618 Thomas Thompson, Rector of Montgomery in Wales, referred to 'the base relikes of Antichristian and Popish opinions, as yet maintained by some particular teachers in some Reformed Churches'. These included, he said, 'that monster of universall election, redemption and vocation, together with those their consequents—the uncertaintie of salvation and deniall of perseverance unto the saints, all flowing from that heathenish, Pelagian, Popish mainteyning of free-will to good in man corrupted'.[48] Given the date, the allusion must be to the Arminian controversy in the United Provinces. Thompson moreover dedicated his remarks to Prince Charles.[49] Arminianism was mentioned by name in Roger Ley's sermon of 1619. Ley, curate of St Leonard Shoreditch in London, preached that

as God loveth to the end, so must his friends be led by the same perseverance. From hence we condemn the Arminian friendship that starteth aside like a broken bow. They imagine a man may have the spirit of God, the graces of regeneration and bee partaker of the priviledges of a saint, yet fall away and bee damned.[50]

Stephen Denison, soon to become curate of St Katherine Cree in London, was equally explicit in a sermon printed the same year. He attacked the 'new upstart Arminians' and their 'doctrine of free will'. They 'denieth the doctrine of the eternall truth of God concerning election and reprobation, maintaining that one person is not elected more than another except it be for foreseene faith or forseene workes'. Hence, too, their claim that 'a Christian might fall finally and totally from saving grace'. In truth the 'child of God is enlightened and quickened, but the reprobate is only enlightened

[47] Charles Richardson, *The Price of our Redemption* (1617), pp. 123, 125–7.
[48] Thomas Thompson, *Antichrist Arraigned* (1618), pp. 221–2.
[49] Ibid., sigs. ¶3–A2.   [50] Roger Ley, *The Scepter of Righteousness* (1619), p. 39.

and not quickened'. Denison also distinguished between sins of 'in-firmitie' and sins of 'presumption', the elect being merely subject to the former.[51]

A sermon of 1620 by Thomas Walkington, Vicar of Fulham in Middlesex, includes a fairly extensive treatment of perseverance, from the Calvinist point of view. 'God's mercy in Jesus Christ . . . never can be broken, for whom the Lord loves once hee loves unto the end.' The 'deare elect of God shall stand fast for ever'. Although they may 'some-while stagger in their faith', appearing like 'trees in winter . . . leafe-lesse and sapless', their 'blessed spring and sun-shine of grace' shall come again making them to 'blossome and bud'. The 'small sparke of faith covered in cold embers' will be rekindled and 'grow to a big flame'. For 'needes must God's eternall determi-nation (in whom there is no shadow of change) stand sure and immutable, of saving his elect'.[52] The 'perseverance of God's chil-dren' was also handled by Michael Wigmore, of Oriel College, Oxford, in a printed sermon of 1620. Such is the 'zeale' kindled 'in the hearts of the faithfull that come there never so many waters, come there never so many gusts, come there never so many flouds to overwhelme them with calamitie, they shall never bee able to quench or smother it'.[53]

Thomas Bedford's sermon of 1621 is dedicated to Bishop John Davenant of Salisbury. Bedford himself was still at Queens' College, Cambridge. In his sermon he distinguished between 'tempor-izers and true beleevers', quoting the Synod of Dort to this effect. 'Illumination and a tast of God's favour' can be lost, whereas 'saving knowledge' cannot. Those 'of Arminius's brood', however, deny the 'difference betwixt them' and 'thereby would hope to confirme their poysonous and uncomfortable doctrine of recidivation and falling from grace once received'. When the godly fall, the divine 'seede remaineth in them'.[54] Immanuel Bourne, Rector of Ashover in Der-byshire, dedicated his sermon of 1622 to William Piers, the Vice-Chancellor of Oxford. (The following year, 1623, Piers was formally to censure Arminianism at Oxford in the person of Gabriel Bridges.)[55] Bourne spoke of regeneration as being 'our new creation' and restricted to 'the elect'. To 'them onely belongs this grace and they either have or shall have it when it shall please God to call them, either at the first, or the third, or ninth, or eleventh houre, either in their youth or middle age, or old age'. He 'that is once

[51] Stephen Denison, *The New Creature* (1619), pp. 15–17, 28, 59.
[52] Thomas Walkington, *Rabboni* (1620), pp. 64–5, 67–9.
[53] Michael Wigmore, *The Good Aventure* (1620), p. 26.
[54] Thomas Bedford, *The Sinne unto Death* (1621), sigs. ¶2–¶4, pp. 18, 23, 51.
[55] See above, pp. 74–5.

engrafted into Christ by faith, though Christ may suffer him to bee shaken with the winde of temptations . . . yet he will never totally and finally forsake him'.[56]

The problem of sin in the elect was again handled in 1622, this time by Samuel Buggs, 'minister' at Coventry. 'God's people' are 'halfe in heaven and halfe in earth, in heaven by reason of their holy and heavenly conversation, in heaven by reason of their assurance of salvation, but on earth by reason of that body of sinne and death which they carry about them, having the flesh pressing with continuall fight and oppressing with often conquest'. Such sins are, however, 'but of infirmity'. An 'evill admitted and perpetrated by a child of God makes God in his holinesse dislike and distaste, though not absolutely and finally the person yet the sinne'.[57] The last Paul's Cross sermon both to touch on these questions and to be printed in the reign of James I is that by Robert Harris, and is dated 1622. He denied that 'we' make God the 'cause of sinne' any more than does 'Arminius'. If 'disputes arise, touching reprobation, which trench farre upon God's rights, say still he is good, all that he decrees and does is of himselfe and for himselfe, and therefore best'.[58] Harris was Rector of Hanwell in Oxfordshire.

Calvinist sermons continued to be preached at Paul's Cross in the remaining years of James, but no more appear to have been printed until after his death. This may have been as a consequence of the royal directions to preachers, issued in mid-September 1622.[59] On the other hand, no anti-Calvinist sermons are known to have been preached at Paul's Cross during the entire reign of King James. Thus there was an even closer fit than in the Elizabethan period between what was printed and what was preached. While the Arminian controversy in the United Provinces gave a certain topicality to Calvinist doctrines, these had been standard since the 1570s and probably earlier. Although these Jacobean preachers included no bishops in their ranks, neither were there many Puritans.[60] Calvinism at this time was clearly the Church of England norm.

III

The accession of Charles I in March 1625 initially made no difference to the regular propagation of Calvinism through the medium of

[56] Immanuel Bourne, *The True Way of a Christian* (1622), sigs. A2–A4, pp. 70–1, 86.

[57] Samuel Buggs, *David's Strait* (1622), pp. 13, 43, 54.

[58] Robert Harris, *God's Goodnes and Mercie* (1622), pp. 15–16.

[59] See above, p. 103, fn. 72.

[60] Samuel Ward of Ipswich and probably a few others were of nonconformist inclination. *DNB*, s.n. Ward, Samuel (1577–1640).

Paul's Cross sermons. Up to and including the year 1628 ten such printed Calvinist sermons survive. From May 1627, however, an alteration set in, marked by a sermon then preached by John Donne, Dean of St Paul's. On this occasion Donne warned against spiritual 'security', for 'when Christ himselfe saith "The children of the kingdome shall be cast into utter darknesse" who can promise himselfe a perpetuall or unconditionall station?' According to Donne, 'filiation' does not preclude disinheritance.[61] As we have seen, by November 1629 Donne had become much bolder in attacking Calvinist predestinarian teaching from the pulpit.[62] Yet these sermons of his were not printed until after the Civil War. In terms of publication, the Arminian breakthrough came in 1632 with the printing of John Gore's sermon *The Way to Prosper*. This was licensed by a chaplain of Laud, as Bishop of London.[63] Apparently the last Calvinist sermon to be preached at Paul's Cross was by Robert Sanderson in April 1627. This was printed the following year, in 1628, as was an earlier Calvinist sermon by him and one by John Gumbledon.[64]

Three Calvinist sermons were printed in 1625. Robert Vase, an otherwise unidentified 'preacher', taught that 'the hand and power of grace' prevents 'God's elect' from 'finall perishing'. There is 'an abiding seede . . . whereof whosoever be quickened never totally lose the life thereof'. The 'vertue' may be obscured for a time, but only 'as the starres in a darke night are not seene to the eye'.[65] William Proctor, 'minister' at Upminster in Essex, handled the question of reprobation.

In God's decree of reprobation there are two acts. The former is negative and that is the eternall purpose and decree of God not to shew mercy nor give grace as hee doth to the elect, but leaves them in that masse of sinne and most woefull estate whereunto all men (in Adam) are promiscuously fallen. The other is positive and that is the eternall purpose and decree of God to inflict that everlasting punishment upon them which is most justly deserved, by that sinne into which they wilfully fall and in which they still abide.[66]

Robert Bedingfield, a student of Christ Church, Oxford, attacked the Semi-Pelagians who deny that the will is 'moved necessarily' and say grace is 'like a suasory or eloquent oration which we are not forced to consent unto'. Whereas the reprobate 'serve sinne', the

[61] Donne, *Sermons*, VII. 423.
[62] See above, p. 182.
[63] See above, pp. 216–17. The printing of Gore's sermon at this time would seem to reflect a growing confidence on the part of the Arminian leadership.
[64] See below, p. 263.
[65] Robert Vase, *Jonah's Contestation about his Gourd* (1625), p. 46.
[66] William Proctor, *The Watchman Warning* (1625), pp. 51–2.

elect 'give it only house-roome'.[67] His sermon was printed at Oxford.

The year 1626 saw the printing of a sermon by Humphrey Sydenham, a fellow of Wadham College, Oxford, which was solely concerned with 'election and reprobation'. Like the sermons of Vase, Proctor, and Bedingfield, this had been preached in the reign of King James. Sydenham described his subject as 'the very battlement and pinacle of divinity'. The will of God is 'the primary and immediate cause' why some are 'marked out as the inheritours of his Sion' and others 'expulsed'. Here 'the Pelagian startles and lately backt with a troope of Arminians takes head against the truth', arguing that 'faith and obedience (foreseene of God in the elect) was the necessary condition and cause of their election'. But 'those whom God from all eternity hath destined to salvation, he hath in a like priviledge destined to the meanes'. He 'will have mercy onely on some, of which some there is a definite and set number incapable of augmentation or diminution'. Arminians, by contrast, make 'our election mutable, incompleat, conditionate, subject to change and revocation . . ., altering no lesse the number than the condition of the elect into the state of the reprobate and of the reprobate into the elect'.[68]

In another sermon of 1626, Anthony Fawkner, of Jesus College, Oxford, argued that 'all things prove to the good of the elect. If they sinne, they shall be punished. Yet their punishment shall be the witnesse of their triall, and that the path-way to their glorie. God will not cocker his children, but correct them and strike hardest where he loves most.'[69] Matthew Brookes's sermon of 1627 defined the 'church' as 'the company of God's elect and chosen'. Christ is 'the sure foundation' and the elect are the 'stones' of the building. Yet 'it is not every kinde of faith that maketh a stone'. For 'there is a common faith which both the elect and reprobate have and there is a faith proper to the elect of God'. Only the latter is 'justifying or saving faith'. Those chosen to be 'stones' are beneficiaries of 'the free mercie of God', and their 'estate is perpetuall'. The rest are 'cast by' according to 'the righteous judgement of God'.[70] Brookes was subsequently to become curate of Great Yarmouth. Stephen Denison, the same year, included Arminians among the religious 'wolves' cur-

[67] Robert Bedingfield, *A Sermon preached at Paul's Crosse* (Oxford, 1625), pp. 18, 35.

[68] Humphrey Sydenham, *Jacob and Esau: Election and Reprobation opened and discussed* (1626), pp. 1, 2, 5, 14, 16. Sydenham quotes both the Synod of Dort and St Augustine, and is unique among Paul's Cross preachers in recognizing that the latter had changed his mind on the subject of predestination. Ibid., pp. 4–6. The printing of Sydenham's sermon may have been intended as a contribution to the controversy aroused by the writings of Richard Montagu.

[69] Anthony Fawkner, *Comfort to the Afflicted* (1626), p. 26.

[70] Matthew Brookes, *The House of God* (1627), pp. 6, 9–10, 19, 34.

rently ravaging England. They 'make a bridge betweene us and Popery', teaching 'conditionall election upon foreseene faith or workes', denying 'the doctrine of reprobation in the true sense thereof', maintaining 'universall redemption of all sorts', and defending 'the totall apostacy of saints'.[71]

John Gumbledon's sermon was printed at Oxford in 1628, and concerned the 'all-sufficient sacrifice' of Christ, who 'in due time bare the sinns of many'. Those for whom Christ 'prayeth continually and for whom hee died effectually shall never be set with the goats' on God's 'left hand'. Gumbledon, 'preacher' at Longworth in Berkshire, restricted the atonement to 'all in all ages that acknowledge their sinnes' and 'believe faithfully'. Such believers can 'never fall'.[72] Robert Sanderson's two sermons were also printed in 1628. According to Sanderson, Rector of Boothby Pagnell in Lincolnshire, there are two 'degrees' of sanctification, one 'common' and the other 'peculiar to the godly'. These correspond to two decrees, the first again 'common' and the second whereby God 'for the merits of Christ Jesus, the second Adam, . . . removeth from the creature that curse wherein it was wrapped through the sin of the first Adam. And in this the wicked have no portion, as being out of Christ . . .'[73] In his second sermon, Sanderson differentiated between 'restraining' and 'renewing' grace, the former being 'common' and the latter limited to 'the elect'. This 'renewing grace springeth from the speciall love of God towards those that are his in Christ'; it 'holdeth out unto the end, more or lesse, and never leaveth us wholly destitute'.[74]

Here this series of fifty surviving Calvinist sermons, from 1570 onwards, comes to a stop. The abrupt ending clearly reflects the religious policy of King Charles and his advisers, who had called a halt to the discussion of such questions for the future.[75] By itself this would have been startling enough, given the one-sided nature of the previous debate. But in practice Arminian views now came to be aired at Paul's Cross, while the Calvinists were silenced. Five printed Arminian sermons are extant. That by Edward Boughen, Rector of Woodchurch in Kent, is particularly interesting because it

---

[71] Stephen Denison, *The White Wolfe* (1627), pp. 37–8. This sermon is dedicated to King Charles. Ibid., sigs. A2–A4ᵛ.

[72] John Gumbledon, *God's Great Mercy to Mankinde in Jesus Christ* (Oxford, 1628), pp. 12, 14, 16–18.

[73] Robert Sanderson, *Two Sermons preached at Paules-Crosse* (1628), pp. 40–1. Sanderson seems to have changed his mind about Arminianism at some date after 1637. Robert Sanderson, *The Works*, ed. W. Jacobson (Oxford, 1854), III. 29.

[74] Sanderson, *Two Sermons* pp. 110, 126.

[75] The relevant proclamation was issued in June 1626 (*Stuart Constitution*, ed. Kenyon, pp. 154–5) but its full implementation had to await the appointment of Laud to the bishopric of London in July 1628 (Le Neve, *Fasti*, II. 303).

Appendix I

seeks to explain the new policy. Preached in April 1630, this sermon was not printed until 1635. Boughen's text (1 John 4: 1–3) concerned 'false prophets' and he warned his auditory 'beleeve not every sermon', for 'every sermon is not the word of God'. The individual must 'consider seriously with himselfe whether the doctrine hee heares, or reades, be agreeable to the received doctrine of the Church'.[76]

Error is both wilful and 'upon simplicity'. A man should 'not be wedded to his own conceit, but upon better instruction when he heares some truth that he hath not beene acquainted with heretofore, when he sees it made evident to be the ancient doctrine of the Church, let him not say this contradicts my former opinion [and] it is a disgrace for me to yeeld or to alter my minde'. Rather 'let him humbly say, with all meeknesse, this is more than ever I knew before. I did not understand this point. I knew not that this was the doctrine of the Church . . . but now . . . I am so much wiser than before. God pardon my former ignorance.' The 'well-minded man that hath beene drawne to evill, through deceitfull and lying doctrine, will much more embrace that which is good—the truth enforcing him'.[77]

Boughen explicitly linked his remarks to the royal declaration of 1628, concerning the Arminian controversy. 'Care is had, you see, that from henceforth yee shall have the ancient and received doctrine to guide you.' The alternative is to 'forsake the universall consent of the Church' for 'some few though ancient and laborious preachers', and to 'be drawne away with two or three puny scholars that are scarce acquainted with the Articles of Religion'. He went on to refer to certain heretics in the past, who claimed to be 'perfect men and the very seed of election', and spoke of 'some such as these that are spurring fast this way . . . of late dayes'. Scriptural interpretation needs to be supported 'from learned and religious antiquity'. The exposition of 'true Catholike tradition' is to be 'gathered out of the most consonant writings of the most ancient fathers and gravest decrees of the eldest councels'. Towards the end of this sermon Boughen returned to the 'false prophets'. By 'these factious men the gates of Heaven are barred up against the infants of Christians, while the grace of baptism is utterly denied'. Instead Boughen proclaimed the universality of the atonement. Christ is indeed 'the saviour of the world'.[78]

Boughen's caricature of his 'few' Calvinist predecessors in the Paul's Cross pulpit, and of the 'puny' scholarship of Calvinist

[76] Edward Boughen, *Two Sermons* (1635), ii. 5, 6.
[77] Ibid., ii. 8–9. [78] Ibid., ii. 10–12, 16, 26–7, 29, 39, 49.

divines in general, is indicative of the dramatic theological change involved here. Certainly his remarks cannot be dismissed as those of an unrepresentative maverick. Boughen had been chaplain to Bishop Howson and this sermon of his was licensed for publication by one of Archbishop Laud's chaplains—William Haywood.[79] The Arminian sermons of James Conyers, John Gore, and Oliver Whitbie have already been discussed above.[80] Published between 1632 and 1638 they, together with that by Boughen, are without precedent in terms of the printed output of Paul's Cross sermons. Conyers and Whitbie adopted a polemical stance similar to Boughen, referring to the 'vaine Catharist' and 'Novation brood'.[81] Gore, on the other hand, was much less combative in tone. None the less, the new Arminian hallmark of the 1630s is unmistakable.

[79] Arber, IV. 313; Greg, *Licensers for the Press*, pp. 45–6.
[80] See above, pp. 216–19.
[81] Conyers, *Christ's Love and Saints' Sacrifice*, p. 13; Whitbie, *London's Returne*, p. 15.

The Arminianism of Archbishop Laud

The claim that William Laud was an Arminian has proved surprisingly contentious.[1] Therefore I print below the main documentary evidence, with an accompanying commentary.

A

May it please your Grace [Buckingham],

We are bold to be suitors to you in behalf of the Church of England and a poor member of it, Mr. Montague, at this time not a little distressed. We are not strangers to his person, but it is the cause which we are bound to be tender of.

The cause we conceive (under correction of better judgment) concerns the Church of England nearly; for that Church, when it was reformed from the superstitious opinions broached or maintained by the Church of Rome, refused the apparent and dangerous errors and would not be too busy with every particular school-point. The cause why she held this moderation was because she could not be able to preserve any unity amongst Christians, if men were forced to subscribe to curious particulars disputed in schools.

Now, may it please your Grace, the opinions which at this time trouble many men in the late work of Mr. Montague are, some of them, such as are expressly the resolved doctrine of the Church of England and those he is bound to maintain. Some of them such as are fit only for schools and to be left at more liberty for learned men to abound in their own sense, so they keep themselves peaceable and distract not the Church; and therefore to make any man subscribe to school-opinions may justly seem hard in the Church of Christ, and was one great fault of the Council of Trent. And to affright them from those opinions in which they have (as they are bound) subscribed to the Church, as it is worse in itself so it may be the mother of greater danger.

May it please your Grace further to consider that, when the clergy submitted themselves in the time of Henry the Eighth, the submission was so made that if any difference, doctrinal or other, fell in the Church the King and the bishops were to be judges of it, in a national synod of convocation, the King first giving leave, under his broad seal, to handle the points in difference.

But the Church never submitted to any other judge, neither indeed can she though she would. And we humbly desire your Grace to consider, and then to move his most gracious Majesty (if you shall think fit), what dangerous consequences may follow upon it.

[1] K. Sharpe, 'Archbishop Laud and the University of Oxford', in *History and Imagination*, ed. H. Lloyd-Jones *et al.* (1981), pp. 160–1; White, 'Rise of Arminianism Reconsidered', pp. 53–4.

1) For, first, if any other judge be allowed in matter of doctrine, we shall depart from the ordinance of Christ and the continual course and practice of the Church.

2) Secondly, if the Church be once brought down beneath herself we cannot but fear what may be next struck at.

3) Thirdly, it will some way touch the honour of his Majesty's dear father and our most dread sovereign of glorious and ever blessed memory, King James, who saw and approved all the opinions of this book; and he in his rare wisdom and judgment would never have allowed them, if they had crossed with truth and the Church of England.

4) Fourthly, we must be bold to say that we cannot conceive what use there can be of civil government in the commonwealth or of preaching and external ministry in the Church, if such fatal opinions, as some which are opposite and contrary to these delivered by Mr. Montague, are and shall be publicly taught and maintained.

5) Fifthly, we are certain that all or most of the contrary opinions were treated of at Lambeth and ready to be published, but then Queen Elizabeth of famous memory, upon notice given how little they agreed with the practice of piety and obedience to all government, caused them to be suppressed; and so they have continued ever since, till of late some of them have received countenance at the Synod of Dort. Now this was a synod of that nation and can be of no authority in any other national church, till it be received there by public authority; and our hope is that the Church of England will be well advised, and more than once over, before she admit a foreign synod, especially of such a Church as condemneth her discipline and manner of government to say no more.

And, further, we are bold to commend to your Grace's wisdom this one particular. His Majesty (as we have been informed) hath already taken this business into his own care, and most worthily referred it in a right course to Church-consideration. And we well hoped that, without further trouble to the state or breach of unity in the Church, it might so have been well and orderly composed as we still pray it may. These things considered, we have little to say for Mr. Montague's person; only thus much we know, he is a very good scholar and a right honest man; a man every way able to do God, his Majesty, and the Church of England great service. We fear he may receive great discouragement and, which is far worse, we have some cause to doubt this may breed a great backwardness in able men to write in defence of the Church of England against either home or foreign adversaries, if they shall see him sink in fortunes, reputation, or health, upon his book-occasion.

And this we most humbly submit to your Grace's judgment and care of the Church's peace and welfare. So recommending your Grace to the protection of Almighty God,

We shall ever rest at your Grace's service,

John Rochester* [Buckeridge]
John Oxford* [Howson]
William St. Davids* [Laud]

2 August, 1625.

(Laud, *Works*, vi. 244–6)[2]

[2] The original of this letter survives in the British Library. Harleian MS 7000, fo. 183ʳ⁻ᵛ.

The foregoing letter, signed by Laud, comprises the most direct evidence of his Arminianism. Not intended for public eyes, it is an unusually frank statement and comes from an early stage in his episcopal career. Laud was the last and most junior signatory of this letter, although he must have agreed with the general tenor. Written in support of Richard Montagu, who at the time was under attack as an Arminian, it is illuminating on a number of counts. First, the letter assimilates the teaching of the Lambeth Articles to that of the Synod of Dort, which had condemned Arminianism in 1619. Secondly, it describes the published doctrines of Montagu as being 'contrary' to those of Lambeth and Dort. Thirdly, it condemns the articles of Lambeth and the canons of Dort as containing 'fatal opinions' incompatible with 'civil government in the commonwealth or of preaching and external ministry in the Church'. Moreover, in so far as it distinguishes between the Lambeth Articles and the Synod of Dort, the former are deemed the more objectionable. 'Queen Elizabeth, of famous memory, upon notice given how little they [the Lambeth Articles] agreed with the practice of piety and obedience to all government, caused them to be suppressed; and so they have continued ever since, till of late *some* of them have received countenance at the Synod of Dort.'

This last point is particularly interesting in the light of modern arguments that the Lambeth Articles do not represent a clear statement of Calvinist doctrine.[3] The letter also exposes as false the subsequent claim by Laud, in the account of his trial, that he never gave his approbation to Montagu's published views. Since this letter was not available to the prosecution, they fell back on circumstantial evidence, such as the possession by Laud of Montagu's books. To which Laud replied 'I have Bellarmine in my study [and] therefore I am a Papist, or I have the Alcaron in my study [and] therefore I am a Turk, is as good an argument as . . . I have Bishop Montague's books in my study [and] therefore I am an Arminian'.[4] (Incidentally, while seeking to dissociate himself from Montagu's doctrines, Laud appears here to acknowledge that Montagu was indeed an Arminian.) There is, however, one further and very important feature of this letter. By describing the content of the Lambeth Articles and the Dort canons as 'fatal', the bishops indicate that they conceived anti-Calvinist or Arminian teaching on predestination to be part of 'the resolved doctrine of the Church of England' and not in the category of disputable particulars.

[3] Porter, *Reformation and Reaction*, pp. 366–71.
[4] Laud, *Works*, IV. 289–90.

B

For many things in the works of providence many men, yea and sometimes the best, are a great deal too busy with . . . They would fain know all the secrets of predestination. But it is one of God's foundations, and such a 'foundation' as he hath set a 'seal' upon it. 'The Lord knows who are his.' It is very dangerous breaking up of 'seals', especially God's. The indorsement is enough for us and very plain to be read. It follows: 'and let every man that calls on the name of Christ depart from iniquity.' If he do not that he is not Christ's, let him talk of predestination while he will.

(Laud, *Works*, I. 130–1)

This passage occurs in a sermon preached by Laud at Whitehall, on 5 July 1626. Thus it dates from a bare three weeks after the issue of the proclamation concerning the Arminian controversy,[5] and can be taken as Laud's comment on current royal policy. Laud goes considerably further than simply endorsing the official ban on the predestinarian dispute. The reference to 'busy' men, prying into 'the secrets of predestination', recalls the allusions of Lancelot Andrewes to the Synod of Dort,[6] while the emphasis on conduct—departing from iniquity—hints that this is the cause rather than the consequence of predestination.

C

Mr. Pryn himself (who hath been a great stickler in these troubles of the Church) says expressly, 'Let any true saint of God be taken away in the very act of any known sin, before it is possible for him to repent; I make no doubt or scruple of it, but he shall as surely be saved as if he had lived to have repented of it.' And he instances in David, 'in case he had been taken away before he had repented of his adultery and murder.' So, according to this divinity, the true saints of God may commit horrible and crying sins, die without repentance, and yet be sure of salvation; which teareth up the very foundations of religion, induceth all manner of profaneness into the world, and is expressly contrary to the whole current of the Scripture . . . [Furthermore] almost all of them say that God from all eternity reprobates by far the greater part of mankind to eternal fire, without any eye at all to their sin. Which opinion my very soul abominates. For it makes God, the God of all mercies, to be the most fierce and unreasonable tyrant in the world. For the question is not here what God may do by an absolute act of power, would he so use it upon the creature which he made of nothing, but what he hath done and what stands with his wisdom, justice, and goodness to do.

(Laud, *Works*, VI. 132–3)

These remarks are to be found in Laud's reply to a speech by Viscount Saye attacking the liturgy of the Church of England. The

[5] *Stuart Constitution*, ed. Kenyon, pp. 154–5.
[6] See above, pp. 45, 103.

reply was written in the early 1640s, when Laud was a prisoner in
the Tower of London. He is here ostensibly talking about 'Brow-
nists', among whom he ranks William Prynne—by this date a
presbyterian. The quotation is from Prynne's book *The Perpetuitie of a
Regenerate Man's Estate*, which had been licensed for the press in 1626
by one of Archbishop Abbot's chaplains.[7] At that time Prynne was a
Calvinist episcopalian. The case of David, in the Old Testament,
was standard among Calvinist exponents of the doctrine of perseverance. They argued that, as one of the truly regenerate, David could
never have fallen totally from grace, and consequently his salvation
was not conditional upon repentance. Nevertheless, they claimed
that such repentance followed inevitably.

Prynne distinguishes here between 'generall' and 'particular'
repentance for every sin committed, maintaining that only the
former is 'absolutely necessary to salvation'. But he also says that
even admitting such particular repentance was essential to salvation, 'when God doth take away any of his saints, in the very act of
sinne, hee doth in that very instance which hee takes them in give
them such an actuall and particular repentance as shall save their
soules'.[8] Clearly, therefore, Laud rejected orthodox Calvinist doctrine concerning the perseverance of the saints, while portraying it in
a highly unfavourable light. The same holds true of his comment on
reprobation. Most Calvinists differentiated between reprobation
and damnation. The latter was indeed the reward of sin, whereas
reprobation was the obverse of God's decision only to elect a minority of fallen mankind. At the very least this comment by Laud means
that, like John Overall,[9] he envisaged a majority of justified persons
who might attain to Heaven by the exercise of their own free will.

---

[7] Prynne, *The Perpetuitie*, p. 339; Arber, IV. 118.
[8] Prynne, *The Perpetuitie*, pp. 338–9, 341.
[9] See above, pp. 24, 37.

Select Bibliography

A NOTE ON MANUSCRIPTS

The unpublished materials for the study of English Arminianism, in its various aspects, lie scattered through numerous repositories. Probably most record offices contain something of relevance. Of the manuscripts consulted for the present book the university archives of Cambridge and Oxford, together with the related holdings of the Cambridge University and Bodleian libraries, are among the most significant. There is no real equivalent at Cambridge of the splendid Oxford series of Congregation and Convocation registers, but this is more than compensated for by a considerable body of letters, notebooks, and Consistory Court records which shed valuable light on Cambridge religious developments. Of the named collections in the Bodleian Library, the Rawlinson and Tanner manuscripts have proved of central importance for the understanding of Oxford and more general religious history. Thus the Tanner collection includes the incoming correspondence of Samuel Ward, who was one of the English delegates at the Synod of Dort. Among the British Library holdings, the Harleian manuscripts have been especially useful. They incorporate, for example, part of the material collected by the Cambridge antiquary Thomas Baker. At the Public Record Office, State Papers Domestic and State Papers Holland have helped to provide both a national and an international dimension, while the wills registered in the Prerogative Court of Canterbury have yielded some welcome information concerning individuals. My discussion of the Arminianism of Archbishop Neile owes much to the Hunter manuscripts in the Durham Dean and Chapter Library. Particularly illuminating on the subject of lay Arminianism are the Dyott papers, deposited at the Staffordshire Record Office. Other collections drawn on include those of the Borthwick Institute, Canterbury Cathedral Archives, Lambeth Palace Library, Trinity College Dublin and a number of Oxford colleges. Details are to be found in the footnotes.

PRINTED WORKS

(The place of publication is London unless otherwise stated)

I. *Primary*

A., J., *An Historicall Narration of the Judgement of some . . . English Bishops, Holy Martyrs and others . . . concerning God's Election and the Merit of Christ his Death* (1631).

Abbot, George, *An Exposition upon the Prophet Jonah* (1600).
—— *The Reasons which Doctor Hill hath brought* (Oxford, 1604).
—— *A Treatise of the Perpetuall Visibilitie and Succession of the True Church in all Ages* (1624).
Abbot, Robert, *De Gratia et Perseverantia Sanctorum. Exercitationes aliquot habitae in Academia Oxoniensi* (1618).
Acontius, Jacobus, *Stratagematum Satanae* (Oxford, 1631).
The Acts of the High Commission Court within the Diocese of Durham, ed. W. H. D. Longstaffe (Surtees Soc., 34, 1858).
Airay, Henry, *Lectures upon the Whole Epistle of Saint Paul to the Philippians* (1618).
Andrewes, Lancelot, *The Works of Lancelot Andrewes*, ed. J. P. Wilson and J. Bliss (11 volumes, Oxford, 1841–54).
The Answere of the . . . Universitie of Oxford (Oxford, 1603).
Anti-Montacutum: An Appeale or Remonstrance of the Orthodox Ministers of the Church of England against Richard Mountagu (1629).
Arminius, Jacobus, *Examen Modestum Libelli quem D. Gulielmus Perkinsius edidit* (Leiden, 1612).
—— *De Vero et Genuino Sensu Cap. VII Epistolae ad Romanos Dissertatio* (Leiden, 1612).
—— *The Writings of James Arminius*, tr. J. Nichols and W. R. Bagnall (3 volumes, Grand Rapids, 1956).
Articles agreed on in the Nationall Synode of the Reformed Churches of France (Oxford, 1623).
Articles of Religion agreed upon . . . in the Convocation holden at Dublin (Dublin, 1615).
Articuli Lambethani (1651).

Babington, Gervase, *A Sermon preached at Paules Crosse the second Sunday in Mychaelmas Tearme last* (1591).
Balcanqual, Walter, *et al.*, *A Joynt Attestation avowing that the Discipline of the Church of England was not Impeached by the Synode of Dort* (1626).
Ball, Thomas, *The Life of the Renowned Dr. Preston writ . . . . in the Year 1628*, ed. E. W. Harcourt (1885).
Barnevel's Apology or Holland Mysterie (1618).
Baro, Peter, *Summa Trium de Praedestinatione Sententiarum* (Harderwijk, 1613).
Bastingius, Jeremias, *An Exposition or Commentarie upon the Catechisme of Christian Religion which is taught in the . . . Low Countries* (Cambridge, 1589).
Baudius, Dominicus, *Epistolarum Centuriae Tres* (Leiden, 1620).
Bedford, Thomas, *Luther's Predecessours or an Answere to where was your Church before Luther* (1624).
—— *The Sinne unto Death* (1621).

Benfield, Sebastian, *Doctrinae Christianae Sex Capita* (Oxford, 1610).

—— *Eight Sermons publikely preached in the University of Oxford . . . begunne in the Yeare 1595* (Oxford, 1614).

—— *De Perseverantia Sanctorum. Praelectiones in Scholia Theologica Oxonii habitae* (Frankfurt, 1618).

—— *A Sermon preached at Wotton under Edge* appended to *A Commentarie or Exposition upon Amos* (Oxford, 1613).

Blair, Robert, *The Life of Mr. Robert Blair,* ed. T. M'Crie (Edinburgh, 1848).

The Book of Common Order of the Church of Scotland, ed. G. W. Sprott (Edinburgh, 1901).

Boughen, Edward, *Two Sermons. The First preached at Canterbury, at the Visitation of the Lord Archbishop's Peculiars . . . April 14. 1635, the Second preached at Saint Paul's Crosse the Eighteenth of April 1630* (1635).

Bradwardine, Thomas, *De Causa Dei contra Pelagium* (1618).

Bramhall, John, *The Works of Archbishop Bramhall* (5 volumes, Oxford, 1842–5).

Brandt, G., *The History of the Reformation . . . in . . . the Low Countries* (4 volumes, 1720–3).

Bridges, John, *A Sermon preached at Paules Crosse* (1571).

Browne, Abraham, *A Sermon preached at the Assizes . . . at Winchester* (1623).

Browne, Thomas, *The Copie of the Sermon preached before the Universitie at St. Maries in Oxford . . . the XXIV of December 1633* (Oxford, 1634).

Browning, John, *Concerning Publike Prayer and the Fasts of the Church* (1636).

Buck, James, *A Treatise of the Beatitudes. Or Christs Happy Men* (1637).

Buckeridge, John, *A Sermon preached before His Maiestie at Whitehall, March 22, 1617 . . . touching Prostration, and Kneeling in the Worship of God. To which is added a Discourse concerning Kneeling at the Communion* (1618).

Burges, Cornelius, *Baptismall Regeneration of Elect Infants, professed by the Church of England, according to the Scriptures, the Primitive Church, the present Reformed Churches, and many particular Divines apart* (Oxford, 1629).

Burton, Henry, *For God and the King. The Summe of Two Sermons preached on the Fifth of November . . . 1636* (1636).

—— *Israel's Fast* (1628).

—— *A Narration of the Life of Mr. Henry Burton* (1643).

—— *A Plea to an Appeale* (1626).

—— *Truth's Triumph over Trent* (1629).

Cade, Anthony, *St. Paul's Agony* (1618).

Calderwood, David, *The History of the Kirk in Scotland*, ed. T. Thomson (8 volumes, Edinburgh, 1842–9).

Campbell, A., *The Doctrines of a Middle State between Death and the Resurrection* (1721).

Cardwell, E., *Documentary Annals of the Reformed Church of England* (2 volumes, Oxford, 1844)

—— *A History of Conferences and other Proceedings connected with the Revision of the Book of Common Prayer* (Oxford, 1840).

—— *Synodalia. A Collection of Articles of Religion, Canons and Proceedings of Convocation in the Province of Canterbury* (2 volumes, Oxford, 1842).

Carier, Benjamin, *A Treatise written by Mr. Doctour Carier* (Liège, 1614).

Carleton, Sir Dudley, *Letters from and to Sir Dudley Carleton, Knt., during his Embassy in Holland*, ed. P. Yorke (1775).

Carleton, George, *An Examination of those Things wherein the Author of the late Appeale* [Richard Montagu] *holdeth the Doctrines of the Pelagians and Arminians to be the Doctrines of the Church of England* (1626).

—— *A Thankfull Remembrance of God's Mercy* (1624).

Cartwright, William, *Plays and Poems*, ed. G. B. Evans (Madison, 1951).

Casaubon, Isaac, *Ephemerides Isaaci Casauboni*, ed. J. Russell (2 volumes, Oxford, 1850).

—— *Isaaci Casauboni Epistolae* (Rotterdam, 1709).

Chamberlain, John, *The Letters of John Chamberlain*, ed. N. E. McClure (2 volumes, Philadelphia, 1939).

Chillingworth, William, *The Religion of Protestants* (Oxford, 1638).

A Christian Letter of Certaine English Protestants (n.p., 1599).

Chown, Thomas, *Collectiones Theologicarum* (1635).

Commons, *Journals of the House of Commons*.

Commons Debates, 1621, ed. W. Notestein, F. H. Relf and H. Simpson (7 volumes, New Haven, 1935).

Commons Debates, 1628, ed. R. C. Johnson, M. F. Keeler, M. J. Cole and W. B. Bidwell (4 volumes, New Haven, 1977–83).

Commons Debates for 1629, ed. W. Notestein and F. H. Relf (Minneapolis, 1921).

The Constitutional Documents of the Puritan Revolution, 1625–1660, ed. S. R. Gardiner (Oxford, 1962).

Constitutions and Canons Ecclesiastical treated upon by . . . the Clergy of Ireland . . . in . . . 1634 (Dublin, 1664).

Conyers, James, *Christ's Love and Saints' Sacrifice* (1635).

Corbett, Richard, *The Poems of Richard Corbett*, ed. J. A. W. Bennett and H. R. Trevor-Roper (Oxford, 1955).

Correspondence of King James VI of Scotland with Sir Robert Cecil and Others in England, ed. J. Bruce (Camden Soc., 1st ser. 78, 1861).

Corro, Anthony, *Dialogus Theologicus, quo Epistola Divi Pauli ad Romanus explanatur* (1574).
—— *Tableau de l'oeuvre de Dieu* (Norwich, 1569).
Cosin, John *The Works of . . . John Cosin . . .* ed. J. Sansom (5 volumes, Oxford, 1843–55).
—— *The Correspondence of John Cosin . . .* ed. G. Ornsby (2 volumes, Surtees Soc., 52, 55, 1868–72).
Cotton, John, *The Way of Congregational Churches Cleared* (1648).
Crakanthorpe, Richard, *Defensio Ecclesiae Anglicanae contra M. Antonii de Dominis* (1625).
—— *A Sermon of Predestination, preached at Saint Maries in Oxford* (1620).
Crosfield, Thomas, *The Diary of Thomas Crosfield,* ed. F. S. Boas (Oxford, 1935).
Crowley, Robert, *An Apologie or Defence of . . . Predestination* (1566).

Davenant, John, *Animadversions upon a Treatise intitled God's Love to Mankind* (Cambridge, 1641).
—— *Determinationes Quaestionum Quarundam Theologicarum . . . publice disputatarum* (Cambridge, 1634).
—— *Dissertationes Duae: prima de Morte Christi . . . altera de Praedestinatione et Reprobatione . . .* (1650).
Davenport, Christopher, *Deus, Natura, Gratia, sive Tractatus de Praedestinatione . . .* (1st edition Lyons, 1634; 2nd edition Lyons, 1635).
Davenport, John, *The Letters of John Davenport,* ed. I. M. Calder (Yale, 1937).
Debates in the House of Commons in 1625, ed. S. R. Gardiner (Camden Soc., NS 6, 1873).
Dee, Francis, *Articles to be enquired of throughout the Whole Diocese of Peterborough* (1634).
D'Ewes, Sir Simonds, *The Journal of Sir Simonds D'Ewes from the Beginning of the Long Parliament,* ed. W. Notestein (New Haven, 1923).
Dominis, Marcus Antonius de, *M. Antonius de Dominis . . . declares the Cause of his Returne out of England* (n.p., 1623).
Donne, John, *The Sermons of John Donne,* ed. G. R. Potter and E. M. Simpson (10 volumes, Berkeley and Los Angeles, 1953–62).
Dove, John, *A Sermon preached at Paules Crosse, the Sixth of February, 1596* (1597).
Dow, Christopher, *Innovations Unjustly Charged upon the Present Church and State. Or an Answere to the most Materiall Passages of a Libellous Pamphlet made by . . . H. Burton . . .* (1637).
Downham, George, *The Covenant of Grace or an Exposition Upon Luke 1. 73, 74, 75* (Dublin, 1631).

Du Moulin, Pierre, *The Anatomy of Arminianisme* (1620).

Duppa, Brian, *Articles to be inquired of throughout the Diocesse of Chichester* (1638).

Dyke, Jeremiah, *A Sermon preached at the Publicke Fast* (1628).

Ecclesiae Londino-Batavae Archivum, ed. J. H. Hessels (3 volumes, Cambridge, 1887–97).

Featley, Daniel, *Cygnea Cantio or Learned Decisions and . . . Pious Directions for Students in Divinitie, delivered by . . . King James at White Hall a few Weekes before his Death* (1629).

—— *A Second Parallel together with a Writ of Error sued against the Appealer* (1626).

—— and Goad, Thomas, *Pelagius Redivivus or Pelagius raked out of the Ashes by Arminius and his Schollers* (1626).

Field, Nathaniel, *Some Short Memorials concerning the Life of . . . R. Field,* ed. J. Le Neve (1717).

Field, Richard, *A Learned Sermon preached before the King at Whitehall* (1604).

—— *Of the Church* (4 volumes, Cambridge, 1847–52).

Fisher, Jasper, *The Priests Duty and Dignity* (1635).

Fletcher, John, and Massinger, Philip, *The Tragedy of Sir John Van Olden Barnavelt.* ed. W. P. Frijlinck (1922).

Forbes, John, *Opera Omnia* (Amsterdam, 1703).

Forbes, William, *Considerationes Modestae et Pacificae,* ed. and tr. G. Forbes (2 volumes, Oxford, 1850–6).

Foxe, John, *A Sermon of Christ Crucified* (1570).

Fuller, Thomas, *The Church History of Britain,* ed. J. S. Brewer (6 volumes, Oxford, 1845).

Gardiner, Samuel, *The Foundation of the Faythfull* (1611).

—— *A Sermon preached at Paules Crosse* (1605).

Goad, Thomas, *Stimulus Orthodoxus sive Goadus Redivivus* (1661).

Gordon, James, *History of Scots Affairs from 1637 to 1641,* ed. J. Robertson and G. Grub (3 volumes, Aberdeen, 1841).

Gore, John, *The Oracle of God* (1636).

—— *The Way to Prosper* (1632).

—— *The Way to Well-doing* (1635).

Grotius, Hugo, *Briefwisseling van Hugo Grotius,* ed. P. C. Molhuysen and B. L. Meulenbroek (11 volumes, The Hague, 1928–81).

Hacket, John, *Scrinia Reserata. A Memorial offer'd to the Great Deservings of J. Williams . . . Archbishop of York* (1693).

Hakewill, George, *An Answere to a Treatise written by Dr. Carier* (1616).

Hales, John, *Golden Remains of the Ever Memorable Mr. J. H.* (1673).

Hall, Joseph, *Epistles* (1608).

—— *The Works of . . . Joseph Hall,* ed. P. Wynter (10 volumes, Oxford, 1863).

Harsnett, Samuel, *A Fourth Sermon* appended to Richard Steward, *Three Sermons* (1656).

Hausted, Peter, *Ten Sermons* (1636).

Hayne, Thomas, *The Equal Wayes of God for Rectifying the Unequal Wayes of Man* (1639).

Hegge, Robert, *The Legend of St. Cuthbert,* ed. J. B. Taylor (Sunderland, 1816).

Heigham, John, *The Gagge of the Reformed Gospel* (Douai, 1623).

Hemmingsen, Niels, *The Epistle of the Blessed Apostle Saint Paule . . . to the Ephesians* (1581).

Herbert of Cherbury, Lord Edward, *De Veritate,* tr. M. H. Carré (Bristol, 1937).

Heylyn, Peter, *A Coale from the Altar* (1636).

—— *Historia Quinqu-Articularis or a Declaration of the Judgement of the Western Churches, and more particularly of the Church of England, in the Five Controverted Points, reproched in these Last Times by the Name of Arminianism* (1660).

—— *Cyprianus Anglicus or the History of the Life and Death of . . . William* [Laud] *. . . Archbishop of Canterbury . . . Also the Ecclesiastical History of . . . England, Scotland and Ireland, from his First Rising till his Death* (1671).

Hickman, Henry, *Historia Quinq-Articularis Exarticulata or Animadversions on Dr. Heylyn's Quinquarticular History* (1673).

Hoard, Samuel and Mason, Henry, *God's Love to Mankind, manifested by disprooving his Absolute Decree for their Damnation* (1633).

Hooker, Richard, *The Works of Mr. Richard Hooker* (2 volumes, Oxford, 1850).

—— *Of the Laws of Ecclesiastical Polity* (4 volumes, Cambridge, Mass., 1977–82).

Hutton, Matthew, *Brevis et Dilucida Explicatio, Verae, Certae, et Consolationis Plenae Doctrinae de Electione, Praedestinatione ac Reprobatione* (Harderwijk, 1613).

—— *The Correspondence of Dr. Matthew Hutton,* ed. J. Raine (Surtees Soc., 17, 1843).

Jackson, Thomas, *The Works of Thomas Jackson* (12 volumes, Oxford, 1844).

James I, King, *His Majestie's Declaration . . . in the Cause of D. Conradus Vorstius* (1612).

—— *A Meditation upon the Lord's Prayer* (1619).

—— *The Workes of the Most High and Mightie Prince, James . . . King of Great Britain, France and Ireland* (1616–20).

Jewel, John, *The Works of John Jewel,* ed. J. Ayre (4 volumes, Cambridge, 1845–50).

Johnston, Sir Archibald, *Diary of Sir Archibald Johnston of Wariston, 1632–9,* ed. G. M. Paul (Scottish History Society, 61, 1911).

The Judgement of the Synode holden at Dort (1619).

Kimedoncius, Jacobus, *Of the Redemption of Mankind . . . wherein the Controversie of the Universalitie of Redemption and Grace by Christ, and of his Death for All Men, is largely handled. Hereunto is annexed a Treatise of God's Predestination* (1598).

King, John, *Lectures upon Jonas* (Oxford, 1597).

Lake, Arthur, *Sermons with Some Religious and Divine Meditations* (1629).

Laud, William, *The Works of William Laud,* ed. W. Scott and J. Bliss (7 volumes, Oxford, 1847–60).

Laurence, Thomas, *A Sermon preached before the King's Majestie at Whitehall* (1637).

—— *Two Sermons. The First preached at St. Maries in Oxford July 13, 1634, . . . the Second in the Cathedral Church of Sarum, . . . May 23, 1634* (Oxford, 1635).

Leech, Humphrey, *A Triumph of Truth* (Douai, 1609).

Leighton, Alexander, *An Appeal to the Parliament, or Sion's Plea against the Prelacie* (Amsterdam, 1628).

—— *An Epitome or Briefe Discoverie . . . of the . . . Great Troubles that Dr. Leighton suffered* (1646).

Le Neve, J., *The Lives and Characters . . . of All the Protestant Bishops of the Church of England since the Reformation* (1720).

Leslie, Henry, *A Sermon preached before His Majesty at Windsore* (Oxford, 1625).

—— *A Sermon preached before His Majesty at Wokin* (1627).

Leslie, William, *Vindiciae Theologicae pro Perseverantia Sanctorum in Gratia Salvifica* (Aberdeen, 1627).

Ley, John, *A Letter against the Erection of an Altar* (1641).

Loe, William, *A Sermon preached at . . . the Funerall of . . . Daniel Featley* (1645).

Lords, *Journals of the House of Lords.*

Maden, Richard, *Christ's Love and Affection towards Jerusalem* (1637).

Marshall, Stephen, *A Sermon preached before the Honourable House of Commons . . . November 17, 1640* (1641).

Matthew, Tobie, 'Two Sermons, hitherto unpublished, of Dr. Tobie Matthew . . . ', *Christian Observer,* 47 (1847).

Meredeth, Richard, *Two Sermons preached before His Majestie* (1606).

Montagu, Richard, *Appello Caesarem. A Just Appeal from Two Unjust Informers* (1625).

—— *Articles to be enquired of throughout the Whole Diocesse of Chichester* (1628).

—— *Articles to be enquired of throughout the Whole Diocesse of Chichester* (1631).

—— *Articles to be enquired of throughout the Whole Diocesse of Chichester* (1637).

—— *Articles of Enquiry and Direction for the Diocese of Norwich* (Cambridge, 1638).

—— *A Gagg for the New Gospel? No. A New Gagg for an Old Goose* (1624).

—— *De Originibus Ecclesiasticis Commentationem* (1636).

Morton, Thomas, *A Defence of the Innocencie of the Three Ceremonies of the Church of England* (1618).

—— *Of the Institution of the Sacrament* (1st edition, 1631; 2nd edition, 1635).

N., O., *An Apology of English Arminianisme* (St Omer, 1634).

A Necessarie and Godly Prayer appoynted by the Right Reverend Father in God John [Aylmer], Bishop of London . . . for the Turning Away of God's Wrath (1585).

Neile, Richard, *Articles to be enquired of within the Diocese of Lincoln* (1614).

—— *Marcus Antonius de Dominis . . . his Shiftings in Religion* (1624).

Notes of the Treaty carried on at Ripon . . . 1640, ed. J. Bruce (Camden Soc., 100, 1869).

Oldenbarnevelt, Johan van, *Bescheiden Betreffende zijn Staatkundig Beleid en zijn Familie*, ed. S. P. Haak and A. J. Veenendaal (3 volumes, The Hague, 1934–67).

Overall, John, *Articles to be enquired of in the Diocese of Norwich* (Cambridge, 1619).

Parker, Henry, *The Altar Dispute* (1641).

Pemble, William, *Vindiciae Gratiae: a Plea for Grace* (1627).

Perkins, William, *A Golden Chaine . . . containing the Order of the Causes of Salvation and Damnation* (1591).

—— *The Whole Workes of . . . W. Perkins* (1612–13).

—— *The Work of William Perkins*, ed. I. Breward (Abingdon, 1970).

Playfere, Thomas, *Nine Sermons* (Cambridge, 1612).

Pocklington, John, *Altare Christianum* (1637).

Polanus, Amandus, *A Treatise of A. Polanus concerning God's Eternall Predestination* (Cambridge, 1599).

Potter, Christopher, *A Sermon preached at the Consecration of the Right Reverend Father in God Barnaby Potter* (1629).

—— *His Own Vindication of Himselfe*, appended to John Plaifere, *Appello Evangelium* (1652).

—— *Want of Charitie* (Oxford, 1633).

Praestantium ac Eruditorum Virorum Epistolae Ecclesiasticae et Theologicae. ed. C. Hartsoeker and P. Limborch (Amsterdam, 1684).

Preston, John, *De Gratia Convertentis Irresistibilitate* (1652).

Proceedings in Parliament, 1610, ed. E. R. Foster (2 volumes, New Haven, 1966).

Proceedings, principally in the County of Kent, in connection with the Parliament called in 1640, ed. L. B. Larking (Camden Soc., 1st ser., 80, 1862).

Proceedings of the Short Parliament of 1640, ed. E. S. Cope and W. H. Coates (Camden, 4th ser., 19, 1977).

Price, Daniel, *The Defence of Truth* (Oxford, 1610).

Prideaux, John, *Lectiones Novem de Totidem Religionis Capitibus* (Oxford, 1625).

Prynne, William, *Anti-Arminianisme or the Church of England's Old Antithesis to New Arminianisme* (1630).

—— *A Briefe Survay and Censure of Mr. Cozens his Couzening Devotions. Proving both the Forme and Matter . . . to be meerely Popish* (1628).

—— *Canterburies Doome or the First Part of a Compleat History of the . . . Tryall . . . of William Laud* (1646).

—— *God no Imposter nor Deluder* (1629).

—— *A Looking-Glasse for all Lordly Prelates* (1636).

—— *The Perpetuitie of a Regenerate Man's Estate* (1626).

—— *A Quench-Coale* (Amsterdam, 1637).

—— *The Unbishoping of Timothy and Titus* (Amsterdam, 1636).

Reeve, Edmund, *The Communion Booke Catechism* (1635).

The Register of the University of Oxford, ed. A. Clark (4 parts, Oxford Hist. Soc., 10, 1887–9).

Renshaw, W.C., 'Notes from the Act Books of the Archdeaconry Court of Lewes', *Sussex Archaeological Collections*, 49, (1906).

Richardson, Charles, *The Repentance of Peter and Judas* (1612).

Rogers, Thomas, *The English Creede consenting with the True Auncient, Catholique, Apostolique Church . . .* (2 parts, 1585–7).

—— *The Faith, Doctrine and Religion, professed and protected in the Realme of England and Dominions of the Same* (Cambridge, 1607).

Rous, Francis, *Testis Veritatis. The Doctrine of King James . . . , of the Church of England* [and] *of the Catholicke Church, plainely showed to bee one in the points of Praedestination, Free-will* [and] *Certaintie of Salvation. With a discovery of the Grounds both Naturall [and] Politicke of Arminianisme* (1626).

—— *Treatises and Meditations* (1657).

Row, John, *The History of the Kirk of Scotland*, ed. D. Laing (Edinburgh, 1842).

Rushworth, John, *Historical Collections* (7 volumes, 1659–1701).

Rutherford, Samuel, *Exercitationes Apologeticae pro Divina Gratia* (Amsterdam, 1636).

—— *Letters of Samuel Rutherford*, ed. A. A. Bonar (Edinburgh, 1894).

Sancti Gregorii Nazianzeni in Julianum Invectivae Duae, ed. Richard Montagu (Eton, 1610).

Sanderson, Robert, *The Works of Robert Sanderson*, ed. W. Jacobson (6 volumes, Oxford, 1854).

Sandys, Sir Edwin, *A Relation of the State of Religion . . . in the Several States of these Westerne Parts of the World* (1605).

Shelford, Robert, *Five Pious and Learned Discourses* (Cambridge, 1635).

Shepherd, Thomas, *My Birth and Life*, in A. Young, *Chronicles of the First Planters of . . . Massachusetts Bay* (Boston, Mass., 1846).

Smart, Peter, *A Sermon preached in the Cathedral Church of Durham* (Edinburgh, 1628).

Smith, Miles, *Sermons of the Right Reverend M. Smith* (1632).

Some, Robert, *Three Questions briefly handled* (Cambridge, 1596).

Sparrow, Anthony, *A Sermon concerning Confession of Sinnes and the Power of Absolution* (1637).

Strafford, Thomas Wentworth, Earl of, *The Earl of Strafford's Letters and Despatches*, ed. W. Knowler (2 volumes, 1739).

The Stuart Constitution, ed. J. P. Kenyon (Cambridge, 1966).

Sweeper, Walter, *Israel's Redemption by Christ. Wherein is confuted the Arminian Universall Redemption* (1622).

Sydenham, Humphrey, *Jacob and Esau: Election and Reprobation opened and discussed* (1626).

Table Talk of John Selden, ed. F. Pollock (1927).

Thomson, Richard, *R. Thomsonii Angli Diatriba de Amissione et Intercisione Gratiae et Justificationis* (Leiden, 1616).

A Transcript of the Registers of the Company of Stationers, 1554–1640, ed. E. Arber (5 volumes, 1875–94).

Twisse, William, *A Discovery of D. Jackson's Vanitie* (Amsterdam, 1631).

—— *The Riches of God's Love unto the Vessels of Mercy* (Oxford, 1653).

—— *Vindiciae Gratiae, Potestatis ac Providentiae Dei* (Amsterdam, 1632).

Two Elizabethan Puritan Diaries, ed. M. M. Knappen (Chicago, 1933).

Ursinus, Zacharias, *The Summe of Christian Religion* (Oxford, 1587).

Ussher, James, *The Whole Works of . . . James Ussher*, ed. C. R. Elrington (17 volumes, Dublin, 1847–64).

Veron, Jean, *A Fruteful Treatise of Predestination and of the Divine Providence of God* (1563).

Ward, Samuel, *Gratia Discriminans. Concio ad Clerum habita Cantabrigiae* (1626).

—— *Opera Nonnulla, viz. Determinationes Theologicae* (1658).

Warmstry, Thomas, *A Convocation Speech* (1641).

Whitaker, William, *Cygnea Cantio* (Cambridge, 1599).

Whitbie, Oliver, *London's Returne* (1637/8).

White, Francis, *The Orthodox Faith and Way* (1617).

—— *A Treatise of the Sabbath-Day* (1635).

White, John, *The First Century of Scandalous, Malignant Priests* (1643).

Whitgift, John, *The Works of John Whitgift*, ed. J. Ayre (3 volumes, Cambridge, 1851–3).

Widdowes, Giles, *The Schysmatical Puritan* (Oxford, 1630).

Willet, Andrew, *An Antilogie or Counterplea to an Apologicall Epistle* (1603).

—— *Ecclesia Triumphans: that is the Joy of the English Church for the Happie Coronation of . . . Prince James . . .* (1603).

—— *Hexapla: that is a Six-Fold Commentarie upon the Epistle to the Romanes* (Cambridge, 1611).

—— *Synopsis Papismi, that is a Generall Viewe of Papistry* (1592).

Williams, John, *The Holy Table, Name and Thing* (1637).

—— *Perseverantia Sanctorum* (1628).

Winwood, Sir Ralph, *Memorials of Affairs of State,* ed. E. Sawyer (3 volumes, 1725).

Wood, Anthony, *The History and Antiquities of the University of Oxford,* ed. J. Gutch (2 volumes, Oxford, 1792–6).

Wotton, Anthony, *A Dangerous Plot Discovered . . . wherein is proved that R. Mountague . . . laboureth to bring in the Faith of Rome and Arminius* (1626).

Wren, Christopher, *Parentalia, or Memoirs of the Family of the Wrens* (1750).

Wren, Matthew, *Articles to be inquired of within the Diocesse of Hereford* (1635).

—— *Articles to be inquired of within the Dioces of Norwich* (1636).

Yates, John, *God's Arraignement of Hypocrites with . . . a Defence of . . . M. Perkins against Arminius* (Cambridge, 1615).

—— *Ibis ad Caesarem or a Submissive Appearance before Caesar, in Answer to Mr. Montague's Appeal, in the Points of Arminianisme and Popery, maintained and defended by him, against the Doctrine of the Church of England* (1626).

II. *Secondary*

Adams, S., 'Spain or the Netherlands? The Dilemmas of Early Stuart Foreign Policy', in *Before the Civil War,* ed. H. Tomlinson (1983).

Addleshaw, G. W. O. and Etchells, F., *The Architectural Setting of Anglican Worship. An Inquiry into the Arrangements for Public Worship in the Church of England from the Reformation to the Present Day* (1948).

Albion, G., *Charles I and the Court of Rome. A Study in 17th century Diplomacy* . . . (1935).

Allison, A. F., 'John Heigham of St Omer c.1568–1632', *Recusant History*, 4 (1957–8).

Archer, M., 'English Painted Glass in the Seventeenth Century: the Early Work of Abraham van Linge', *Apollo*, 101 (1975).

—— '17th Century Painted Glass at Little Easton', *Essex Journal*, 12 (1977).

Armstrong, B. G., *Calvinism and the Amyraut Heresy. Protestant Scholasticism and Humanism in Seventeenth-Century France* (Madison, 1969).

Aylmer, G. E., *The King's Servants. The Civil Service of Charles I, 1625–1642* (1961).

Babbage, S. B., *Puritanism and Richard Bancroft* (1962).

Bangs, C., *Arminius: a Study in the Dutch Reformation* (Nashville, 1971).

—— 'Arminius and the Reformation', *Church History*, 30 (1961).

Blethen, H. T., 'Bishop Williams, the Altar Controversy and the Royal Supremacy, 1627–41', *Welsh History Review*, 9 (1978–9).

Christianson, P., *Reformers and Babylon: English Apocalyptic Visions from the Reformation to the Eve of the Civil War* (Toronto, 1978).

—— 'Reformers and the Church of England under Elizabeth I and the Early Stuarts', *JEH* 31 (1980).

Cliffe, J. T., *The Puritan Gentry: the Great Puritan Families of Early Stuart England* (1984).

Colie, R. L., *Light and Enlightenment. A Study of the Cambridge Platonists and the Dutch Arminians* (Cambridge, 1957).

Collinson, P., 'A Comment Concerning the Name Puritan', *JEH* 31 (1980).

—— *The Elizabethan Puritan Movement* (1967).

—— 'The Jacobean Religious Settlement: the Hampton Court Conference', in *Before the Civil War*, ed. H. Tomlinson (1983).

—— 'Lectures by Combination: Structures and Characteristics of Church Life in 17th Century England', *BIHR* 48 (1975).

—— *The Religion of Protestants. The Church in English Society, 1559–1625* (Oxford, 1982).

Cooper, C. H., *Annals of Cambridge* (5 volumes, Cambridge, 1842–1908).

Costin, W. C., 'The Inventory of John English, B.C.L., Fellow of St. John's College', *Oxoniensia*, 11–12 (1946–7).

Cremeans, C. D., *The Reception of Calvinistic Thought in England* (Urbana, 1949).

Curtis, M. H., *Oxford and Cambridge in Transition, 1558–1642. An Essay on Changing Relations between the English Universities and English Society* (Oxford, 1959).

Davies, G., 'Arminian versus Puritan in England, ca.1620–1640', *Huntington Library Bulletin*, 5 (1934).

Dawley, P. M., *John Whitgift and the Reformation* (1955).

Den Tex, J., *Oldenbarnevelt* (2 volumes, Cambridge, 1973).

Dent, C. M., *Protestant Reformers in Elizabethan Oxford* (1983).

Deursen, A. Th. van, *Honi soit qui mal y pense?* (Amsterdam, 1965).

Donaldson, G., *The Making of the Scottish Prayer Book of 1637* (Edinburgh, 1954).

Dorsten, J. A. van, *Thomas Basson 1555–1613: English Printer at Leiden* (Leiden, 1961).

Eason, C., *The Genevan Bible. Notes on its Production and Distribution* (Dublin, 1937).

Faction and Parliament. Essays on Early Stuart History, ed. K. Sharpe (Oxford, 1978).

Fincham, K. and Lake, P., 'The Ecclesiastical Policy of King James I', *JBS* 24 (1985).

Finlayson, M. G., *Historians, Puritanism and the English Revolution: the Religious Factor in English Politics before and after the Interregnum* (Toronto, 1983).

Fletcher, A., *A County Community in Peace and War: Sussex 1600–1660* (1975).

Foster, A., 'The Function of a Bishop: the Career of Richard Neile, 1562–1640', in *Continuity and Change*, ed. R. O'Day and F. Heal (Leicester, 1976).

Foster, H. D., 'Liberal Calvinism', *Harvard Theological Review*, 16 (1923).

Foster, J., *Alumni Oxonienses, 1500–1714* (4 volumes, Oxford, 1892).

Foster, S., *Notes from the Caroline Underground: Alexander Leighton, the Puritan Triumvirate and the Laudian Reaction to Nonconformity* (Hamden, Conn., 1978).

Fuller, M., *The Life, Letters and Writings of John Davenant, D.D., 1572–1641, Lord Bishop of Salisbury* (1897).

Gardiner, S. R., *History of England, 1603–1642* (10 volumes, 1896).

George, C. H. and K., *The Protestant Mind of the English Reformation, 1570–1640* (Princeton, 1961).

Gibson, M., *A View of the Ancient and Present State of the Churches of Door, Home-Lacy and Hempsted* (1727).

Goode, W., *The Doctrine of the Church of England as to the Effects of Baptism in the Case of Infants* (1850).

Grayson, C., 'James I and the Religious Crisis in the United Provinces, 1613–19', in *Reform and the Reformation: England and the Continent, c.1500–1750*, ed. D. Baker (Oxford, 1979).

Greaves, R. and Zaller, R., *Biographical Dictionary of British Radicals in the Seventeenth Century* (3 volumes, Brighton, 1982–4).

Green, I., 'The Persecution of "Scandalous" and "Malignant" Parish Clergy during the English Civil War', *EHR* 94 (1979).

Greg, W. W., *Licensers for the Press, Etc. to 1640* (Oxford Bib. Soc., NS 10, 1962).

—— *Some Aspects and Problems of London Publishing between 1550 and 1650* (Oxford, 1956).

Gruenfelder, J. K., 'The Election to the Short Parliament, 1640', in *Early Stuart Studies*, ed. H. S. Reinmuth (Minneapolis, 1970).

Hall, B., 'Calvin against the Calvinists', *Proceedings of the Huguenot Soc.*, 20 (1962).

—— 'Puritanism: the Problem of Definition', in *Studies in Church History*, ed. G. J. Cuming, II (1965).

Haller, W., *The Rise of Puritanism . . . 1570–1643* (New York, 1957).

Harrison, A. W., *The Beginnings of Arminianism to the Synod of Dort . . .* (1926).

—— *Arminianism* (1937).

Hauben, P. J., *Three Spanish Heretics and the Reformation. Antonio Del Corro—Cassiodora De Reina—Cypriano De Valera* (Geneva, 1967).

Henderson, G. D. *Religious Life in Seventeenth-Century Scotland* (Cambridge, 1937).

Herefordshire. Royal Commission on Historical Monuments, England (3 volumes, 1931–4).

Hibbard, C., *Charles I and the Popish Plot* (Chapel Hill, 1983).

Hill, C., *Antichrist in Seventeenth Century England* (1971).

—— *The Collected Essays of Christopher Hill, Volume II: Religion and Politics in 17th Century England* (Brighton, 1986).

—— *Economic Problems of the Church from Archbishop Whitgift to the Long Parliament* (Oxford, 1956).

—— *Puritanism and Revolution. Studies in the Interpretation of the English Revolution of the 17th Century* (1958).

Hill. J. W. F., 'The Royalist Clergy of Lincolnshire', *Lincoln Architectural and Archaeological Soc.*, 2 (1938).

Howell, R., *Newcastle-upon-Tyne and the Puritan Revolution* (Oxford, 1967).

Hunt, W., *The Puritan Moment: the Coming of Revolution in an English County* (Cambridge, Mass., 1983).

Hutton, S., 'Thomas Jackson, Oxford Platonist, and William Twisse, Aristotelian', *Journal of the History of Ideas*, 39 (1978).

Iken, J. F., 'Bremen und die Synode zu Dordrecht', *Bremisches Jahrbuch*, 10 (1878).

International Calvinism, 1541–1715, ed. M. Prestwich (Oxford, 1985).

James, M., *Family, Lineage and Civil Society. A Study of Society, Politics and Mentality in the Durham Region, 1500–1640* (Oxford, 1974).

Jones, R. F., *Ancients and Moderns: a Study of the Rise of the Scientific Movement in Seventeenth Century England* (Berkeley, 1965).

Kearney, H. F., *Strafford in Ireland, 1633–41. A Study in Absolutism* (Manchester, 1959).

Kendall, R. T., *Calvin and English Calvinism to 1649* (Oxford, 1979).

Kirby, E. W., 'Sermons before the Commons, *1640–1642*', *American Historical Review*, 44 (1939).

Lake, P., *Moderate Puritans and the Elizabethan Church* (Cambridge, 1982).

Lamont, W., 'The English Revolution: Sunbeams and Lumps of Clay', *Encounter*, 42 (1974).

—— *Godly Rule: Politics and Religion, 1603–1660* (1969).

—— *Marginal Prynne, 1600–1669* (1963).

Laplanche, F., *Orthodoxie et predication. L'Œuvre d'Amyraut et la querelle de la grace universelle* (Paris, 1965).

Le Neve, J., *Fasti Ecclesiae Anglicanae*, ed. T. D. Hardy (3 volumes, Oxford, 1854).

Lockyer, R., *Buckingham: the Life and Political Career of George Villiers, First Duke of Buckingham, 1592–1628* (1981).

MacLure, M., *The Paul's Cross Sermons, 1534–1642* (Toronto, 1958).

McGee, J. S., *The Godly Man in Stuart England. Anglicans, Puritans and the Two Tables, 1620–1670* (New Haven, 1976).

—— 'William Laud and the Outward Face of Religion', in *Leaders of the Reformation*, ed. R. L. DeMolen (1984).

Malcolm, N., *De Dominis (1560–1624): Venetian, Anglican, Ecumenist and Relapsed Heretic* (1984).

Marchant, R. A., *The Puritans and the Church Courts in the Diocese of York, 1560–1642* (1960).

Mason, T. A., *Serving God and Mammon: William Juxon, 1582–1663, Bishop of London, Lord High Treasurer of England, and Archbishop of Canterbury* (Toronto, 1985).

Mayor, J. E. B., 'Materials for the Life of Thomas Morton, Bishop of Durham', *Cambridge Antiquarian Soc.*, 3 (1865).

Milward, P., *Religious Controversies of the Elizabethan Age. A Survey of Printed Sources* (1978).

—— *Religious Controversies of the Jacobean Age. A Survey of Printed Sources* (1978).

Morrill, J., 'The Attack on the Church of England in the Long Parliament, 1640–42', in *History, Society and the Churches*, ed. D. Beales and G. Best (Cambridge, 1985).

—— 'The Religious Context of the English Civil War', *TRHS* 34 (1984).

New, J. F. H., *Anglican and Puritan. The Basis of their Opposition, 1558–1640* (1964).

Newcourt, R., *Repertorium Ecclesiasticum Parochiale Londinense* (2 volumes, 1708–10).

Nijenhuis. W., *Adrianus Saravia (c.1532–1613): Dutch Calvinist, First Reformed Defender of the English Episcopal Church Order on the Basis of Ius Divinum* (Leiden, 1980).

Nobbs, D., *Theocracy and Toleration. A Study of the Disputes in Dutch Calvinism from 1600 to 1650* (Cambridge, 1938).

Oman, C., *English Church Plate, 597–1830* (1957).

Ovenell, R. F., 'The Library of Brian Twyne', *Oxford Bib. Soc.*, NS 4 (1952).

Parker, T. M., 'Arminianism and Laudianism in Seventeenth-Century England', in *Studies in Church History*, ed. C. W. Dugmore and C. Duggan, 1 (1964).

Patterson, W. B., 'King James I's Call for an Ecumenical Council', in *Councils and Assemblies: Studies in Church History*, ed. G. J. Cuming and D. Baker, 7 (1971).

—— 'King James I and the Protestant Cause in the Crisis of 1618–22', in *Studies in Church History*, ed. S. Mews, 18 (1982).

—— 'The Peregrinations of Marco Antonio de Dominis, 1616–24', in *Studies in Church History*, ed. D. Baker, 15 (1978).

Platt, J., 'Eirenical Anglicans at the Synod of Dort', in *Reform and the Reformation: England and the Continent, c.1500–1750*, ed. D. Baker (Oxford, 1979).

Porter, H. C., *Reformation and Reaction in Tudor Cambridge* (Cambridge, 1958).

Quintrell, B. W., 'The Royal Hunt and the Puritans, 1604–1605', *JEH 31* (1980).

Rabb, T. K., 'The Editions of Sir Edwin Sandys's Relation of the State of Religion', *Huntington Library Quarterly*, 26 (1962–3).

Reid, R. R., *The King's Council in the North* (1921).

Richardson, R. C. *Puritanism in North-West England: a Regional Study of the Diocese of Chester to 1642* (Manchester, 1972).

Russell, C., 'Arguments for Religious Unity in England, 1530–1650', *JEH 18* (1967).

—— 'The Parliamentary Career of John Pym, 1621–9', in *The English Commonwealth, 1547–1640*, ed. P. Clark *et al.* (Leicester, 1979).

—— *Parliaments and English Politics, 1621–1629* (Oxford, 1979).

Schaff, P., *The History of the Creeds* (3 volumes, 1877–8).

Schwartz, H., 'Arminianism and the English Parliament, 1624–1629', *JBS* 112/2 (1973).

Seaver, P., *Wallington's World: a Puritan Artisan in Seventeenth Century London* (Stanford, 1985).

Sharpe, K., 'Archbishop Laud and the University of Oxford', in *History and Imagination*, ed. H. Lloyd-Jones *et al.* (1981).

Sheils, W. J., *The Puritans in the Diocese of Peterborough, 1558–1610* (Northampton, 1979).

Shriver, F., 'Hampton Court Re-visited: James I and the Puritans', *JEH* 33 (1982).

Stevenson, D., *The Scottish Revolution, 1637–44. The Triumph of the Covenanters* (Newton Abbot, 1973).

Stieg, M. F., *Laud's Laboratory: the Diocese of Bath and Wells in the Early Seventeenth Century* (Lewisburg, 1982).

Stone, L., *The Crisis of the Aristocracy, 1558–1641* (Oxford, 1965).

Strype, J., *The Life and Acts of John Whitgift* (3 volumes, Oxford, 1822).

Tatham, G. B., *The Puritans in Power. A Study in the History of the English Church from 1640 to 1660* (Cambridge, 1913).

Thomas, K., *Religion and the Decline of Magic. Studies in Popular Beliefs in Sixteenth and Seventeenth Century England* (1971).

Trevor-Roper, H. R., *Archbishop Laud, 1573–1645* (1965).

—— 'Archibishop Laud', Friends of Lambeth Palace Library (1978).

—— *Edward Hyde, Earl of Clarendon* (Oxford, 1975).

—— *Religion, the Reformation and Social Change* (1967).

Tyacke, N., 'Arminianism and English Culture' in *Britain and the Netherlands*, ed. A. C. Duke and C. A. Tamse, VII (1981).

—— 'Puritanism, Arminianism and Counter-Revolution', in *The Origins of the English Civil War*, ed. C. Russell (1973).

—— 'Science and Religion at Oxford before the Civil War', in *Puritans and Revolutionaries*, ed. D. Pennington and K. Thomas (Oxford, 1978).

Usher, R. G., *The Reconstruction of the English Church* (2 volumes, 1910).

Venn, J. and J. A., *Alumni Cantabrigienses . . . Pt. I* (Cambridge, 1922–7). 4 volumes.

Wallace, D. D., *Puritans and Predestination: Grace in English Protestant Theology, 1525–1695* (Chapel Hill, 1982).

Welsby, P. A., *George Abbot. The Unwanted Archbishop, 1562–1633* (1962).

White, P., 'The Rise of Arminianism Reconsidered', *Past and Present*, 101 (1983).

UNPUBLISHED THESES

Adams, S., 'The Protestant Cause: Religious Alliance with the West European Calvinist Communities as a Political Issue in England, 1585–1630', Oxford D.Phil. thesis, 1973.

Beddow, H., 'The Church in Lincolnshire, *c*.1595–*c*.1640', Cambridge Ph.D. thesis, 1980.

Fincham, K., 'Pastoral Roles of the Jacobean Episcopate in Canterbury Province', London Ph.D. thesis, 1985.

Foster, A., 'A Biography of Archbishop Richard Neile, 1562–1640', Oxford D.Phil. thesis, 1978.

Grayson, C., 'From Protectorate to Partnership: Anglo-Dutch Relations, 1598–1625', London Ph.D. thesis, 1978.

Kitshoff, M., 'Aspects of Arminianism in Scotland', St Andrews M.Th. thesis, 1968.

Macauley, J., 'Richard Montague Caroline Bishop, 1575–1641', Cambridge Ph.D. thesis, 1965.

Shriver, F., 'The Ecclesiastical Policy of James I: Two Aspects: the Puritans (1603–5)—the Arminians (1611–25)', Cambridge Ph.D. thesis, 1967.

Index

Abbot, George, Archbishop 15, 21–2, 37, 41, 43, 45–6, 56, 62, 68, 75, 79 n., 88, 91–3, 97–102, 105, 109, 157, 164–5, 167–8, 171, 181, 191 n.; and altars 214; attitude to Puritanism 185–6; on baptism 21; Calvinism of 21, 62, 91, 97; chaplains of 47, 65, 92, 149, 255–6; definition of the church, 153 n.; and House of Commons 149–52; opposes Laud 68; and preaching 202

Abbot, Robert, Bishop 65 n; Calvinism of 41, 60–1, 72, 74, 97; opposes Laud 70

Abdy, Anthony 221

Abel 179

Aberdeen 231–2; King's College 230; Marischal College 232

absolution, priestly 222

absolutism 158–9, 170, 239–45

Acontius, Jacobus 82

Adam 29, 31, 94, 96, 102, 229, 255–6

Adams, Sylvester 222

Airay, Adam 84

Airay, Henry 21, 61–2, 79; Calvinism of 79

Allen, Francis 65

Allen, Giles 189 n.

Allen, Thomas 63 n.

Allenson, John 117

altars 52, 55, 84, 116–18, 120, 176, 194, 197–216, 223, 225, 228–9, 233, 237, 239, 241–2, 246; bowing towards 55, 84, 198; Cathedrals and royal chapel precedents for 200–1, 203, 208, 214; on a dais 206, 246; and God's grace 84, 197; objections to 116–18, 199–201, 203–6, 208–15, 225, 228, 237, 242; railing of 199, 203–5, 237–9, 246; seats above 200; stone 118, 206, 216, 221, 233

Alvey, Richard 58–9

Amsterdam 36, 87, 232

Ananias 257

Andrewes, Lancelot, Bishop 22, 36, 45, 91, 103, 113–14, 123, 166–7, 179, 190; anti-Calvinism of 20, 45, 103, 269; chalice of 71; dislike of excessive preaching 186; printing of collected sermons 184

Andrewes, Nicholas 195 n., 197

'Anglican' viii

Annesley, Sir Francis 134 n.

Antichrist 1, 55, 64, 149, 172, 186, 215, 247

antinomianism 16

Anyan, Thomas 75

Aquinas 174, 223

Archer, M. 193 n.

Arches, Court of 204

Arminians, Arminianism: and absolutism 158–9, 247; avant la lettre 4; Baptist 8 n.; and Catholicism 5–6, 35, 55–6, 62–4, 122, 125–6, 147, 162, 227–8; and church patronage 50, 79, 106–24, 133–4, 159, 161–2, 167, 169–70, 181, 247; and clerical status 221, 247; and convocation 75–6, 101, 105, 129 n., 154, 156, 236; declaration concerning 50–1, 77, 80–2, 103, 181–3, 206–7, 228–9, 243 n., 264; definition of vi, 20, 28–30, 39, 46, 50, 53, 67, 74–5, 91, 128, 149, 245; Dutch 9, 20, 28, 36, 41, 45, 55, 69–70, 83, 86, 88–9, 91, 95–6, 100, 119–20, 127, 156, 164, 171; economic outlook of 141–5, 219; and Ireland 229–30; lay support for 34, 38, 67, 91, 123–5, 140–7, 166–7, 184–5, 192–4, 216–23; moderate 79–82, 84–6; and modernism 120, 141–2, 145; named in Paul's Cross sermons 257–60, 262–3; at parish level 53–6, 185, 195–9, 216–18; party of 87, 106–24, 133–5, 159, 166–8, 180–1; petition against 181–2; popularization of term 127; proclamation concerning 48–9, 76–7, 103, 107, 133, 154–5, 157, 160, 167, 182, 229, 263, 269; proposed legislation against 152, 154–5, 160; publishing of 7, 36, 47, 53, 58–9, 72, 75–6, 81, 83–5, 101, 103–4, 121, 126–7, 136–7, 151, 159–60, 182, 184–5, 192, 198, 216–19, 232, 263–5; and royalism 142, 144, 146, 181, 247, 267; and science 7, 66–7, 120; and Scotland